"Design for four hundred."

HIS WORK AT
ALFRED A. KNOPF
MADE CHIP KIDD
A SUPERSTAR IN
DESIGNING THESE

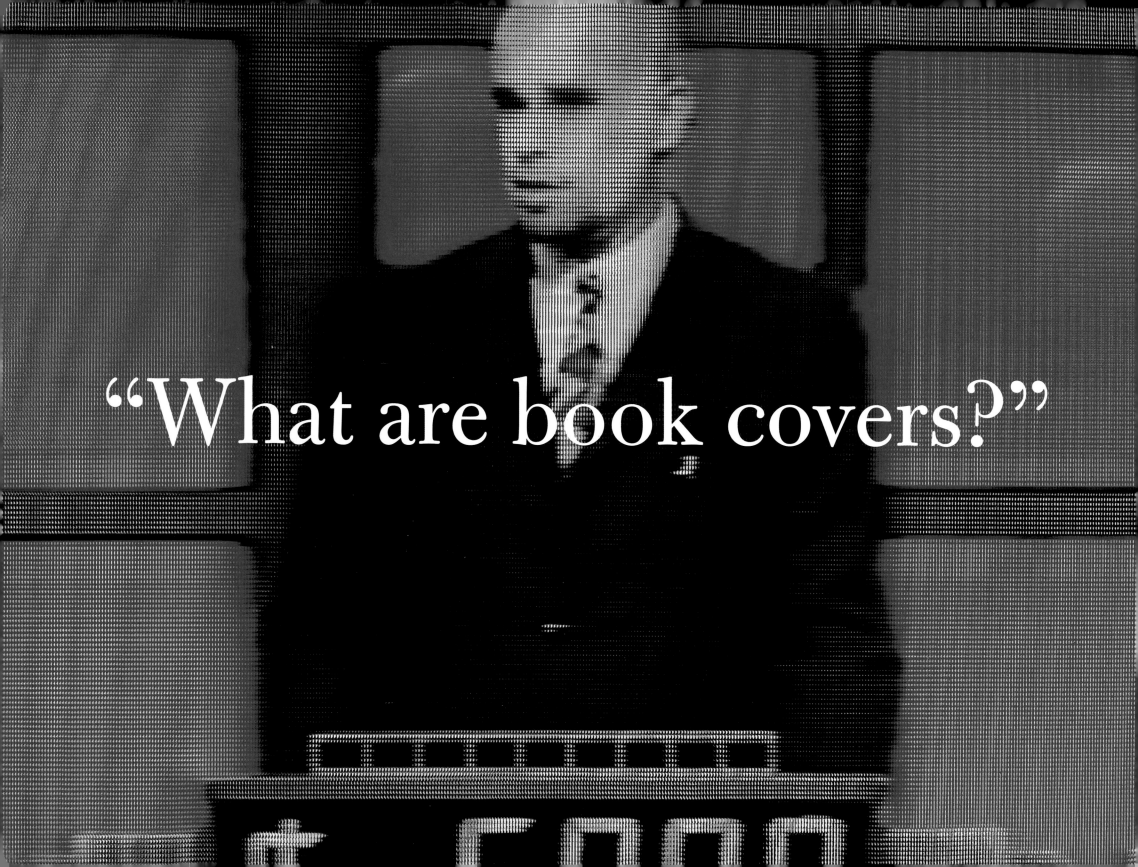

201 LITTLE ART DIRECTORS ONLY $1⁹⁸

2 COMPLETE ARMIES

EVERY PIECE OF PURE MOLDED PLASTIC, EACH STANDING ON ITS OWN MUTUAL FUND — SOME UP TO SIX FIGURES! RE-LIVE THOSE FAMOUS BATTLES FOR ACCOUNTS LONG LOST, PETTY INTER-OFFICE CONFLICTS, AND UNQUENCHED CAREER LUSTS

HERE'S WHAT YOU GET:

36 Illustrators
12 Designers
12 Marching "Idea Men"
12 Shooting "Idea Men"
12 Fleeing "Idea Men"
6 Creative Teams
6 Promo guys
30 Production Peons
12 Macintoshes
1 Pencil
1 Caterer
2 Bankrollers
10 Sports Cars
24 Cellular Phones
96 "Interns"
1 Job

PLEASE R.S.V.P.

No C.O.D.'s

The Art Directors Club. 250 Park Avenue South. New York, New York. Telephone (212) 674-0500.

Gentlemen: Please rush my reservation today. I realize that if I am not satisfied with Mr. Kidd's talk, there is nothing I can do about it, except, perhaps, to impulsively challenge him to a drunken brawl.

Name ....

Nicest Neighborhood Lived in thus far.....................

Education................Projected Retirement Age..........

FIRST PUBLISHED IN THE UNITED STATES OF AMERICA BY RIZZOLI INTERNATIONAL PUBLICATIONS, INC. | 300 Park Avenue South, New York, NY 10010 | www.rizzoliusa.com | Copyright © 2005 Chip Kidd. All rights reserved. No part of this publication may be reproduced, stored in a retrieval system, or transmitted in any form or by any means, electronic, mechanical, photocopying, recording, or otherwise, without prior consent of the publishers. 2006 2007 2008 / 10 9 8 7 6 5 4

ISBN-10: 0-8478-2748-8 (HC) ISBN-13: 978-0-8478-2748-0 (HC) / ISBN-10: 0-8478-2785-2 (PB) ISBN-13: 978-0-8478-2785-5 (PB) | Library of Congress Control Number: 2005928316 | Printed in China | All DC Comics characters TM & © 2005 DC Comics. All rights reserved. All PEANUTS characters and comic strips are © 2001 by United Features Syndicate, Inc. All Sin City characters © 2005 Frank Miller, Inc. | **COVER DESIGN:** Chip Kidd & Mark Melnick | **BOOK DESIGN:** Mark Melnick

ChipKidddesign

bad drawings & stupid ideas just right for your business

CURATED & DESIGNED BY MARK MELNICK

INTRODUCTION BY JOHN UPDIKE

PHOTOGRAPHS BY GEOFF SPEAR

ART DIRECTION, TEXT, FIDDLING, WHINING, POKING, WINCING, HOT TEAR-SOAKED REGRETS, & CATERING BY CHIP KIDD

RIZZOLI INTERNATIONAL PUBLICATIONS, INC., NEW YORK, 2005

OPPOSITE: Verso of an invitation to one of my lectures at the Art Director's Club in New York. Art and copy by Chris Ware, 1994. **ABOVE:** Early post-collegiate business card idea. Soon abandoned, 1986. **RIGHT:** As time goes by

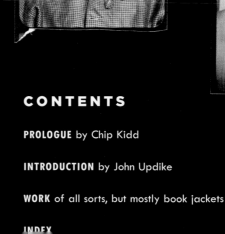

CONTENTS

"Books are *awfully* decorative, don't you think?"

—Gloria Upson, *Auntie Mame*

F. A. IACONE, INC.

The Men's Store of Reading

519-521 PENN ST.

ABOVE: The logo for my maternal grandfather's custom clothier shop in Pennsylvania, 1930s. **BELOW:** Undated photo of my maternal grandparents, Ferruccio Alexander and Mary Louise Iacone (Iacone is my middle name), with my aunt Gloria. Ferruccio came from near Rome, Mary from Trieste. They settled in America in the 1930s. They died long before I was born.

For J. D. McClatchy,

and for my family.

ABOVE: My paternal grandmother, Ruth Edna Matthias (later Ruth Kidd) as a teenager in Philadelphia, late 1910s. **LEFT:** My mother, Cornelia Ann Iacone, in Reading, Pa., 1952. Two paintings by my aunt Gloria hang in the background. **BELOW:** My dad, Thomas Iden Kidd, on Army leave in Morocco in 1952.

Prologue.

THIS IS A BOOK ABOUT BOOKS. IT IS ALSO ABOUT people's heads, trees, ducks, the Congo, bestiality, wrinkly yellow plastic, Batman, God, banana taffy, sex, booze, crippling despair, eucalyptus trees, horse hair, penises, boundless joy, black paint, and milk. It is about these things, and many others, because that is what the books are about. I could never have thought of all of these things in a million years, and here's the secret that is no secret at all: I didn't have to. One of the great advantages to designing book covers is that you don't ever have to have an idea, much less a thought, ever, in your head. That is the author's job. Through a manuscript, he or she will give you all the ideas and thoughts that you could possibly need to design a jacket. What you have to do is sort through them, figure out which ones to use, and make them look interesting. Give them a visual meaning. Sometimes it is easy, sometimes it is impossible, always it is worth trying.

Most of what I've worked on are jackets for hardcover books. This was not a matter of choice, it was just one of the givens of my job at Knopf. What you must remember about hardcover books is that they are like tattoos. Once you get one, it's never really going to go away. That may sound like the delusion of a navel-gazing book designer, but really—when was the last time you tossed a hardcover book into the trash? Yes, you may have boxed it up and left it on the doorstop of the Salvation Army, but only because you could no longer care for it and wanted to give it a good home. I've found that for most people, the financial commitment made to a book eventually becomes an emotional one (especially if the read is good enough), and they will hang onto it. So I always try to keep that in mind—what will something I work on look like in five years? In ten, twenty, a hundred?

Another thing to keep in mind about hardcover books when designing their jackets is that you're dealing with luxury items. They are, in most cases, the more elaborate version of something that's going to come out in about a year for half the price. But that doesn't mean they're supposed to be bound in mink and stamped with platinum (Trump books notwithstanding). What it means is that the luxury extends to the intellect as well as the wallet. It is almost embarrassing to have to point out that the audience for a book designer reads, and if they read they probably think, and if they think they should be receptive to something they may actually have to think about. There was an editor I worked with once who used to dismiss certain jacket ideas by airily decreeing, "Oh, come on—let's give the reader a *break*." To which I would always reply, in silence, to myself: "Oh, come on—let's give the reader some *credit*."

And that's exactly what Sonny Mehta, the head of Alfred A. Knopf since 1987, has always done. A well-known axiom in the graphics trade says that good clients make good design. Translated for publishing: a great editor-in-chief makes great book jackets. You could spend the better part of a week designing your latest little masterpiece, but if it never sees the light of day it's all for naught. Sonny has consistently enabled and encouraged the Knopf design team to challenge ourselves and him, and the readers. More on that later.

I DID NOT GROW UP YEARNING TO BECOME A BOOK DESIGNER. What I wanted to be was Chris Partridge on *The Partridge Family*. To me he represented the pinnacle of human achievement: an eight-year-old professional rock drummer performing with his rock-group family on primetime TV. His mother, Shirley Jones, sang lead and also found the time to make spaghetti and stitch together the group's vested velour maroon leisure suit costumes. They toured the country in a bus that looked like it was designed by Piet Mondrian, though it would be many years before I understood this. Chris was not at all the star of the show (that would have been David Cassidy, who in my book was an over-rated, arrogant skag), but that was okay—discerning viewers like myself nonetheless recognized him as the literal backbeat of the group, the Partridge driving force. He rarely had any scripted lines, but that just made him all the more intriguing. So I took up the drums, at the rather ripe age of nine, in hopes of following in his bass-pedal foot-taps. That was fun but didn't exactly lead to a career, alas. By the end of high school *The Partridge Family* had long since been cancelled, and I had to decide between music and art as a viable vocation. I didn't drink or take drugs, so professional musicianship was out. Art won by default. And then Graphic Design trumped Art. But I'm getting ahead of myself.

OPPOSITE LEFT: Bookshelves in my apartment, New York, fall 2004. Photo by Ellie Miller. **RIGHT:** The library in my apartment, New York, fall 2004. Photo by Ellie Miller. **ABOVE:** Annoying the neighbors, Lincoln Park, Pa., 1974. **LEFT:** Halloween, 1970. My parents always made costumes for me and my brother, Walt, and did an amazing Job. The problem with Zorro was that it was too easy for my first grade teacher, Miss Kinsel, to figure out who I was. That bitch.

BEFORE COLLEGE, I DIDN'T KNOW WHAT GRAPHIC DESIGN WAS. Or, more accurately, I didn' know that's what it was called. But I did know that Roger Dean did all of the album covers fo Yes. Did I want to be him? Maybe. I wanted to be a lot of things and still do. But a graphi designer? Never heard of it. What I loved was to make stuff, and when I "grew up" that's wha I wanted to do—whether it was music or comics or art (whatever that was) or some other media In tenth grade, on a whim, I joined the Wilson High TV Crew, and what a revelation: a full operational television studio within the school that covered its many sports and extracurricula events. We had a full-time faculty instructor (John Dallas, who is still there as of this writing) but otherwise it was completely staffed and run by students, and we put on a weekly live shov called *Wilson Highlights* every Monday night, going out on local cable access. This is fairl common now, but back then it was a real novelty and a total blast. We were all AV nerds ir AV nerd heaven. Everyone took turns running the camera, directing, presenting on-air, doing live interviews, remote feed, etc. It was so much fun that I soon decided my future was in televi sion, and I applied to Penn State to major in Communications. But in my senior year two pivota things happened to change my mind. First, I took advanced 5th-year Spanish with Mrs. Loraine Kovary, who introduced us to the work of El Greco, Goya, Picasso, and the Lord God of ado lescent notebook fodder, Dalí. This was the first serious exposure to art history that I'd eve had, and it completely changed my approach to drawing and painting. I'd actually never taker an art class in high school, and this was better—if you're going to learn, learn from the mas ters. The second thing that altered my career path was starting to do graphics for *Highlights* I soon found creating the titles and other ancillary artwork for the variously themed shows to be the most satisfying job of all. So, having been accepted at Penn State, that spring I switchec my major to Art. This did not sit well with Mom and Dad—nearby Kutztown U was much more renowned locally for its art program. But it was too late; I was determined and PSU bound. I wouldn't be the last time I made a random decision that turned out to be utterly prescient.

LEFT: The back cover of my 8th grade English notebook, Wilson Southern Junior High School Sinking Spring, Pa., 1978. How mortifying: not ONE cool band represented (all right, The Cars *maybe*). It would be another year before I discovered the B-52's, the Clash, Gang of Four, etc Note that The Outlaws didn't exist—it was a name I was considering for the band my friend Brad and I were constantly scheming to take over the world with. **BELOW LEFT:** Front cover o my high school senior yearbook. I did NOT design this, but in all fairness to whoever did, I prob ably couldn't have done much better. **BELOW RIGHT:** Wilson HS band spring concert, 1982

PENN STATE

WHERE I GREW UP, PENN STATE WAS THE THIRTEENTH GRADE. That isn't a knock, it's just a way of saying that if you knew you had to go to college and didn't want to deal with researching schools (me, in spades), good old State was it. But for art? Well, yes, if you wanted, but early on my freshman advisor told me about a relatively obscure area of concentration within the department called Graphic Design. How obscure? Well, they graduated 18 seniors a year. On a campus of 30,000+ kids. Now *that* was for me. The way it worked was you took foundation courses for two years, put together a portfolio, and then submitted it to see if you made the cut to study for two more. It was rather competitive, as you can imagine. During my freshman year two names kept surfacing: Lanny Sommese and Bill Kinser. The former was the head of the department and the latter the senior professor. Both had formidable reputations for brilliant work and brutal critiques. There were far more students than room, and if you didn't like it, there was the door. Or so the rumors went. I poured myself into Introduction to Typography, Life Drawing 101 (naked people in school!), Still Life, Color Theory—a world of ideas and techniques I'd never seriously thought about, at least not the way I was thinking about them now. Obviously, come submission time my portfolio was accepted, but back then I didn't see it as a sure thing by any means and knew I was going to have to work like mad.

Senior year everyone was assigned a work cubicle, and we practically lived in the studio. The idea was to learn from each other as much as from the teachers, and the two I learned the most from were a skinny little firecracker brunette named Sandy Chambers and an avant-blond with the improbably cool name of Barbara deWilde (which we pronounced dee-wild). Barbara had just returned from a year off in New York to study with Milton Glaser, so we all sort of bowed before her. Sandy was like a cross between Siouxsie Sioux and Audrey Hepburn with a little Exorcist-era Linda Blair thrown in just to keep us all guessing. They were both as smart as they were unpredictable, and years later in my novel *The Cheese Monkeys* (see p. 354) I fused them together to become the ultimate art school chick named Himillsy Dodd. **BELOW:** In the photolab with Barbara deWilde, mid-1980s.

see p. 354

AMNESTY INTERNATIONAL

ABOVE: Hitchhiking sign assignment from junior year with Bill Kinser, which I cribbed for a scene in *The Cheese Monkeys*. Kinser kept the crit in the classroom but always said he would have made us road-test the signs in the middle of nowhere if he could. So in the book, I did. **ABOVE RIGHT:** With Lanny Sommese at my graduation party, spring 1986. **RIGHT:** A Sommese Amnesty International poster using split-font silk-screen. He worked right in the studio among us and would pull all the sheets by hand with an assistant, usually a grad student. **BELOW:** A typical all-nighter with Sandy Chambers. Her senior film project was a gorgeous five-minute black-and-white montage of a man being savagely beaten with a pair of stiletto-heeled black leather pumps. It was called *These Shoes Are Killing Me*. She got an "A."

How to Dress
Yourself While
Drawing A
Profile of
Imogene Coca

And Balancing
A Big Stuffed
Chair On
Your Head

Blindfolded.

Now You Try it.

TIME AND SEQUENCE

THE FIRST SEMESTER OF FOURTH-YEAR GRAPHIC DESIGN Lanny has the students not really making conventional graphic design at all but studying the properties of time and sequence. Slide shows, film, flip-books, morphing one abstract shape into another step by step, and hand-marking blank film leader to sync with a soundtrack are all on the roster, and it can become a little frustrating to someone who just wants to dive right into print design. But it's an ingenious approach—we came to understand that all graphic design relies heavily on these tools, which require a careful consideration of scale and pacing. The second semester, the lessons are applied to magazines, corporate identities, posters, and yes, books. The main strength of the program Lanny started in 1970 is that it is conceptually based and free of the stylistic dogma of schools like Cranbrook and SVA in the 1980s. Sommese and Kinser heavily stressed that the solution to a problem always lies in the problem itself, and that any preconceived notion of an approach to take before you properly define the problem was folly. This was the greatest lesson I learned—I use it to this day and always will. I've been described as not having any recognizable style and that's one of the greatest compliments I could hope for. I want each book to have as much of its own individual personality as possible, based on what it is and what it's about. If that risks falling short of "the cutting edge," then so be it. In school, bowing to fads was discouraged, not that I didn't succumb now and again—Memphis had just landed and New Wave was running riot—but for the most part I tried to learn from the timeless quality of masters like Piet Zwart, Herbert Bayer, and El Lizzistky, just to name three. If I did betray a stylistic fallback, it was humor—strip-mining any given assignment for it's inherent absurdity or just injecting some of my own. Sometimes it worked, sometimes it didn't. **LEFT:** Penn State, fall 1984. Assignment: Using twenty slides, show someone how to do something. I'd reached my Imogene Coca phase, having grown out of my Ruth Gordon fixation.

As part of the last generation of pre-computer graphic design students, I am deeply grateful I was educated during this time. Not that I don't use the computer now—of course I do, and I give thanks to Apple on a daily basis. But I was schooled to solve problems with my hands as well as my head, and one influenced the other constantly, back and forth. And still do, regardless of the tools. When I interviewed Milton Glaser in 1993 for *The Believer*, he theorized that no graphic designer should be allowed to touch a computer until reaching the age of 40. I find that a bit drastic. I was 30, and that seems about right.

Anyway, Barbara graduated a year ahead of me, in 1985, and moved back to New York, extending an open invitation for me to crash at the loft she was sharing with her boyfriend in Williamsburg, Brooklyn. After another year of study and a summer stint at Lorish Advertising in Reading, Pa., I felt I was ready to come to the city and took her up on it. Portfolio in one hand and suitcase in the other, I was determined, eager, and scared to death. Growing up and going to school in Pennsylvania was great, but I'd outgrown it—as for so many others, New York was it for me. Whether or not I was for it was going to be the most daunting problem yet I would attempt to solve.

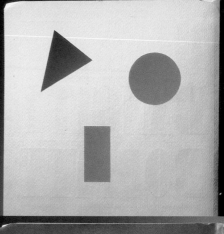

BiPPiTY
BANGiTY
BOPPiTY

BiPPiTY
BANGiTY
BOPPiTY

BOOM

TOM

The
purpose
of the
Tom-Tom
is to
provide a
perfect
pulse.

It
can be
played
to produce
anything
from a
penetrating
pounding
to a
piercing
ping.

A
round
of rythms
rapidly repeated
is readily
refered to as a
drum...

ROL

TOM

The
purpose
of the
Tom-Tom
is to
provide a
perfect
pulse.

It
can be
played
to produce
anything
from a
penetrating
pounding
to a
piercing
ping.

A
round
of rythms
rapidly repeated
is readily
refered to as a
drum...

ROLL

the
long
ROLL ROLL ROLL

ABOVE: I played drums in the Penn State Blue Band for four years, culminating in this glamorous photo-op. It was actually a hell of a lot of fun and a great respite from designer's block. **RIGHT:** My senior thesis, a typographic children's book about percussion instruments printed entirely with letter-press lead and wood type on a Vandercook proof press. The finished book itself has gone AWOL, but the maquette, seen here, survives. Working with movable type was one of the most engrossing experiences I had in college, and I definitely recommend it to any serious graphic design student.

IF I CAN MAKE IT THERE . . .

ONE GLANCE AT MY FALL 1986 APPOINTMENT DIARY MAKES IT ALL LOOK SO EASY—move to New York, go on a zillion interviews, get a great job. In exactly a month. But it was harrowing at the time and a lot more complicated than that. I dragged my portfolio to anyone and everyone who would see me, and if they weren't hiring I asked for a referral to someone else. After just a few weeks I began to understand that I was in the biggest small town in the world, and I was starting to get the same names. And I was starting to panic. People were great and relatively accessible, but no one had a position open, or they'd just filled one. "We'll call you if they don't work out." And they always worked out. At some point someone said, "Why don't you go to Random House and get freelance book cover work?" I was hesitant at first—I wanted the security of a full-time staff position, and I wanted to work for a multidisciplinary graphic design firm, designing all sorts of things. But I phoned anyway, and to my surprise a woman named Judith Loeser, then the art director at Vintage Books, agreed to see me. She was charming—all tomboy bubbly enthusiasm—and though I had absolutely no professional book cover experience, she gave me my first assignment. It was ironically called *How to Work for a Jerk*, a self-help book for people who hate their bosses but don't want to quit. She gave me a freelance contract and two weeks to show sketches.

I was elated, and terrified. So terrified, in fact, that I decided I would make the cover look like an old EC Horror Comic. I worked up colored-pencil-on-tissue layouts in the style of *Crypt of Terror* and *Vault of Horror*, with dripping, gooey type and shrieky colors. Would they go for something like this? Only one way to find out. It was on my trip a few days later to the building on East 50th Street to show my sketches when I discovered Judith's office was just two doors down the hallway from Louise Fili's—and that's when terror turned to awe. I'd become aware of Louise's book jacket work the previous year with the publication of *The Lover* by Marguerite Duras. As did every other graphic designer who was paying attention—that ghostly, delicately beautiful cover was the highlight of every design annual, and as art director of Pantheon she regularly produced a ravishing array of others on a regular basis. Amazing.

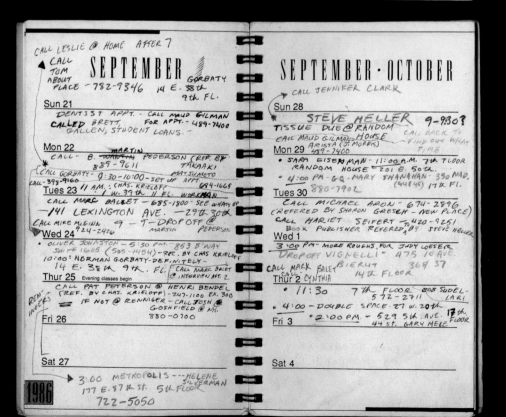

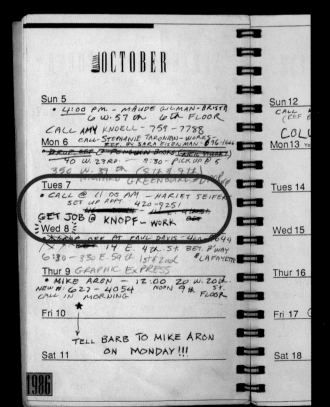

ANYWAY, BACK TO MY SKETCHES—the editors hated them. But Judith thought they were a hoot and showed them to Sara Eisenman, the young art director of Alfred A. Knopf—whoever that was—and asked: did I want to show her my portfolio? Sure, what the heck. Sara was the yin to Judith's yang: very sweet but quiet, careful, thoughtful. I would later learn she descended from graphic design royalty: her father was Alvin Eisenman, head of the department at Yale for many years. After going over my work, she looked up from it and uttered the magic phrase: "Well, you know I'm looking for an assistant." Whoa. I hadn't the slightest idea. I wanted to be it, him, whatever. Now. And said so. But not so fast—she'd just started looking, and needed to show my stuff to her boss, the vice-president in charge of art direction, Bob Scudellari. A torturous week passed. In the meantime I got an offer to assist the assistant doing in-store graphics at Macy's, which was starting to sound like the chance of a lifetime. But I resisted. And on the eighth day the phone rang. Hallelujah. The Knopf job was mine. My plan: I would design book jackets for a year or two, build up my portfolio, and then go on to work for a design firm, like I really wanted. Yes, that's what I would do.

THE KNOPF DESIGN LEGACY.

THOUGH I WAS FRANKLY IGNORANT ABOUT IT AT THE TIME OF MY HIRING, the history of Knopf has always been marked by its commitment to smart, distinctive book jackets (see Borzoi Credo, page 28). Herewith a microscopic sampling from the 1930s, '40s, and '50s. I should point out that all of these artists worked freelance, and that the art director for much of this era at Knopf was Sidney R. Jacobs, who also oversaw all of the production.

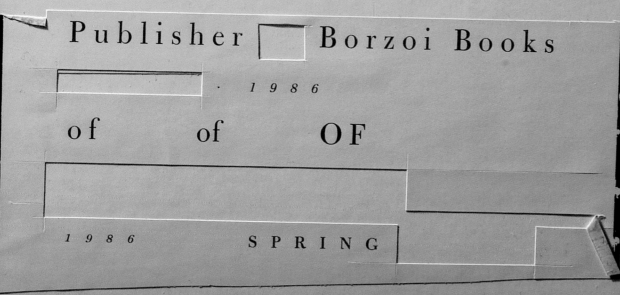

WILLIAM A. DWIGGINS (1880–1956)
Prolific, genius type designer and illustrator, he also coined the term "Graphic Design" in 1928.

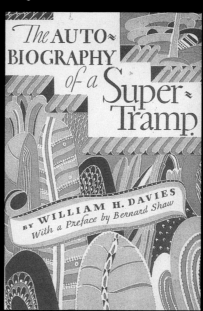

ARTHUR HAWKINS, JR. (1903–1987)
Hawkins mainly relied on abstract decorative patterns, but still somehow conveyed a book's emotional content.

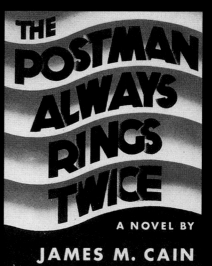

GEORGE SALTER (1897–1967)
Salter drew as well as designed, and his career spanned three decades. His nephew, Peter Salter, taught me typography and color theory at Penn State.

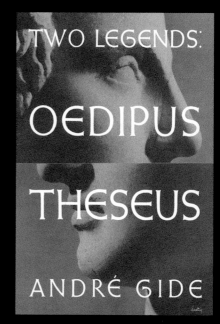

ALVIN LUSTIG (1915–1955)
The designer I've been most compared to, which is extremely flattering. His ingenious photo montages and his work for New Directions completely reimagined what book jackets could look like.

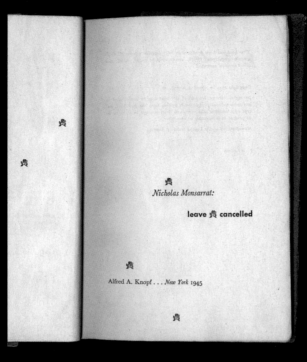

PAUL RAND (1914–1996)

The modernist master. I found *Leave Cancelled* (1943) in the Knopf library shortly after I was hired and for the first time really understood how the design for a novel could be carried through the entire book in a way that was both radical and elegant at the same time. The margins, the folios, the whisper of the title page spread, the die-cut jacket that gave way to the binding stamped with 1-24 in a grid representing the number of hours during which the action takes place. Of course it's beautiful, but it all *means* something too, and that's what mattered.

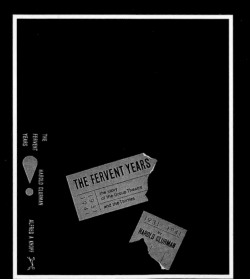

LEFT: Rand's design for *The Fervent Years* (1945) was also tremendously influential for me—the use of negative space, the integration of the type in the ticket, the way it carries over onto the spine. Not an inch wasted or unconsidered, the concept clear while avoiding clichés. This is as near to perfect as it gets and years ahead of its time. **RIGHT:** Summer, 1987. I met Rand for the first and only time at Sara's wedding. She very sweetly made sure that we were introduced and talked. He is probably laughing at my dorky hat and clip-on bowtie.

WHAT CHIP BRINGS TO DESIGN IS DECEPTIVELY SOPHISTICATED AND ULTIMATELY SIMPLE. First he finds meaning, and then he tinkers with the complexity of his message or interpretation. Can he reveal his idea simply, or does that become too predictable? Is it too boring or obvious? How can he invite the viewer to work for meaning? His designs challenge the viewer and break the rules, defiantly merging types that are incompatible or cropping pictures so that the perception is skewed or meaning redefined. Sometimes he does it with the position of the elements and sometimes by the images he chooses to combine. Sometimes Chip just turns everything inside out. His work is bold and sometimes loud, and always smart. It never fails to catch your attention.

How did I see this in his portfolio? As a new art director of two years in 1986, I was still evolving with the job and had made a firm decision to transition away from the retro design trend. Designers were making lovely art deco and Russian constructivism inspired posters and book jackets, and I was looking for something very different for Knopf. I wanted to explore more conceptual design and downtown influences that were all around me, so I was looking for an assistant who was headed in that direction. It is not that he arrived with the portfolio that he has now. There were no daring face transplants or altered typefaces or startling croppings, but it was quirky and fresh, in both senses of the word. It was his illustration that most caught my attention. In one portfolio piece, Chip had interpreted the sounds a drum makes using wood type and his own hand-drawn images. It was clear that he understood certain things about rhythm in a book, transitions, image and meaning, and how to surprise the reader while translating sound and percussion in two dimensions. He was not afraid to experiment by throwing unlikely things together, such as cartoon drawings with traditional wood type. In another piece he used cigar wrappers and other things that he had collected in very fresh and unusual contexts. Apparently I told him his work reminded me of Léger, and looking back at the early work now I can see why I said that. His sense of color and spatial arrangement have a big bold griddy quality; never predictable or subtle but still formal.

Chip had been rejected already, so he was a little discouraged. I don't think I was exactly what he had in mind when he set out on his journey to find his first job, but Knopf was absolutely the perfect place for him to be. When I left a year later to move to Boston, he stayed on with the newly appointed Sonny Mehta and Carol Devine Carson for the next nineteen years (and counting).

—Sara Eisenman

MR CHARLES KLOD
KNOPF PUB ART DEPT
201 E 50TH ST FL 7
NEW YORK NY 10022

THE NAME'S KLOD.
CHARLES KLOD.

LITTLE COULD I (OR ANYONE) HAVE KNOWN that I had just landed when a pivotal era of change was about to dawn at the firm. I'd scarcely figured out where the coffee machine was when Robert Gottlieb announced in December 1986 that he was leaving as editor-in-chief to replace William Shawn at *The New Yorker*. This event warranted no less than an above-the-fold headline on the front page of *The New York Times*, sent the magazine's staff into a mutinous frenzy, and left everyone at Knopf shellshocked and wondering what was going to happen next. I have to admit it was not the worst news in the world for a certain entry-level book jacket designer. While Gottlieb was clearly brilliant and one of the most oddly charismatic personalities I've ever encountered (especially presiding over the sales force, which was like watching a rat take command of a villageful of pied pipers), it seemed clear from our few meetings that his idea of a good cover and mine were at odds. But heck, who was I?—just some dumb kid from Lincoln Park, Pa. However, I also sensed this discrepancy between him and Sara. I was mystified as to how she ever got designs by people like Mark Cohen, Francis Jetter, and Henrik Drescher approved. But she did, so I knew there was hope. I just hunkered down and was thrilled to be working and tried to stay under everyone's radar, which wasn't hard—most of the company was preoccupied with the question of Gottlieb's successor.

And in the early spring of 1987 the answer arrived in the form of Ajai Singh Mehta. Sonny, as he was and is called, was about as different from Bob as anyone could possibly be. Much has been written about this, but suffice it to say: if Gottlieb was the Joker, Sonny was Batman. Which I thought was great, but it threw a lot of the Gottlieb acolytes for a loop. He was immediately perceived as dark, mysterious, and aloof. I just thought he was cool.

Then the other shoe fell: in late spring that year Sara married the publisher David Godine and moved to Boston. Which, amazingly, didn't mean she gave up her job. She actually commuted, spending three days in the middle of the week in New York working on the Knopf list, and Friday through Monday in beantown. It's a testament to how much she loved the job and the degree to which Bob Scudellari gave her the chance to make it work that this arrangement lasted several months. But it was too much of a strain, both on her and a new editor-in-chief who needed a full-time art director. By June, she reluctantly withdrew to Boston full time and went to work there for Beacon Hill Press.

With Sara gone, Scudellari had to figure out what to do. First he sat me down and explained that he just couldn't promote me—all

of 22, with less than a year's experience—to art director. "If you just had six more months, we could try it, but I just can't. You have to understand." Ambitious upstart that I was, frankly I didn't. I was very disappointed, but I had to accept it. And how absurd was that—not nine months previous I was selling balloons in Avalon, New Jersey (a long, sad story), and now I couldn't understand why I wasn't being put in charge of jackets for the most prestigious publishing house in America—which, incidentally, I'd never even *heard* of before I started working there. Insane. So Bob screened applicants. For weeks. And as the process dragged on, the summer of 1987 became my trial by fire. Without an assistant and no replacement for Sara in sight, I effectively *became* the Knopf art director. And it wasn't fun. There was a ton of follow-up work to do for the upcoming fall list, which Bob helped me with, but it meant dealing with both editors and freelance designers impatient for the real art director to show up. Even though there was little new work to dole out, I did manage to slip a jacket to Barbara deWilde to illustrate and design—it was called *The Boys and Their Baby*, a novel by Larry Wolff—the least I could do as thanks for her help the previous fall. Finally, in September Bob had made a choice. And it was worth the wait: Carol Devine Carson was smart, well-read, witty, talented, radiant, and well-equipped with the requisite sense of humor. With a background primarily in magazine design, she had never done a book jacket in her life, but Bob saw the potential in her; just as he'd seen it in me a year earlier. And she more than met the challenge, winning over the editorial staff with passion and skill. Soon I introduced her to Barbara, and they hit it off immediately, with Carol eventually bringing Barb on as a full-time freelancer in 1988. Archie Ferguson, another exceptional designer in the department who'd been an assistant at Times Books, also caught Carol's eye. After he designed the jacket for the companion book to Ken Burns's landmark Civil War series as a freelancer, the deck was cleared to make him a Knopf staff designer too. By 1990 what became known informally as the Knopf Design Team was firmly in place.

LEFT: In my first office, circa 1987. Less than a year, and already it's a pigsty. You can't tell, but I'm still in my ponytail period. Sad. Dig all of the Stone Age trappings: rubber cement, colored pencils, rapidiographs, T-square, pterodactyl meat. **LOWER LEFT:** Return to sender. Collecting name-mangled mailing labels from the envelopes sent by clueless wannabe vendors and freelancers was an officewide sport. Carol Carson had some of the greatest, including Crasno Calo. The all-time best was when she got a letter in her mailbox addressed to Random House author Carl Sagan. Someone in the mailroom had fallen off the wagon. Again.

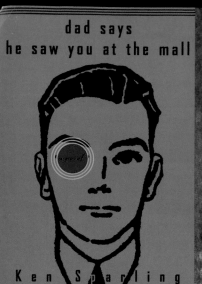

dad says
he saw you at the mall

Ken Sparling

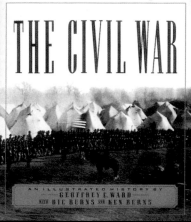

THE CIVIL WAR

AN ILLUSTRATED HISTORY BY
GEOFFREY C. WARD
WITH RIC BURNS AND KEN BURNS

THE KNOPF DESIGN TEAM

PHOTOGRAPHED BY MARION ETTLINGER, 1995, for *ID Magazine's* design annual the year we won for Best of Category, Packaging. This came as a bit of a surprise, because we sent our entries in separately. But the judges felt the work was strongest as a whole and gave the award to us as a group. This recognized the dynamic Carol creates so well—that of a design collective or laboratory, in which ideas, approaches, and resources are constantly exchanged. This line-up lasted nearly ten years, from 1990 to 1999, after which Archie became art director for Pantheon and Barbara took on the same role for *Martha Stewart Living.* **LEFT:** Covers by Archie. **BELOW:** Covers by Barbara. **RIGHT:** Covers by Carol.

ARCHIE FERGUSON

CAROL DEVINE
CARSON

BARBARA deWILDE

C. K.

DAMAGE
A NOVEL BY
Josephine Hart

DEGREE
OF
GUILT

A NOVEL BY

RICHARD
NORTH
PATTERSON

Stories in the Worst Way

Gary Lutz

*For
the Relief
of
Unbearable
Urges*

stories by
Nathan Englander

Birds of America

stories by
Lorrie Moore

MEN IN THE OFF HOURS

ANNE CARSON

THE NEXT GENERATION.

AS CAROL NEARS THE CLOSE OF HER SECOND DECADE AS Vice President and art director of the Knopf Publishing Group, she can take pride in having carefully assembled what I would say is the finest art department of its kind in publishing, anywhere. With Archie helming Pantheon; the addition of Knopf junior designers Abby Weintraub, Gabrielle Wilson, and Peter Mendelsund; and at Vintage, Megan Wilson as senior designer and John Gall as art director—the team has never been stronger. All right, call me biased, but the quality level of the group's vast annual output cannot be denied.

A lot of art directors lord over their staff, reducing them to pairs of hands, relinquishing little or no creative work. Carol does exactly the opposite and fosters an environment in which the designers she's responsible for do their own thing, play to their particular strengths, and figure things out for themselves. Certainly when she started at Knopf she was under no obligation to give me the extraordinary amount of freedom that I've had over the years, and I'll be forever grateful for it, as we all are. When intervention is needed, she's there, but she is loathe to dictate and treats her department like a family. Everyone on staff adores her, and in addition to the warm and inspiring atmosphere that lends the office, better yet: it shows in the work.

But there is no resting on our laurels, either. What has always mattered as much as talent and a love of literature is consistency. The unspoken Knopf design axiom: You're only as good as your last list. Or preferably, your next. No sooner do we finish a season's worth of jackets (and sometimes before we even get a chance to) than another arrives, and the manuscripts are distributed and dates are set for the sales meetings and catalogue deadlines, and our collective hamster wheel is kept spinning. This, as exhausting as it sounds (and often is), is also curiously sustaining and makes Knopf that rarest of things: the source of a steady stream of challenging, enthralling, rewarding work. If you're a graphic designer who likes to read (and think), there is simply no better job in the world.

TOP ROW: Design by Abby Weintraub. **MIDDLE ROW:** Design by Gabriele Wilson. **BOTTOM ROW:** Design by Peter Mendelsund. Knopf is publisher for all shown.

ABBY WEINTRAUB
designer

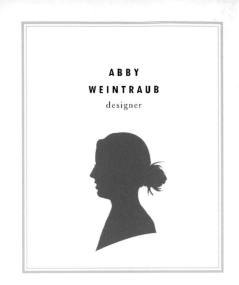

GABRIELE WILSON
designer

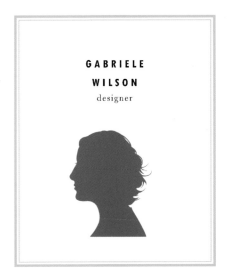

PETER MENDELSUND
designer

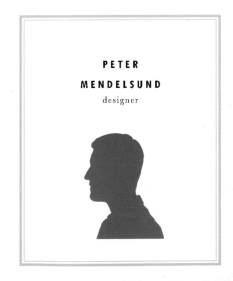

IN BLACK AND WHITE
THE LIFE OF SAMMY DAVIS, JR.
WIL HAYGOOD

BALZAC
and the
LITTLE CHINESE SEAMSTRESS

a novel

Plain Heathen Mischief
a novel

Martin Clark
author of
The Many Aspects of Mobile Home Living

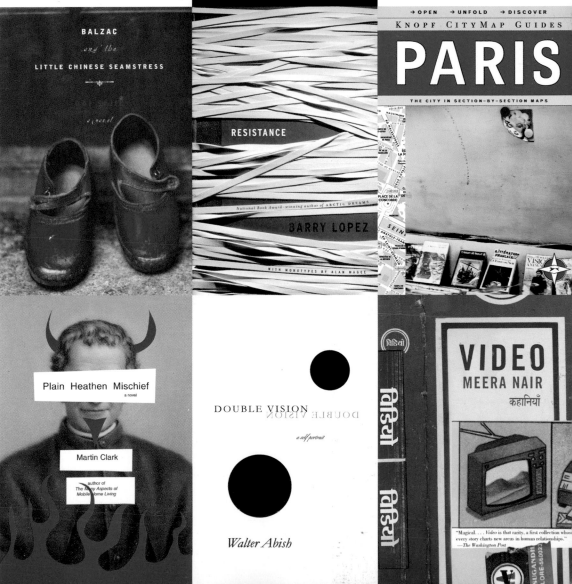

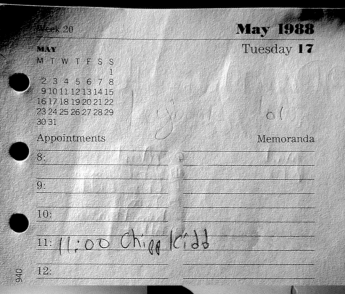

Tuesday 17

MAY
M T W T F S S
            1
2 3 4 5 6 7 8
9 10 11 12 13 14 15
16 17 18 19 20 21 22
23 24 25 26 27 28 29
30 31

Appointments   Memoranda

8:

9:

10:

11: 11:00 Chipp Kidd

12:

GEOFF

GEOFF SPEAR IS MY MERLIN, THE ETHEL TO MY LUCY—or, more butch, the Norton to my Kramden, except that our hare-brained schemes actually work. It wasn't long after I got to New York that I saw a photographic interpretation of the Talking Heads' *Don't Worry About the Government* in the book *What the Songs Look Like* and was mesmerized by it. It depicted figurines of Washington and Lincoln under siege of what appeared to be a giant burning condom. Don't worry! Then a year or so later a photographer named Jeff called and asked to show me his portfolio because he'd seen some of the jackets I'd done. So into the office he comes, and it's Geoff not Jeff, and he's the burning condom guy! And so we began what has become a long creative partnership. Although our first collaboration in 1988, *The Global Rivals* (right), made it all the way to the printed proof stage only to get killed (for reasons I can't recall), we persisted and have since worked on literally thousands of shots together, for dozens of book jackets and projects like *Batman Collected*, *Batman Animated*, and *Peanuts: The Art of Charles M. Schulz*. Geoff's skill with lighting and focus are peerless, and you'll see many examples herein. He also shot all the books for this book. I don't know how else to say it: he's the best. **ABOVE:** Readying a Superman prototype action figure for its close-up in *Mythology: The DC Comics Art of Alex Ross* (p. 386). Photo by Paul Amador. **ABOVE RIGHT:** Geoff's appointment log marking the day we met. Note the two "p"'s.

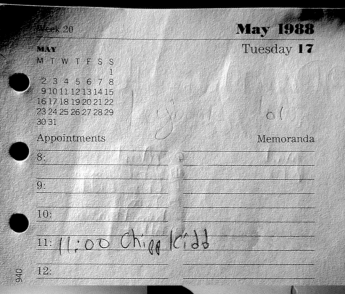

THE GLOBAL RIVALS • BIALER + MANDELBAUM

THE GLOBAL RIVALS

The forty-year contest for supremacy between AMERICA and the SOVIET UNION

SEWERYN BIALER
+
MICHAEL MANDELBAUM

A companion book to the Public Television Series

KNOPF

AUGUSTEN BURROUGHS

MAGICAL THINKING

TRUE STORIES

MAGICAL THINKING

TRUE STORIES

St. Martin's Press

AUGUSTEN BURROUGHS

The *New York Times* bestselling author of RUNNING WITH SCISSORS and DRY

THE LITTLE FRIEND
Knopf
DONNA TARTT

THE LITTLE FRIEND

a novel by the author of THE SECRET HISTORY

DONNA TARTT

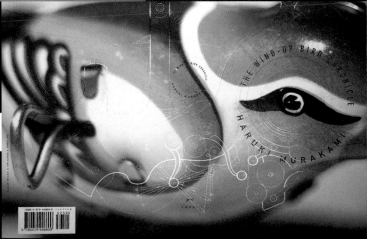

THE WIND-UP BIRD CHRONICLE

HARUKI MURAKAMI

SO MANY BOOKS, SO LITTLE LOGIC.

OKAY, SO YOU'VE DESIGNED OVER 800 BOOK JACKETS and you want to collect them all in one big fa
volume. How do you organize them? By date? By subject matter? Alphabetically by author? By title
The answer was a little of all of these, and none of them exactly. The original idea was to divide
everything into sub-categories, like a bookstore—Fiction, Non-fiction, Biography, Poetry, Comics, etc.—
and then arrange them chronologically within each. This made sense in theory, but once we tried it we
abandoned the idea almost immediately. It was aesthetically arbitrary. More important, many of the
authors wrote both fiction and non-fiction—do you split up their titles among different sections? Tha
seemed wrong. So we started with a core group of writers for whom I've done a lot of work over the
years and built layouts around all of their titles, regardless of subject matter. Once we did that, we
let the remaining jackets organize themselves into groups that seemed to belong together. Thus, a nove
about Africa seemed to belong next to a historical study of Africa, and so on. So the ultimate method
was no method, really, as much as an intuitive sense of what worked. Which is about as close to any
kind of "definitive approach" to design that I could offer.

We (that is, myself and Mark Melnick, the invaluable curator and designer of this book) originally
attempted to show everything I've done here, warts and all. Well. Here's the short story: there wasn'
room. We deduced this, to our horror, after we were well into the layout stage. To show everything, i
any kind of proper fashion, would require more pages than we were allotted, even after begging fo
a good many more and actually getting them. So there was trimming. But we still managed to include
a good amount of the failed sketches, dismissed ideas, and ghastly designs that resulted because
just gave up or ran out of time. Whenever I give a lecture, especially at a school, I always make sure
to show plenty of misguided attempts to solve problems. Because this happens to everyone, all of the
time, no matter who they are or how "well-known" they become. The important thing is that no matte
what, you mustn't stop trying. More important, you must look at rejections as opportunities to do some
thing better than what you did the first time. Or reasons to drink more. Or in my case both.

It's been said that most graphic design monographs are adventures in narcissism and self-absorbtion
That is certainly the case here, but I'm hoping it's as much about the books and the authors as it i
about me. (I know, nice try). To this end, I have asked several writers I've worked with over the year
to comment, in the hopes that their insight might be helpful. Please believe me—purely gushing testi
monials were discouraged. Regardless, I thank all of them for their contributions. If there's anyone I lef
out, I apologize, but there was too much to sort through and keep track of, and I am not the mos
organized person in the world (that would be Mark). Also note that in no way is this intended as a
definitive history of contemporary Knopf book jacket design. Many publishers are represented here
though of course my heart belongs to the Borzoi.

IT HAS BEEN A PRIVILEGE TO DO THIS WORK—I've always understood that and have never taken it fo
granted. Which doesn't mean that a lot of it wasn't a struggle and still is, or that I didn't spend extend
ed periods of time wondering how the hell I got into this business and how and when I could get out
But then—that manuscript lands on your desk, and you read it and it seizes your imagination and fill
your head with ideas like a balloon with helium, and then you chance upon the perfect art, and the
editor likes it, and the author loves it, and it gets printed and it looks great in your hands, and all i
right with the world. And you're mortified that you ever could have thought of books and publishing
as anything less than the most noble effort on the planet. I have been so lucky. It's obvious. What else
but luck could explain everything in this book?

Which reminds me of . . .

Faculty 1946

WESLEY R. UPDIKE

A.B., Ursinus College
M.S., University of Pennsylvania

Mathematics

Sunset and fall . . . "My Wild Irish Rose" is his favorite song . . . football and bowling . . . ambition as a child— to be a policeman . . . often heard saying "Wait a minute!" . . . likes gardening . . . Harry James . . . desires to visit San Francisco . . . roast beef and mashed potatoes . . . George Raft and Lucille Ball . . . dislikes people who forget their pencils.

Hi-Life 1946

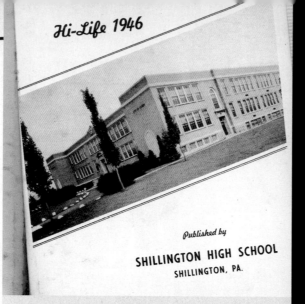

Published by
SHILLINGTON HIGH SCHOOL
SHILLINGTON, PA.

THIS PAGE: All images are from my dad's high school yearbook, senior year. Wesley Updike was one of his favorite teachers and one of the most eccentric. Dad remembered his son John as a gangly, sweet-natured kid four years his junior.

Seniors-1946

THOMAS KIDD

"T" is crazy about chop suey . . . claims he hasn't been thrilled . . . childhood ambition was to grow up . . . enjoys sleeping, eating, and loafing . . . "Bugs Bunny" rates high . . . is thrilled by Spike Jones and his City Slickers . . . says he's usually found in school . . . would like to travel . . . marine corps— big favorite branch of the service.

Chatterbox 1946

CO-EDITORS IN CHIEF, ARTISTS, FACULTY SUPERVISERS
Standing, left to right: W. Haeussler, Mrs. Lewis, Mrs. Ehrhart, A. Wentzel, L. Bert.
Sitting: J. Updike, A. Speck.

Editors

. . . a true story.

MY FIRST GRAPHIC DESIGN ASSIGNMENT IN COLLEGE was to create a jacket for John Updike's collection of short stories entitled *Museums and Women*. Well. I knew I had the inside track on this one. It was family lore growing up that Updike's father had been my father's math teacher at Shillington high school, which of course John had gone on to immortalize in many of his books, including the *Rabbit* series and especially *The Centaur*, which was specifically about his dad. I myself had grown up in Lincoln Park, Pa., a scant mile or two from Shillington (where my grandmother still lived) but separated by a highway that left bicycle access out of the question, so I rarely went there on my own.

Anyway, the narrator of the title story recalls attending his first museum as a child on a class field trip, and sure enough, it's the Reading Museum, where I'd gone at his age—it was a rite of passage for any kid in the county. So that weekend I returned home, went to the scene of the crime as it were, and took pictures. *This is shooting fish in a barrel*, I thought, aiming my lens at the fountain described on page 4 and clicking the shutter. *Only MY book cover will be authentic. Only MINE will be honest and true to the subject! I shall crush them all! Ha ha! Fools!!* So I went back to school and had the pictures developed, and arranged the best ones in a cunningly attractive scheme, and as a crowning touch for the title treatment I duplicated the M of *Museums* and flopped it so it became the W of *Women*. Oh, yes.

The next morning we had our first critique. I got there early and was the first to tack mine to the cork board that lined the front of the room. Soon everyone's solutions were up, and we waited nervously for the teacher's wisdom. As she strolled slowly from one end to the other, inspecting each carefully, she settled on mine and and turned to address the class.

"Who's is this?"

I sat up straight, very pleased, and beamed "Why, it's mine."

And she replied, and I will never forget it:

"Well, this is one area of graphic design we may have to steer *you* away from."

And then, for what seemed like hours (probably five minutes), she methodically, calmly, and succinctly dissected my solution, exposing each of its faults like a dentist going over my x-rays and pointing out the root rot. In one fell swoop my swelled breast became a chicken chest. I was mortified.

So, do I tell this story out of disdain or malice? The avenging shriek of ultimate vindication? I do not. I tell this story because that teacher, one Edith Friedman, was right. What I'd done was silly, amateurish, and forced. It hardly mattered that the photos had a direct connection to the subject if they were clumsy and dull, which they were; and the typography was needlessly gimmicky. Presto: because of her, I could see that now. What a revelation. Edie Friedman was a damned good teacher, doing her job. Had she not, you wouldn't be reading this.

And so I learned from her. A lot. And I went on and studied graphic design for three more years at Penn State with Bill Kinser and Lanny Sommese and worked very hard—and well, you'll see.

But of course the weirdest part of the story is that after I graduated I came to Knopf, and eventually designed jackets for . . . John Updike (see page 316). Such an irony makes you want to ask for a rewrite—it's just too contrived. Certainly it is unworthy of the finest writer Shillington has ever produced. —C. K.

Introduction by John Updike

FOR A FEW YEARS IN THE MID-1940s, between the ages of eleven and thirteen, I used to deliver movie circulars for the local cinema in Shillington, Pennsylvania. My pay was a week's movie pass. Wartime taxes had put the ticket price up to eleven cents, and to buy into all three of the features that The Shillington (as it was flatly called) projected each week, at seven and nine p.m. Mondays through Saturdays, would have taken too huge a bite from my thirty-five-cent allowance, leaving only two cents for the Sunday-school collection. A bunch of us boys gathered at the theater on Saturday mornings, and each team of two was given its sheaf of circulars and its territory. Shillington, a town of nearly five thousand, was divided into several sections, and then there were the outlying satellites like Mohnton, Pennwyn, and Lincoln Park. Some were a trolley-car ride away, and others a stiff walk. Lincoln Park I remember as being just a little beyond the old quarry on the Shillington line, a no-man's land of no-nonsense middle-class brick homes whose offspring wound up in the Shillington public schools. Imagine my sense of eternal return, of geographical ambush, when, decades after leaving the area, I learned that Chip Kidd, my publisher's dashing young virtuoso of book-jacket design, was from Lincoln Park.

Bucks County, on the Delaware, was in those distant days a weekend resort for New York writers and theater types, and Chester County a play-ground for the Philadelphia horsey set, but Berks County was a laboring county, divided between farmers plowing its loamy fields and millworkers crammed into the rowhouses of Reading, the county's perpetually depressed and crime-friendly metropolis. The region was not unfriendly to popular culture. Radios babbled their daily soap operas in every dentist's office; any town of any size had its movie palace and Reading had five (Loew's, the Warner, the Astor, the Embassy, the Ritz) along Penn Street alone; art and music still rode high in public-school curricula; and shops carrying craft and art supplies were common. Art, of the practical, sign-painting, enroll-in-our-course-and-become-a-well-paid-cartoonist sort, had its place in the local enterprises. We wallowed in kitsch—even the Amish had their hex signs—and relied, pre-television, pre-computer, on the print medium to bring us imagery from the metropolitan centers of consumerism and entertainment. It was a golden age of comic strips, animated cartoons, movie fan magazines, comic books; we would all be a little richer had we kept the Superman and Batman comics we bought for a nickel and saved until the next wartime paper drive. The sensory and romantic deprivations of provincial existence call for avid consumption of news from fantasylands.

Though the cultural climate of southeastern Pennsylvania has surely changed in the two-and-thirty years between my boyhood and Chip Kidd's,

the soil must still be fertile for the young homebody and media-maven, "for all of us," as Kidd wrote in his epic album *Peanuts: The Art of Charles M. Schulz* (Pantheon, 2001), "who ate our school lunches alone and didn't have any hope of sitting anywhere near the little red-haired girl and never got any valentines and struck out every single time we were shoved to the plate for Little League." Véronique Vienne, in introducing her monograph *Chip Kidd* (Yale University Press, 2003), claims on doubtless good authority that his greatest design influence was daytime television; that at age two he was already a Batman fan, complete with mask, cape, and gloves; and that "he developed a love of graphic design by staring in supermarkets at the packaging of Batman playthings." He majored in graphic design at Penn State, studying under Lanny Sommese (an experience with some relation to the antic events of Kidd's one novel, *The Cheese Monkeys*), and at the tender age of twenty-two was hired by Knopf as a junior assistant to Sara Eisenman.

The rest is, so to speak, graphic history. In a field, book-jacket design, where edge, zip, and instant impact are *sine qua non*, Kidd is second to none, and singular in the complexity of the comment his book jackets sometimes deliver upon the text they enwrap. His jackets, for example, for the novels *My Name Is Red*, by Orhan Pamuk, and *Was*, by Geoff Ryman, suggest with their dizzyingly variegated panels the vertiginous, layered contents within.

On the biographies of William Blake by Peter Ackroyd and of Jim Thompson by Robert Polito, Kidd's tightly tiled imagery fairly shouts out with the pain of a life. His series of jackets for Elmore Leonard form a suite of photographic motifs from the nation's psychic underworld.

In the intensity of his wish to use a jacket's few square inches to arrest and intrigue the bookstore browser, he exploits every resource of modern printing. On Richard North Patterson's *Silent Witness*, embossing uncannily duplicates the feel of crinkled and stretched police tape; on Haruki Murakami's *The Wind Up Bird Chronicle*, a semi-visible diagram concocted by Chris Ware (a cartoonist frequently engaged by Kidd) underlays a partially blurred photo of a mechanical bird taken by Geoff Spear (another favorite collaborator); on Kurt Anderson's *Turn of the Century* not only is the cover image of New York mirrored in the lower half but the word "century" is inverted also. Not that Kidd's jackets are always complicated. Katherine Hepburn's autobiography, *Me,* was done with simple typography; a tyrannosaur silhouette starkly adorned Michael Crichton's *Jurassic Park*; and rather famously (in the whispering galleries of jacket design) a stuffed bunny on its head presented an enigmatic, vaguely horrific image for Paul Golding's *The Abomination*. Ditto an enlarged doll's head on Donna Tartt's *The Little Friend*. Kidd reads the books he designs for and

locates a disquieting image close to the narrative's dark, beating heart. The eyes on his jacket for Richmond Lattimore's translation of the New Testament may have bombed with booksellers but in two seconds achieved what Mel Gibson strived to do in two hours: made Christ's death real.

Can Kidd draw? Presumably, yet the mark of his pen or pencil rarely figures into his work. His tool is the digital computer, with its ever more ingenious graphics programs. In the ever-expanding electronic archives of scannable photographic imagery, he is a hunter-gatherer. His jackets for books of poetry, exempt from any demand for mass-market appeal, show him at his freest and—see the snuggled spoon and fork of Vikram Seth's *All You Who Sleep Tonight*—witticst. There is a playful thinginess and a stern dimension of concreteness to Kidd's designs: Robert Hughes's essays on art are fronted by the back of a canvas, a Cuban novel by Cristina Garcia is wrapped in cigar-box imagery. A book on Samuel Beckett, stunningly, floats the subject's miniaturized head in a sea of black. And so on, idea after idea after idea.

What remains to be said is that Chip Kidd, my fellow Berks Countian, is wonderfully easy to work with—open and adaptable and unflappable, when faced with authors who have ideas of their own. I had the notion, on my novel *Seek My Face*, of an abstract-looking mess of brushstrokes that would resolve at a distance into a face. Kidd actually went down to Soho, bought an inexpensive, broadly worked portrait, and had the face photographed under a raking light, to bring up the shadows of the impasto. He has the good humor and spendthrift resourcefulness of an artist who trusts the depth of his own creativity. In an edgy field, he is not only edgy but deep.

John Updike

THE BORZOI CREDO

I *believe that* a publisher's imprint means something, and that if readers paid more attention to the publisher of the books they buy, their chances of being disappointed would be infinitely less.

I *believe that* good books should be well made, and I try to give every book I publish a format that is distinctive and attractive.

Appeared originally as an advertisement in The Atlantic Monthly, November 1957.

28

The Borzoi Credo

I *believe that* I have never unknowingly published an unworthy book.

I *believe in* keeping the price of the books as low as is compatible with quality, production costs, and the financial resources of the reader for whom they are intended.

I *believe that* a publisher has a moral as well as a commercial obligation to his authors to try in every way to promote the sales of their books, to keep them in print, and to enhance his authors' prestige.

I *believe in* the innate good taste of book readers and in their ability to recognize a superior book when they have it brought to their attention.

I *believe that* a review by an incompetent critic is a sin against the author, the book, the publisher, and the publication in which the review appears.

I *believe that* the basic need of the book business is not Madison Avenue ballyhoo, but more booksellers who love and understand books and who can communicate their enthusiasm to a waiting audience.

I *believe that* magazines, movies, television, and radio will never displace good books.

29

1989

SPRING

KNOPF

PUBLISHER OF BORZOI BOOKS

LEFT: Alfred A. Knopf's heartbreakingly earnest publishing manifesto. Who wouldn't want to work for this company? I think he would now add "the internet" to the last article. **ABOVE:** Knopf catalogue, spring 1989, featuring an art deco brooch from the 1920s. Photo by Geoff Spear. **BELOW:** Since its inception in 1915, Knopf's logo has been a borzoi (Russian Wolfhound) running to the left. Its most ingenious aspect is that it can be interpereted any number of ways and has been throughout the firm's history. These are a few of my versions.

DRIBS 'N DRABS BORZOI · MATTISSEAN/AB-EX BORZOI · MESA FLATS BORZOI · CONSTRUCTIVIST BORZOI · MY ALL-TIME FAVE: THE EXISTISTENTIAL BORZOI, REDUCED TO ITS MOST ESSENTIAL PARTS

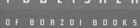

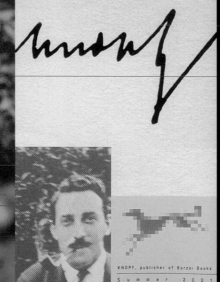

IN THE ART DEPARTMENT WE TAKE TURNS DESIGNING THE CATALOGUE cover for each season's list of titles. Of course it has to have a borzoi on it somewhere, but other than that it can be anything. We publish three seasons of books a year—Fall, Spring and Summer (there was a short-lived Winter season, soon re-thought), which means that each staff member gets a crack at it every year and a half. **THIS PAGE:** (clockwise from top left) Fall 1991; Fall 1994 (illustration by Carol Carson); Spring 2003; Winter 1996; Summer 2001; Fall 1998; Spring 1993. My favorite is the above right, which I had Peter Mendelsund shoot in our temporary location on Park Avenue and just outside Carol's office, as one of the denizens of her extensive borzoi collection appears to be venturing into the hallway for a stroll. That's me trying to look busy next to Natalie Slocum, one of our rights and permissions people at the time, who went on to design numerous book covers herself.

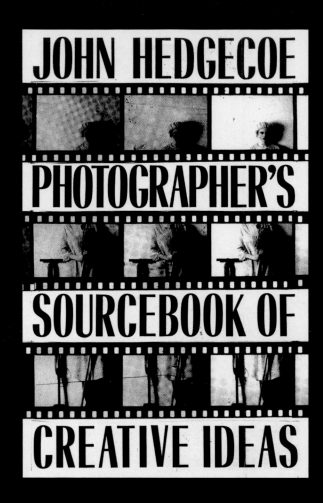

On your marks, get set . . .

SO HERE IT IS, THE FIRST JACKET I EVER DESIGNED. PRETTY INAUSPICIOUS, ISN'T IT? I seem to remember that it was a holdover from the previous list and had to get done very quickly. That situation, I've come to learn, can be the best facilitator. As much as they are a dreadful burden, deadlines can also be your best friend—when something simply must get done and time has run out, the people in charge tend to finally focus and the approval process suddenly gets easier.

I remember I kept trying to impart a "concept" to the jacket, to have images in the frames interacting with each other or otherwise expand beyond their borders (above). This was not wanted. Many years later Archie Ferguson revamped these for new expanded editions and did a much, much better job. **ABOVE:** The first rejected sketch for the first jacket. Too "arty." **RIGHT:** Knopf, 1986. That's it, man—naked chicks and hot rods! Awesome! Note my attempt to be "sequential" in the first strip, "purely" black and white in the middle, and then just giving up and succumbing to sleaze and cliché at the bottom. Approved!

Next!

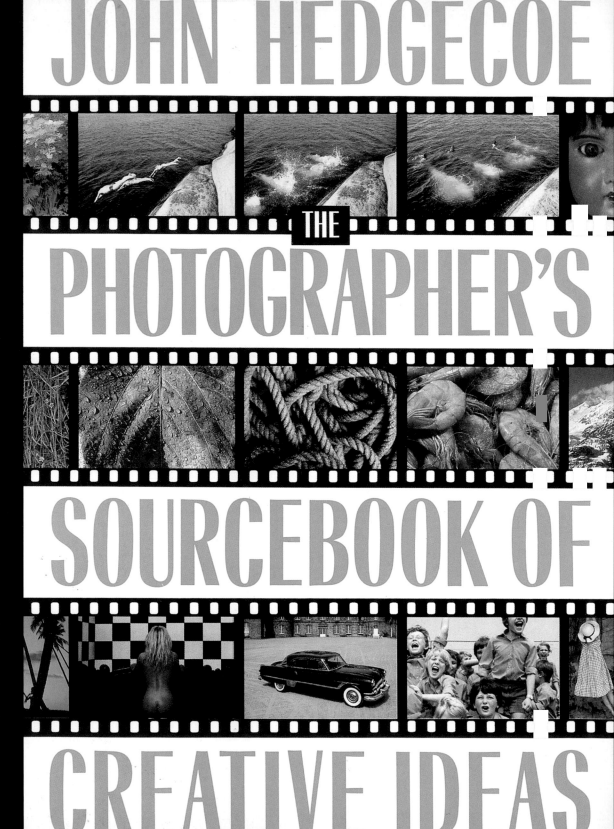

ARCHAIC FIGURE

POEMS BY

AMY CLAMPITT

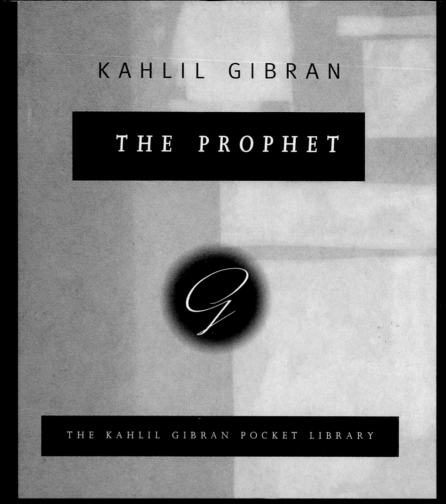

KAHLIL GIBRAN

THE PROPHET

G

THE KAHLIL GIBRAN POCKET LIBRARY

What's Etruscan for 'Eureka?'

AS WITH THE HEDGECOE, THE FIRST ASSIGNMENTS I GOT WERE FOLLOW-UPS on previously assigned and rejected covers. This was hardly surprising—Sara Eisenman had been without an assistant for several weeks, and plenty had backed up. But nor was it disappointing, because it was all so new, and not having to come up with designs completely from scratch was a good way to start. The first jacket I felt I really brought something to came along after a couple of months and was for a collection of poems by Amy Clampitt called *Archaic Figure*. Now, I was given the art—the rather uninspiring subject of the title you see to the left—but in the photo the statue was in a truly dull context (a museum? I can't remember). So I thought why not silhouette it and make it part of a more alluring milieu? The result is purely decorative, but now looked more interesting to me than what I'd been given to work with. And *that* was the revelation—you have to force yourself to see beyond what's initially in front of your eyes. **LEFT:** Knopf, 1987. **ABOVE:** Knopf, 1995. This jacket doesn't really belong here chronologically, but we couldn't find any other place to put it. Originally published in 1923, *The Prophet* is the single bestselling Knopf title of all time and was due to soon enter the public domain. Thus this design for a series of "pocket library editions," which included Gibran's other titles.

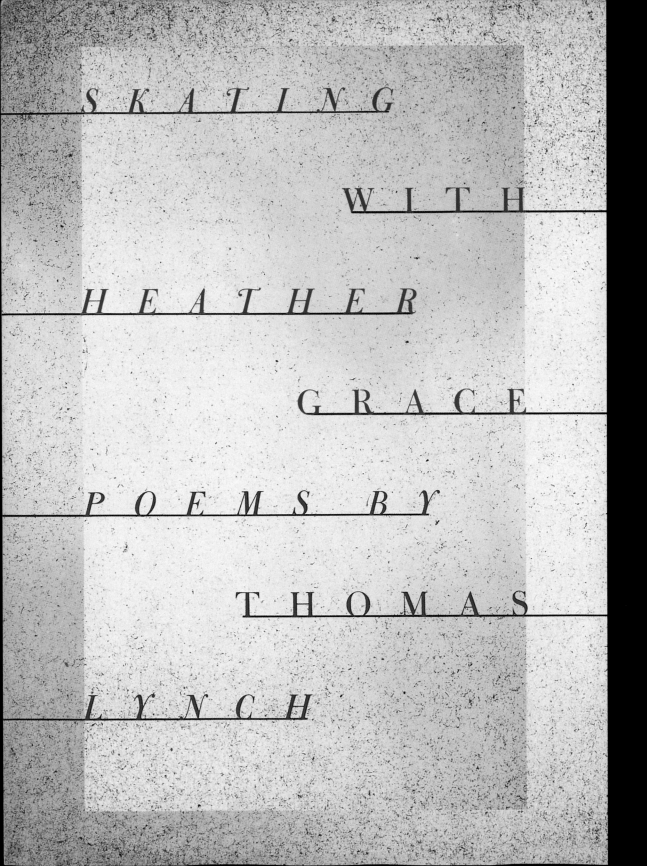

S K A T I N G

W I T H

H E A T H E R

G R A C E

P O E M S   B Y

T H O M A S

L Y N C H

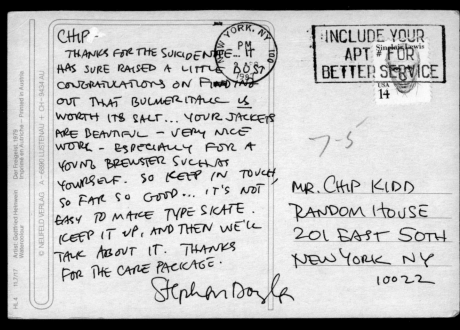

CHIP—
THANKS FOR THE SUICIDE NOTE... IT
HAS SURE RAISED A LITTLE BOOST.
CONGRATULATIONS ON FINDING
OUT THAT BULMER ITALIC IS
WORTH ITS SALT... YOUR JACKETS
ARE BEAUTIFUL — VERY NICE
WORK — ESPECIALLY FOR A
YOUNG BREWSTER SUCH AS
YOURSELF. SO KEEP IN TOUCH,
SO FAR SO GOOD... IT'S NOT
EASY TO MAKE TYPE SKATE.
KEEP IT UP, AND THEN WE'LL
TALK ABOUT IT. THANKS
FOR THE CARE PACKAGE.
                    Stephen Doyle

INCLUDE YOUR
APT # FOR
BETTER SERVICE

MR. CHIP KIDD
RANDOM HOUSE
201 EAST 50TH
NEW YORK NY
              10022

Cold snap.

BEFORE I SETTLED IN NEW YORK FOR GOOD in the fall of 1986, I'd made a short trip to scout things out the previous June and found myself at the offices of the newly formed Drenttel Doyle Partners design firm. Stephen Doyle was smart, urbane, and enormously talented, having cut his teeth at *Rolling Stone* and M&Co. He and partner Bill Drenttel weren't hiring but said they'd hold onto my résumé if something came up. That August, while I was still in Reading, to my disbelief they contacted me about coming in to assist on a big new project they'd taken on. Could I start in a day or two? Family obligations kept me home that summer, and I hadn't planned on heading into the city until September. Could they wait 'til then? They very politely said they couldn't, but thanks. And several months later I realized I'd given up the chance to work on the launch of, yes, *Spy* magazine. I kicked myself repeatedly. But I stayed in touch with Stephen, and when I was getting desperate with no prospects in October he told me to keep looking for a little while longer and if nothing came up, to call him again and he'd give me something to do. The next week Knopf called and that was that. But I never forgot Stephen's kindness, and we've remained friends throughout the years. The postcard from him above refers to a letter I wrote to *Spy* early on, saying, "I was going to kill myself because there are so many ugly magazines, but then *Spy* came along and now I live month to month." When he says "keep it up and we'll talk about it," he's referring to my constant badgering about working for him. The reference to skating type is to the jacket for Thomas Lynch (left).

THE FOURTH WORLD

THE HERITAGE OF THE ARCTIC

AND ITS DESTRUCTION

BY SAM HALL

OPPOSITE LEFT: Knopf, 1987, co-designed with Sarah Eisenman. I made the art by hand-tinting an underexposed photostat with water-based dyes. I think the rules are way too thick; they would have worked much better in hairline thickness. **OPPOSITE RIGHT:** Knopf, 1987. Illustration by Peter deSéve. **ABOVE:** Knopf, 1987. This looks so dated to me . . . those heavy initial caps on every word are the typographic equivalent of Joan Collins's shoulder pads on *Dynasty*. **RIGHT:** Knopf, 1989. Photo by Drew Pleak. One of my first designs for editor Gordon Lish (see p. 50).

THE ICE AT THE BOTTOM OF THE WORLD

stories

MARK RICHARD

THE DAY ROOM

A PLAY BY DON DeLILLO

WHEN KNOPF DID A HARDCOVER EDITION of my play *The Day Room*, there was very little time, I recall, for customary niceties. They wanted the book to be available when the play opened in New York, and that meant Right Away. So when I saw Chip Kidd's cover design I was surprised and delighted by the way in which he managed to convey the grim mystery of the text so quickly and deftly. The split grin of the straightjacketed man, the significant gap between the acts, the subtle background of transparent stage flats arranged in a somewhat anxious cubist block—all these elements make his design a faithful flat-earth rendering of the world inside the play.

—Don Delillo

LEFT: Knopf, 1987. This was the first jacket I felt I was allowed to give a strong personal stamp to, and the first that got into the AIGA's book show. **BELOW:** The original art—a photo by Thomas Derrah that I enhanced with pencil and spray-fix (check out that faux-cubist background!). The yellow marks around his crotch were not meant to be seen and only eventually emerged with time, the scars of a now-outdated "stat eradicator pen."

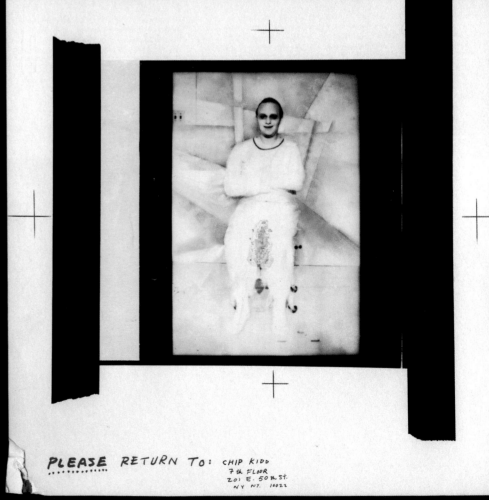

PLEASE RETURN TO: CHIP KIDD 7th FLOOR 201 E. 50th St. NY NY. 10022

OPPOSITE LEFT: Random House, 1992. One of the few jackets I illustrated. **OPPOSITE RIGHT:** TCG, 1997.

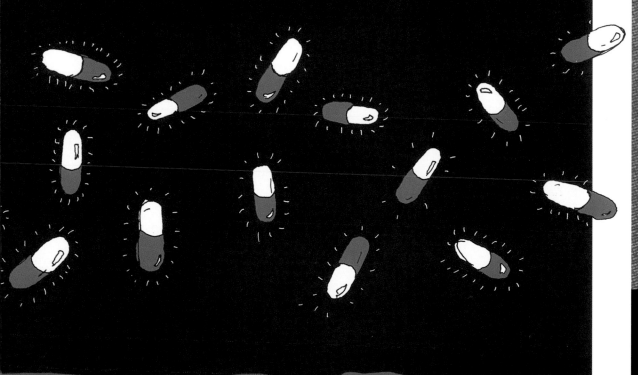

KICKING

TOMORROW

DANIEL RICHLER

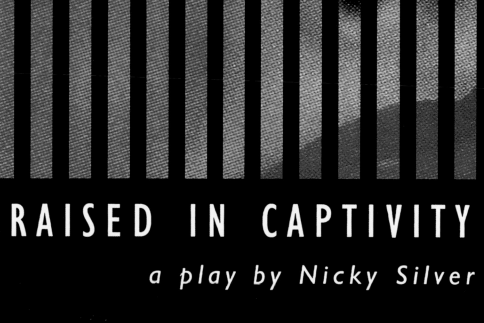

RAISED IN CAPTIVITY

a play by Nicky Silver

MY HARD BARGAIN

STORIES

WALTER KIRN

"I ate these stories! I gobbled them right up! I swallowed them whole—
while in bed, while riding in the back of a truck, while driving the truck,
while sitting in the yard cooking elk steaks on the grill! Thank goodness
for Walter Kirn, whose heart has fed me — whose heart has fed my
heart!"
—Rick Bass

"The weight of these stories is something remarkable. They are big-
hearted, readable, original. This is the perfect place to get used to Walter
Kirn; he is going to be around for a long time."   —Thomas McGuane

9 780394 583037

51895>

ISBN 0-394-58303-5

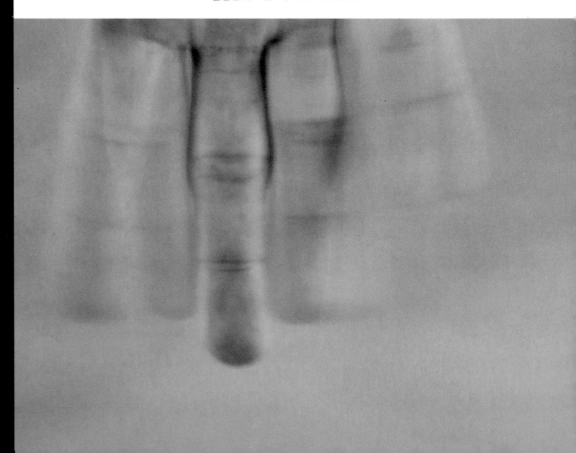

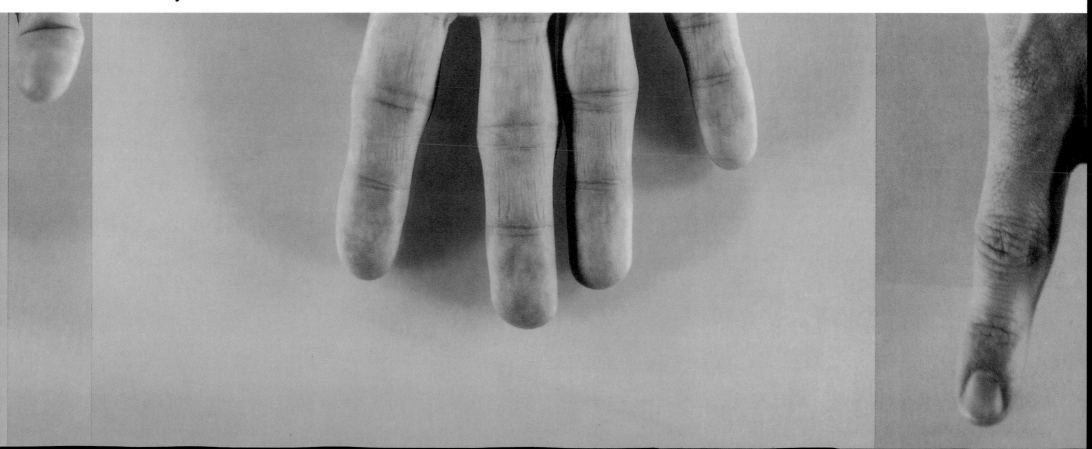

MY
hard
bargain

WALTER

KIRN

KNOPF   stories by   **WALTER KIRN**

MY hard bargain

hand-job

'MY HARD BARGAIN' WAS THE FIRST of what I came to informally dub "the weird-art half-jackets." These consist of a bisected picture plane (usually through the center) with the art (usually a "quirky" photograph) relegated to one half (usually the bottom), and the type in the other. As much as I've tried to diversify my design approaches over the years, when I'm stumped I inevitably fall back to this formula (*All the Pretty Horses, SlackJaw, Naked*, etc.). Why does it work so well? I think one reason is that it makes everything so neat, like organizing someone's closet—the type goes up there and the picture down there, and no muss no fuss. **LEFT:** Knopf, 1990. That's (surprise!) my hand, which I shot myself on the stat camera. In the first story of this collection, a team of Mormon basketball players is told by their coach to record every time they masturbate by marking an X in invisible ink onto a large sheet of cardboard. Before the big game he has them bring their boards into the locker room, kills the lights, and turns on a big ultra-violet bulb. Bright yellow X's suddenly appear everywhere. The story is called *Planetarium*. **OPPOSITE LEFT:** I was heartsick when this sketch was nixed—it got the kibbosh not because the title ran vertically, but because there was no model release for the man in the photo. But I do think what we ended up with was more interesting.

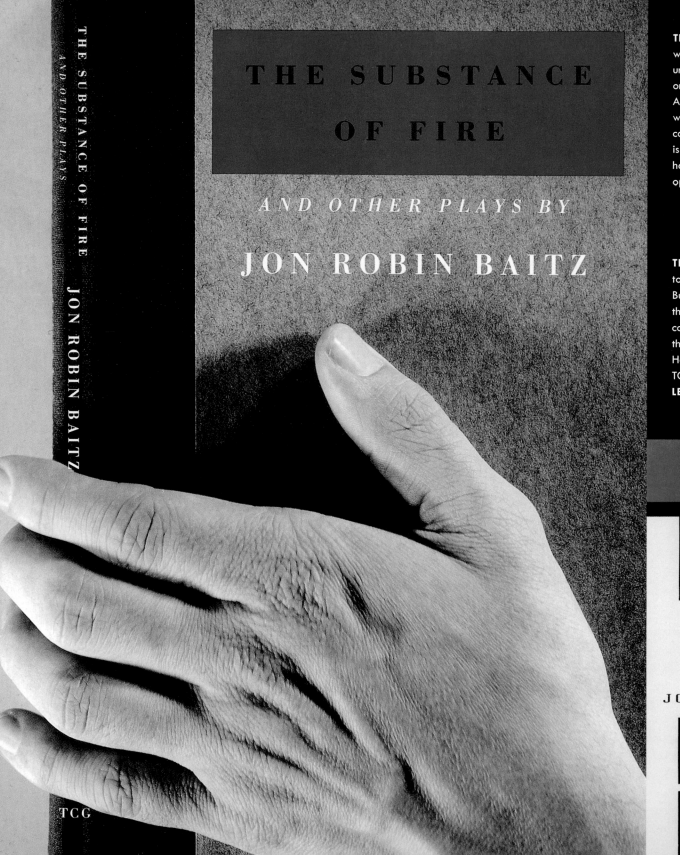

THE SUBSTANCE
OF FIRE

AND OTHER PLAYS BY

JON ROBIN BAITZ

THE HAND RESTING ON THE BOOK, AS IF FOR COMFORT. A very good image for my plays, which seem often to concern themselves with the predicaments of clever people being undone by their own weakness, and having nowhere to go for comfort. On first glance, one begins to suspect the great exhaustion of the body and spirit connected to that hand. Am I "projecting," as the radio psychologist would say? Sure. And isn't that a wonderful way into a book? To see one's own condition reflected on its cover? *The Substance of Fire* concerns the state of being that occurs when one has lost almost everything, and all that is left is an anemic internal life, one tumultuously imagined, and fueled by memory. That hand on the cover is instantly recognizable; someone seeking refuge, someone about to open a book and escape.

—Jon Robin Baitz

THE MOST UNCANNY THING TO ME ABOUT 'THE SUBSTANCE OF FIRE' was that it seemed to be directly based on what was happening at Pantheon at the time the play premiered. But of course it couldn't have been, unless Baitz wrote it and had it produced in about three days (not the case). The ousting of editor-in-chief Andre Schiffrin was unpleasant, complicated, and very public, and directly mirrored the plot and protagonist of the play— the heartbreaking dismissal of an idealistic book publisher (primarily of Judaic and Holocaust literature) whose fiscal irresponsibility is destroying his own company. **LEFT:** TCG, 1993. The nice thing was the way the fingers wrapped around the spine. **BELOW LEFT:** Unused idea for *Three Hotels*, 1994. **BELOW RIGHT:** Trade ad for the *New York Times*.

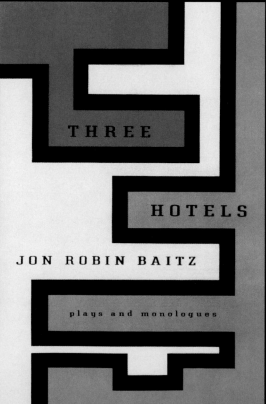

39

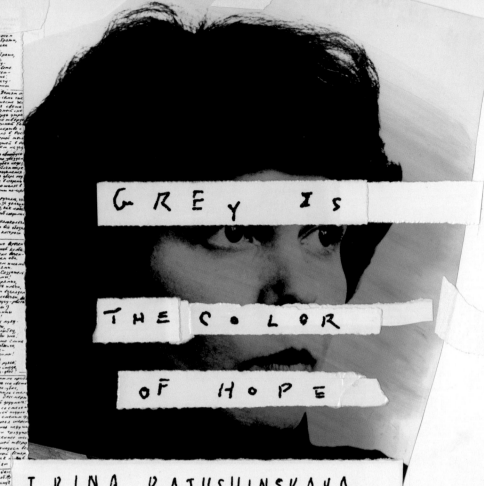

GREY IS
THE COLOR
OF HOPE

IRINA RATUSHINSKAYA

PANTONE®
433C

PANTONE®
412 C

PLEASE
RETURN TO:

CHIP KIDD
7th FLOOR
201 E. 50th St.

Hope is the color of design.

LIKE SO MANY BEFORE HER, IRINA RATUSHINSKAYA SPENT YEARS OF HER LIFE in a Soviet prison because of her poetry. Labeled a dissident and jailed in 1983, she surreptitiously wrote on whatever scraps of paper she could find, scrolled them up into tiny capsules, and hid them from guards. Upon being freed in 1986, she fled to America and published two sets of memoirs and a collection of poetry. The strips of paper were both her doom and her salvation, so I wanted to use their form to represent the terms of her confinement. On the cover of *Grey Is the Color of Hope*, they hover above her sensory inputs, as she survives despite their threatening to choke her.

PAGE 39: Experiments on the stat machine using copies of Ratushinskaya's texts. **OPPOSITE LEFT:** Sketch comp for *Grey is the Color of Hope*, which became the original art. **OPPOSITE RIGHT:** Knopf, 1988. **ABOVE:** Knopf, 1989. **RIGHT:** Knopf, 1991. Photo by Geoff Spear. In order to properly achieve the trompe l'oeil effect of something like this, you have to have it photographed.

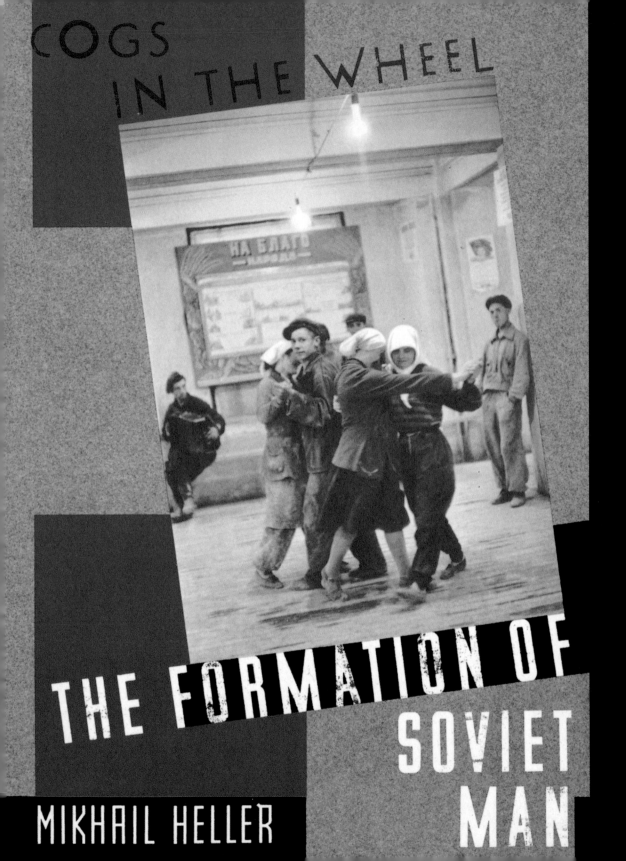

COGS IN THE WHEEL

THE FORMATION OF SOVIET MAN

MIKHAIL HELLER

EDWARD

W. SAID

OUT

OF

PLACE

KNOPF

OUT OF PLACE

A MEMOIR

GORE VIDAL ONCE REMARKED, "IT IS NOT ENOUGH TO SUCCEED. OTHERS MUST FAIL." What a guy. So he must have been thrilled with the cover for *Palimpsest*, because while I wasn't the first to work on it, I definitely was the last. **OPPOSITE RIGHT:** Random House, 1995. Andy Carpenter, art director. This is how I displayed the semi-transparent vellum jacket in my portfolio at the time—a vintage Victorian photo album (see title page). **LEFT:** Knopf, 1988. I'm trying to channel my inner Rodchenko here, with Emigre type no less. Hey, I was young. **ABOVE:** Knopf, 1999. I had the honor to work directly with Edward Said on this jacket, carefully sifting through his personal photos at his home on the Upper West Side. This memoir only extends up through his mid-twenties, so he "ages" on the spine as you start at the top and read downward. The front uses the negative space to heighten Said's sense of unease and displacement. What you can't see is that he's leaning against his mother.

YES, EARTHLINGS, THERE IS A 'STAR TREK' PERSONALITY QUIZ. When the Vulcan ambassador offers a series of meditative courses designed to renew energy and encourage inner harmony you are: a) not really interested or, b) very interested. A Borg sphere appears in front of the Enterprise, weapons at the ready, and your first instinct is to: a) destroy them or, b) figure out what's going on. Upon beaming down to a mysterious planet in the Delta Quadrant, you discover that the aliens are capable of reading your mind and instantly transforming your slightest wish into a harmless and fun reality for all to see. You: a) stay for a week or, b) beam back up to the ship and read a book. Maybe this one . . . **BELOW:** HarperCollins, 1994. Limited signed edition. Joseph Montebello, art director.

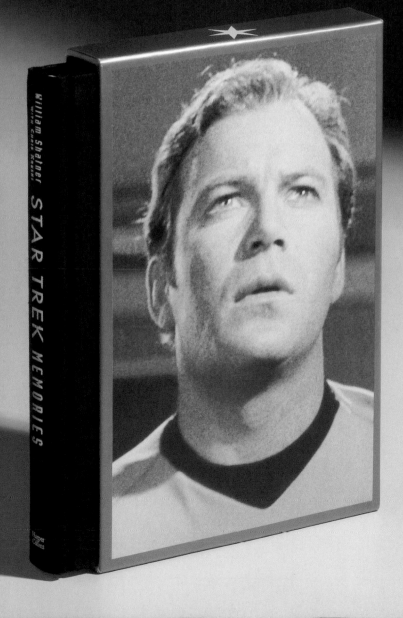

GORE VIDAL

PALIMPSEST

A MEMOIR

VÁCLAV HAVEL

DISTURBING THE PEACE

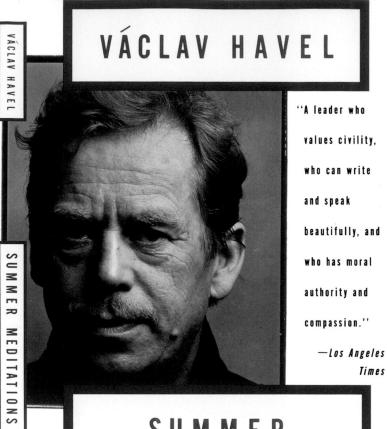

VÁCLAV HAVEL

"A leader who values civility, who can write and speak beautifully, and who has moral authority and compassion."

—*Los Angeles Times*

SUMMER MEDITATIONS

Vintage

The SPIRIT OF PRAGUE

STATES OF INJURY
POWER AND FREEDOM IN LATE MODERNITY

Ivan Klíma

WENDY BROWN

THE ANGEL OF HISTORY

Carolyn Forché

"A voice that spoke, speaks, and will continue to haunt the future." —DEREK WALCOTT

Prague Spring break.

IT'S A TESTAMENT EITHER TO MY LONGEVITY AT KNOPF, or how much times have changed in Czechoslovakia, or both, but here is a fact: not long after joining the firm I was sitting in a pre-sales meeting when editor Bobbie Bristol pitched jailed dissident playwright Václav Havel's book of prison writings to his wife (*Letters to Olga*), and *he was still in prison at the time.* And I remember people remarking at the meeting that it was unlikely he'd ever be freed. The idea that he would eventually become president of the country? Completely unthinkable. **CLOCKWISE FROM OPPOSITE LEFT:** Knopf, 1990; Vintage, 1993. Photograph by Annie Leibowitz; HarperCollins, 1995. Joseph Montebello, art director; unused comp for *The Angel of History*. I knew it was a long shot, but had to try. Not even the mighty Joseph could railroad this one through; Princeton University Press, 1995; Granta, 1995.

THE ANGEL OF HISTORY

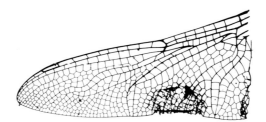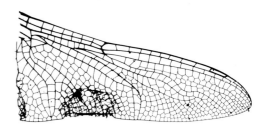

Carolyn Forché

○

AUTHOR OF **THE COUNTRY BETWEEN US**

THE GREEN DARK

POEMS BY

MARIE PONSOT

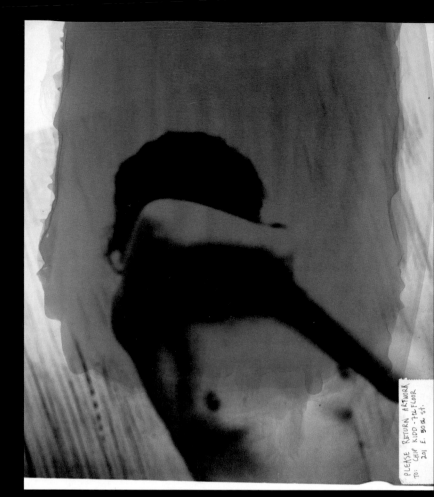

THE BIRD CATCHER

poems

Marie Ponsot

Marie Ponsot

Springing

NEW AND SELECTED POEMS

Springing green.

EVERYONE IN THE ART DEPARTMENT WANTS TO WORK on the poetry books, because they afford the chance to design something, well, poetic. Marie Ponsot's certainly do—*The Green Dark* was the first poetry title that allowed me to construct the art entirely from scratch. **OPPOSITE LEFT:** Knopf, 1988. I was still in my continuous-tone photostat and watercolor dye phase. The dye deeply saturates the paper, and the color just glows. **OPPOSITE RIGHT, TOP:** The original art. At first I wanted to use this in its entirety, as you see it, to emphasize the idea of a "green dark" literally descending on the figure. But the boobies made it awkward, and zooming in for a closeup detail always amps up the drama. **OPPOSITE RIGHT, BOTTOM:** Knopf, 1998. **LEFT:** Knopf, 2002. The painting of the fireworks is by Stephen Hannock. The portrait is the author, by her husband, Claude Ponsot. **BELOW:** Knopf, 2002.

SIR GAWAIN & THE GREEN KNIGHT

a new verse translation by W. S. MERWIN

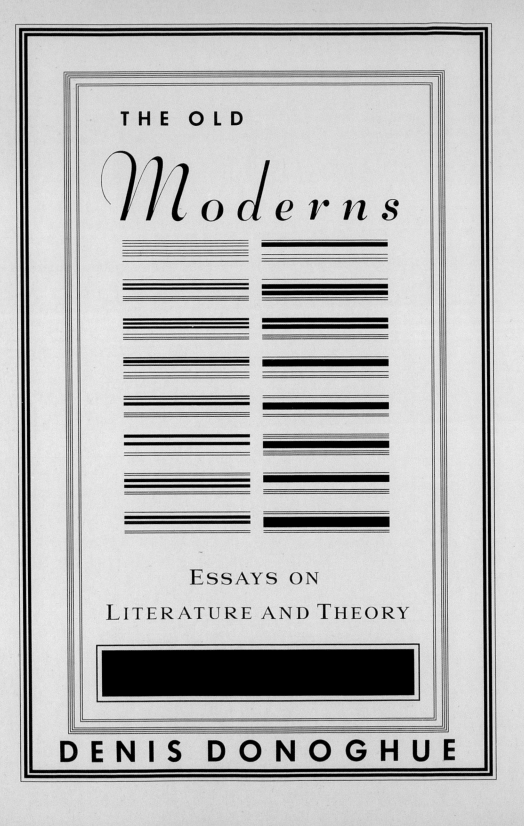

THE OLD

Moderns

ESSAYS ON
LITERATURE AND THEORY

DENIS DONOGHUE

Picking up the pieces.

I HADN'T BEEN EXPOSED TO MANY TYPOGRAPHIC SPECIMEN books—especially older ones—in college because we never spec'd actual type for projects and couldn't have afforded it even if we wanted to. We used Letraset rub-down type for headlines and display, or if we had time, set it ourselves with lead or wood type in the print shop (tedious but worth it).

So when I first encountered these tomes, both from Knopf co-workers and from antiquarian book-dealers (thank you, Irving Oaklander), it was a revelation. The fascinating configurations of the myriad assortments of bars, brackets, and dingbats were not meant for anything other than cataloguing purposes, but we in the jacket department saw them as unintended but undeniable typographic poetry. Barbara and I seized on this for Dennis Donoghue's collection of essays analyzing and deconstructing some of the great modernist writiers of the early twentieth century—we literally lifted a Monotype specimen page line for glorious line and used it as a metaphor for this collection of challenging fragments. The real fun was on the back, as we then let them fall like leaves from the authorial tree. Boy, would we have LOVED to do the same to the barcode, which seems to have taken up where they left off. **LEFT & RIGHT:** Knopf, 1994, co-designed with Barbara deWilde. **BELOW:** Just one example of the visual language of type spec books. It's when you remove all the copy from them that they *really* get interesting. **OPPOSITE RIGHT:** HarperCollins, 1997. Yet another design championed by Joseph Montebello. It's a little extreme, but if you've ever seen a Beckett play . . .

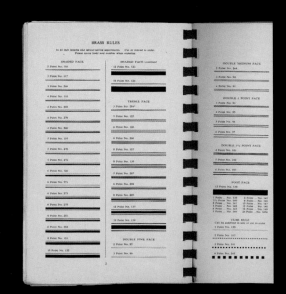

BILL HAYWARD

SAMUEL **BECKETT**

THE LAST MODERNIST

ANTHONY CRONIN

Harper
Collins

THE LAST MODERNIST

SAMUEL **BECKETT**

ANTHONY CRONIN

Call me Lishmael!

GORDON LISH WAS KNOPF'S CHE GUEVARA, WILLY WONKA, and P. T. Barnum, with a little Little Richard tossed in for good measure. Only he was more articulate than any of them and wore safari outfits to the office. (Every. Single. Day.) A kamikaze editor who honed his craft at *Esquire* in the mid-1970s, Lish joined Knopf in the early '80s and was immediately dubbed "Captain Fiction" by the media. I found him to be equal parts fearlessness, insanity, brilliance, and a by-product of his own skewed brand of pathologically fierce dedication. As Gordon would be the first to tell you, he was endlessly searching for nothing less than a new fiction form. And, putting his money where his mouth was, that meant book jackets to match—the more outlandish, the more unexpected, the more completely against the traditional Knopf grain, the louder he clapped. But beyond shock, Gordon understood that a jacket had to effectively represent the book—especially if the text was completely over the top. Which was inevitably the case. Working with Gordon was an exhilarating, delirious treat, and all of us in the design department practically tripped over each other for the privilege. *Watching the Body Burn* was not the first of his books I worked on (that would be Mark Richard's *The Ice at the Bottom of the World*, p. 33), but it *was* my first comprehensive design (jacket, binding, and text) for a novel. More important, it was my first real breakthrough—the manuscript inspired me to cut loose and try something I'd never done before: create more than a book's facade, but its unique sense of visual self—to give it an inner life dictated by its own origins. To this end, I reinterpreted the visual vernacular of vintage matchbooks, using extracts of the text in the manner of advertising slogans for cigarettes. **RIGHT AND OPPOSITE:** Knopf, 1989.

HOLY SHIT!! WHAT HAVE YOU DONE TO MY BOOK JACKET?? What is this? You're not going to use those colors, are you? OK, I'm not looking at the real book jacket, right? Now you're going to do the real book jacket, right? I mean, you wouldn't use those colors, would you? Aren't they too, garish? And that figure, that face, those arms and legs, that type face, they all look so weird. The whole thing kind of jumps out at you, startles you, shocks you . . .

Isn't that what you were doing in the novel?
Well, yes, but a novel is one thing; a book jacket, that's . . .
Different?
Yea, a novel is . . . well, a novel is . . .
Shouldn't it be a part of the whole? Shouldn't it fit?
Well . . . hmmm . . . sonafabitch, yes!

—Thomas Glynn

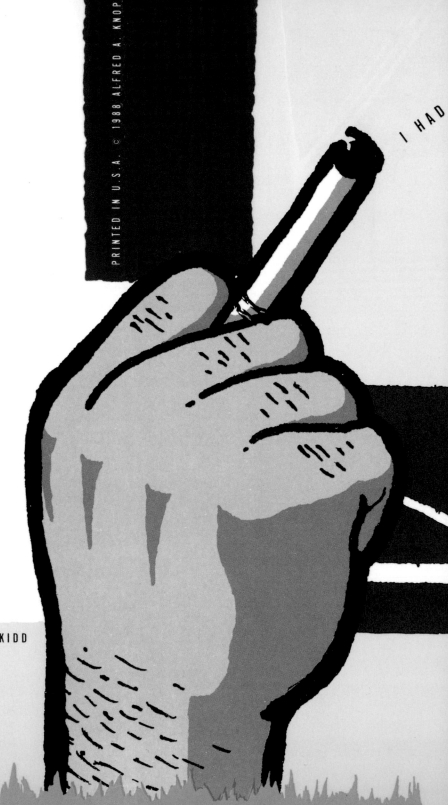

THOMAS GLYNN has had fiction in *The New Yorker, The Paris Review,* and *The Quarterly.* He was educated at the University of Chicago, and now makes his home in Brooklyn. Mr. Glynn's previous novels are *Temporary Sanity* and *The Building.*

PRINTED IN U.S.A. © 1988 ALFRED A. KNOPF INC.

JACKET DESIGN & ILLUSTRATION BY CHIP KIDD

ALFRED A. KNOPF

PUBLISHER, NEW YORK

1/89

I HAD

WATCHING
THE
BODY
BURN

WATCHING THE BODY

Burn

THOMAS GLYNN

FPT

R SEEN ANYONE ON FIRE BEFORE, CERTAINLY NOT MY FATHER.

HE STOOD IN THE MIDDLE OF THE FLOOR, MUMBLING,

TRYING TO

SHAKE THE FL

Th
fat
But
it's
doze
and
went
all o
man's
and s
turns
body
Body
fierc
Watc
ing a
hims
fathe
poles
must

THOMAS GLYNN

KNOPF

51895

80394 571768

BN 0-394-57176-2

right,

burning

a metaph

al fire! Th

h a cigarette

on going—

flame, and hir

it—and if you

you have to com

and watch as y

it is no metaphor—

eaten by fire. *Wa*

ome inert meditat

between father a

y Burn is instead

w one boy manage

ood on the back o

immolation mark

us march that e

FROM HIS

ABOVE: Binding for *Watching the Body Burn.* Here's to the old days, when we had unlimited stamping options! **RIGHT:** Interior spreads. The hat over the word "Body" on the title page layout is pure M&Co. (or so I intended at the time). The numbers above the first line of text refer to the ages of the narrator in the chapter.

WATCHING THE BODY

Burn

THOMAS GLYNN

ALFRED A. KNOPF
NEW YORK
1989

SMOKING

7

14

HE SMOKED PHILIP MORRIS. PHILIP MORRIS WAS ADVERTISED over the radio by a midget whose face looked like a piece of wood left out in the sun and rain until the grain had run to sharp ridges. The midget had a cutting, high-pitched, ball-less voice. The midget used to say: *Call for Philip Morris.* That is, he tried to say it, or was supposed to say it, but what he said was something else: *Kawl fo-re* (or *ka-well fo-were*, turning two or three syllables into four, stretching them into an invocation, like a Muslim's call to prayers) *Fil-leep,* or *Phil Leap* (sometimes spending two seconds on the first vowel and running quickly through the next vowel so he could get to his favorite part in the pronunciation, the final *p*, which he loved to explode over the radio, as if making the first part of the

sound effects for a bomb going off, or sometimes deciding to reduce the first vowel to but a second's duration and then really jumping into the next, letting it rise and fall as if on a roller coaster, and then in a switch he would ignore the last consonant, slurring over the *p* that he had exploded just the previous night), and then the midget's crescendo, the witch's whine that he turned into a Wagnerian solo, *Morris,* which was not really Morris but *Mo-reeiiss,* or *More Reeece,* or, when he was drunk, *Mo-reeze.* (He seemed to prefer leaving off the *r*, that being a letter unsuitable for utterance by the tiny vocal cords of midgets, and get right to the meat of the matter, everything that came after the *r*, so that *Mo* was more an introduction to what would follow, a prologue, a guide to the song ahead. But attention paid to the midget's moment of glory revealed that the *r* never disappeared, it just transferred itself to the second syllable, where it served as a convenient bookend, a beginning, a justification to the spiel, the *Reeece,* the triple *ee* hitting the high end of the midget's register, held for what seemed an interminable length of time, and then suddenly dropped, dismissing the *c*, as if one had run up a mountain screaming and reaching the highest pitch on top of the mountain, held it, and then jumped off.) The midget was a drunk who had to be watched by a normal-sized man and kept sober enough to shout these four words over the radio. The midget was despondent over his size, his tiny prick, and the ravines of flesh in his face, and he loved to go to bars and complain. He would shout his famous four words before he passed out, his head bouncing off the bar or the barstool if he was lucky or in attendance with his male nurse, sometimes bouncing off the floor, if he was unlucky or his attendant slow. The midget had many women, large and small. They were fascinated with his tiny prick, fascinated by how it turned into a small prick; performance rather than size was what they counted on, but the midget could not persuade himself to believe that.

The boy's father was a drunk, and he shared that with the midget, along with the Philip Morris cigarettes, but beyond that little else. Smoking had a hypnotic effect on him. It calmed him

217

28 April 95

Dear C'm'l,

No, not a parsnip. A rutabaga, yes, but never a parsnip. Maybe a kholrabi but I can't spell it, and it may even be rutebaga or rootoobooguh. All I know is no outfit wants even a taste of me.

Since when is Chip Kidd an author? He's a great designer and a great guy, but an author? Lish is an author! Make a column about Lish authoring!

Here's for Chip.

"Ladies and gents, look alive, because, boy oh boy, am I, Lish, just the very fellow in just the very position to be the very person to tell you just what you need to hear about this Chip Kidd you have all been hearing so wondrous much about, which is, hey, if you have an empty surface somewhere, then go ahead and let this Chip Kidd go to work on it with his demonic devices of the designer's art. You want my guarantee? Swell, you have my guarantee--that what gets produced from any Kidd-ized planar occasion will knock them back on their heels or knock them out of their socks or anyhow do something knocklike to first their footy parts and then, a whipstitch thereafter, to their entire entirely alerted corpus. What Chip Kidd has done for The Quarterly for me and what Chip Kidd has done for about four tons of Knopf books for me, and what Chip Kidd has done even for some of my own Gordon Lish books for me never fails to do less than a miracle and a half for every object and party concerned--because what Chip Kidd does (first and foremost for himself!--and here's, ladies and gents, Chip Kidd's, shh, secret, okay?) is delight in the planar occasion to discover the dimensions of himself in every catastrophe wherein the empty must be made to have something in it, in every instance where absence must be made presence, every blessed time when life must be put where no life is."

Hope this does you--and our friend.

Racing,

G

GORDON LISH

Lish life.

BY 1995 IT WAS DETERMINED THAT GORDON AND KNOPF WERE NO LONGER a good fit. Sonny gave him every chance, but I think ultimately the problem with Gordon's books wasn't their eccentricity, it was that they simply didn't sell—the fate of most experimental writing. There were the occasional critical bright spots (Amy Hempel, Lily Tuck), but another Raymond Carver was just not in the offing. I suppose I could selfishly say that the efforts of Lish's writers were most effective as an excuse to design mondo-bizarro book jackets that really pushed the form and inevitably aced all the design competitions. And for that, I will forever give Gordon my sincerest gratitude. To say I was sorry to see him go doesn't begin to describe it. **ABOVE:** For the life of me I can't remember what this testimonial was for, but when called upon for quotable references, Gordon always delivered. **RIGHT:** Pantheon, 1993.

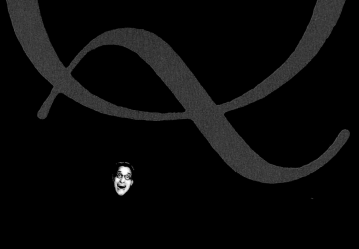

Extravaganza

A JOKE BOOK

Gordon Lish

Buddy, can you spare a . . .

'THE QUARTERLY' WAS GORDON LISH'S VERSION of *The Paris Review* for people who didn't really care for *The Paris Review*—or, as some wags said, any kind of narrative coherence whatsoever. That he was able to keep it going for as long as he did is something of a minor publishing miracle. Initially published by Vintage Books (the trade paperback arm of Knopf), it consisted chiefly of short fiction pieces by students of Gordon's private writing classes. I took over the cover design from Lorraine Louie at issue 13, and saw it through to its end in 1995. **ABOVE**: White Pine Press, 1990. The cover of Gordon's astonishing, eerie novel about the Holocaust, represented by a self-portrait photo of my wrist.

I4

THE QUARTERLY IS

THE MAGAZINE OF NEW WRITING

THE QUARTERLY IS

THE MAGAZINE OF NEW WRITING

I7

THE QUARTERLY IS

THE MAGAZINE OF NEW WRITING

I3

THE QUARTERLY IS
THE MAGAZINE OF NEW WRITING

I5

THE QUARTERLY IS
THE MAGAZINE OF NEW WRITING

I8

THE QUARTERLY IS
THE MAGAZINE OF NEW WRITING

I9

THE QUARTERLY IS
THE MAGAZINE OF NEW WRITING

INSIDE : THE AWFUL REVENGE OF CLAIRE!

21

THE QUARTERLY IS

THE MAGAZINE OF NEW WRITING

INSIDE : THE POKEY PIGGIES!

INSIDE: JOEL McCREA'S SECRET WARDROBE!

22

23

THE QUARTERLY IS

THE MAGAZINE OF NEW WRITING

THE QUARTERLY IS

THE MAGAZINE OF NEW WRITING

¼ LY Q

¼ LY Q

THE MAGAZINE OF NEW WRITING

¼ LY Q

26

27

LEFT: A sampling of covers for *The Quarterly* 13-16, 1990, featuring a quartet of tiny heads; then 17-20, 1991, which was four multi-colored views of my hand and wrist; and finally 21-24, 1992, sporting images of lard-laden meals from a 1950s cookbook. However . . .

WHEN GORDON WAS FINALLY BANISHED from the Vintage kingdom, he kept *The Quarterly* going for six more issues with private funding. This demanded a complete redesign to distinguish its new incarnation, and the concept was that each year's four covers would combine to make a single image. **ABOVE:** We got halfway there. The last two issues. The next two would have completed a stylized pictogrammic face. **RIGHT:** The new logo on Gordon's business card. In my opinion, this design was far more successful than anything I'd previously done—the idea that the *Quarterly* logo was only one fourth of a larger whole was perfect for the nature of Gordon's ultimately unfulfillable mission.

¼ LY Q

Gordon Lish

650 Madison Avenue Suite 2600
New York, New York 10022
Tel: 212-888-4769

The Quarterly

"I stroke my cow and hold her dewlap, lay my hand against her throat and feel the irrigating heart. She thumps a life lived up in her. She maybe thinks that I'm not bull enough, can see I'm not her kind."

—*Darling*, p. 107

Darling

William Tester

Moo.

LET'S NOT MINCE WORDS: 'DARLING' IS THE STORY OF THE FIERCE RIVALRY between two brothers for the love of their family cow. And I mean LOVE. As in *let's make a calf*. I will forever cherish the spectacle of editor Gordon Lish feverishly pitching this novel to the Knopf sales force during the launch meeting—it was like watching Larry Flynt trying to solicit *Hustler* subscriptions from the Junior League. I couldn't *wait* to work on it. **LEFT:** Knopf, 1991. Photography by Geoff Spear. I found the painting at Reninger's flea market in Adamstown, Pa. I'd bought it for fun (above) before the book came along, charmed by its naive snapshot quality. But now I realized it was *Darling*'s narrator and his brother, Jeab. I rented the cowhide from a taxidermist in Chelsea and used it as a backdrop to overwhelm the protagonists. The red crayon hand-scrawl added just the right twisted touch. This jacket tipped the weird-o-meter and breezed into the top honors of every design competition extant, arguably eclipsing the book itself.

```
                          William Tester
                        New York, NY 10014


        Mr. Chip Kidd, Esq.
        c/o Alfred A Knopf
        201 E 50th St
        New York, NY 10022
                                                      11/24/91
        Dear Chip,

        Gorgeously, brilliantly, wonderfully done. My
        hat and spurs off to you. The cover is, well,
        in a word, fabulous.

                                       My best wishes,


                                       William Tester
```

CONTINUED FROM FRONT FLAP

But the agony of their need, of their shame, is newly wild with violence when the rivals meet again in the flyblown kitchen of a New York City tenement, a loaded pistol reposing malignantly on the table between them as the drunken night careens helplessly towards the inevitable crisis of morning. Which of them—all for the precious, saving love of Darling—will pick up the pistol and fire it? As with certain antecedents whose contents severed all touch with convention—William Tester's *Darling* chances scandalizing us in order to disclose to us the nature of us. It is in these dangerous terms that the appearance of this book anticipates an extraordinary literary episode.

KEN COLLINS

WILLIAM TESTER is a native of South Carolina, and now lives in New York City. This is his first work of fiction.

JACKET DESIGN
BY CHIP KIDD

ALFRED A. KNOPF, PUBLISHER, NEW YORK 1/92

PRINTED IN U.S.A. © 1991 ALFRED A. KNOPF, INC.

I WANTED TO IMPART A SENSE OF OBSESSION AND made it look like the narrator couldn't stop writing the name of his intended on the back of the jacket, as if he's practicing endlessly in an effort to do the very best version to fill in the blanks on the front. On the spine he obviously wasn't following the directions and drew in the borzoi and the imprint name in the same box as the author name, instead of using the allotted space at the bottom.

William Tester
Knopf

GEEK
LOVE

GEEK LOVE

A NOVEL

KATHERINE DUNN

ALL I EVER HOPED FOR IN A BOOK COVER WAS NOT BEIGE. Not that bland cream-to-tan range that is so tastefully discreet and complacently qual-lit that you want to scrawl lewdisms all over it before it sedates you completely. This cover arrived in the mail with a note inquiring cautiously whether I thought this was too, too . . . anything. No, it's not too, I thought. It's visible. And you could fry eggs on it.

The cover fired as much attention as the book. People talked about it everywhere I went. "What, ahem, do you, think . . . ?" Trying not to offend. "A bit bright . . . " "Not exactly Knopfian . . . " Some Pleistocene rigidity was apparently jarred by color. "It certainly jumps off the shelves," they'd concede. Then there was that five-legged borzoi. Nervous giggles among the famous over that. The alphabet had its own fans. "No two letters alike!" they'd crow, "a subtle and witty demonstration of the text." The wild one called it an Ironic triumph, a joyous heresy. Yeah, I'd say, and it doubles as a night light.

—Katherine Dunn

FROM BOLD TO SAFE: *After Chip Kidd at Knopf designed the hardcover (left), the paperback (right) was 'toned down' for wider appeal.*

Freakish.

WITHOUT SONNY MEHTA'S ADVICE, THIS JACKET WOULD HAVE BEEN VERY DIFFERENT. I could say that about a lot of them, but this was one of the first. In the original design, the type was as you see here, but I had added a photo at the bottom of a primitive wood carving, a sort of grotesque head that was meant to symbolize . . . I don't know, the freakish characters? Sonny looked at it and said "Can you try it with just the type?" And boy, was he right. For those who don't know, *Geek Love* is the story of the Binewskis, a carny family whose mater- and paterfamilias set out—with the help of amphetamines, arsenic, and radioisotopes—to breed their own exhibit of human oddities. This was the first book that Sonny bought for Knopf, and it represented a bold new direction for the house. **OPPOSITE:** Proof that I actually used to put pen to paper to make type. **LEFT:** Knopf, 1989. Try to imagine the orange as flourescent. **ABOVE LEFT:** This got me into a little trouble. I altered the colophon on the spine of the jacket to match the content. No one noticed it, until they did. When the book had been out for a month. And then I was called upstairs. Gulp. **ABOVE RIGHT:** From the *Christian Science Monitor*, November 19, 1990. This accompanied an article in which I publicly dumped on the paperback cover. It was the first time (but not the last) that I should have been more prudent when talking with the press.

BETTER GET
YOUR
ANGEL
ON

STORIES

JENNIFER
ALLEN

divine concepts of physical
beauty

A NOVEL BY

michael bracewell

Freaks

MYTHS AND IMAGES OF THE SECRET SELF

"A fascinating and sensitive exploration of human freakishness and what it means in our waking and subconscious lives."
—*Publishers Weekly*

LESLIE FIEDLER
Author of
Love & Death in the American Novel

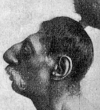

WHEN ALL ELSE FAILS, SEND IN THE DWARF. I figured that out long before I ever saw *Twin Peaks*. When I was looking for an image to represent the alienated topor of Barbara Gowdy's characters, the first Photonica stock catalogue had just been released. In it I found a picture of a girl wearing a ballet costume and a gold lamé half-moon on her head. Her hands were crossed demurely in front, and she was standing next to a dwarf with a top hat, a giant bow tie, and white gloves. They were in a swamp, ankle-deep in marsh water. I didn't know why, but it was perfect. When I called the agency, they apologized and said a Japanese firm had just bought the image outright and it was no longer available. Furious, I hired a friend to recreate it in acrylics, with enough subtle changes to avoid litigation. **ABOVE:** Anchor Books, 1993. **RIGHT:** HarperCollins, 1993. Painting by Tom Hubben.

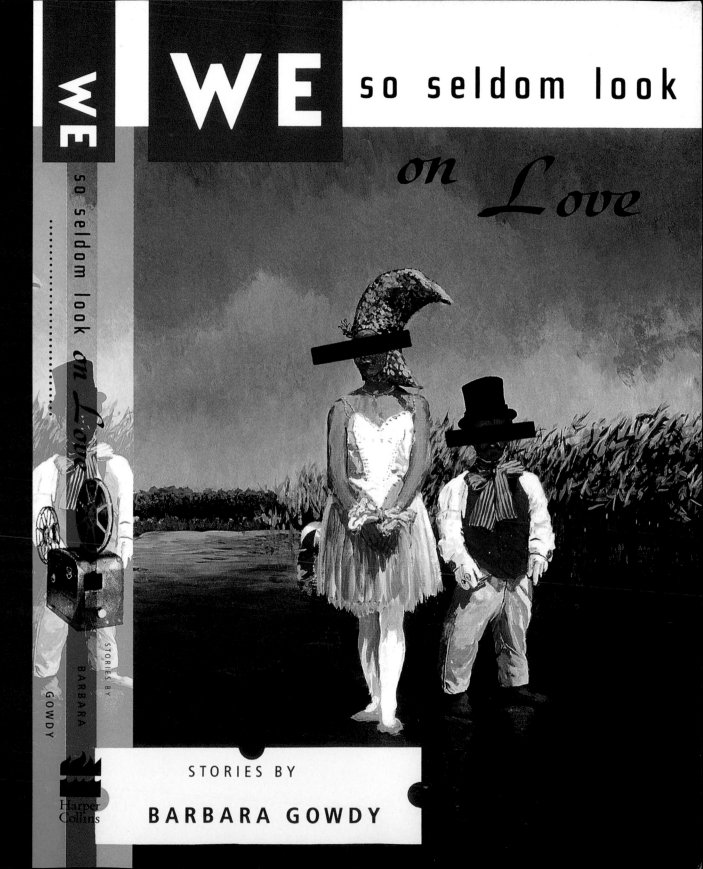

WE

so seldom look *on Love*

STORIES BY

BARBARA GOWDY

HarperCollins

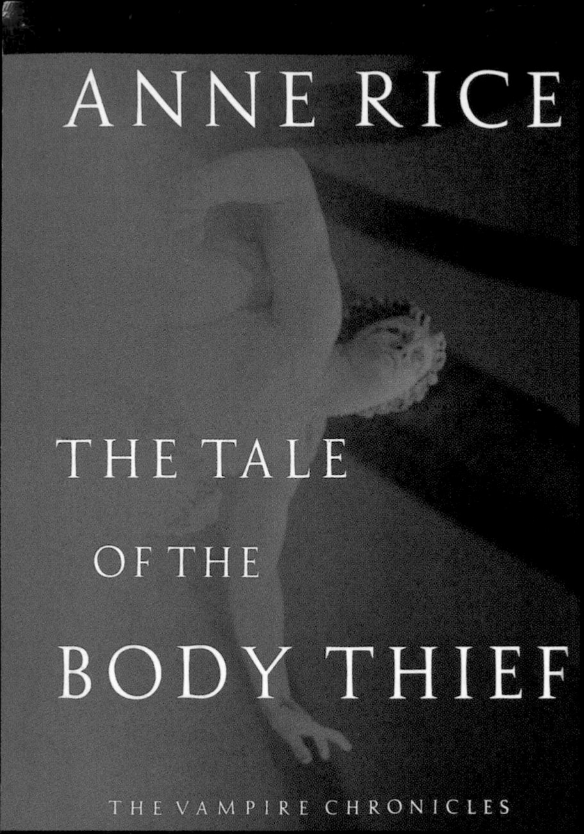

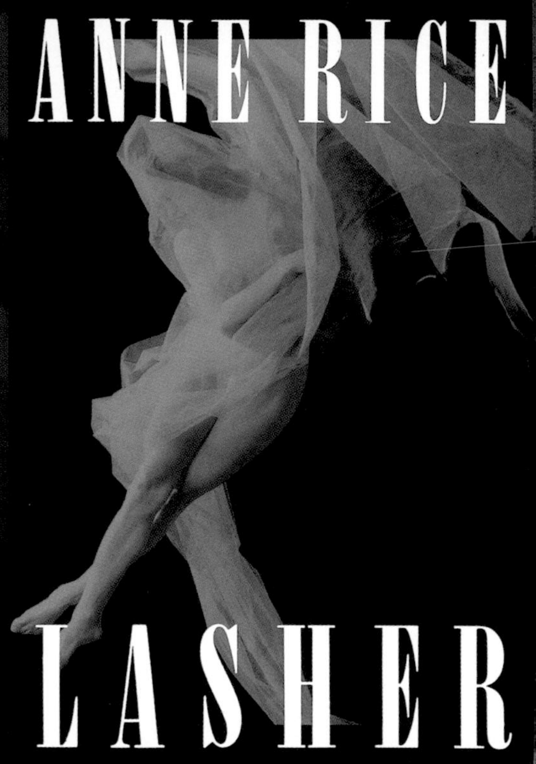

ANNE RICE

THE TALE
OF THE
BODY THIEF

THE VAMPIRE CHRONICLES

ANNE RICE

LASHER

MEMNOCH
THE DEVIL
THE VAMPIRE CHRONICLES

ANNE RICE

LeStat camera.

I ONCE ATTENDED A NOCTURNAL ANNE RICE BOOK SIGNING FOR 'MEMNOCH THE DEVIL' in the Garden District of New Orleans, and the line was so long it stretched all the way into a less reputable part of town and two people waiting at the end of it got mugged. Or so the story goes—by the looks of things it certainly was plausible. I ultimately designed three jackets for Anne, but I had the most fun putting together an audiotape boxed set of her first three vampire titles (opposite). I hired the photographer Amy Guip, who went all out and tested models to portray LeStat, Louis, and Claudia (the results of which, in my humble opinion, looked much more the part than Cruise, Pitt, and Dunst ever did). The conceit for the box was a coffin, naturally, and depending on how you put the cassettes to rest you either see Claudia or Louis lying in it. LeStat is on a separate card that slides in and "oversees" the other two characters. I created various fake pagan symbols and motifs, surprinting in black and gold. Andy Hughes oversaw the production brilliantly as usual. **ABOVE LEFT**: Knopf, 1992. **ABOVE RIGHT**: Knopf, 1993. Photo by Lauren Greenfeld. **RIGHT**: Knopf, 1995. **OPPOSITE**: Random House Audio, 1995.

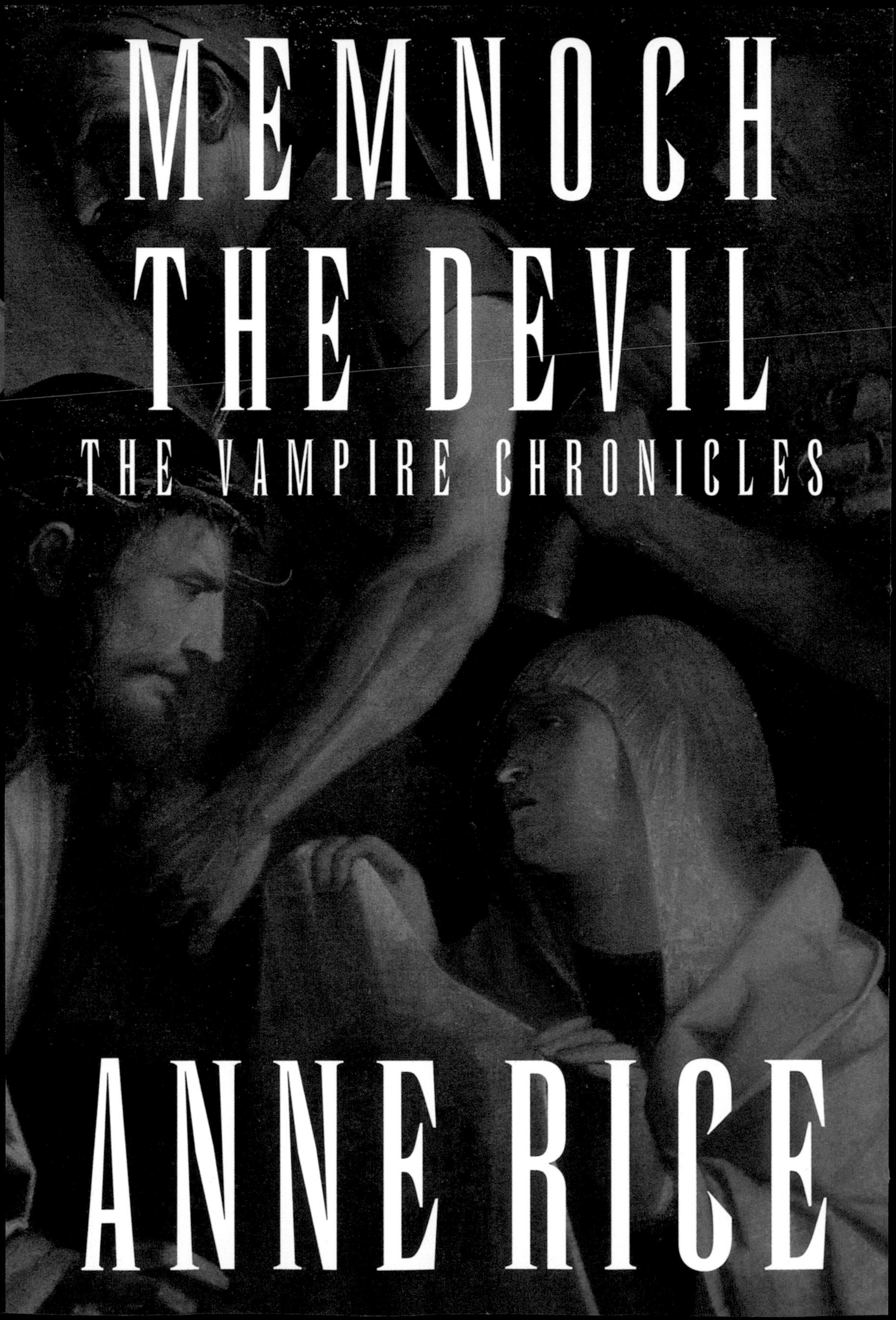

Jurassic? What's a Jurassic?

"REMEMBER WHAT HAPPENED WITH 'JAWS'," Sonny said, shortly after acquiring something called *Jurassic Park* by Michael Crichton in 1992. What he meant was, simply, that the original book jacket image (by Paul Bacon) on Benchley's 1974 novel became the basis for the shark-and-nude-swimming-lady movie poster, which was then universally embraced as a pop-culture icon. The implication was that I was supposed to accomplish the same, with this.

Right.

"Okay," I said, safe in the knowledge that no such thing would ever, ever happen, even though the two projects did have in common Steven Spielberg. He'd bought the movie rights, pre-publication, for a tidy sum. Regardless, the idea that I could devise a cover as iconic as *Jaws* was unthinkable. So I didn't think about it. Instead, I read the manuscript. Which I LOVED, and which naturally led me to the Museum of Natural History on the Upper West Side, to plunge into books on dinosaurs.

In the meantime, Carol had commissioned a painting of what dinosaur skin might look like up close. The result was very interesting—I remember a lot of pebble-like shapes that almost looked like an aerial view of a park itself. This was smart. Too smart. At the time, no one knew what "Jurassic" meant, so the enigmatic title paired with the abstract imagery was too confusing.

We needed a dinosaur, but how to render one without making it look like a pulp magazine? Somehow we had to show it . . . without showing it. And it would have to be as scientifically accurate as possible—this was a Crichton book. So back to the reference (right). When trying to recreate one of these creatures all anyone has to go on is bones, right? So that was the starting point. On the stat machine I blew up a diagram of a Tyrannosaurus Rex skeleton, laid a sheet of vellum over it, and traced it with a Rapidograph mechanical pen. As I went along, I selectively obscured parts of it, so the the effect was more like that of an x-ray in reverse. To give it as much of a sense of menace as possible I sharpened the teeth, the claws, the ribs. I also "cheated" the holes in the head a bit to give a clearer sense of where the eyes and nose would be.

I thought the final result (opposite) was just graphic enough while not giving too much away—it was a suggestion of a dinosaur that could actually exist.

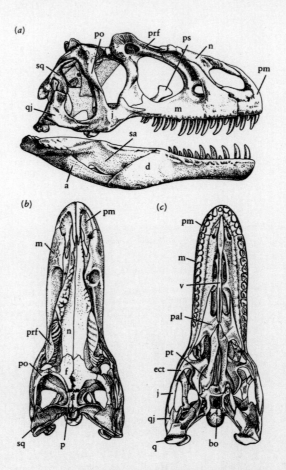

Figure 14-14. SKULL OF *ALLOSAURUS*. (*a*) Lateral, (*b*) dorsal, and (*c*) palatal views. Abbreviations as in Figure 8-3. *From Madsen, 1976.*

The upper Jurassic genus *Allosaurus* is the best-known representative of a conservative lineage that extends into the Upper Cretaceous. *Allosaurus* reached 12 meters in length and was among the most powerful carnivores of its time (Figure 14-13; see page 295). The body was strengthened to support the extra weight, and the sacrum had five fused vertebrae.

The skull is high and laterally compressed; the orbital opening is triangular and smaller than the principal antorbital fenestra (Figure 14-14). The teeth are long, laterally compressed, and recurved. In contrast with more primitive megalosaurs, the cervical vertebrae have well-ossified anterior condyles that contribute to well-defined ball-and-socket joints between the vertebrae. The more posterior trunk vertebrae retain a shallowly amphicoelous configuration. The tail is long, and the posterior prezygapophyses are considerably elongated.

The forelimb is considerably shorter than the rear limb and could not possibly have supported the body. Only three digits of the manus are retained. Each has a long recurved claw. Metatarsals II, III, and IV are closely integrated elements. The first digit, like that of birds, was oriented posteriorly.

Tyrannosaurids

The gigantic tyrannosaurids of the Upper Cretaceous were the largest of all theropods (Figure 14-15). Specializations of this family include the further reduction in the length of the forelimbs (which could not have reached the mouth) and the retention of only two functional digits, the first and second, which bear respectively two and three phalanges.

The skull is distinguished by the shape of the parietals, which form a sharp sagittal crest between the upper

vertebrae and a single antorbital opening. The femur is slightly longer than the tibia.

The early megalosaurs radiated during the Jurassic and led to specialized forms that included *Spinosaurus* from the Upper Cretaceous and its relatives, which had neural spines of the trunk vertebrae that were 2 meters long, and the Upper Jurassic *Ceratosaurus*, which had a short "horn" that was borne on the nasal bones (Stromer, 1915; Gilmore, 1920).

Figure 14-15. THE GIGANTIC UPPER CRETACEOUS THEROPOD *TYRANNOSAURUS*, WHICH REACHED A HEIGHT OF 6 METERS. The forelimbs are much shorter than those of *Allosaurus* and have only two digits. *From Osborn, 1916.*

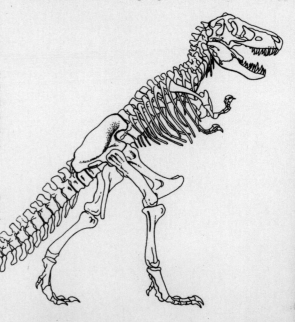

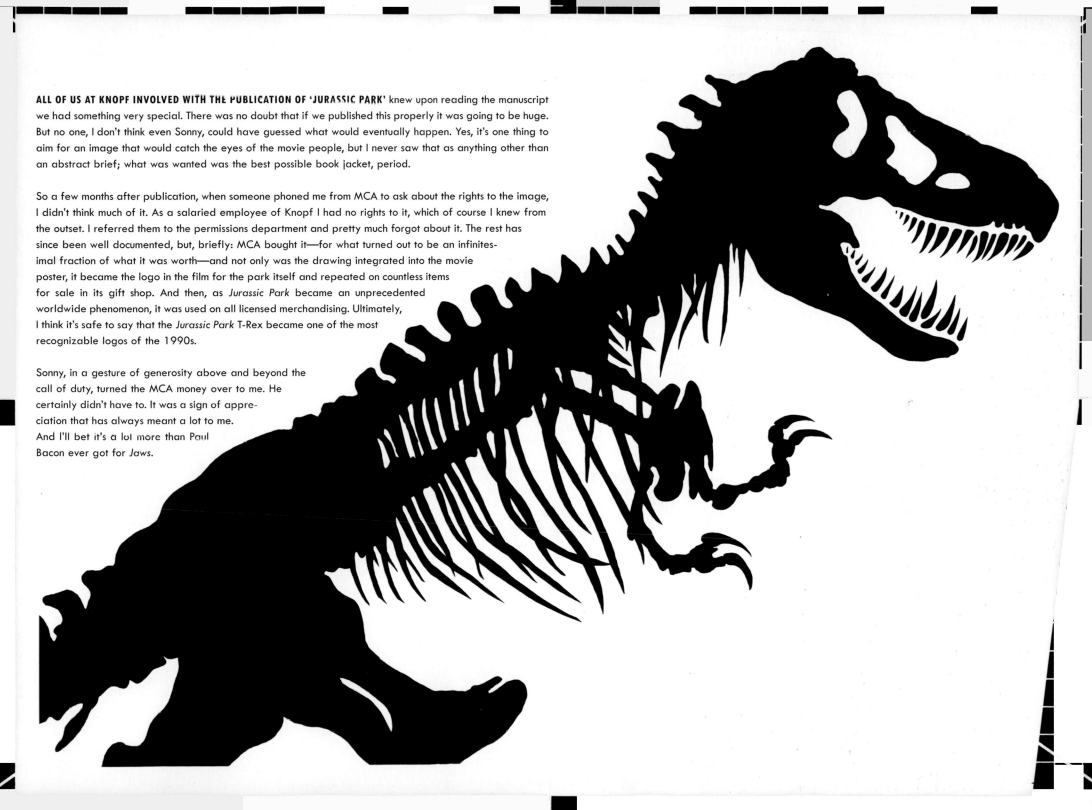

ALL OF US AT KNOPF INVOLVED WITH THE PUBLICATION OF 'JURASSIC PARK' knew upon reading the manuscript we had something very special. There was no doubt that if we published this properly it was going to be huge. But no one, I don't think even Sonny, could have guessed what would eventually happen. Yes, it's one thing to aim for an image that would catch the eyes of the movie people, but I never saw that as anything other than an abstract brief; what was wanted was the best possible book jacket, period.

So a few months after publication, when someone phoned me from MCA to ask about the rights to the image, I didn't think much of it. As a salaried employee of Knopf I had no rights to it, which of course I knew from the outset. I referred them to the permissions department and pretty much forgot about it. The rest has since been well documented, but, briefly: MCA bought it—for what turned out to be an infinites-imal fraction of what it was worth—and not only was the drawing integrated into the movie poster, it became the logo in the film for the park itself and repeated on countless items for sale in its gift shop. And then, as *Jurassic Park* became an unprecedented worldwide phenomenon, it was used on all licensed merchandising. Ultimately, I think it's safe to say that the *Jurassic Park* T-Rex became one of the most recognizable logos of the 1990s.

Sonny, in a gesture of generosity above and beyond the call of duty, turned the MCA money over to me. He certainly didn't have to. It was a sign of appre-ciation that has always meant a lot to me. And I'll bet it's a lot more than Paul Bacon ever got for *Jaws*.

JURASSIC PARK

MICHAEL CRICHTON

The Transom ——— *By Frank DiGiacomo* ———

Giving Away the Dino-store

Alfred A. Knopf graphics designer Chip Kidd must have particularly enjoyed the scene in *Jurassic Park* where the theme park's lawyer is plucked, head first, off a toilet and devoured by a Tyrannosaurus rex.

Mr. Kidd is the 28-year-old designer who created the menacing skeletal dinosaur image that first appeared on the cover of Michael Crichton's 1990 Knopf book and now has become the centerpiece of a logo that will adorn approximately 1,000 different product tie-ins to Steven Spielberg's adaptation of *Jurassic Park* (and countless bootleg ones) that are expected to generate hundreds of millions of dollars for Universal/MCA Studio's merchandising division and Mr. Spielberg's Amblin Entertainment, which co-own the logo's copyright. But nowhere in the film's credits is Mr. Kidd identified.

Sources familiar with the negotiations say that Universal purchased the copyright to Mr. Kidd's skeleton graphic more than a year ago when the studio began moving into high gear to promote the film. At the time of the deal, a source said, Mr. Kidd was promised a financial reward for his work. The studio's artists substituted new typography and added tropical plants and flowers to the image before plastering it all over the movie (it is the logo for the theme park within the movie) and its tie-in T-shirts, bed ruffles, gummy candies, toys and other keepsakes.

It is unclear how much money Random House, Knopf's parent company, made from the sale, but a source familiar with the arrangement suggested that the publisher's legal wranglers never imagined that the film might turn out to become the second largest box-office grosser in history (as is now projected)—even though the wide appeal of dinosaurs, Mr. Spielberg's films and Mr. Crichton's books are certainly not unknown quantities. "The legal department handled the whole thing," said the source. "I think Knopf could and should have gotten a lot more." Elise Solomon, a lawyer with Random House who is said to have worked on the deal, declined to comment.

The source added that Knopf editor in chief Sonny Mehta, who did not return The Transom's calls, was put in the unenviable position of explaining to Mr. Kidd that his design would not be credited in the film.

Mr. Kidd, who designed the covers for Anne Rice's last two books and Mr. Crichton's *Rising Sun*, and who co-designed the jacket for Donna Tartt's *The Secret History*, has apparently received a modest bonus for creating an image that will be burned onto the brainpans of the public by the end of the summer. And his artwork is credited on the movie's official paperback tie-in, published by Ballantine.

For his part, Mr. Kidd, who has worked for Knopf for six and a half years, has chosen to say little about the incident. "Random House and I worked out an agreement," he said, adding: "I'm happy. I really like working here." After some prodding, Mr. Kidd, who is currently working on the design for Mr. Crich-

ton's upcoming novel, *Disclosure*, admitted that "it would have been nice" to have been credited for creating an image "that's all over the movie." In one scene, the artist remembered, "They're eating off of plates with the logo. I thought, I'd love to have a set of those dishes. It would be a great settlement."

Roehm Fiddles, Kravis Spins

When a chorus of gossip columnists identified French-Canadian economist Marie-Josee Drouin as the new lady on the arm of Henry Kravis, the news was greeted with more than a little skepticism. Followers of the privacy-loving leveraged-buyout king's personal life found it odd that Mr. Kravis would choose the most social weekend of the summer—the Fourth of July holiday—to let the Canuck out of the bag, so to speak, given that relatively little time had passed since the announcement that he had separated from his second wife, fashion designer Carolyne Roehm. That is, unless Mr. Kravis, who's no stranger to media manipulation, was looking to play a little game in public this summer.

Social contrarians speculate that Ms. Drouin, who's said to be equal parts policy wonk and femme fatale, may be a red herring that Mr. Kravis has fed to the press to quash ru-

LEFT: Knopf, 1990. I can't remember why I put the drop-shadow of black under Michael's name. I suppose to give it weight. I'm not a fan of drop-shadowed type at all and only use it when there is a legibility issue, which wouldn't have been the case here. **ABOVE:** Gossip from *The New York Observer*. I never did get a set of those dishes . . . **OPPOSITE:** Imagine my surprise when I came upon this full-page ad in *The Licensing Book*. What's always amazed me is that aside from tilting both of the arms a bit higher, the drawing was left completely intact, down to the last incisor.

LEFT: Bad dinosaur doodle from my *Jurassic* period. **BELOW:** Another satisfied customer. Once when I was giving a lecture at Rhode Island School of Design an apparently fully grown graphic designer told me that he used to draw the *JP* T-Rex in his notebook in 6TH GRADE. I found that simultaneously charming and mortifying. I am not that old. I am NOT.

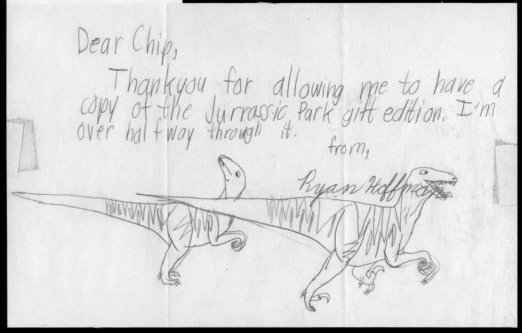

Dear Chip,
    Thank you for allowing me to have a copy of the Jurassic Park gift edition. I'm over halfway through it.
                    from,
                    Ryan Hoffman

'JURASSIC PARK' WENT THROUGH MORE DRAFTS THAN ANY BOOK I'VE EVER WRITTEN, and the cover went through more iterations than any other. Everybody agreed the graphic approach needed to be oblique, but that proved more easily said than accomplished. The first cover consisted of a background of pebbled brown texture, meant to be dinosaur skin. To me it looked like a close-up of a football, or a woman's handbag. I was cranky. My editor, Sonny Mehta, said not to worry, because Chip was now stepping in to do the cover. We moved on to dinosaur shadows and dinosaur footprints, scales and tails, silhouettes and reptilian eyes peering through jungle fronds. Nothing worked. As the days passed, we began to understand that finding a menacing image that also suggested genetically recreated dinosaurs was probably impossible. We were asking too much of a single image. I became discouraged. Sonny said, "Don't worry, Chip will get it." But Sonny wasn't sending me covers anymore. Finally he called and said, "Chip thinks we can do something with skeletons." I said I didn't think it would work, and anyway, skeletons missed the point. The point was, they were alive. Sonny said they'd probably try something anyway. He called a few days later to say he was sending some new cover art for me to look at. I asked how many covers. "Just one," he said, in his laconic way. "I think you might like it."

And of course I did. Everybody liked it at once, and the image was used for both the book and the movie. To pack so much meaning into so simple an image was really extraordinary.

—Michael Crichton

MICHAEL CRICHTON

Wow! Fucking Fantastic Jacket

RISING SUN

GEE, MICHAEL, WHAT ARE YOU TRYING TO SAY? Sonny gave me a copy of this enigmatic fax regarding the jacket for *Rising Sun*. **LEFT:** Knopf, 1992. Photograph by Melissa Hayden. Everyone wanted to know who the girl was. Imagine Carol Carson's and my horror when Melissa later confessed (after the book came out, thanks Missy) that she shot it off a random television broadcast and had absolutely no idea. **OPPOSITE:** Knopf, 1993. I especially liked the spine on this, with the animal's ribs tickling Michael's name. Also note the Jurassic borzoi.

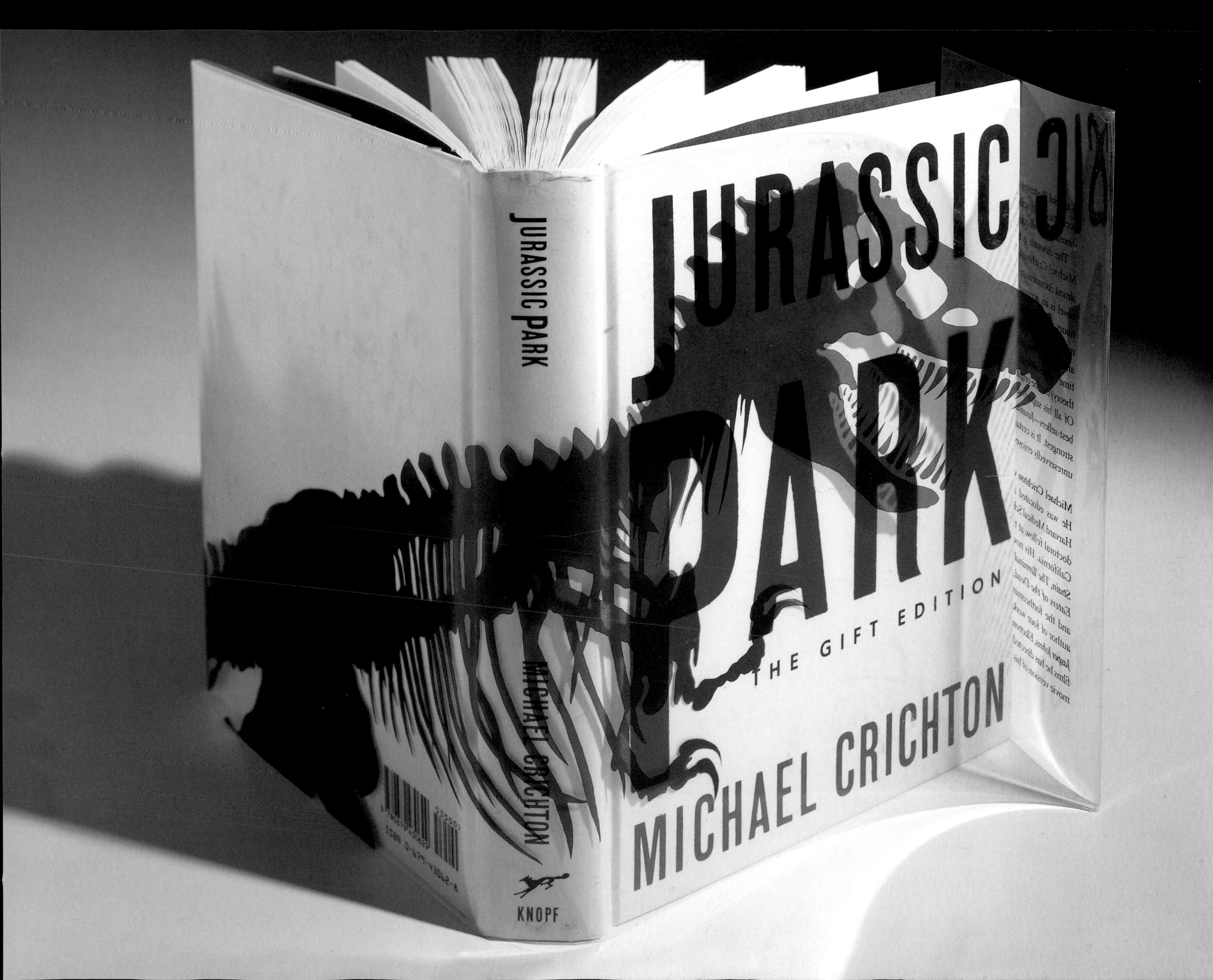
JURASSIC PARK
THE GIFT EDITION
MICHAEL CRICHTON
JURASSIC PARK
MICHAEL CRICHTON
KNOPF

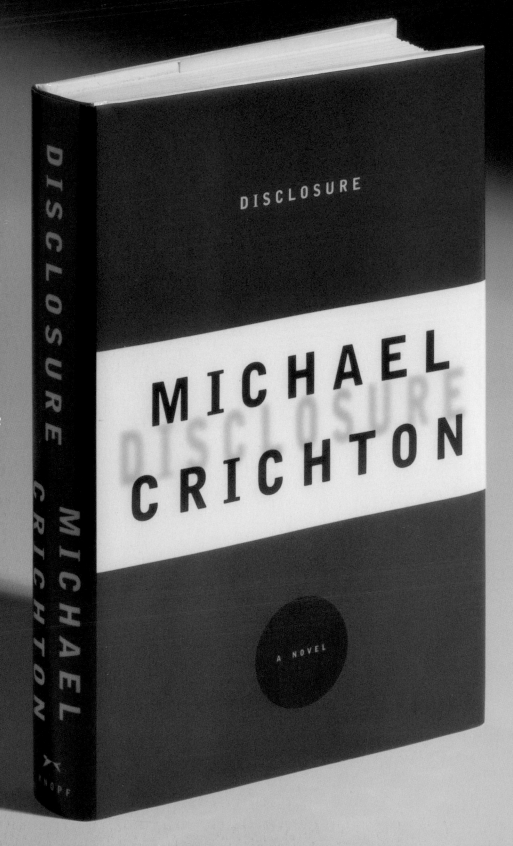

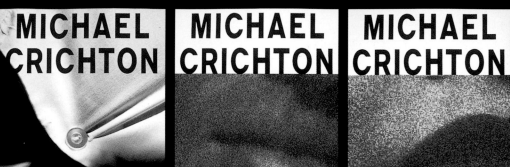

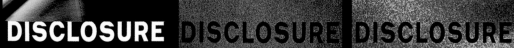

'DISCLOSURE' WAS PROBLEMATIC BECAUSE THE ORDINARY IMPULSE, to make a cover with hot sexual imagery, might be construed as exploitative. And the idea of subterfuge and concealment does not lend itself to any image at all. The usual business imagery—file cabinets and so forth—was, well, usual. After a lot of experimentation, Chip created a layered image that literally had something behind it. It was quite elegant and I thought it worked very well. I later heard criticism that it was not a bestseller image. In the words of one publisher, "too arty, too classy." But I thought it was perfectly suited for the novel itself.

—Michael Crichton

ABOVE: The long, hard road to *Disclosure*. The first idea (upper left), shot by Geoff Spear, was meant to depict a moment of button-popping passion, but Sonny thought it looked instead like a novel about rampant obesity. So I came up with the two ideas to the right, meant to be issued simultaneously—for this he-said-she-said novel of sexual harassment and corporate intrigue the idea was you could literally buy his story or hers. Michael wasn't crazy about it and in the meantime someone in his office worked up the sketch at the middle left (lesson: disk drives are *not* sexy). So then I started thinking about materials and the nature of book jackets as "cover-ups" of books. What can they afford to hide, and to what extent? **LEFT:** Knopf, 1994. This, to me, represents the ideal confluence of the commercial and the aesthetic—an instant #1 bestseller that also won all the design competitions. That's very, very rare, and the only non-fiction equivalent that I can think of is *Naked* by David Sedaris. **MIDDLE RIGHT:** It was amusing to see how *Disclosure* showed up in book club ads.

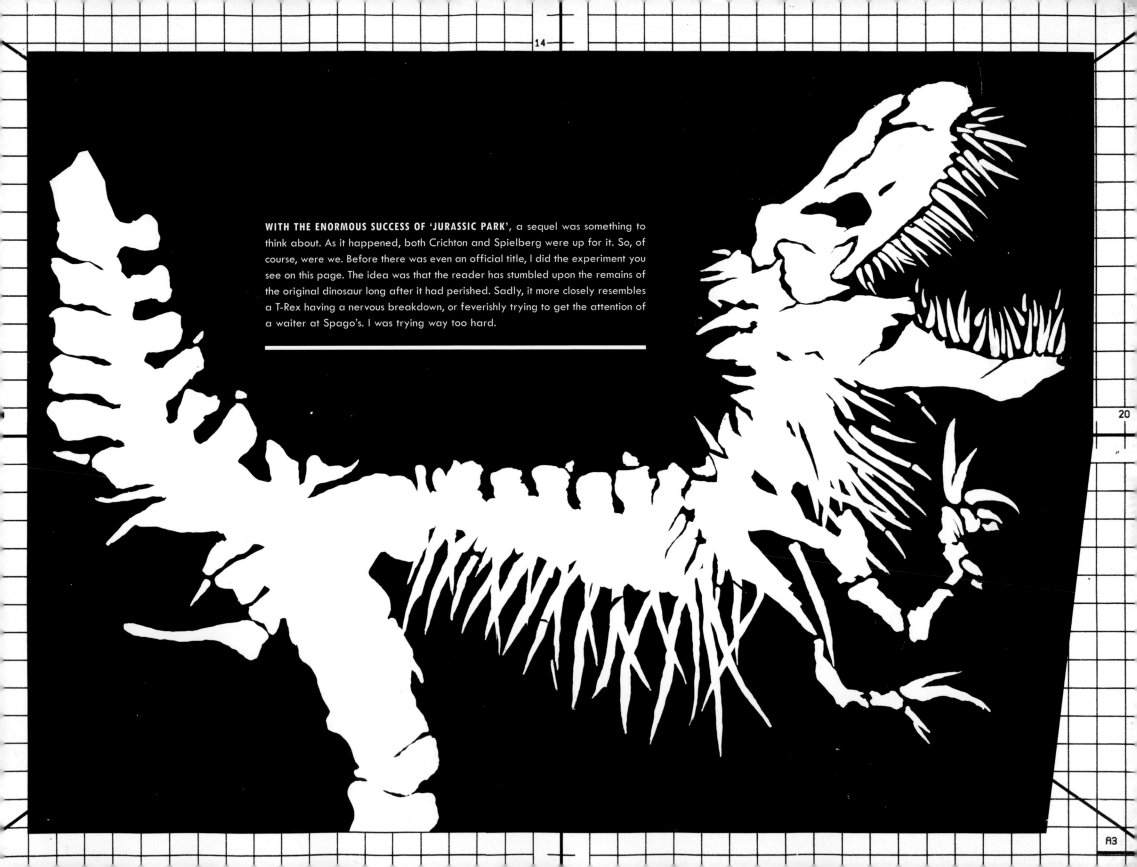

WITH THE ENORMOUS SUCCESS OF 'JURASSIC PARK', a sequel was something to think about. As it happened, both Crichton and Spielberg were up for it. So, of course, were we. Before there was even an official title, I did the experiment you see on this page. The idea was that the reader has stumbled upon the remains of the original dinosaur long after it had perished. Sadly, it more closely resembles a T-Rex having a nervous breakdown, or feverishly trying to get the attention of a waiter at Spago's. I was trying way too hard.

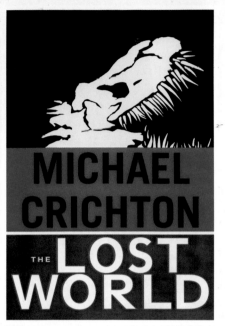

THE LOST WORLD

MICHAEL CRICHTON

LEFT: Early comp for *The Lost World*. NOT successful in any way. Ugh. I was having the typographic equivalent of a bad hair day. Michael never saw it, thank God. **RIGHT:** Knopf, 1995. The solution was to take the original art and use it in a different way. There was no need to redraw anything. **BELOW:** I just loved this little guy, yet couldn't figure out any way to use him. Sad.

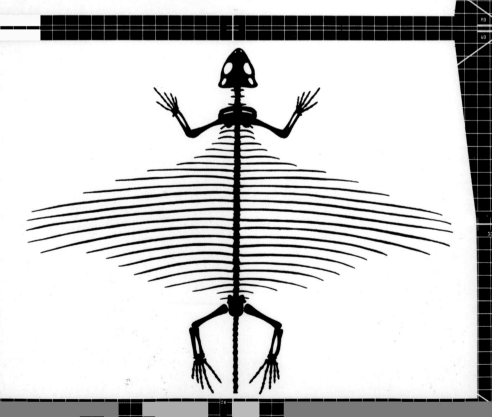

SOMETHING HAS SURVIVED

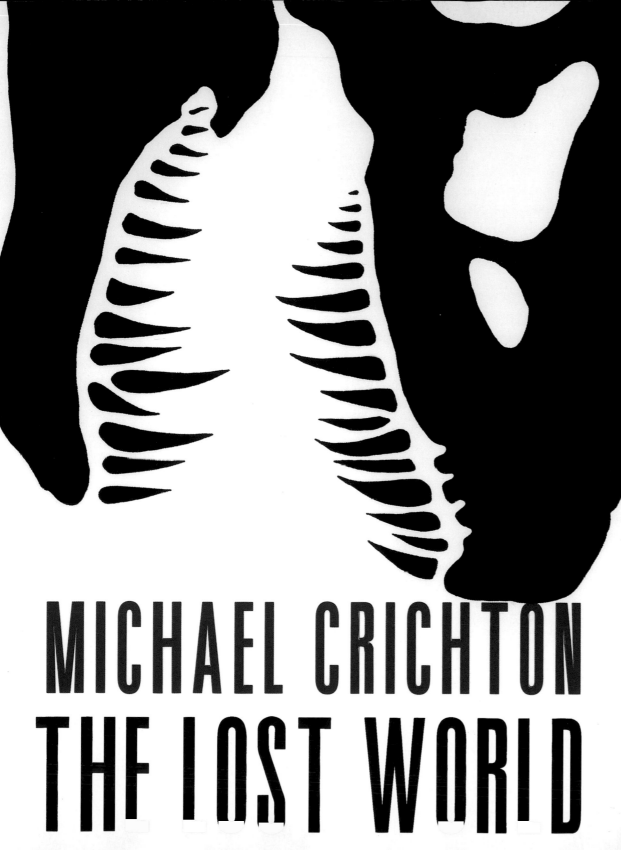

MICHAEL CRICHTON

THE LOST WORLD

KNOPF

"Aaaaaaaaaaah!"

THE BACK COVER COPY OF 'THE LOST WORLD' comes from Karen Latuchie, who is a wonderful writer and coined the phrase for the flap copy of the jacket, which she wrote as part of her duties on staff at Knopf. I merely seized upon it and splayed it large as a slogan for the book. I mean, really: that says it all.

So then, there I am, a couple of months after the book has come out, sitting in a movie theater, as a trailer for a new film begins to burst onscreen. There is thunder. There is lightning. There is typography.

> "SOMETHING"
> Oh, no.
> "HAS"
> Please don't.
> "SURVIVED!"
> Cacophonous crashes. Pandemonium.
> They've done it again.

If you look to the left, you may notice something significant considering this was one of the most high-profile sequels of the decade: on the front it doesn't mention or refer to the name *Jurassic Park* anywhere. This is a testament to the Knopf approach and Sonny's respect for the reader. The fact was *The Lost World* held up as an adventure novel in and of itself and everyone knew it was the sequel to *Jurassic Park*, so why belabor the point on the cover? There were enough visual cues, along with the accompanying storm of publicity, so we let all of that state the case for us and let the cover be as stark as possible.

MICHAEL CRICHTON

AIRFRAME

A NOVEL

AIR FRAME

A NOVEL

MICHAEL CRICHTON

A

AIRFRAME

MICHAEL CRICHTON

MICHAEL CRICHTON

AIRFRAME

A NOVEL

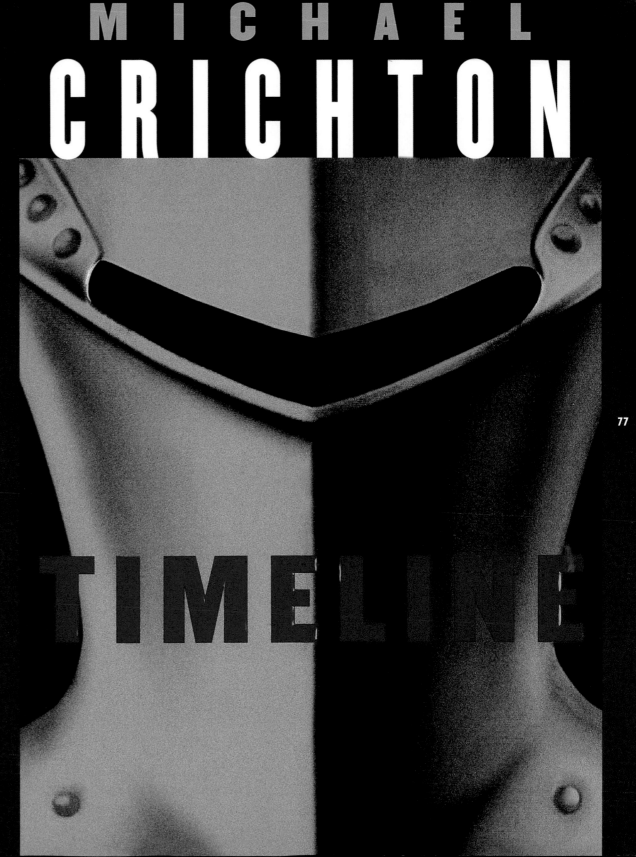

MICHAEL CRICHTON

TIMELINE

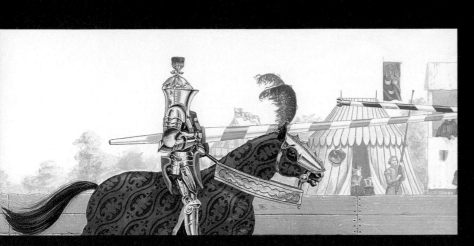

FOR MICHAEL'S FOLLOW-UP BOOK AFTER 'THE LOST WORLD', the catalogue deadline came and went and we still didn't even have a title to work with. But sure enough, someone from marketing or promotion (I can't remember which) phoned me, and the following conversation took place:

Marketing person: "Is there anything on the Crichton yet?"
Me: "I'm sorry?"
"A jacket. Do you have a jacket?"
"There's . . . no title, yet."
"I know."
"Much less a plot."
"Right." Long pause. "So . . . you don't have a jacket yet?"
Amazed silence, then, "No. I do not. Alas."
Heavy sigh. "All right. Thanks." Click.

Eventually, handed over with the utmost secrecy, there was the manuscript for *Airframe*, a thriller about corruption and intrigue in the airline industry. **OPPOSITE RIGHT:** Various stages of development for *Airframe*. The one with just the big "A" on it is supposed to mimic signage in an airport (and doesn't, really, at all). The image on the lower right is the apparatus of the title, and when applied geometrically to the type scheme to the left of it (**OPPOSITE LEFT:** Knopf, 1996), rather nicely recalls the logos of Pan Am and TWA.

For *Timeline*, there was the same secrecy and dearth of information. But Sonny eventually briefed me, and I did research on 15th-century France at the Metropolitan Museum of Art. **ABOVE:** Inspiration for the jacket. **RIGHT:** Knopf, 1999. The nice thing about this is it recalls a woman's corseted torso, which isn't at all inappropriate.

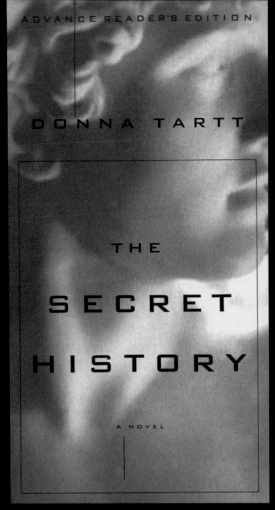

ADVANCE READER'S EDITION

DONNA TARTT

THE

SECRET

HISTORY

A NOVEL

THE
SECRET
HISTORY
—
DONNA
TARTT
KNOPF

The secret historian.

EVERY SO OFTEN A BOOK COMES ALONG THAT SEEMS DESTINED TO DEFINE A MOMENT IN PUBLISHING, and before there was even a manuscript one could sense that *The Secret History* was going to be such a work—the buzz was that strong. Once we read it, we knew why. Donna Tartt's mesmerizing story—an eccentric group of Greek classics students at a northeastern college (based on Bennington) murder one of their own and then methodically cover it up—left everyone in the office spellbound. Barbara deWilde and I teamed up to devise the visual approach, both for the jacket and the interior. What was needed was a unification of the classical and modern worlds, so we took a cue from antiquarian bookdealers, who sheath their tomes in clear acetate to protect them, regardless of the vintage. What if they printed modern type on the covering, suspended above a classical statue on the binding? To us that was the way to go, but as far as we knew no one had done it on a novel before—we had no idea if anyone else would get it. But Carol Carson did, Gary Fisketjon did, Sonny Mehta did. To produce it properly was a nightmare, capped by the issue of how to print an author photo onto plastic. For that we turned to our intrepid head of production, Andy Hughes, as we always did. He figured it out—a pass of opaque white ink beneath the black halftone made it show up. **ABOVE LEFT:** Advance reader's copy for reviewers, with a photograph by Robert Mapplethorpe, who had just died. His estate in chaos, we couldn't get permission to use the image for the hardcover and continued our search for the right statue. We eventually found *Discobulos*, the discus thrower by Myron, through a stock agency. **ABOVE CENTER:** *The New York Times*, November 16, 1992. **ABOVE RIGHT:** Entirety of case design—front, spine, and back. The acetate jacket ate up the budget for a three-piece case, so we simulated a leatherette texture for the spine. The thin red lines represent a combination of blood and modernism, literally cutting across the images. **RIGHT:** The inevitable mass-market paperback edition (which I did not design), an object lesson in how different markets can be perceived for the same book, and so drastically. **OPPOSITE RIGHT:** Knopf, 1992, co-designed with Barbara deWilde. An instant hit, debuting on *The New York Times* bestseller list, lingering there for weeks. To this day it never ceases to amaze me: not once did *anybody* ever question or bring up the subject of legibility. And let's face it, this has to be one of the most subtle uses of typography on a major, popular novel in recent memory. As ever, the credit goes to Sonny for taking the chance on a design that ultimately redefined what a bestseller could look like. And sure enough, the following season acetate jackets sprang up in bookstores like mushrooms on a murdered tree.

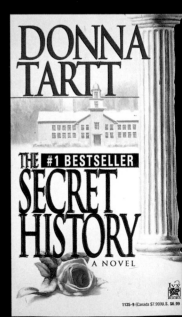

DONNA TARTT

THE #1 BESTSELLER

SECRET HISTORY

A NOVEL

WHEN I FIRST SAW THE DESIGN FOR 'THE SECRET HISTORY', I was apprehensive. I'd envisioned something much more traditional, but when Chip and Barbara showed me their design I felt like I was looking at The Book of the Future (which I suppose in some ways I was). I liked the images from Greek sculpture, which I'd chosen myself; and I loved the tall, narrow shape because it felt reminiscent of 18th-century books, but the rest of the package—acetate cover and all—was so radical looking that I was a little worried: what did all this cutting-edge modernism have to do with a book about classicism? Even though it was all very beautiful, I wasn't at all sure I wanted my first novel—which had taken me ten years to write—to be a testing ground for book design; and I left the Knopf offices thinking: well, either this will work or it won't.

BUT OF COURSE IT DID WORK, BRILLIANTLY. The very first time I walked into a bookstore (the old Rizzoli's in midtown) and saw a pile of my own books, they stood out across the room. People were gravitating around them and talking about them as objects: picking them up, showing them to each other, opening and shutting them to see how the acetate cover worked. ("Aren't these great?" someone said, when I drifted over to look at them myself, as if I was just another anonymous shopper drawn by the display). They were beautiful and distinctive en masse, stacked on tables or in a pyramid, but a single copy, held in the hand, was just as eccentric and extraordinary. Nobody (I was told again and again, in book shops throughout America that fall) had ever seen a book that looked quite like it before; and now, twelve years later, the design is still so inextricably intertwined with perceptions of the novel that (in America anyway) readers have come to see the hardcover design as an organic extension of the novel itself. This all happened fairly early in both our careers; and I think it was soon very plain to both Chip and me that our names would always be linked because of this book. (CONTINUED ON FOLLOWING PAGE)

MY SECOND NOVEL WAS VERY DIFFERENT from the first—much more ambitious in style and tone; and the only person who saw the relationship between the first book and the second and who could translate it visually for the publisher was Chip. He immediately saw the irony and creepiness of the title; and the cover image he came up with for *The Little Friend* was so powerful that all of a sudden everybody else got it, too. So—even though I have all sorts of other reasons to be grateful to Chip—I will always be especially grateful to him for allowing me to keep the title of my second book.

Chip and I talked more about the design of *Little Friend* than we did the first book—we had lots of discussions about the endpapers and the front matter—but the doll's head was all his idea (later he told me he'd envisioned this tiny object—which is not actually a doll, but a hatpin—as the cover for my second book years before I'd finished the book or before he even knew what it was about). Chip's design picks out the whisper of kinship between *Little Friend* and *Secret History* and makes it visually very clear that they're siblings. They're the same size, they look good on the shelf together, but even the doll's head has an eerie little echo of *The Secret History* about it; the black brush-stroke in the doll's eye is archaic and terrifying, like the painted eye on the bow of a Greek trireme. But as understated as Chip's work often is, there's almost always a little fizz to his cleverness, a pop kick that makes it irresistible. I laughed out loud when I saw that, on the cover of *Little Friend*, he'd put the doll's red lips directly beneath my name on the spine of the book, so it looks like I'm blowing a kiss to the reader.

Wherever I go, I'm asked about Chip in reverential tones. ("Will you share with us what it's like to work with him?") His admirers show up in droves at my readings (very conspicuous in the crowd, because they're always so stylish), and occasionally I'm even asked to sign autographs for him in proxy. I feel very, very fortunate to have worked with him from the beginning, and I hope he designs every book I ever write.

—Donna Tartt

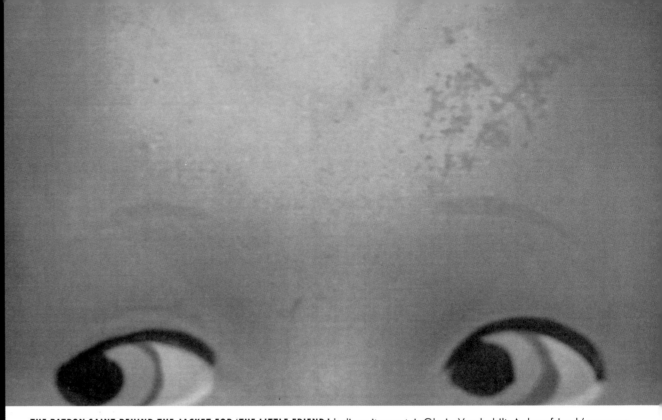

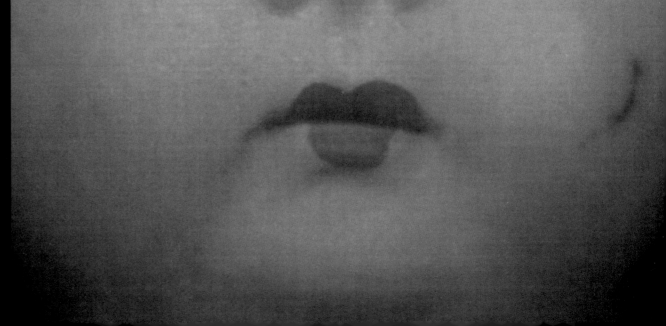

THE PATRON SAINT BEHIND THE JACKET FOR 'THE LITTLE FRIEND,' believe it or not, is Gloria Vanderbilt. A dear friend (see page 278), she had been working on an extraordinary series of 3-D assemblages of Depression-era ephemera when I made a visit to her studio. And I saw it: in one corner was a baby bonnet display stand from the 1930s, consisting of a molded doll's head with a pole jutting out of the center of its cranium, an expression of utter apprehension on its face—as if it were about to be bludgeoned. I recognized it as perfect for Donna's book, which hinged on the murder of a little boy. And now I had found him. Gloria sweetly allowed me to borrow the piece, and I did a crude scan (seen here) in order to acclimate Gary and Sonny to the idea, and they gave the go-ahead to the actual shoot. **LEFT:** Cavorting with Donna at my 40th birthday party.

THIS PAGE: Knopf, 2002. Photo by Geoff Spear. Once the concept was approved, Geoff photographed the same model head you see opposite and lit it to heighten the sense of dread and foreboding. Gary asked, "Can you make its eyes look to the right instead of the left?", which only required flopping it. He was absolutely right—this way the glance leads you directly into the book.

THE LITTLE
FRIEND

Knopf

DONNA
TARTT

THE LITTLE FRIEND

a novel by the author of THE SECRET HISTORY

DONNA TARTT

James Ellroy

A NOTE

ON THE TYPE

NOVELISTS BE-BOP THROUGH AN EPHEMERAL WORLD: fame, critical hurrahs, and money come and go book to book. The books themselves remain: largely on the shelves of strangers—loved, liked, or repudiated in ways the writer can never assess. Individual novels hold sway in their creator's mind for indeterminate periods, until they are eclipsed by new concepts and ideas—call it the serial monogamy of authoring fiction.

The transient nature of it all is frustrating.

White Jazz is a blunt, dark, stylized novel about police corruption. Chip Kidd frames the front cover in pristine white—a color at once stark, innocent, and inviting. Centered in that white expanse: an LAPD patrol car door shot full of holes. The potential book buyer/reader has been presented with a statement and a challenge—forceful, simple, elegant: Read This Book! It's both artful and powerful.

Killer instinct:

Mine, of course, for writing the book;

Chip Kidd's for knowing that the book is a story of epic bureaucratic dysfunction and for symbolizing it through a design concept that states the case plainly.

—James Ellroy

RIGHT: Knopf, 1992. This was an early attempt at the notion of an "incongruous spine." The idea that the only color on the whole jacket rests on what is usually considered the least important part of it reaffirms the novel's reliance on the unconventional method (of investigation, interrogation, suspicion, etc.). At least that's what I told myself. It also happens to look good spine-out on the shelf. Re: the photograph, here's the illusion-shattering truth: this police car door, so beautifully shot (sorry) by Robert Morrow, arrived at this condition not as the result of some dire standoff in Compton, but as the subject of target practice by the LAPD itself. This subliminal injection of authorial duplicity is more than apt for Ellroy's sensibility—when the cops aren't busy wasting perps they're wasting each other. Whether anyone got it or not was beside the point. As for the image, I was immediately taken by its de-contextualization—where's the rest of the sedan? And what happened to who was in it? Or rather, where are they buried?

James Ellroy
HOLLYWOOD NOCTURNES

something for the girls

CUSTOM HIGH FIDELITY MG 20141

featuring
DICK CONTINO
and his accordion

with the
DAVID CARROLL
orchestra

OTTO PENZLER BOOKS

Woof, daddy-o!

IT'S JAMES ELLROY'S WORLD. WE JUST LIVE IN IT. And lucky for us—because everyone else tends to die in it. I first became aware of the work of Mr. Ellroy (aka The Devil Dog of Death, self-named) through the photographer Melissa Hayden, an ardent fan. So at her behest I read *The Big Nowhere* and came away from it shellshocked: someone had finally managed to take what Mickey Spillane started forty years ago and advance it to the next level. This was before Knopf took him on, and little did I know that not only would I eventually work on his books but also through the years find him to be a trusted friend.

The tragedy of Ellroy's childhood is well known and documented (see overleaf), but what impresses me most about him is how he overcame seemingly insurmountable odds in order to solve the mystery of not only how to survive but how to become what can only be called an artist. He took the horror of his life and burned it—converting the resulting terrible energy into fuel for his savage chronicles of complex intrigue and piercing social comment.

I felt this work demanded an entirely different visual approach from what is expected when one thinks of "noir." I recast it in broad daylight. Which, by the way, offered no protection whatsoever.

LEFT: Mysterious Press, 1992. One of James's endearing obsessions is with the '50s accordionist Dick Contino. Those are his fingers on the keyboard spine. **OPPOSITE:** Knopf, 1993. Though James posits that eyeball is you, the reader, here's who it really is: Frank Sinatra. See? It's blue. So's the one on the spine. Really. Take my word for it.

THE BIGGEST THRILL OF MY 25-YEAR CAREER IS being published by Knopf. I came to Knopf for its literary reputation. I understood that legacy going in. Knopf imparts immortality. I crashed an elite circle and stayed for six books to date. I expected superb treatment at Knopf—and got it. What bushwacked me and surpassed my expectations was the art of Chip Kidd.

Six books. Fourteen years. Six Chip Kidd covers—hardcover and paperback. Six brilliant conceptualizations of the book text with visual recreations that supplant and in every way enhance and densify the force of the Knopf imprimatur.

I write large, historical crime novels full of institutional corruption and complexly layered collusion. Chip Kidd's jacket designs display entire criminal worlds with smashing concision. The colors are always stark. Archival photographs merge with bold contemporary typefaces and entice and warn the reader: a horribly real dramatic environment lives right here. The images summarize the prose. A paranoid eyeball clipped from a '50s scandal rag. A notice that the eyeball is you and that literary voyeurism is your game. A photocollage centered around a snapshot of my murdered mother. A stunning announcement that in death she lives. More photos—the Vegas strip circa '67 and a sheet-covered stiff. The message that murderous history unrolls in snap-crackle-pop prose.

I'll die one day. My books will live on. My stories will be one leg up on immortality. Chip Kidd's art will enclose them. I'm honored and grateful for that. Knopf and Kidd: synchronous and sizzlingly symbiotic. A rich and continuous joy for me.

—James Ellroy

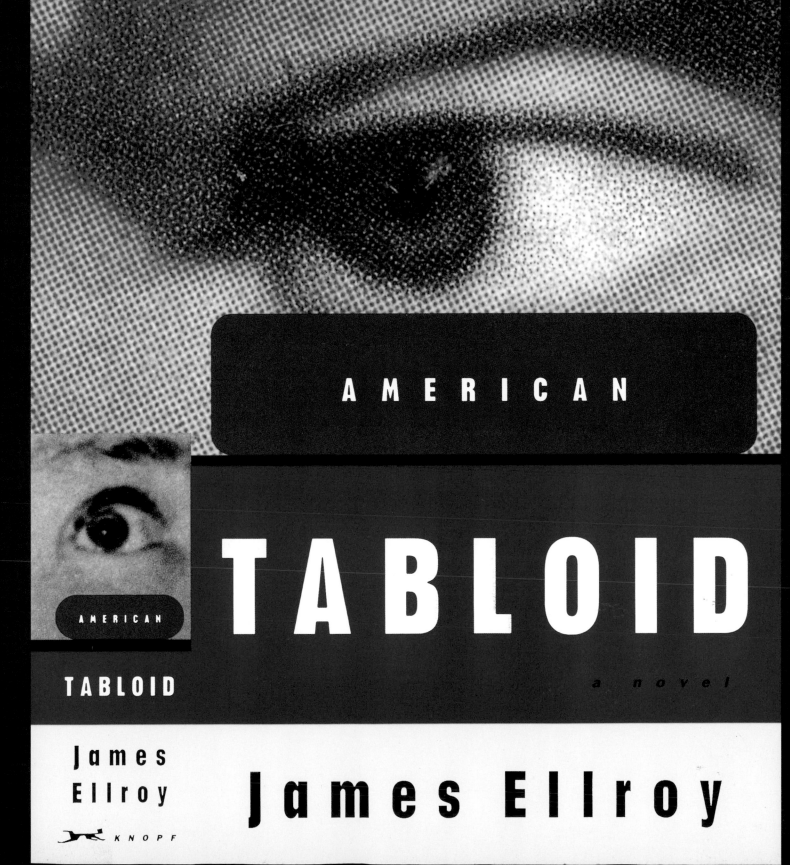

MY DARK PLACES

On the reverse of the jacket for Ellroy's *My Dark Places* I printed a detail of the newspaper report on the murder of Ellroy's mother. This is one of those—okay, gimmicks—that the reader may or may not ever see, and yet it is literally underlying everything. Sonny, as he so often did and does, indulged me on that one and its extra expense. **LEFT:** Knopf, 1996. Ellroy's memoir of trying to come to grips with, and solve, the crime. A vintage photo of the victim looms large beside the image of her son. Her smile makes it all the more unsettling. **ABOVE:** A crime scene photo from the jacket verso. **OPPOSITE LEFT:** A variety of those cool target practice and general crime dingbats that were often featured in midcentury pulp magazine ads, courtesy of the invaluable CSA archives. **OPPOSITE RIGHT:** Vintage, 1998. **OVERLEAF:** (from left to right) A fax from Ellroy regarding *The Cold Six Thousand*; Knopf, 2001. **FOLLOWING SPREAD:** Vintage, 2001; Vintage, 2001. Adapting *American Tabloid* and *White Jazz* to trade paperback to follow the visual scheme of *The Cold Six Thousand*. The key element in all three is a genuine crime scene photograph by Mell Kilpatrick, who was the unsung Weegee of 1950s and '60s southern California. Most of his work was only discovered after his death in the 1970s.

JAMES
ELLROY
author of L.A. CONFIDENTIAL and MY DARK PLACES

REPORTAGE AND FICTION FROM THE UNDERSIDE OF L.A.

CRIME WAVE

VINTAGE CRIME

6/13/00 A.D.

From:
James Ellroy

To:
Chip Kidd
Alfred A. Knopf
299 Park Ave.
New York NY 10171
212-572-2363 (phone)
212-940-7676 (fax)

Dear Chip:

Hey, Daddy-O!!! How's the hammer hanging? Long and strong, I hope.

I'm fucking hopped up to get all the good production shit going on my magnum opus, *The Cold Six Thousand.* As we discussed, and as I know you expect, it's a motherfucker of a book. Karen Latuchie and I have koncocted Knopf kover kopy, along with the "About the Author" blurb. Sonny moved the book to May 2001, so it's in the Summer 2001 katalogue. That probably gives you more time to koncoct your dust-jacket art.

*   *   *

When we discussed your jacket ideas, I gave you a rundown of the real-life characters who will appear in the book. I realize now that I left a few out. Here, once and for all, is the kast of real-life fiends:

J. Edgar Hoover; Howard Hughes; Robert F. Kennedy; Martin Luther King; Jimmy Hoffa; Carlos Marcello (celebrated mobster); Sam Giancana (celebrated mobster); Bayard Rustin (civil rights fiend); Sonny Liston; Sal Mineo; James Earl Ray; Sirhan Sirhan.

That covers it. Marion Ettlinger took some bonaroo pix of me for the katalogue and dust jacket. Black and white photos rule; color photos drool. I'm working out a strategy to request -- rather than demand -- that my fucked-up foreign publishers use your jacket on their editions. It may work; it may not work; I'm going to try.

I hope this fax finds you in a moon-howling, Borzoi-boffing, mood. (I hear they give good snout.) Tell Sandy I'm trying to find him a first of *Brown's Requiem.*

Woof!

Dog

Dog

Paw print

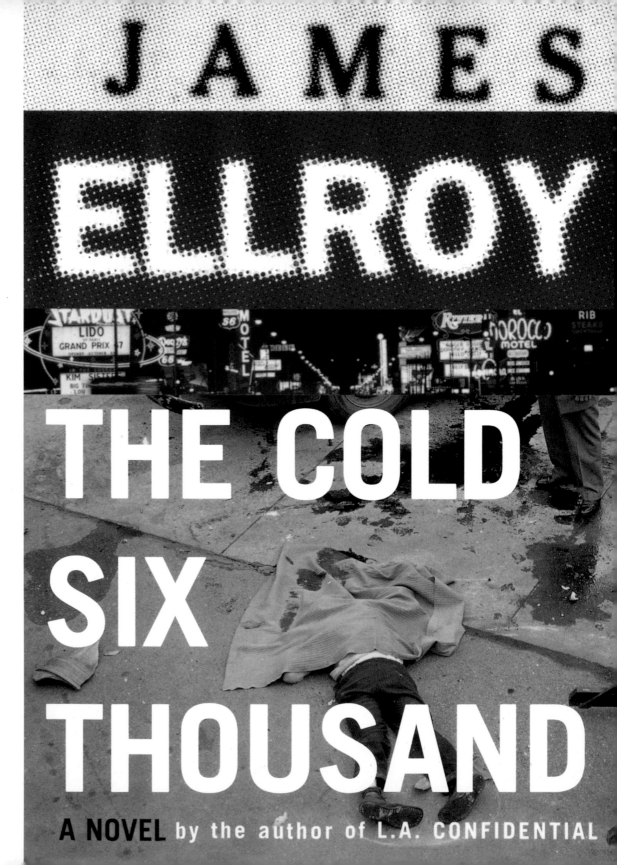

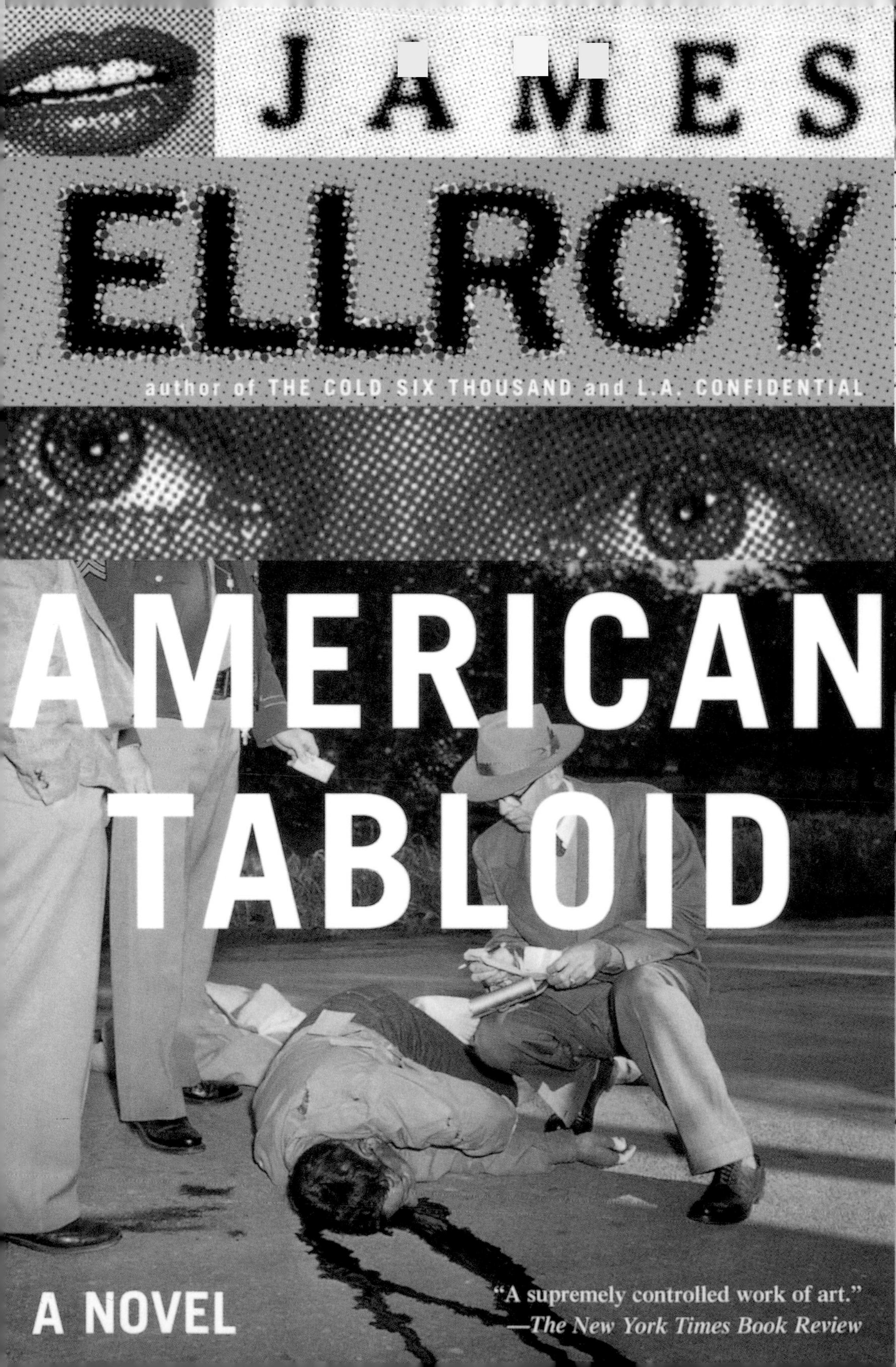

JAMES ELLROY

author of THE COLD SIX THOUSAND and L.A. CONFIDENTIAL

AMERICAN TABLOID

A NOVEL

"A supremely controlled work of art."
—The New York Times Book Review

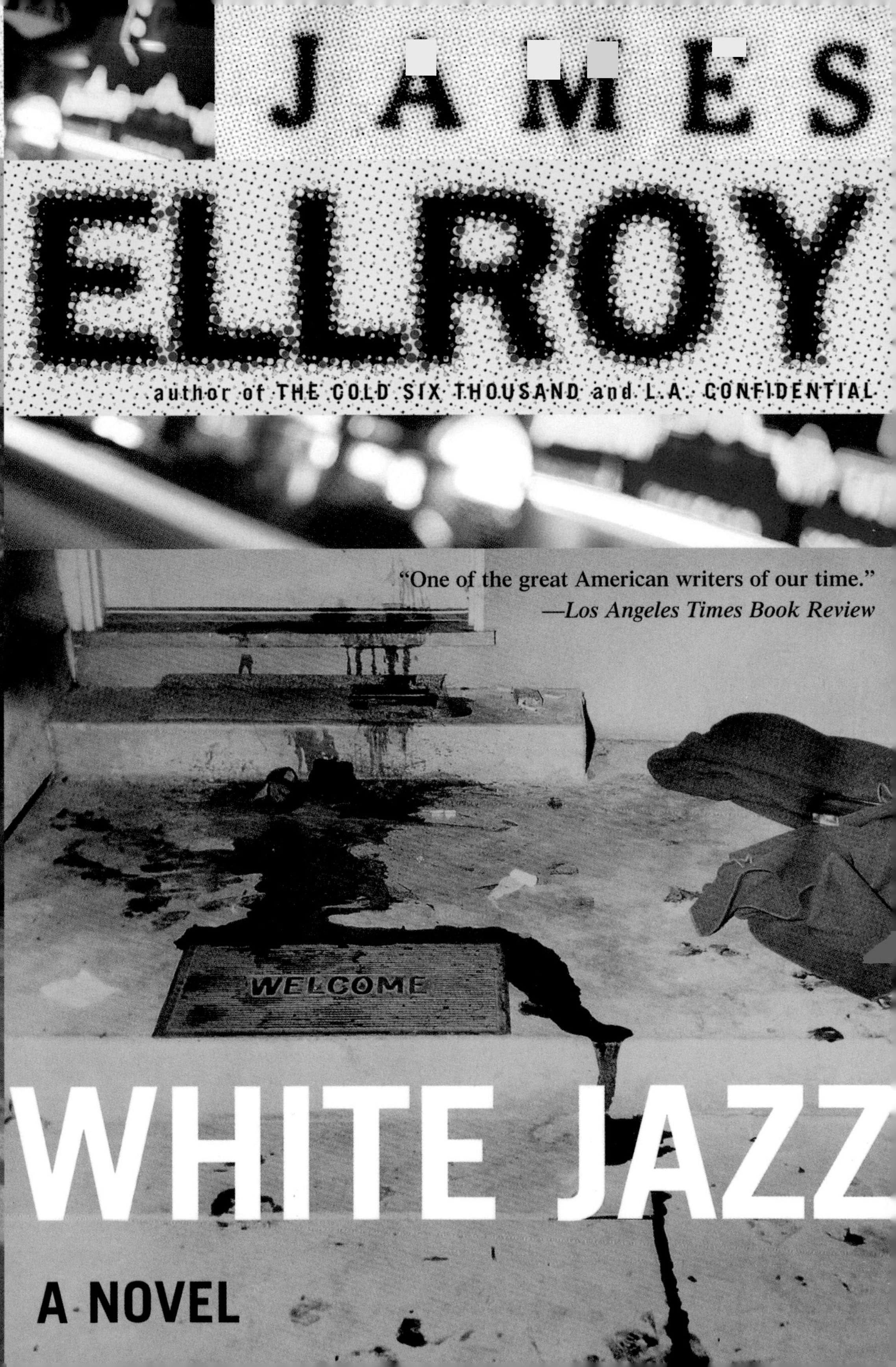

JAMES ELLROY

author of THE COLD SIX THOUSAND and L.A. CONFIDENTIAL

"One of the great American writers of our time."
—Los Angeles Times Book Review

WELCOME

WHITE JAZZ

A NOVEL

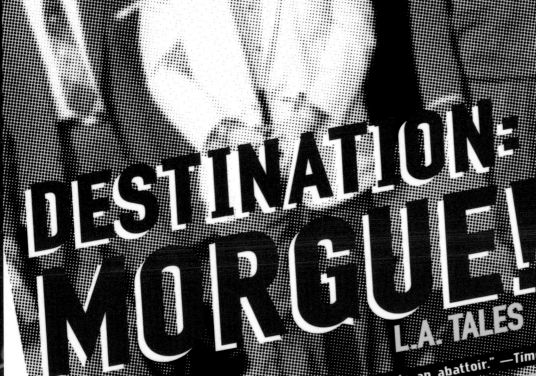

JAMES ELLROY

Bestselling author of The Cold Six Thousand and L.A. Confidential

DESTINATION: MORGUE!

L.A. TALES

A VINTAGE ORIGINAL

"Ellroy rips into American culture like a chainsaw in an abattoir." —Time

INCLUDING THREE NEVER BEFORE PUBLISHED NOVELLAS

ABOVE: Donald Keith Bashor, sentenced to death for the murders of two women in the mid-1950s. He figures prominently in the plot of *Hot-Prowl Rape-O*, a short story in 2004's *Destination: Morgue!* (left, Vintage). I superimposed his mug shot over a photo of him being led to the electric chair. Everything is tilted 10 degrees counterclockwise, to impart a sense of twistedness and descent. **OPPOSITE LEFT:** Vintage, 2005. **OPPOSITE RIGHT:** Vintage, 2005. Redesigning Ellroy's early backlist for trade paperback presented the challenge of where to go next with his covers. Vintage art director John Gall wanted something different from anything I'd done before. When I discovered the amazing work of artist Thomas Allen, who photographs ingeniously deconstructed pulp paperbacks, I knew I'd found it. Ellroy's writing, to me, always leapt from the page, and now the covers did too.

James
ELLROY

author of L.A. CONFIDENTIAL

BLOOD ON
THE MOON

a novel

"A brilliant detective and a
mysterious psychopath come
together in a final dance of
death."
—*The New York Times*

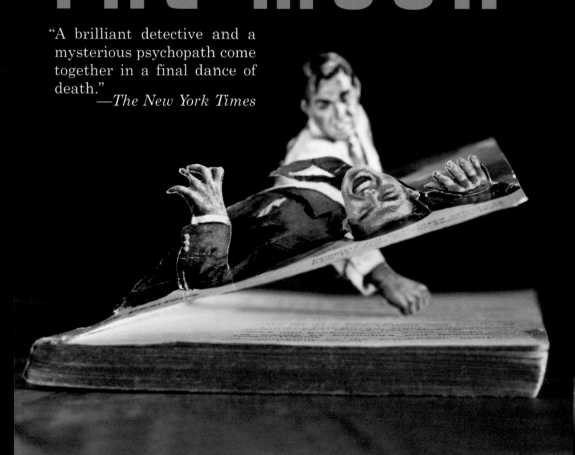

James
ELLROY

author of L.A. CONFIDENTIAL

BECAUSE
THE NIGHT

a novel

Complete and
Unabridged

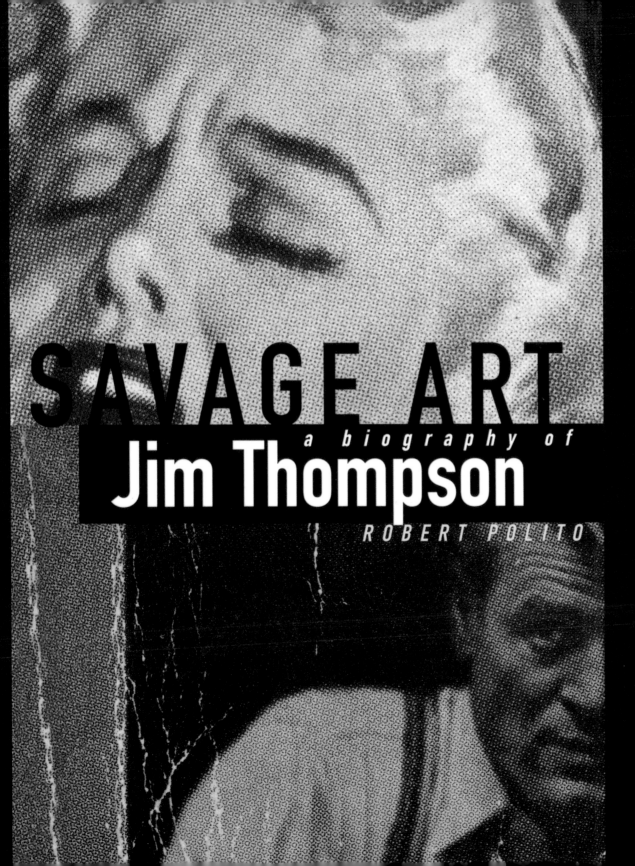

SAVAGE ART
a biography of
Jim Thompson
ROBERT POLITO

RAYMOND
CHANDLER

LEFT: Knopf, 1995. Jim Thompson, author of *The Grifters* and *The Killer Inside Me* is the relatively "forgotten man" of American noir letters. Rather than show a conventional portrait on the jacket of his biography, I used two details from vintage pulp covers of his novels. They imply both a narrative of dread and a closer examination of things than is normally taken. **ABOVE:** Knopf, 2005. In this case I thought it was amusingly appropriate for a guide to life to have a gun on the front. **OPPOSITE:** Harper Collins, 2000. For this gripping tale of deception based on a true story, the vellum jacket covers up more information than it would at first appear to.

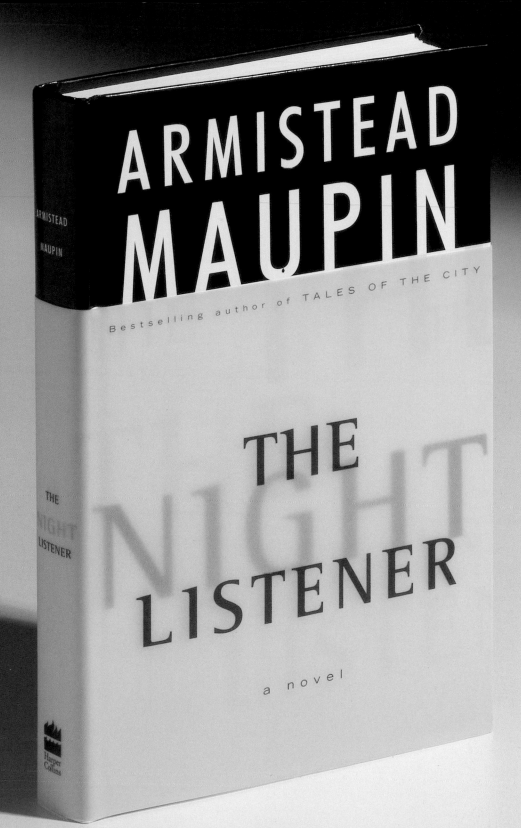

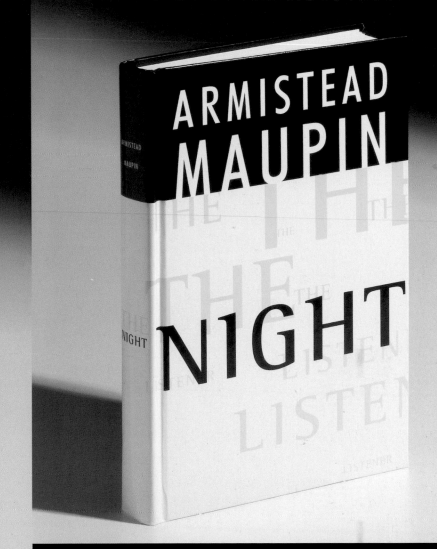

IT TOOK ME A WHILE TO GET ENOUGH CLOUT WITH MY PUBLISHERS, but when I did, I asked for a Chip Kidd cover. Chip's earliest efforts for *The Night Listener* disappointed me, however. (Several of them involved large ears, which struck me as a little too—well, on the nose.) I confess to having been nervous about sending the King of Covers back to the drawing board, but Chip was more than accommodating. The end product was perfectly suited to a novel of psychological suspense; bright yellow and black, like a highway caution sign, and partially jacketed with a see-through vellum miniskirt that gave the word NIGHT an eerie ectoplasmic shimmer. Best of all, the book could be seen on a shelf from miles away. The vellum was a bitch, however, refusing to accept Annie Leibovitz's author photo during the initial print run. It also had a nasty tendency to slip. When Charlie Rose interviewed me, he held the book up for the money shot and the jacket shimmied all the way to the top, thereby losing its ectoplasm. "The novel is called *The Listener*," Charlie said, as indeed it appeared to be. To this day the word vellum incites naked terror at HarperCollins.

—Armistead Maupin

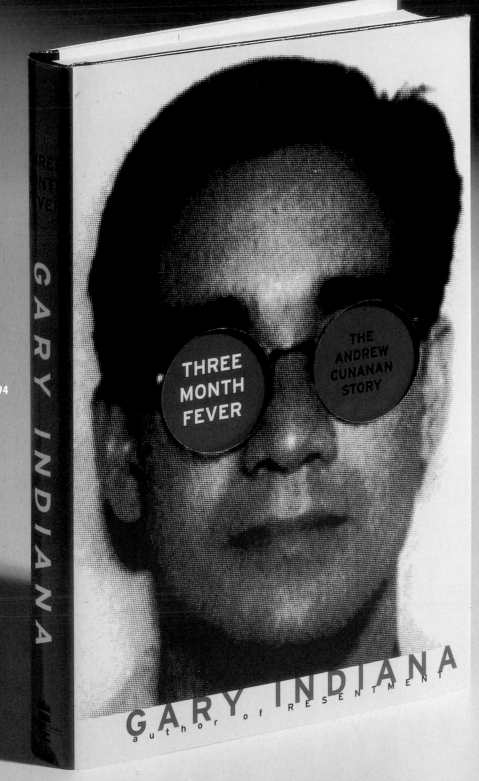
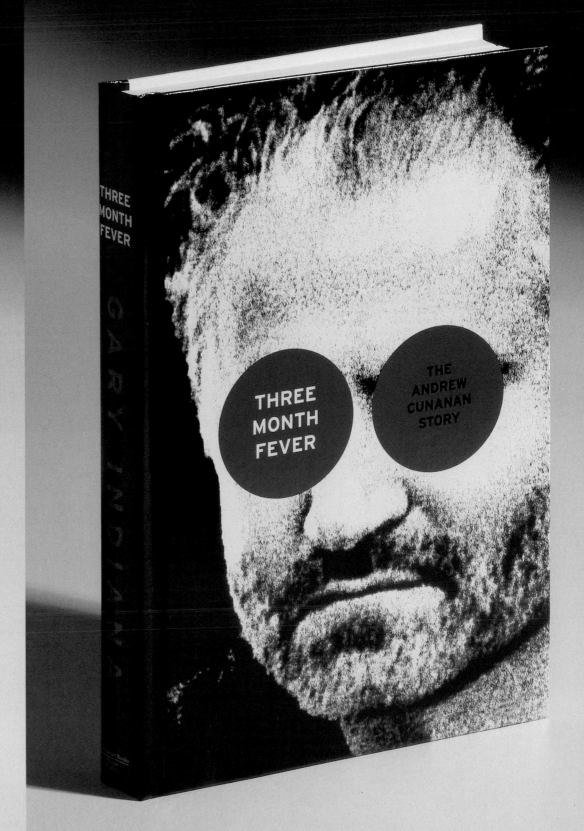

ARMING AMERICA

THE ORIGINS OF A NATIONAL GUN CULTURE

MICHAEL A. BELLESILES

ORIGINAL ART FOR "DEPRAVED INDIFFERENCE" BY GARY INDIANA

HANDLE w/CARE!!
RETURN TO: CHIP KIDD
299 PARK AVE.
3RD FL. NYC 10171

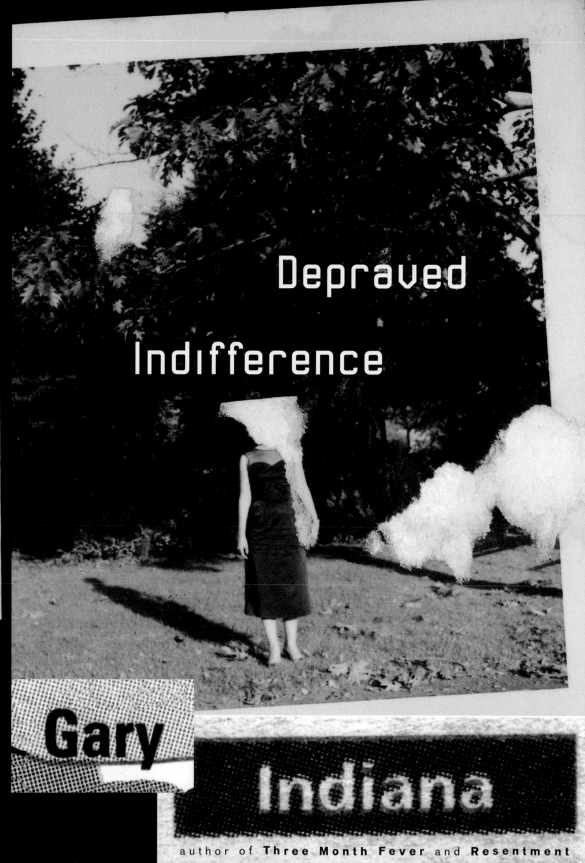

Depraved

Indifference

Gary

Indiana

author of **Three Month Fever** and **Resentment**

OPPOSITE: Jacketed and unjacketed, HarperCollins, 1999. The hunter covers up the hunted. **ABOVE LEFT:** Knopf, 2000. **ABOVE RIGHT:** I got this old Polaroid snap as a gift from a fan at a book signing. I knew it would be good for something if I held onto it long enough and—lo and behold!—Gary Indiana's novel based on the exploits of those adorable sociopaths, Santee and Kenneth Kimes, dropped into my lap. **RIGHT:** HarperCollins, 2002. The author name was culled from bits of a road atlas. I mean, how could I not?

ELMORE LEONARD

LEONARD

CUBA
LIBRE

A NOVEL

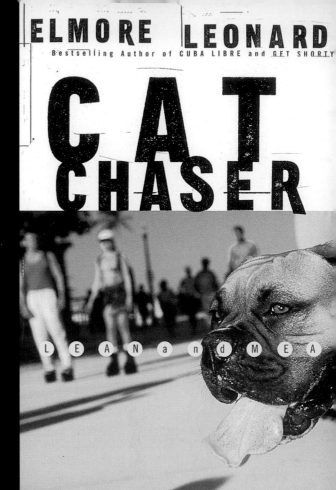

ELMORE LEONARD
Bestselling Author of CUBA LIBRE and GET SHORTY

CAT
CHASER

YORK OBSERVER

the unidentified model posing vampishly in a black lace negligee, left hand pressed to right breast, in a decorating book published on April 9 by Regan Books, *The Paris Apartment: Romantic Decor on a Flea Market Budget*. Now, who could that be?

TICKLE ME, ELMORE

Literary agent Andrew Wylie, who now represents mystery master Elmore Leonard, has hatched a scheme to crank up Mr. Leonard's already high profile by giving a trademark design to the entire Leonard backlist—both trade paperback and mass market—as well as future books. He has given Knopf designing whiz Chip Kidd a shot at the makeover. A proposal is due by June 1.

The idea is highly unusual because of Mr. Leonard's publishing arrangement: His backlist is divided between Avon, the paperback division tied to his former publisher, William Morrow, and Dell, part of Delacorte Press, his current house. Between them, the companies have 17 Leonard titles in print. Mr. Wylie said that designers from both Avon and Dell would also be submitting designs. Mr. Leonard's next novel, according to Jackie Farber, his editor at Delacorte, is called *Cuba Libre*. An "adventure story, romance and historical novel" set in Cuba during the Spanish-American War, it will have a February 1998 release date to coincide with the centennial of the sinking of the *Maine*. Once a unified look has been chosen, said Mr. Wylie, "it won't matter whose logo is on the cover."

Dutch treat.

ELMORE LEONARD IS SYNONYMOUS WITH COOL, SO HOW COULD I REFUSE THE OPPORTUNITY to redesign all of his books? At the behest of his agent (the formidable Andrew Wylie), I took on the welcome task of taking Dutch (as he is known to friends) into a new visual direction, starting with the hardcover novel, *Cuba Libre*. That title was something of an anomaly for him—a period piece revolving around the wreck of the *Maine* and the onset of the Spanish-American war—but I devised a scheme using distressed type culled from current *New York Post* headlines, which I could then apply to his more contemporary titles. In my opinion *Glitz* was as good as it ever got—that oh-so-unglitzy hirsute gut embodies the perils of Iris, the naive heroine-victim of the book, who falls for the false promises of a ruthless and possessive casino mogul in Atlantic City and pays the ultimate price. To me the discrepency between the title and image embody the ugly truth Leonard's work is all about. My thanks to the photographers Juddha Harris, Batienne Schmidt, and Martin Parr, whose photos grace the various covers. You're all such good sports.
LEFT: Delacorte, 1998. **ABOVE CENTER:** *The New York Observer*, April 21, 1997. **ABOVE RIGHT:** Quill, 1998.
OPPOSITE PAGE: (clockwise from top left) Delta, 1998; Delta, 1998; Quill, 1998; Quill, 1998; Quill, 1998.

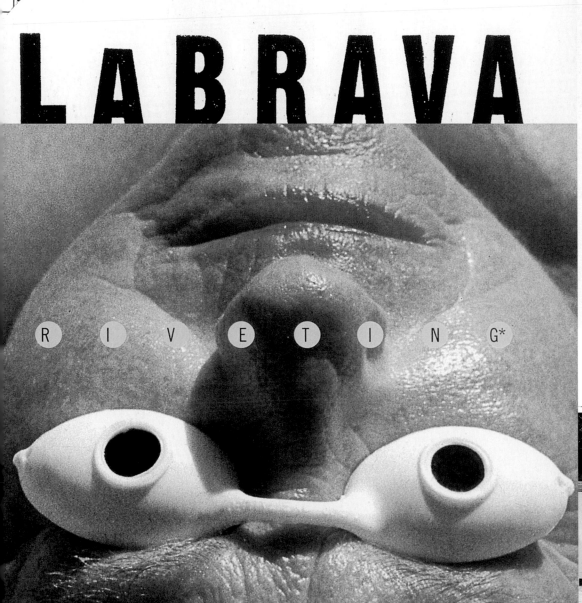

ELMORE LEONARD

LaBRAVA

R I V E T I N G*

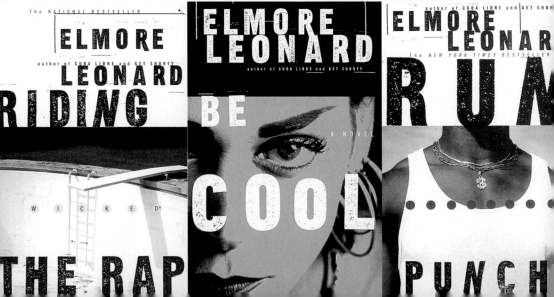

Elmore Leonard

January 3, 2005

For Chip Kidd's Book One

I didn't get to see most of my books as they were published
until it made no difference whether or not I liked the cover
design. Most were okay, they looked like book covers; one,
in 1976, won a New York art directors' award. But with 40
books to dress there were few if any socko ~~visial~~ Visual images
until Chip came along, bless his heart, and the covers came
alive with visuals you had to stare at and wonder about.
What's an empty swimming pool doing in the design? Or the
bloack guy's chest and his jewelry. Or the white guy's
belly, or the bare feet on the balcony with the view of the
ocean. Do they tell anything about the novel? Not much.
But who cares? I love them.

Dutch

The boss of deboss.

I TRY NOT TO USE ANY "SPECIAL EFFECTS" UNLESS THERE'S A COMPELLING, meaningful reason to do so. For Richard North Patterson's political and legal thrillers, I tried to impart a real tactile quality as well as an added element that would immediately draw the reader into the story. *Silent Witness*, for instance, emits a high-pitched wailing sound when opened; *Dark Lady* is printed with an ink that causes temporary blindness; *No Safe Place* gives off an odor that attracts bears. Our production department works very hard to constantly keep up-to-date with the latest printing and paper engineering techniques. **ABOVE LEFT:** Knopf, 1997. Photograph by Geoff Spear. **ABOVE RIGHT:** Knopf, 1999. I got this effect by scanning a color Xerox in "transparency" mode by mistake. Must have been a late night. Looked pretty good, though, so that was that. **RIGHT:** Knopf, 1998. Photo by Geoff Spear. **OPPOSITE:** Quill, 1998; Delta, 1998; Delacorte, 1999; Delta, 1998.

NORTH

OF

MONTANA

A NOVEL

APRIL SMITH

BE
THE
ONE

A NOVEL
3 10 1
APRIL
SMITH

BE

A NOVEL

APRIL SMITH

BE
THE
ONE

THAT'S MONTANA AS IN MONTANA AVENUE IN
Los Angeles. It acts as a sort of border between
the right and wrong side of the tracks—north of
it is the Haves, south is the Wanna Haves. When
a detective from the latter investigates a crime
in the former, classes clash. **LEFT:** Knopf, 1994.
ABOVE: An unused idea for April Smith's thriller
about the only female talent scout in the decid-
edly male-dominated world of major league
baseball. **RIGHT:** The final jacket, Knopf, 2000.

DENNIS LEHANE

Shutter Island

A novel by the New York Times bestselling author of

DENNIS LEHANE

a novel by the author of PRAYERS FOR RAIN

Mystic River

WELCOME TO THE CITY OF CRYSTAL LAKE. You may know us only by our reputation for hosting sleep-away camps that are regularly attacked by a psychotic post-adolescent in a hockey mask, but we're so much more! The City of Crystal Lake is committed to artisanal jams & jellies! Crystal Lake is located 50 miles northwest of Chicago, is a short drive from O'Hare Airport, is near several major highways and interstates, and has regularly been attacked by a pathologi . . . nevermind. The Union Pacific rail line provides easy access to Chicago. As a result, Crystal Lake residents enjoy the employment, cultural, & recreational opportunities of a major city, yet live in a friendly small-town atmosphere, where they are only infrequently hacked to bits. **ABOVE:** William Morrow, 2003. Photographs by Christopher Myers and Ilka Hartmann. **RIGHT:** William Morrow, 2001. Photograph by Jonathan Safir. Richard Aquan was art director on both jackets.

Happy ending.

THE WORKING TITLE OF 'BANGKOK 8' was *Kung Threp*, which is the Thai name for the city. Personally, I thought that was cool, but it was deemed too obscure and replaced with the district designation where most of the action takes place.

This is a terrific crime novel that traffics in the steamy atmosphere of Bangkok and its strip clubs, brothels, massage parlors, and criminal underworld. The narrator is a young half-breed Thai police detective (with the riotous name of Sonchai Jitpleecheep) who's also a practicing Buddhist, thus the figure on the spine looks down over all the wanton sin on the front. Three die-cut holes, through which the type appears, indicate that there's plenty lurking under the surface.

RIGHT: Knopf, 2003. **OPPOSITE:** Case detail. For a book featuring the sex trade in Bangkok's Pat Pong district, how can you not have a peek-a-boo jacket?

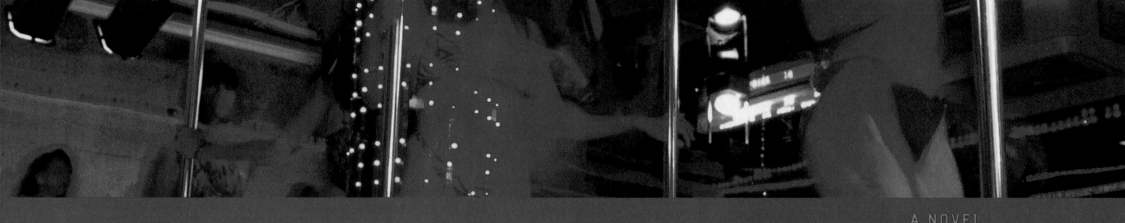

BANGKOK 8

A NOVEL

JOHN BURDETT

KNOPF

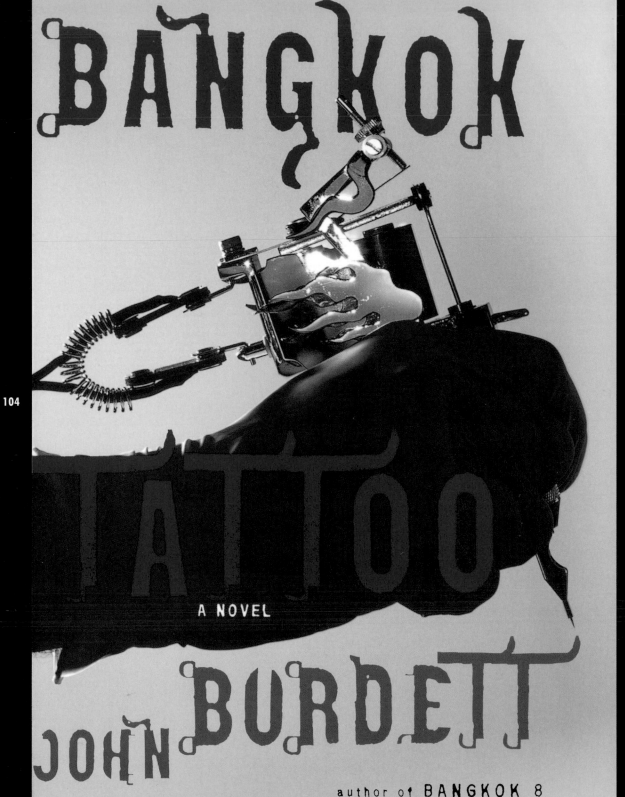

Tattoo Story.

'BANGKOK TATTOO' ISN'T SO MUCH THE SEQUEL TO 'BANGKOK 8' as it is the next installment in what the author plans as an ongoing series. Our narrator Detective Jitpleecheep is back, this time investigating a series of grisly murders in which the victims have large pieces of their skin removed. What comes to light is that what's being "harvested" is their astonishing tattoos, the work of an eccentric Japanese genius of the form.

I felt from the beginning that attempting to show any of the tattoos (which are beautifully described) would be a mistake. Part of the pleasure of the book is imagining what they really look like. Instead I wanted to show a close-up of the hand of the artist himself, his needle poised on a pristine patch of skin. My hope was that this would look menacing. Geoff researched tattoo equipment on the web, and he quickly found a huge supplier just around the corner from his studio, in Chinatown.

It was a fascinating place, a second floor walk-up on Canal Street that you'd never notice if you didn't know it was there. They had all sorts of tattoo guns along one wall, and we were about to settle on one when I spied two others, in a black velvet-lined case under a glass counter next to the cash register. These, it turned out, were collector's items—custom chrome one-of-a-kinds by a Dutch craftsman of apparently huge renown in the world of "body artists." The one with the chrome flames was especially appealing. "Those will be worth a lot when he's dead," said our sales clerk, a boy who wore black rubber gaskets the size of half-dollars in his earlobes. Luckily for us, our man was still among the living, and the price to buy was actually less expensive than renting one of the others for a week.

The sheer flamboyance of the mechanism made me alter my approach: we didn't need the skin now. If we lit this thing well and introduced the right amount of color it should work on its own. Any confusion about what you're looking at is taken care of by the title itself.

RIGHT: Standard-issue tat guns. **LEFT:** The deluxe version, Knopf, 2005. My hand, *again*.

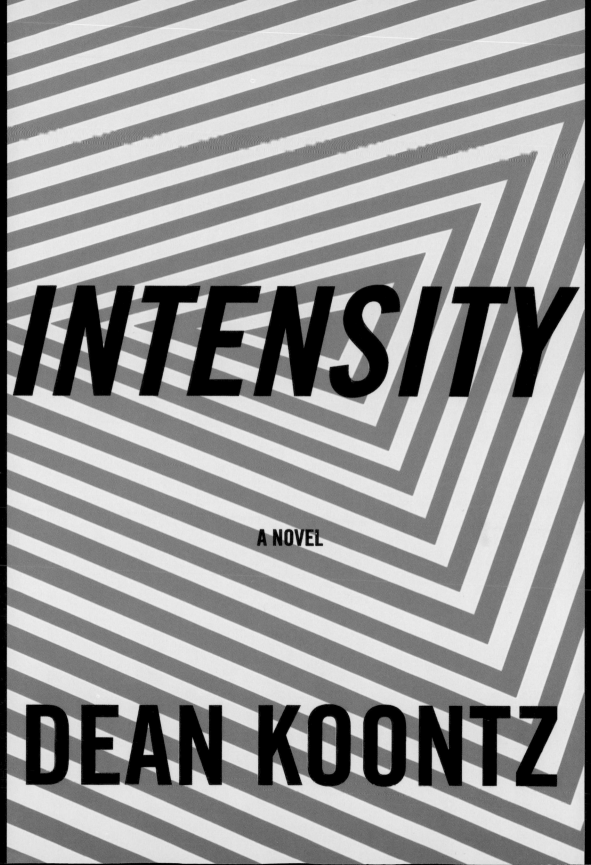

INTENSITY

A NOVEL

DEAN KOONTZ

DEAN KOONTZ'S TENURE AT KNOPF was as triumphant as it was relatively shortlived. Amid much fanfare he was signed to a three book deal in 1994, turned in a book a year, and promptly left. From the outset Sonny wanted me to completely "start over" with the look of his books, which was music to my ears. In my mind, Koontz had already established a reputation for what he does (mostly psychological thrillers), so there was no need to make these look "scary." The important thing was to announce in the book store that there was a new Koontz book, and now he was being published in a completely different way. I think *Intensity* was the most successful, aestheticially as well as commercially. All three of these books went to number one on the *New York Times* Best-Seller List. That phenomenon doesn't happen very often (see *Disclosure*, by Michael Crichton, p. 72). **ABOVE:** Knopf, 1994. **LEFT:** Knopf, 1997. **RIGHT:** Knopf, 1996.

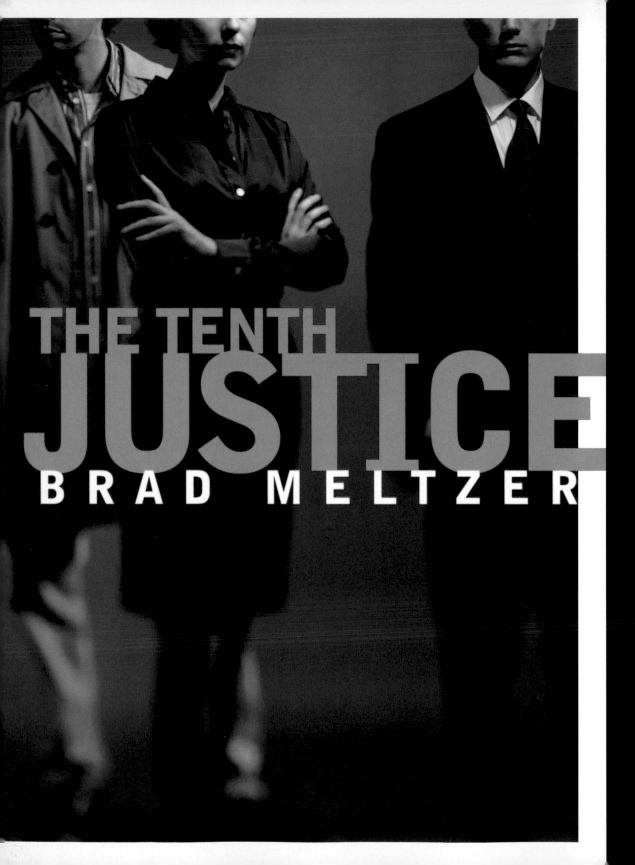

THE TENTH
JUSTICE
BRAD MELTZER

THE FIRST MOCKED-UP COVER FOR MY DEBUT NOVEL, THE TENTH JUSTICE, wasn't done by Chip. In fact, when they presented it to me, my editor Rob Weisbach brought me into hi office and pointed to his bookshelf, where he'd set up six or seven rows of books, all o them with the cover facing outward. His instructions were simple. "Find your book."

The theory was, if this first mocked-up cover was good, I'd be able to find it easily, which was absolutely necessary for a new, first-time writer. With no name to rely on, freshman attempts, I was told, were always judged by their covers. So . . . I did a quick scan of the shelves, figuring it'd be easy. All I had to do was find my name. But as I scanned . . nothing. I took another look, this time going a bit slower. Nothing again. I took a third try being more methodical-starting with the book on top left, then going book by book, paus ing on each one. Still nothing. One last attempt. Book number one . . . no . . . book numbe two . . . no . . . book number three . . . nothing. What the hell was going on?

Finally, my editor pulled "my" book from the shelf. Now let me say, I consider myself a fair ly enlightened person. So I didn't beat myself up too much when my so-called "fresh and different" cover design was so "fresh and different" that the designer decided that the book I'd labored two years on didn't need the title or my name on the cover. Genius, huh?

The next day, we hired Chip. What you see here is the final result—a result that took a brand new book by an unknown author and did the impossible with it. He made it stand out. It sounds so simple. It's not.

A month after *The Tenth Justice* was published, the TV show "Law & Order" filmed one of thei scenes in a New York bookstore. In the far, unfocused background of the scene was a huge wall of books, most of them facing outward (presumably to convince us doubting skeptic in the audience that this was, indeed, a real bookstore). The entire scene was barely a minute or two long. No one in their right mind was looking at the books in the background (okay, let's be honest: the whore that I am, all I cared about was looking at the books in the background). Even worse, the actors blocked most of them. But then, in the final moments of the scene, the camera panned to the door, blurring all the books in the process All except for one. I screamed for my wife. "Honey, I just saw it! You can't miss those brigh orange letters!" The way she rolled her eyes, I knew she was unconvinced. Then the phone started to ring. Friends, relatives, neighbors . . . all saying the same thing: "Did you see it?" "You saw it, right?" "It was just on 'Law & Order'—you couldn't miss it!" And the commen I heard most of all: "It just jumped right out at you."

The following year, my editor started a collection of books that were rip-offs of Chip' design for *The Tenth Justice*. Some stole the style. Others just a mild variation on the colors Few of them worked.

It sounds so simple. It's not.

I owe Chip Kidd more than he'll ever realize. And not just because he put my name and title on the cover.

—Brad Meltzer

T WAS ALWAYS ABOUT THE EYES. TAKE AWAY SOMEONE'S EYES, and they instantly become more mysterious. For *The Tenth Justice*, Chip cut the tops of the characters' heads off, eliminating their soul windows. For *Dead Even*, he used the title to the same effect. That was the easy part.

The hard part was trying to decide how two close-up headshots could possibly tell the story of what was inside. *Dead Even* was about two married lawyers competing against each other in court. Easy to describe in a sentence. Harder to sell in a picture (without going for the cheesy overused pillars and columns that have plagued every legal thriller since the genre was invented). On top of that, between the two photos, which do you choose for the actual cover? The man or the woman?

As always, Chip thought outside the cover. Don't choose just one. Do both. Half of the covers would have the man on the front. Half would have the woman. Individually, the book was just a headshot. But in a display in a bookstore, when they were side by side, they became competing images. Both begging for your attention. Man vs. woman. Husband vs. wife. Get it? Get it? Get it?

We did too.

The image was always amazing (thank you, Geoff Spear). But expanding the canvas beyond the individual cover . . . that's what made it Chip's.

—Brad Meltzer

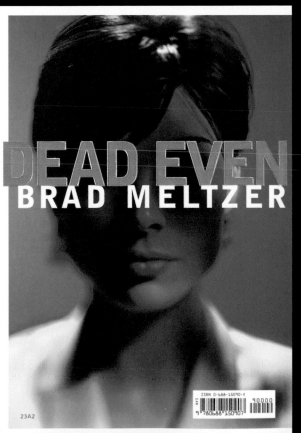

OPPOSITE: Rob Weisbach, 1997.
THIS PAGE: Rob Weisbach, 1998.
Photographs by Geoff Spear.

DEAD EVEN
BRAD MELTZER
The NEW YORK TIMES bestselling author of THE TENTH JUSTICE

A NOVEL BY THE

tours of the black clock

Arc d'X

STEVE
ERICKSON

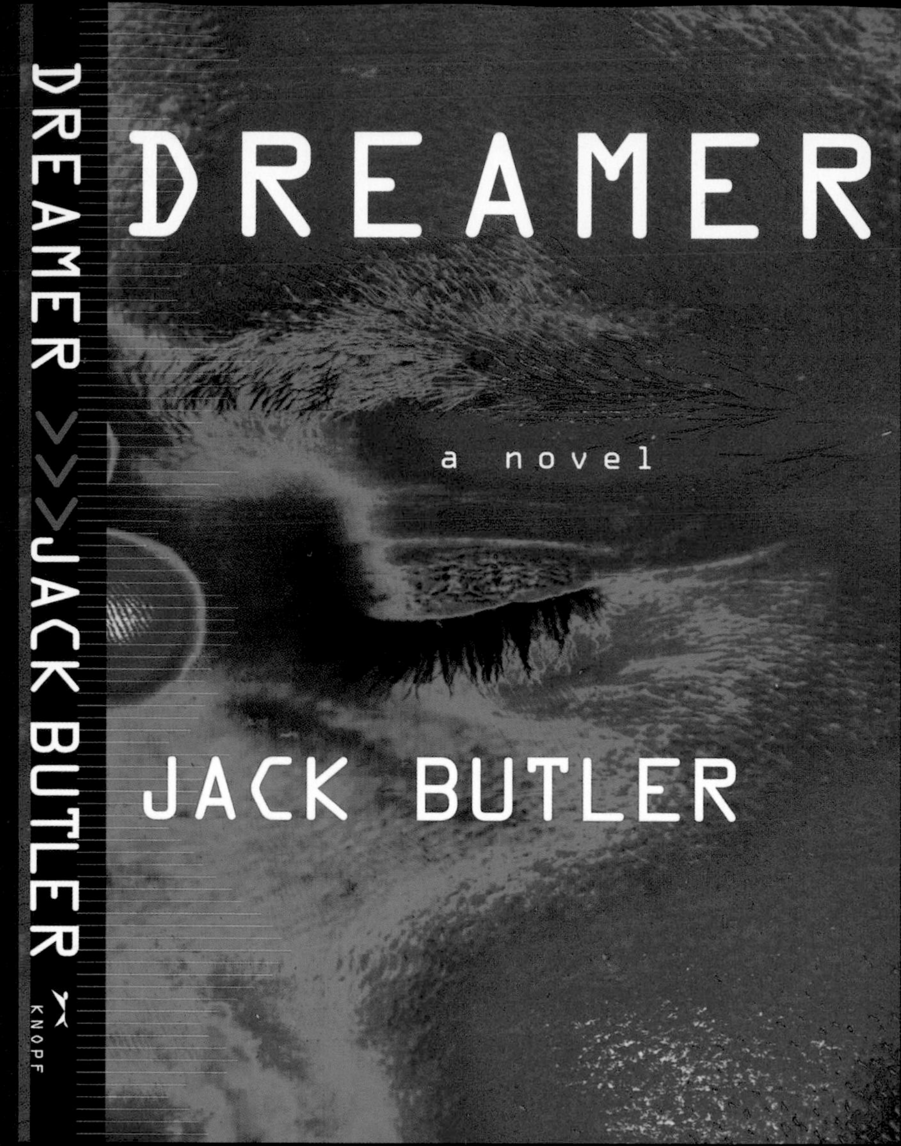

DREAMER

a novel

JACK BUTLER

DREAMER

DREAMER

JACK BUTLER

KNOPF

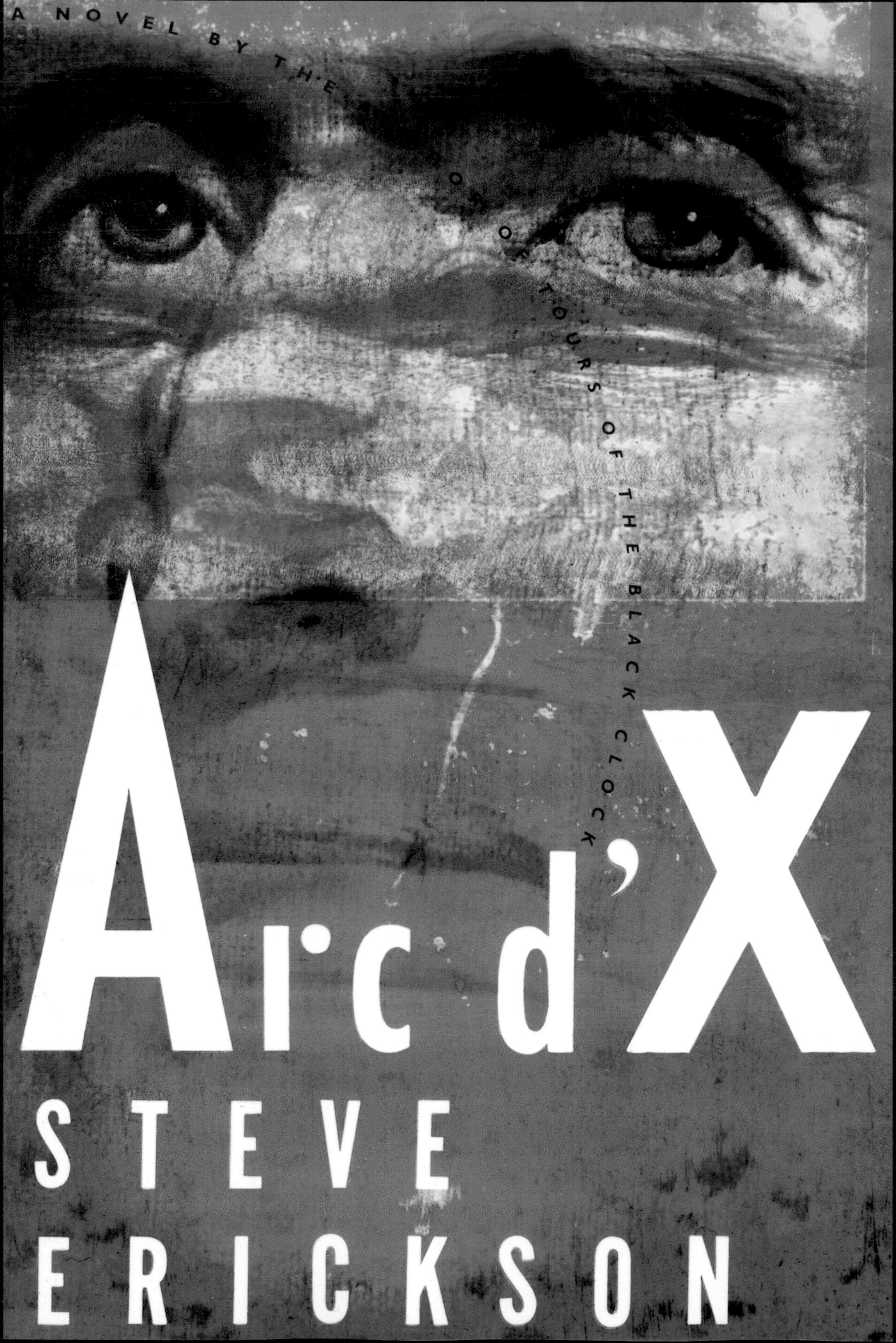

Scan *this*.

WITH THE ADVENT OF COMPUTERS CAME THE OPPORTUNITY TO MAKE IMAGES IN A way we hadn't before. Of course, they'd been doing that in the movies for a good fifteen years, but we're talking about book publishing—at least a decade behind almost every other kind of mass media and proud of it. Soon I was putting anything within reach onto the scanner to see what would happen. This included my face, which I plopped onto the cover of *Dreamer*, a novel about a dream researcher who is targeted by rival CIA factions. Adjusting the curves function in Photoshop turned my sleepy visage into something out of the video for *Go Ask Alice*. **LEFT:** Poseidon Press, 1993. *Arc d'X* is your average science-fiction thriller about Thomas Jefferson. **ABOVE:** Knopf, 1998. **OPPOSITE LEFT:** Pantheon, 2002. **OPPOSITE RIGHT:** *Winnipeg Free Press*, May 19, 2002.

PHILIP K. DICK......................
....

THE

MiNOriTY

rEPOrt

"COOL FACTOR"

Publisher hopes gimmicky design will boost sales of movie tie-in book

By Morley Walker

I T'S a book. But it's not quite the shape of a normal book.

The publishing tie-in for Minority Report, the highly anticipated new Tom Cruise movie opening June 21, has a glossy hard cover and type running across its pages, as books tend to have.

But it's about two-thirds the size of a normal hard cover. And instead of being bound vertically on the left side, it's hinged horizontally along the top.

It flips open like a note pad, in fact, like a police officer's notebook, which it is designed to suggest.

"This project was a total wet dream to work on," says Chris Kidd, Alfred A. Knopf's New York-based associate art director in charge of special projects.

It is the latest in a spate of gimmicky ideas

"For one thing, the author is dead, so you don't have to worry about him. For another, it's just a cool story."

In its original form, *The Minority Report* was a short story published in 1956 by American science-fiction master Philip K. Dick, whose work has also been adapted into the movies Total Recall and Blade Runner.

Stripped of that pesky definite article, Minority Report is destined to be a 2002 summer movie blockbuster, an $80-million US high-tech thriller directed by Mr. Midas Touch himself, Steven Spielberg. And suddenly that little story by a writer who died in 1982 has renewed caché in bookstores, which received their initial shipments of the jazzed-up $20 Cdn version last week.

It is the latest in a spate of gimmicky ideas that have changed the face of book design in the last 20 years.

"Chip and the other designers at Knopf had started finding ways to create packages for books that did not... just illustrate the content," the *Boston Globe* reported last fall.

"They came up with something that was much more tangential or metaphoric or enigmatic or provocative."

Kidd, 37, who hit bestseller lists last year with his own cleverly devised debut novel, *The Cheese Monkeys*, has designed jackets for such bestsellers as Dean Koontz's *Intensity* and Michael Ondaatje's *The English Patient*.

His most recognizable projects are his Batman art books and the Jurassic Park logo. *New York* magazine has called him a "design demigod."

Tricky tomes

Here are some noteworthy books for grownups that employ gimmicky designs.

GRIFFIN & SABINE (1991) — Vancouver-based writer and illustrator Nick Bantock hit the jackpot with his first love story told via postcards.

SEX (1992) — Rock star Madonna's picture book celebrating the world's favourite recreational activity was bound in an orginal format involving two sheets of metal, each numbered, and sealed in a Mylar plastic sleeve.

HOUSE OF LEAVES — (2000) — Mark Z. Danielewski used multiple typefaces, vertical footnotes and color text in a story about a family whose house is bigger inside than outside.

THE CHEESE MONKEYS (2001) — American book designer Chip Kidd wrote his coming-of-age novel in the computer graphics program Quark Express.

GOULD'S BOOK OF FISH (2002) — Tasmanian novelist Richard Flanagan's tale of a 19th-century convict uses different colours of ink and paper for each chapter and lots of detailed fish illustrations.

'THE MINORITY REPORT' WAS THE KIND OF DREAM assignment I'd never had before: design a movie tie-in book that couldn't look anything like the movie. Pantheon had the rights from Philip K. Dick's estate to publish the story in time to coincide with the release of the film, but only in hardcover, and only if it bore no resemblance whatsoever to the efforts of Spielberg and Cruise, who'd passed on the idea. Music to my ears. The story is relatively short, so I had to pad it out with pages of graphics representing the three "pre-cogs" of the story. I also used the old-fashioned gimmick of putting the first word of the next page at the bottom of the preceding recto page, as a sort of "pre-cognition" of the text.

THE N E W N E W N E W THING

] A SILICON VALLEY STORY [

MICHAEL LEWIS

AUTHOR OF *LIAR'S POKER*

MICHAEL LEWIS

author of THE NEW NEW THING

"*Liar's Poker* is the funniest book on Wall Street I've ever read."
—Tom Wolfe, author of *Bonfire of the Vanities*

] #1 BESTSELLER [

LIAR'S POKER

MICHAEL LEWIS

author of LIAR'S POKER and THE NEW NEW THING

"He is the funniest and most trenchant commentator on the money-mad moguls reshaping our world today."
—*USA Today*

] NATIONAL BESTSELLER [

THE

MONEY CULTURE

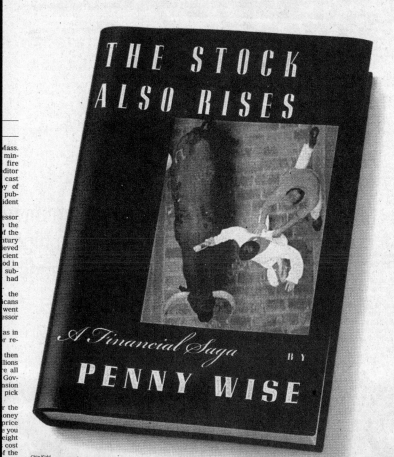

THE NEW YORK TIMES **OP-ED** TUESDAY, JULY 13, 1999

THE STOCK ALSO RISES

A Financial Saga

BY

PENNY WISE

Chip Kidd

AND GLORIOUS FUTURE

OF WORK

2

WHEN IT COMES TO BUSINESS-RELATED BOOKS, I try to turn them into typographic problems that can be solved though simple visual suggestions. **OPPOSITE LEFT:** W. W. Norton, 1999. How does "NEW" become newer? **OPPOSITE RIGHT, TOP:** Penguin, 1999, adapting the scheme of the hard cover to the backlist. **OPPOSITE RIGHT, BOTTOM:** *The New York Times* Op-Ed page, July 13, 1999. **ABOVE:** Doubleday Currency catalogue, 1991. **RIGHT:** Unused idea for *All I Could Get*, a novel about a day trader who's desperately trying to make it on Wall Street. The implication is that the stock figures are steadily rising like a flood, and will eventually drown him. 2002.

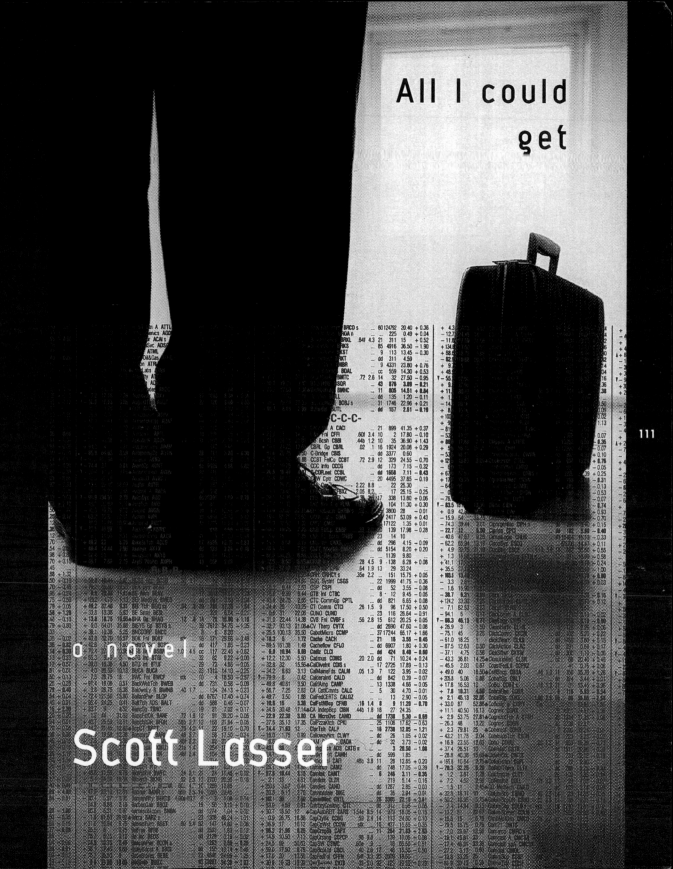

All I could get

a novel

Scott Lasser

Michael Quan for The New York Time

The confusion surrounding the future of information technology has created a brisk market for books on the subject. Nicholas Negroponte, above, director of the Media Lab at the Massachusetts Institute of Technology has taken the early lead with "Being Digital," published by Knopf.

I'LL NEVER FORGET VISITING THE M.I.T. MEDIA LAB WITH *Being Digital* editor Susan Ralston in early 1994 and encountering their demonstrations for this new "internet" thing they kept promising us was going to be so big. We smiled and marveled and nodded our heads and thought they were completely out of their minds. But we had a book to publish, so we said "Cool! We're all for it!" Nicholas kept telling me he wanted a design "that would win awards." That is never a goal one achieves on purpose. Instead you have to focus on the subject matter—I thought the revelation of the book was that all digital material is broken down into ones and zeros. Black and white. On and off. So the jacket shouldn't be able to function properly without the book and vice versa. Cringe-inducing moment: we had coincidentally just gotten computers in the department when this project came along, and Nicholas showed up in my office one day asking to see the design onscreen. So warily I opened it in Quark and tried to advance it to the second page, without success. Finally, I gave up and confessed: "Mr. Negroponte, could you please show me how to scroll down in this program?" Without missing a beat, he cheerfully offered: "Me? I've never seen that program in my life. I have no idea!" **LEFT:** Knopf, 1995. Nicholas did the code for the spine himself, and it actually means something, though for the life of me I can't remember what. **ABOVE:** The author is puzzled as to why all the copy on his book jacket is backwards. From *The New York Times*. P.S.: It *did* win awards.

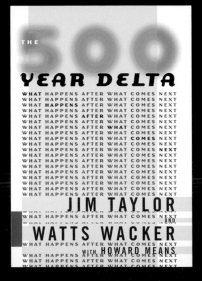

KEN AULETTA

WORLD WAR

MICROSOFT AND ITS ENEMIES

3.0

JAMES GLEICK

author of CHAOS

FASTER

THE ACCELERATION OF JUST ABOUT EVERYTHING

ABOVE: Random House, 2001. More Typography 101—it becomes more pixelated as you read it. Andy Carpenter, art director. **RIGHT:** Pantheon, 1999. Archie Ferguson, art director. **OPPOSITE RIGHT, MIDDLE:** Harper Business, 1997. Joseph Montebello, art director.

THE REMAINS OF THE DAY

a novel by

KAZUO ISHIGURO

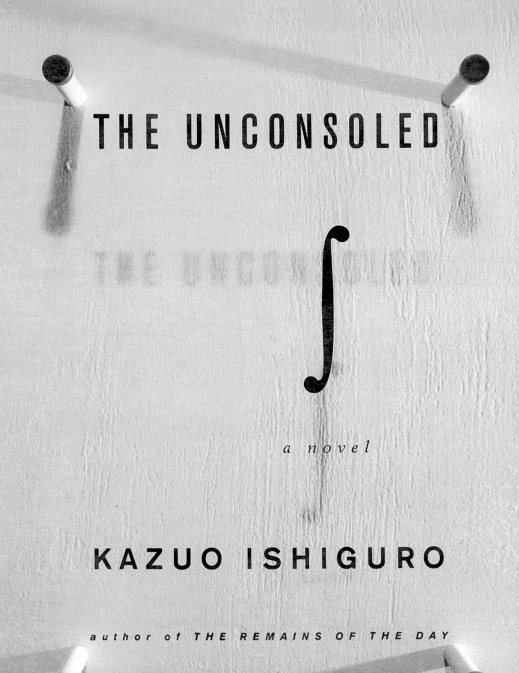

THE UNCONSOLED

∫

a novel

KAZUO ISHIGURO

author of THE REMAINS OF THE DAY

TIME REMAINING

STORIES

JAMES McCOURT

Tempus fugit.

KAZUO ISHIGURO'S 'THE REMAINS OF THE DAY' was one of those rare come-out-of-nowhere novels that took the literary world by storm and went on to win the Booker Prize. After designing the jacket I gave the book to a friend, Remak Ramsey, an actor playing a supporting role at the time in the 1990 Merchant Ivory film *Mr. and Mrs. Bridge*. He claims he loved the book so much he personally put it into the hands of Ismail Merchant on set, a gesture which eventually led to its Oscar-winning adaptation starring Anthony Hopkins and Emma Thompson. Hey, I'm just repeating what he told me. **OPPOSITE LEFT:** Knopf, 1993. Photo by Robert Butler. **OPPOSITE RIGHT:** Unused idea for Ishiguro's *The Unconsoled*. Photo by Geoff Spear. An extremely obtuse and difficult novel, it frankly stumped me, and I tried to execute a typographic solution that would put the the viewer at a physical remove from the book. We went with something entirely different. **LEFT:** Knopf, 1993. Photo by Jarry Lang. **ABOVE:** The 1942 Justice Society of America secret decoder, the basis for . . . **RIGHT:** The Swatch Decoder watch, 1996, an open-ended commission from Swatch that was originally supposed to be part of the company's Artist Series. The art director who hired me to create it was dismissed halfway through production and things got more than a bit chaotic. It eventually was produced the way I envisioned it, but not as part of the Artist Series, as promised.

Peppers

AMAL NAJ

A STORY OF HOT PURSUITS

MAKING BEER
Revised Edition

How to produce excellent home-brewed lagers, ales, and stouts, with note
and comments on the pleasures and pitfalls of this delightful craft

And how to avoid the temptation of starting up your own brewery

William Mares

Buuuuuurrrrrp!

PARDON ME. One area I haven't had to deal with much is cookbooks. They are extremely involved
and complex, and I don't have the head for them. Carol is much better at the genre than I am.
But I have worked on my share of food-related covers. The idea of mimicking food packaging
is hard to resist, so in most cases I don't resist it. Hot sauce, beer, wine—what do they look like?
LEFT: Knopf, 1992. **ABOVE:** Knopf, 1994.

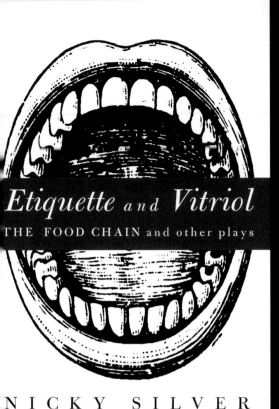

Etiquette and Vitriol
THE FOOD CHAIN and other plays

NICKY SILVER

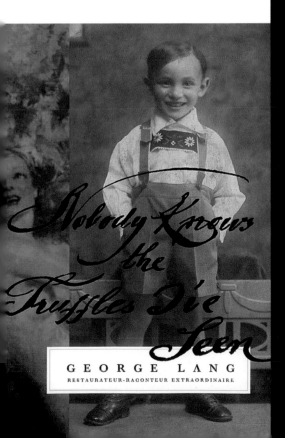

Nobody Knows the Truffles I've Seen

GEORGE LANG
RESTAURATEUR-RACONTEUR EXTRAORDINAIRE

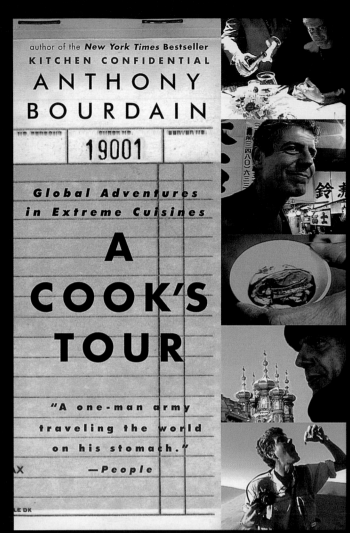

author of the **New York Times** Bestseller
KITCHEN CONFIDENTIAL
ANTHONY BOURDAIN

19001

Global Adventures in Extreme Cuisines

A COOK'S TOUR

"A one-man army traveling the world on his stomach."
—People

THE NEW CONNOISSEURS' HANDBOOK OF CALIFORNIA WINES

THIRD EDITION

THE DEFINITIVE GUIDE TO WEST COAST WINES

Fully updated and expanded to cover more than 800 wineries and labels, with critical ratings of thousands of individual wines and vintages, plus information on winemaking techniques, grape varieties, growing areas, best producers, and much more — *including 1994 harvest reports*

Norman S. Roby
and
Charles E. Olken

ABOVE LEFT: TCG, 1996. **ABOVE:** Ecco, 2002. **RIGHT:** Knopf, 1991. **BOTTOM LEFT:** Knopf, 1998. The impish George Lang gleefully declared his book a "combination cookbook and Holocaust memoir."

Julia Phillips

You'll Never Eat Lunch in This Town Again

ONCE UPON A TIME IN HOLLYWOOD

MOVIE MAKING, CON GAMES, and MURDER in GLITTER CITY

ROD LURIE

Check, please.

JULIA PHILLIPS'S IDEA OF SOBRIETY WAS A VODKA MARTINI that didn't have three lines of cocaine sprinkled on top of it. That's not a value judgment, it's just a probable ingredient in the recipe for the destruction of her successful film-producing career. But, in her Hollywood-Babylon memoir *You'll Never Eat Lunch in This Town Again,* she also attributed her flame-out to a lot more: naming the names of the studio creeps, shooting stars, and black holes, all of whom conspired to screw her. As Phillips would have said, the book opened huge, at the top of the bestseller lists, and had amazing legs. The cover concept was obvious to me before I ever read a word (but of course I devoured the manuscript anyway, with horrified relish). The jacket became somewhat iconic, but I think that had more to do with the book's wild success than the other way around. **LEFT:** Random House, 1991. Photograph by Christine Rodin. With the perspective of 14 years this looks way too ornate to me—restaurants in Los Angeles (at least those whose doorways Julia would deign to darken during her heyday) are sleek, cool, and modern. Yet all the props I chose were so girly-gooey. We set this up and shot it in (then Random House editor-in-chief) Joni Evans's apartment in Olympic Tower, a spectacular glass box high above Rockefeller Center. I suppose with all the frills and elegant details I was trying to offset the feral cold-bloodedness of the knife. And in the end, I can't say it didn't work. That switchblade, by the way, is actually my dad's—he acquired it during his European tour of Army duty. **ABOVE:** Unused, appallingly obvious idea for a book about the movie business.

HIP KIDD, 29, graphic designer   from left: SYLVIA KRUG (aunt), THOMAS and ANN KIDD,
ft shop proprietors, JOSEPH KRUG (uncle).

homas Kidd: "I tried to make a lawyer out of Chip at one point, but I was always comfortable with him going into art as a career."

ip's virgin-wool suit by Hugo Boss, $725. Viscose shirt by Byblos, $275.

WHEN 'DETAILS' MAGAZINE ASKED TO PHOTOGRAPH me with my family in 1993 for a feature on "young men up and coming in their fields," I naturally agreed, as did my mom, dad, Aunt Sylvia, and Uncle Joe. The photographer was to be someone named David LaChappelle. A month later we found ourselves in the dining room of my parents' house in Reading, Pa., caked with make-up amid a blizzard of balloons and streamers, a melting birthday cake, and enough camera equipment and crew to film *Exodus*. How did this happen? To this day we're still not sure, but the resulting image has gone on to appear on greeting cards (the proceeds going to AIDS research), the cover of the Italian magazine *Panorama*, and in *LaChappelle Land*, David's first monograph. And, of course, he has since become the Cecil B. DeMille of fashion photography. **LEFT:** *Details*, January 1994. **BELOW:** *Details* magazine subscription card. **RIGHT:** A poster announcing Paul Rudnick's evening of three one-act plays produced by Drama Dept., 2001. Photo by Kate Raudenbush. Tomatoes by God.

Join the Party!

SPECIAL CHRISTMAS RATE

Details
JUST $1 AN ISSUE!
(12 issues $12)

4L14

Name _____ (please print) _____

Address _____ Apt. _____

City _____

State _____ Zip _____

☐ Payment enclosed
☐ Bill me

In Canada, Details is $27 including GST. Your first issue will be mailed within 6 weeks.

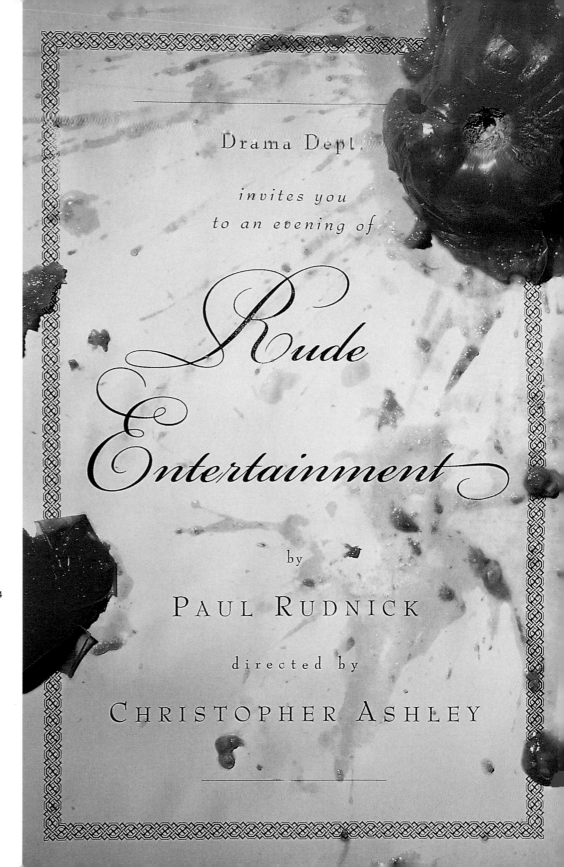

Drama Dept.

invites you

to an evening of

Rude

Entertainment

by

PAUL RUDNICK

directed by

CHRISTOPHER ASHLEY

THE MAN
WHO ATE
EVERYTHING

AND OTHER GASTRONOMIC
FEATS, DISPUTES, AND
PLEASURABLE PURSUITS

JEFFREY
STEINGARTEN

THE MAN
WHO ATE
EVERYTHING

JEFFREY
STEINGARTEN

Knopf

JEFFREY STEINGARTEN IS THE SORT OF GASTRONOME who coerces a good friend to bring six pounds of rendered Austrian horse fat through US customs on her way back from a trip to Vienna so that he may use it in an attempt to produce the most supreme french fry on Earth. And he does. For *The Man Who Ate Everything*, his collection of hilarious and virtuoso food essays culled from *Vogue* (for which he writes regularly), I drew from his piece about the travails of trying to bake the perfect loaf of bread. I wanted an example of it for the cover. He was all too eager to comply and created it in his very own kitchen. The bite-shaped die-cut around the spine was the *coup de grâce*. I wanted the jacket to look good enough to . . . you know. **LEFT:** Knopf, 1997. Photo of bread by Geoff Spear.

(fiction)

THE SLEEP-OVER ARTIST

THOMAS BELLER

Staples of life.

USING OBJECTS WE ALL IDENTIFY WITH CAN MAKE BOOKS seem immediately familiar even though we know we've never seen them before. Then when you place those objects out of context, a new layer of meaning can be added where the familiar becomes intriguing alien territory. **ABOVE:** Norton, 2000. Photos by Oote Boe. **RIGHT:** Knopf, 1990. Photo by Anton Stankowsky. I was doing research for Vikram Seth's new book of poetry when I saw this picture in a history of German photography and nearly wept—mostly because I knew no one would ever go for it. But one must try, and happily I'd underestimated both Sonny and Vikram, who both loved it. This is yet another example of an image I never could've come up with on my own—the photographer did it for me a half-century earlier.

✢ ALL YOU WHO SLEEP TONIGHT ✢

✢ POEMS BY ✢ VIKRAM SETH ✢

LYING AWAKE

a novel

MARK SALZMAN

CHIP KIDD CAN MAKE OR BREAK A BOOK WITH HIS cover designs; that's how powerful they are. In the spring of 2000 he designed the cover for *Lying Awake*, my book about a group of people (nuns) who sleep in cells, have no personal possessions, eat in silence, wear identical uniforms, and who cannot leave their walled community except by special permission. In the spring of 2003 he did the cover for *True Notebooks*, my book about a group of people (incarcerated juveniles) who sleep in cells, have no personal possessions, eat in silence, wear identical uniforms, and who cannot leave their walled community except by court order. Both books were poignant, thought-provoking, humorous, elegantly written, intelligent, surprising, and life-affirming. *Lying Awake* flew out of the bookstores; *True Notebooks* sank like a stone.

How can we explain this? For the cover of *Lying Awake*, Chip selected a black-and-white photograph of a stark hallway in a convent, with a ghostly figure of a nun at the far end of the hall. You can't quite see her face. For *True Notebooks*, he chose a black-and-white photograph of a stark hallway in a prison, with a ghostly figure of an inmate at the far end of the hall. You can't quite see his face. Both beautiful images, both perfect representations of themes encountered in the books. So far, so good. But what style of lettering did he choose for the titles? For *Lying Awake*, he used fragile, vulnerable letters in white, red, and gold, evoking both the material world and the spiritual one, the sacred and the profane. They say to the reader: this is a book that goes right to the heart of the human condition. For *True Notebooks*, he used plump, jaunty lettering in colors reminiscent of childhood: cherry red, sky blue, lemon yellow. Set against the harsh prison image, they say to the reader: this book is about complexity. Was he right? Yes. Was he right to advertise this on the cover? The sales figures show that acknowledging complexity did for *True Notebooks* what it did for John Kerry.

Thanks, Chip Kidd.

—Mark Salzman

I confess.

BELIEVE IT OR NOT, IT WASN'T UNTIL I READ MARK'S ESSAY that I realized how embarrassingly similar these two covers are, for such completely different books. My bad. I didn't plan it that way, I swear to . . . well, you know. My first idea for *True Notebooks* was an actual notebook that looked like it had been "tagged" by a West Coast gang member (yeah, right, as if I know what *that* looks like), but Mark didn't want anything that evoked graffiti because the kids are stereotyped enough as it is. He also didn't want any prison photos, but I remembered that Bastienne Schmidt's series of images from a desolate Texas penitentiary transcended what one usually sees and bore a uniquely ethereal mix of hope and hopelessness. After I finished reading the manuscript (which is enthralling and heartbreaking, by the way), I knew they would be perfect. Which of course isn't always a guarantee of anything, but in this case Mark agreed. Though I take umbrage with his theory on why the numbers on the titles were so disparate. He's wrong.

Two words I learned long ago: Nuns. Sell.

OPPOSITE: Knopf, 2000. Photograph by Shannon Taggart, courtesy of Blind Spot Representation. **RIGHT:** Knopf, 2003. Photograph by Bastienne Schmidt.

TRUE NOTEBOOKS

MARK SALZMAN

TRUE NOTEBOOKS

MARK SALZMAN

author of LYING AWAKE
and IRON & SILK

KNOPF

I ONCE WORKED FOR A PUBLISHER WHO HAD A FRAMED NEEDLEPOINT SAMPLER IN HIS OFFICE that read, "The person who said 'You can't judge a book by its cover' never had to sell a book in his life." Selling books is incredibly difficult. The revenue from the most lucrative titles rarely approach the millions generated by even a flop movie. That's why publishers love subtitles; books need all the help they can get. It's also why authors hate them (subtitles, that is, not publishers, never publishers). It's that classic "What kind of girl do you take me for" moment, when you realize that your book, your beloved child, is nothing more than a commodity. Suddenly, the hot, malodorous breath of the marketplace is licking about your ear, and there, beneath your carefully crafted, agonized-over title, is another line. A blaring, sledgehammer-subtle further explanation of what the book is about, lest a potential reader lose interest and move on.

Chip had warned me about the jacket before he showed it to me. "It's the most obvious cover," he apologized. I know a thing or two about this kind of expectation-lowering prophylaxis—I had given my book of self-loathing personal essays a self-loathing title, after all; a way of beating any eventual detractors to the punch—but I could not for the life of me come up with what the most obvious cover of a book called *Fraud* might be. Until he showed it to me. And then yes, I had to agree with him. Of course, obvious isn't the word I'd use. A spot-on visual approximation of the book's flavor that was more elegant and economical than anything I had managed on the pages inside, certainly. But only obvious in that it seemed like I wrote the book to fit the cover. No one ever mentioned a subtitle.

—David Rakoff

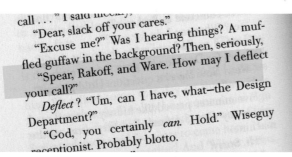

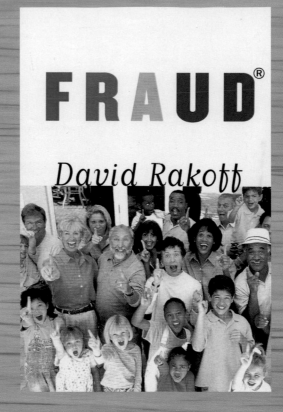

DAVID RAKOFF WRITES ABOUT TRYING TO BE WHAT HE IS NOT. So I thought the cover to his book should try to do the same. At first I experimented with making it look like a box of cereal for people of a certain age who cherish a rare successful bowel movement. Too obscure. Then I moved on to the curious visual language of Viagra™ ads, and how they can't possibly depict the product in use, so instead they use helplessly banal stock photography (so, too, with *The F-Word*, p. 236). Too hard to figure out. Then I tried the concept of name tags, and openly declaring your worthlessness on your sleeve. Too obvious. And then I wondered: what if some poor schmuck bought this book and took it home, read it, and decided that Rakoff was a sham? Why, he'd take out a big red magic marker and scribble all over it! And then he'd do it again on the spine! And especially over the testimonials on the back! **ABOVE:** My nod to David (and Geoff Spear, and Chris Ware) in *The Cheese Monkeys*, 2001. **RIGHT:** Early, abandoned comps. **OPPOSITE:** Doubleday, 2001. John Fontanna, art director.

US $21.95

ISBN 0-385-50084-X

52195

9 780385 500845

FRAUD
David Rakoff

Doubleday

VERTIGO park

AND OTHER TALL TALES

MARK O'DONNELL

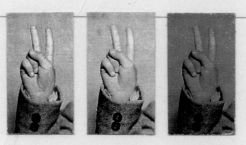

Which way is up?

MARK O'DONNELL IS A HUMORIST of the old *New Yorker* school. The fingerprints of Thurber, Parker, Wolcott, and their like tickle his prose, and he's published his own cartoons in the magazine, too. He also writes for the theater, and he won a Tony award for co-writing the book for the musical *Hairspray* with Tom Meehan, an old hand from *The New Yorker* himself. *Vertigo Park* is a collection of humor pieces that I designed interior for as well. My first idea (left) was one of those "too obvious" things that you execute just to get it out of your system. Then I came across a page in an old commercial artist's how-to book that was so unintentionally funny and haunting I had to give it a try. Mark loved it, and I've worked on his two subsequent books. They're all different but share the puckish quality of the characters and their creator. **LEFT:** Early idea for *Vertigo Park*, 1992. We had just gotten a color Xerox machine in the department, and I was copying everything in sight. As you can see, "image quality" was still in its infancy. **ABOVE:** Art used for the title page of the book's interior. **RIGHT AND OPPOSITE:** Front, spine and verso for *Vertigo Park*, Knopf, 1993. The black-and-white images are from a 1930s manual on air-brush technique. The eye over the mouth on the front is exactly as it appeared in the book.

RIGHT: David Rakoff & Mark O'Donnell, 2004, on hearing the news of David Sedaris's latest book advance.

Just kidding.

VERTIGO PARK

KNOPF

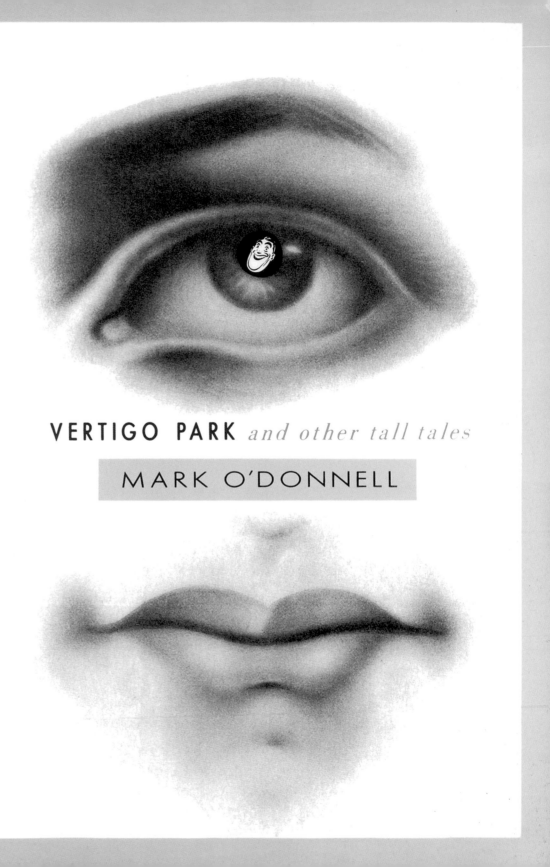

VERTIGO PARK *and other tall tales*

MARK O'DONNELL

GETTING OVER HOMER

GETTING

OVER

HOMER

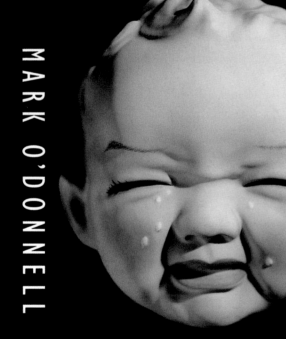

MARK O'DONNELL

A NOVEL

KNOPF

MARK O'DONNELL

UNRETOUCHED - *Please return* ALL *proofs*

Photographs by Chesshire

I was in Cleveland last
weekend & saw this
photo of Steve & me —
It evokes your cover,
don't you think?
Yours cherubically,
Mark O.

CHIP—HIS VERY NAME IS EDGY!—designs images that are simple, prankish, beautiful, and eloquent all at once. For my heartbreak novel, *Getting Over Homer,* Chip devised a visual that summarized a complex plot and made Easter Island look "busy" by comparison: two porcelain baby-doll faces, one weeping and one glad. Apparently, they were vintage wall hangings a friend of his found at a flea market, like those antipodal angel-and-devil salt and pepper shakers. My lovelorn protagonist gets over Homer, so he goes from sad to happy. The protagonist is also a twin—look, twins, with slightly different dispositions!—and he has a gay romance—two guys, at odds, but human. A triple play and funny ha ha and funny peculiar simultaneously. Then, for my madness-bound Christmas novel, *Let Nothing You Dismay,* he lit a plastic front-lawn choir-boy decoration to look as if the flames of hell were tormenting him from within. Plain, yet gnarly. Chip subtly intrigues and prepares readers for the show to come. Authors, of course, like starlets, must be judged for their performances, but it doesn't hurt to be dressed by the best when you get your critical media close-up.

—Mark O'Donnell

OPPOSITE LEFT: Knopf, 1996. Photo by Geoff Spear, using ceramic wall plaques from the 1940s. This story about a lovelorn man with a twin brother was based on an episode of Mark's life. **OPPOSITE RIGHT:** O'Donnell's uncannily bizzaro find, after the book's publication, of a publicity photo of him and his brother Steve. The coincidence would be downright scary if it weren't so cute. **RIGHT:** Knopf, 1998. Photo by Geoff Spear. Check out the "Rudolph" borzoi. The idea was obvious to me from page one, but I kept reading to make sure. Then Geoff found a huge Christmas-supply depot in Michigan and custom-ordered this baby. The light it came with was far too dim for the shot, and Geoff had to substitute one of his own. The title is directly lifted from my aunt Sylvia's holiday piano sheet music.

FPT U.S.A. $18.00   Canada $23.50

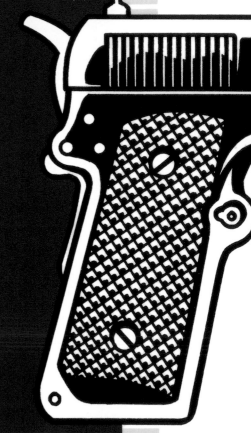

Michael Hickins lives in Paris now. But he was born in a particularly unlovely precinct of Queens, one of the five boroughs constituting the City of New York—and it was there in the hardpan of Queens that Hickins went to school in the lessons of the street and in the higher learning of the back room. A scholarship sent him to Columbia, where he acquired an interest in making a record of what he knew. The result is this book. But do not look in it for the kind of report one has come to expect from the formerly angry, the hitherto deprived. Because to see it the way Michael Missing sees it—Michael Missing being Michael

(c o n t i n u e d   o n   b a c k   f l a p)

MICHAEL
HICKINS

KNOPF

THE
Actual
ADVENTURES of MICHAEL MISSING

AND THAT I

(continued from front flap)

Hickins's favorite stand-in—what's to be angry about, who was deprived? On the contrary, the dirty-mouthed, dirty-minded hotshot hero of these lovable, affiliated fictions is definitely the kid-in-charge. Talk about your wisenheimers, young Michael Missing is banking on making it all the way to the White House. Okay, so what if he's aced a few civilians, perpetrated every stinking, lousy, rotten, crummy, nasty deed in sight, and even tried to nail his own sister? We ask you, what's so awful? Besides, isn't this child just doing his best to have himself a really cool time? Better get out your laughing towel. Plus your shock-proof boots. Because here comes a very bad boy.

And a criminally funny literary debut.

JACKET ILLUSTRATIONS BY CHARLES BURNS

JACKET DESIGN & HAND LETTERING BY CHIP KIDD

Alfred A. Knopf, Publisher, New York

3/91

Missing in action.

THE FIRST JACKET I COMMISSIONED AN ILLUSTRATION FOR was *The Actual Adventures of Michael Missing* by Michael Hitchens. This was one of Gordon Lish's books, which meant that I could push the degree of eccentricity of the design to fit the text. The stories are wild, interconnected tales of inner city street life and strife in deepest Queens involving the title protagonist and his rather nasty disposition. Guns, murders, pit bulls, sexual skullduggery, and other assorted savageries abound. I hired master cartoonist Charles Burns to interperet these various elements (including the narrator), which I then placed in a composition that emphasizes the negative space. This gives it a sense of living in a void. The text, hand-lettered, acts as a sort of visual supporting player for the whole thing, which was unusual for commercial fiction at the time. Normally you're supposed to read the type first, not last. I didn't think it mattered, as long as the result made you pay attention to it.

The flaps feature classic over-the-top Lish promotional copy, including admonishments to the readers to grab their laughing towels and shock-proof boots. Such fare was considered by many within the company to be distinctly "un-Knopfian" and won him his share of detractors, though I certainly was not among them. After all, he loved this jacket.

LEFT: Knopf, 1991. **ABOVE:** Charles Burns's original drawing of his "pit bull" borzoi for the spine, which almost got nixed by our legal department. 1991. **RIGHT:** Burns, photobooth, 2004.

**CREATED
IN DARKNESS
BY TROUBLED
AMERICANS**

THE BEST OF McSWEENEY'S HUMOR CATEGORY
(1 9 9 8 - 2 0 0 3)

EDITED BY DAVE EGGERS, KEVIN SHAY,
PAUL MALISZEWSKI, LEE EPSTEIN & JOHN WARNER
Introduction by Harry Magnan, Exalted Ruler of Elks Lodge No.3

**CREATED IN DARKNESS
BY TROUBLED AMERICANS**

THE BEST OF *McSWEENEY'S* HUMOR CATEGORY

EDITED BY DAVE EGGERS, KEVIN SHAY, LEE EPSTEIN,
JOHN WARNER, AND SUZANNE KLEID
Introductions by Harry Magnan, Exalted Ruler of Elks Lodge No.3, and Dave Eggers

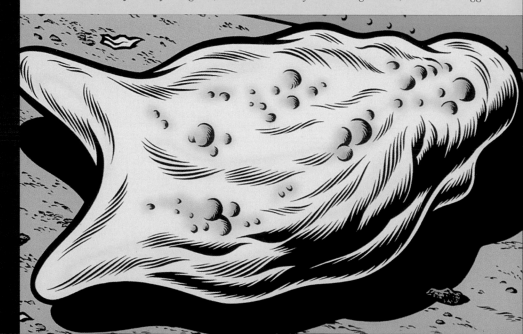

THE TILT OF THE WOMAN'S HEAD—THAT'S WHAT I FIRST LOVED about the cover when I saw it. *And Now You Can Go* is about a young woman, Ellis, who's held up at gunpoint on a Riverside Park bench, and how her life spirals in unexpected ways after that encounter. So she's questing, and there's something about the tilt of the woman's head, and her eyes, tender yet haunted, that instantly conveyed that to me. I also appreciated a very small detail: in the book Ellis is teased for having a Kentucky waterfall—that is, a mullet—and it struck me that the woman in the painting looked like perhaps she had gone to the same hairdresser as Ellis.

The original cover was slightly more . . . sexy than the final version. The original showed the painting, *Seated Figure with Timer* by James Adkins, in its entirety: a woman sitting naked on the floor. The same deli ticket was covering up some parts of her, but she was quite visibly nude. While I really liked the painting—I wanted to own the painting!—I didn't feel entirely comfortable with an unclothed woman on the cover of the book. I didn't think of Ellis as a victim, and yet there was something about a woman naked that I thought other people might interpret as vulnerability. Or maybe I just like modesty.

A week after I received the cover, Chip happened to be in San Francisco, and we went out for lunch; he and I sat in two chairs and a posterboard-enforced cover sat propped on a third. I told Chip that I loved the painting, but I asked if we could maybe put some clothes on the woman. He couldn't have been more understanding, and instantly suggested alternatives. There was talk of asking the artist, James Adkins, to do a new, similar yet clothing-enhanced painting. Eventually, we decided to use a detail of the painting, with a park bench covering up the naked parts. The deli ticket, which, as I said, was there from the start, is a stroke of pure Kidd genius. He got at something that's integral to the book—the idea that what happened to Ellis was random and impersonal; it could have happened to anyone in a city—and expressed it in a bold visual.

Months later, I received an envelope from Lorrie Moore. Inside was an explanatory note, and a pair of cocktail napkins on which Chip had drawn, in blue ink, various sketches of *And Now You Can Go* cover versions. In her note, Ms. Moore explained that Chip had sketched various approaches to the cover one night over drinks, while he and Moore were at a Wisconsin bar. I was pleased to have them, but I did wonder: is there a moment when this guy isn't thinking about his work? I also couldn't help noticing that after a couple beers Chip's penmanship isn't so good.

What I love about the way the cover turned out is its nuance and sensitivity to the atmosphere of the novel, as well as to the protagonist. You appreciate the jacket one way before you read the book, and, I think, in a different way when you're done. Readers often ask me, "Who's the woman on the cover?" and it inevitably takes me a second to remember that the painting is of someone else, someone unrelated to the book. Because to me, the woman on the cover has become Ellis, questing.

—Vendela Vida

a novel

AND NOW YOU CAN GO

VENDELA VIDA

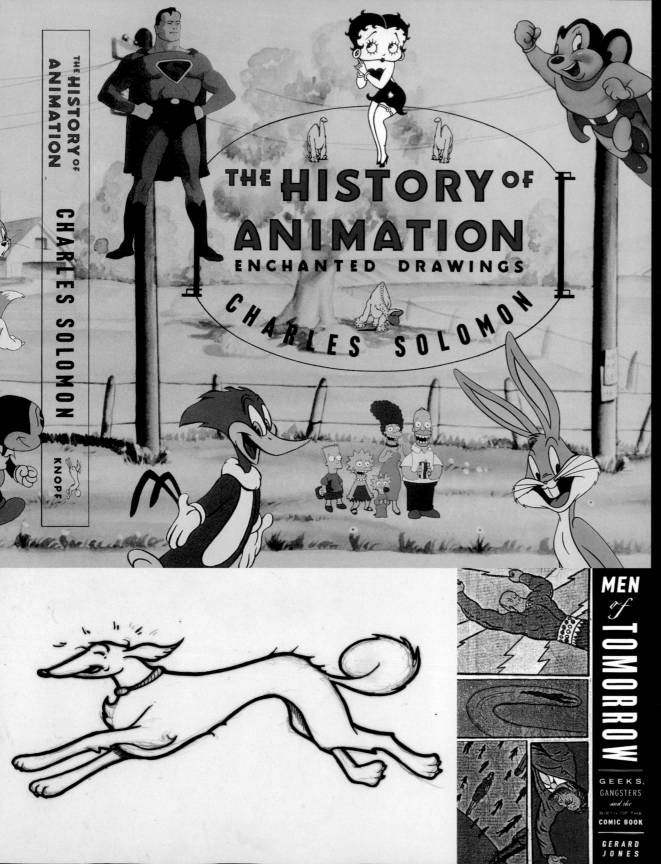

Toon in, turn on.

AS I WAS GOING THROUGH THE ART for Charles Solomon's *History of Animation* to look for jacket material, I came across several frames of a cartoon short I'd just seen on the Tracy Ullmann show. This was in 1988. It was called *The Simpsons,* and it was brilliant. So I put them front and center—so what if they were totally obscure? When I showed the jacket to Bob Gottlieb he singled them out and said "Who are *they*?" I feebly explained, and he acquiesced, sarcastically adding, "They're *adorable.*" I should've played the lottery that day too, dammit. **ABOVE LEFT:** Knopf, 1989. Preceding *The Secret History* by three years, this was my first jacket printed on acetate. **FAR LEFT:** A "Disneyfied" borzoi I drew for the spine. **LEFT:** Basic Books, 2004. **ABOVE:** Knopf, 2003. Illustration by Mark Zingarelli, Photo by Daniel Hennessey. **OPPOSITE:** St. Martin's, 1990. *Further Adventures* is the epic story of Ray Green, a radio actor who portrays a superhero called The Green Ray.

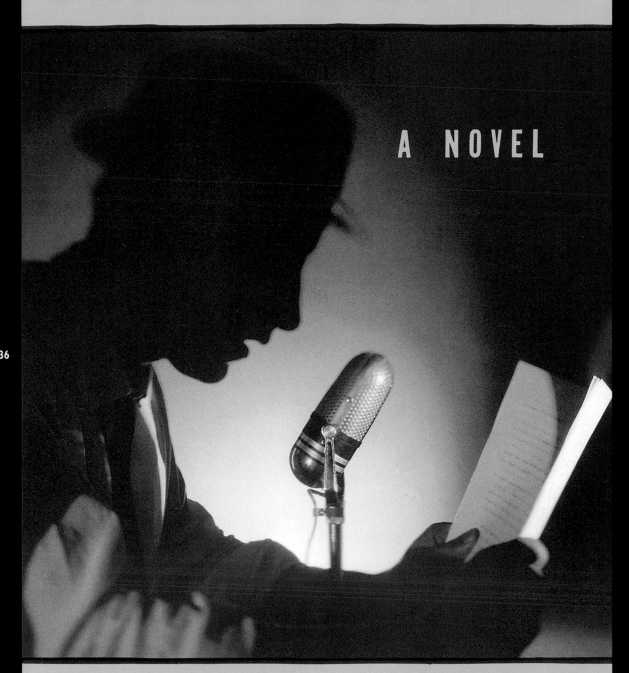

WALTER WINCHELL

A NOVEL

MICHAEL HERR

GOOD EVENING MR. & MRS. AMERICA,

and All the Ships at Sea

a novel   RICHARD BAUSCH

February 24, 1993

Dear Chip Kidd,

Maria Guarnaschelli has shown me a color Xerox of your design for my novel, *The Very Air*, and I just want you to know that I am utterly delighted with it.

As you always do, you've captured the themes and the tone of the book exactly, without in the least sacrificing any aesthetic appeal. It's brilliant work, and I thank you deeply.

With admiration,

Doug Bauer

Ham radio.

WHY PAY A MODEL'S FEE WHEN YOU CAN DO IT YOURSELF? I am a shameless ham and use the slightest excuse to go before the camera. There are bits and pieces of me on dozens of the covers I've worked on, usually my hands or fingers, including the cover of this book (I'm all thumbs). For Michael Herr's novel about the life of notorious gossip reporter Walter Winchell, I got to pull out all of my 1940s period drag and get into snarly, career-destroying mode. Geoff and I staged two scenarios, one of a radio broadcast and one at the Stork Club. The silhouetted mic shot was much more immediate and that's what we went with, but I didn't do my research well enough—only after the fact did I see footage of the man himself, and I will forever regret I didn't wear a hat with a wider brim. Winchell wouldn't have been caught dead in such a skimpy toppe. It really should be a proper fedora. **OPPOSITE LEFT:** Knopf, 1990. Photo by Geoff Spear. **OPPOSITE RIGHT, TOP:** HarperCollins, 1996. Joseph Montebello, art director. Winchell's famous opening line from his radio dispatches formed the title of this novel about coming of age in 1960s America. **OPPOSITE RIGHT, BOTTOM:** Outtake overhead shot from *Walter Winchell*. For some reason the same hat looks big enough here. Regardless, there's no feeling of intensity or drama. It's too quiet. **RIGHT:** William Morrow, 1993.

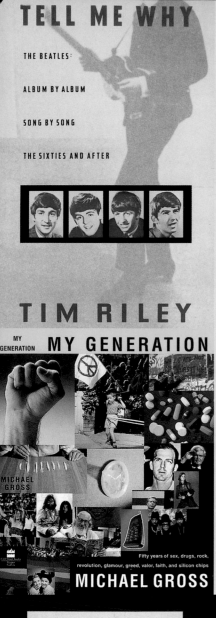

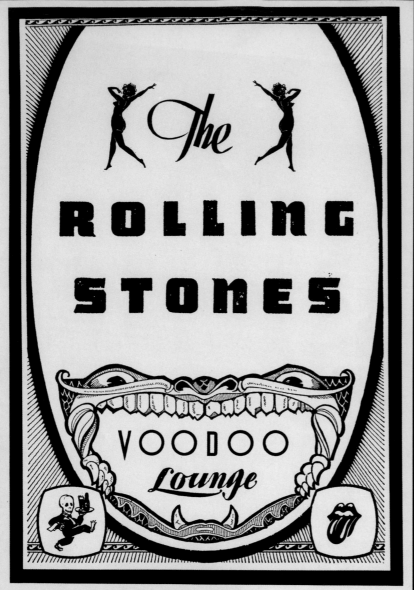

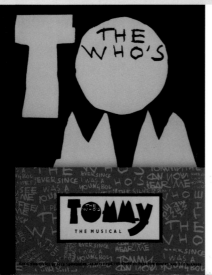

KURT
COBAIN

JOURNALS

Yeah, Yeah, Yeah.

EVERY NOW AND THEN WHEN I FEEL FED UP WITH THE PUBLISHING BUSINESS, I have to remind myself that at least I'm not in the music business (to say nothing of—*shiver*—the movie business). I've worked on scant few album covers, but enough to know that authors are a piece of cake to work with compared to musicians (the exception in my case being John Spencer—see overleaf). I've found that for the most part authors are most concerned with how their work is presented, while musicians are most concerned with how *they* are presented. **THIS PAGE:** (counterclockwise from top left) Knopf, 1988; HarperCollins, 2000; Knopf, 1992. Illustration by Matt Mahurin; Pantheon, 1993. For this coffee-table book of the Broadway version of *Tommy* I adapted the original graphics. **ABOVE:** Penguin, 2003. My first idea for this (and the most obvious) was to just show one of the covers of Cobain's actual notebook, but the editor wanted something more stark and graphic. **ABOVE LEFT:** I was one of a group of designers commissioned to submit preliminary ideas for The Rolling Stones' *Voodoo Lounge*. I was also one of the first to be dismissed from the project.

Fall down, go boom.

MARTY ASHER ISN'T JUST AN AUTHOR, he's also the editor-in-chief of Vintage books and someone I'd worked with on and off for years. So his Knopf book *The Boomer*—a tale of middle-class American soul-searching—lent not only the opportunity to construct an unusual kind of visual novel, but also a rare look into a colleague's psyche. After I read the part about the protagonist calmly gunning the engine, backing up a hill, and then launching his car into the living room of his suburban split-level house I never really looked at Marty the same. Originally the book was intended to be text only, but I thought to tell the story more effectively it needed a visual component and called upon Charles Spencer Anderson's trusty archive of vintage spot illustrations. When I couldn't find what I needed there, I drew the pictures myself. **ABOVE AND LEFT:** Knopf, 2000; illustrations from CSA Archive.

BLUES EXPLOSION

PLASTIC FANG

ABOVE & BELOW: *Plastic Fang* mania. Art Direction by Mark Ohe at Matador and Paul Taylor at Mute (UK). **RIGHT:** Incredibly detailed comic book version of an interview between Jon and me for *Gum* magazine #1, which brilliantly plays to our pop culture fixations. Inks by Steve Illing, pencils by Colin Metcalf, story by Kevin Grady and Colin Metcalf.

LIKE I SAID, I'VE NEVER HAD LUCK WITH THE MUSIC BUSINESS, with the literally outrageous exception of Jon Spencer and his group the Blues Explosion. He contacted me pretty much out of the blue (sorry) in 2001 to design their album *Plastic Fang*. I was dubious, but agreed to meet with him. For someone who roars like a werewolf on stage he was remarkably soft spoken and . . . could it be? sane. He brought some old horror comics as reference, and I immediately saw the possibilities. I always wanted to make a CD in a polybag with a header card, and it was now or never. Jon not only approved it, he helped oversee the production. A musician who knows Quark! For their next album, *Damage*, we did a stylistic 180 and went with all photography and a completely different palate and sensibiltiy. And when the next record comes along, I'm sure we'll go in yet another direction altogether. Many thanks to art directors Mark Ohe at Matador and Paul Taylor at Mute for their invaluable help in producing all this stuff.

THIS PAGE: Materials for *Damage* by the now shorter-named Blues Explosion. All photos shot on location at the Memory Motel in Montauk by Ashkan Sahihi. For the packaging I mimicked the form of a matchbook, then had matchbooks made for promotion (above). Art direction by Paul Taylor at Mute Records.

141

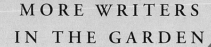

THE WRITER
IN THE GARDEN

Selections from the work of 44 authors including:

Colette
Gertrude Jekyll
Andrew Marvell
Henry Mitchell
Nancy Mitford
Beverley Nichols
Eleanor Perenyi
Vita Sackville-West
Edith Wharton
E. B. White
Louise Beebe Wilder

CONTAINS TWO AUDIOCASSETTES

MORE WRITERS
IN THE GARDEN

An Anthology of Garden Writing
Edited by Jane Garmey

Abby Adams
Karl Capek
Geoffrey B. Charlesworth
Robin Chotzinoff
Robert Dash
Helen Dillon
Charles Elliott
Patti Hagan
Susan Hill
Cynthia Kling
Allen Lacy
Stephen Lacey
Elizabeth Lawrence
Christopher Lloyd
W.S. Merwin
Henry Mitchell
Mirabel Osler
Rayford Clayton Reddell
Eleanour Sinclair Rohde
Marty Ross
Felder Rushing
Rory Stuart
Celia Thaxter
Rosemary Verey
Emily Whaley
Bunny Williams

CONTAINS TWO AUDIOCASSETTES

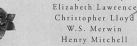

Callas, lillies.

MARIA CALLAS BURNED OUT HARDER AND FASTER
than any punk rocker could ever dream of, with
enough horribly gorgeous fire to scorch Courtney
Love to a crisp. This audio documentary of her life
(opposite) plays like a totally engrossing operatic
novel and will have you weeping copiously by the
fourth tape. Highly recommended. All the projects
on this spread were produced by my dear friend
Jane Garmey. **OPPOSITE:** Highbridge Audio, 1997.
FAR RIGHT: Algonquin Books, 1999. The interior
was designed with Abby Weintraub. **ABOVE:** Highbridge Audio, 1997, 1998. **RIGHT:** Brochure for the
Bogliasco Foundation, 2001, designed with Mark
Melnick. Bogliasco is sort of the Yaddo of Italy's
Ligurian coast, except with much better food and
views, and none of the backbiting or sensible shoes.
(A poem!) Sheer heaven. *The Cheese Monkeys* would
never have been completed without its generosity.

The

BOGLIASCO

FOUNDATION

THE FIRST FIVE YEARS

1996 - 2001

The

WRITER

in the

GARDEN

edited by

JANE GARMEY

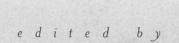

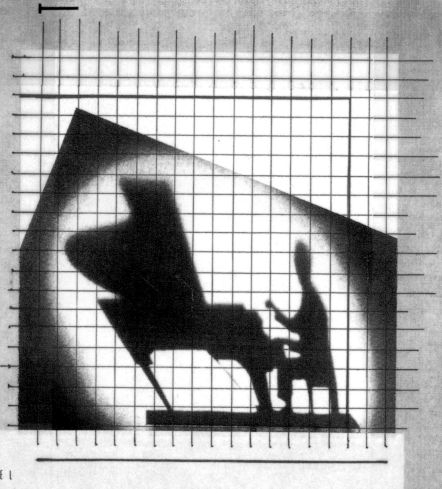

THE TANGO PLAYER

PLAYER

A NOVEL

CHRISTOPH HEIN

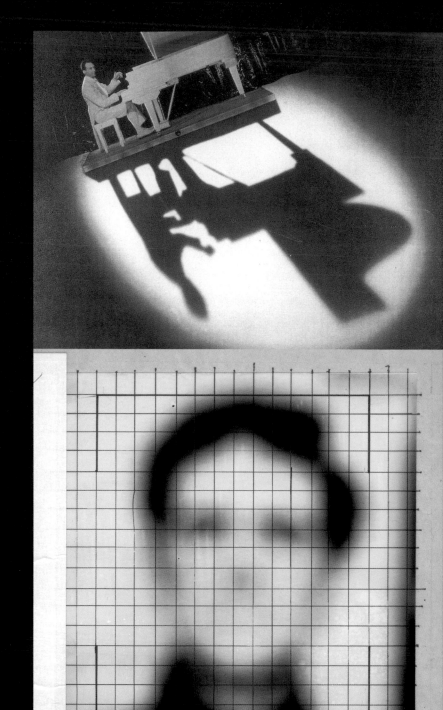

![Wagner Androgyne book cover]

WAGNER Androgyne

JEAN-JACQUES NATTIEZ

TRANSLATED BY STEWART SPENCER

PRINCETON

the
Queen's Throat

OPERA, HOMOSEXUALITY,
AND THE MYSTERY OF DESIRE

"HIGH-SPIRITED.... BRILLIANT... A DAZZLING PERFORMANCE."
—NEW YORK TIMES BOOK REVIEW

WAYNE KOESTENBAUM

NEW INTRODUCTION BY TONY KUSHNER

DA CAPO PRESS

OPPOSITE LEFT: FSG, 1991. A tale of Cold War–era East German persecution, *The Tango Player* is about a pianist who is jailed as a dissident for performing at a politically subversive cabaret revue. The grid over the picture is a metaphor for the oppressive Communist regime. **OPPOSITE RIGHT, TOP:** Source photo. By turning it over and using just the shadow it suggests the title figure rather than literally showing him. **OPPOSITE RIGHT, BOTTOM:** Early experimental illustration inspired by Chuck Close's grided preparatory studies for his paintings. **ABOVE:** Princeton, 1993. **RIGHT:** DaCapo, 2001.

THE HEART THAT BLEEDS

Latin America Now

ALMA GUILLERMOPRIETO

THE HEART THAT BLEEDS

Letters from Latin America

ALMA GUILLERMOPRIETO

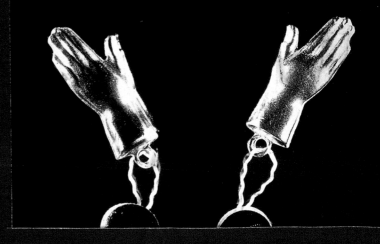

ALMA GUILLERMOPRIETO WRITES ABOUT LATIN AMERICA the way a mother might write about her beloved but deeply troubled child. Her reportage from the slums of Mexico City to the Samba festivals of Rio is unparalleled, and she is an enormously talented, compassionate, and lovely person. I so wanted to do my best for her, and I just don't think I did her justice. **LEFT:** Knopf, 1994. The final jacket featured a blind-embossed memento mori heart with a knife stuck through it. **ABOVE:** Unused idea, though that is the heart represented on the finish. Those are, for once, not my hands.

THE HEART
THAT BLEEDS

Latin America Now

ALMA GUILLERMOPRIETO

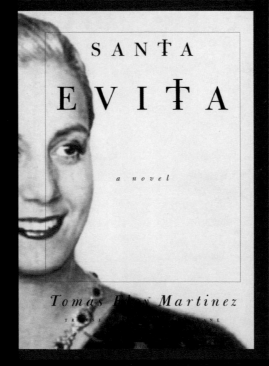

SANTA
EVITA

a novel

Tomás Eloy Martínez

THE HEART THAT BLEEDS

Latin America Now

SANTA
EVITA

A NOVEL

TOMÁS ELOY MARTÍNEZ

TRANSLATED BY HELEN LANE

ALMA GUILLERMOPRIETO

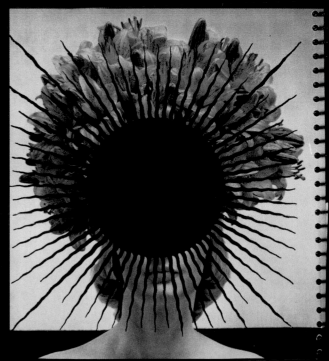

ABOVE & NEAR RIGHT: More unused sketches for Alma. I actually think either of these would have been better than what we ended up with, and I can't remember why we didn't go with one of them. It could have been that someone thought they looked too much like novels rather than journalism, but that was the idea—Guillermoprieto's work reads like exquisite fiction. **NEAR UPPER RIGHT:** Unused approach for Tomás Eloy Martínez's novel about the life of Eva Perón, *Santa Evita.* **TOP FAR RIGHT:** Knopf, 1996. **BOTTOM FAR RIGHT:** Concept art for *Santa Evita.* Too weird, but there's something worth using here.

DREAMING IN CUBAN

CRISTINA GARCIA

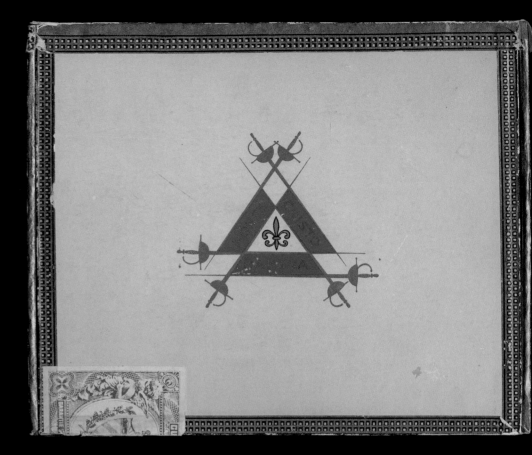

WHEN MY EDITOR CALLED TO TELL ME ABOUT THE JACKET DESIGN for *Dreaming In Cuban*, I could hear the contained excitement in her voice. She wanted me to see it for myself. The next day, the carefully wrapped package arrived. After fussing with layers of cardboard and paper and tape, I slipped out what was to be the cover of my first novel. Yes! I cried out. Yes! Yes! Yes!

—Cristina Garcia

LEFT: Knopf, 1992. **ABOVE:** The cigar box I appropriated for the jacket. This is one of the first examples of "the book that looks like it's something else" school of design, along with the William Boyd cigarette pack (*Brazzaville Beach*, p. 200) and the Stephen Wright detergent box (*Going Native*, p. 203). All are geared to the book's content, but in a bookstore what ultimately matters is that they are striking to the potential reader. The fact they are based on other vernacular material is beside the point.

"DREAMING IN CUBAN IS A MAR-
VELOUS NOVEL AND THE DEBUT OF A
BRILLIANT STORYTELLER. I SUSPECT
WE'LL BE HEARING FROM CRISTINA
GARCIA FOR SOME TIME TO COME—
SHE HAS A GREAT DEAL TO SAY, AND
SHE SAYS IT WONDERFULLY WELL."

—RUSSELL BANKS

DREAMING IN CUBAN

CRISTINA GARCIA

KNOPF

CALL AGAIN

J. A. DOLL
CIGAR CO.   CALL AGAIN   MT. WOLF
PENNA.

ABOVE: The original cigar box label for Call Again, which I shamelessly stole for Cristina. Too sexy. I bought it at one of my favorite places in the world—Renninger's Antiques in Adamstown, Pa. Just a half-hour's drive from my hometown of Reading, Renninger's is among the oldest, largest, and best flea markets in the United States. More than one of my book jackets owes its life to this astonishing repository. Their biggest claim to fame came in the early 1990s, when someone bought an old painting there, just for the frame. As it was dismantled, an original copy of the Declaration of Independance was revealed underneath. It sold at Christie's for millions.

I can't claim anything like that; but once, I found a 1941 Ideal Superman doll for a couple of hundred bucks. And to me that was worth millions at Christie's too.

The AGÜERO SISTERS

a novel

CRISTINA GARCÍA

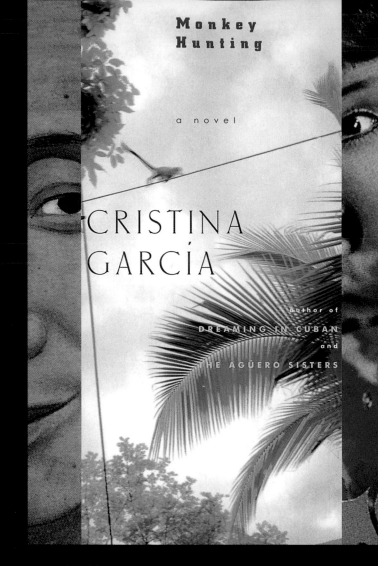

Monkey Hunting

a novel

CRISTINA GARCÍA

author of
DREAMING IN CUBAN
and
THE AGÜERO SISTERS

LEFT: Knopf, 1997. **ABOVE:** Knopf, 2003. Photo by Chris Jones. That actually *is* a monkey, photographed in Havana. **BELOW:** Source material for *The Agüero Sisters*, left.

I DID MY FIRST BOOK, **TYPICAL AMERICAN**, with Seymour (Sam) Lawrence at Houghton Mifflin, who did spoil his writers unconscionably. For example, when the in-house designer was having trouble coming up with something we all liked, Sam told me to go to a bookstore and look at some jackets and see who did them. If I could find someone I liked, he said, he would hire this person. So I went to a bookstore and picked out four jackets I liked. And lo and behold—different as they were, they were all four by this guy Chip Kidd. So I went to Sam and I said, I liked these four jackets and they were all by this guy, but I think he works for Knopf, because all four books are published by Knopf—isn't that a problem? But Sam said no, it was not; and sure enough, he went and got Chip to do the cover, I'm still not sure how. I was thrilled with the results, though. Back then—this was 1991—it was hard to imagine what sort of cover might signal a kind of Americanness that included Chineseness, and a new take on things generally. Chip came up with a design I still love—a collage with the suggestion of an American flag across the bottom, with a Mao stamp in place of the blue part. Brilliant!

When I moved to Knopf, one of the things I most looked forward to was working with Chip, and I have not been disappointed. The only difficulty I can remember was over the noodles for the cover of *Mona in the Promised Land*, which featured a bagel superimposed over a bowl of what looked to me to be, not Chinese noodles, but spaghetti. I did win that one; Chip got Chinese noodles for the picture. He retaliated, though, by putting an Asian eye in the middle of the bagel, which I did think looked familiar. Did I like the eye? Chip asked. To which I replied, Well, yes. That's good, he said, because it's yours!

—Gish Jen

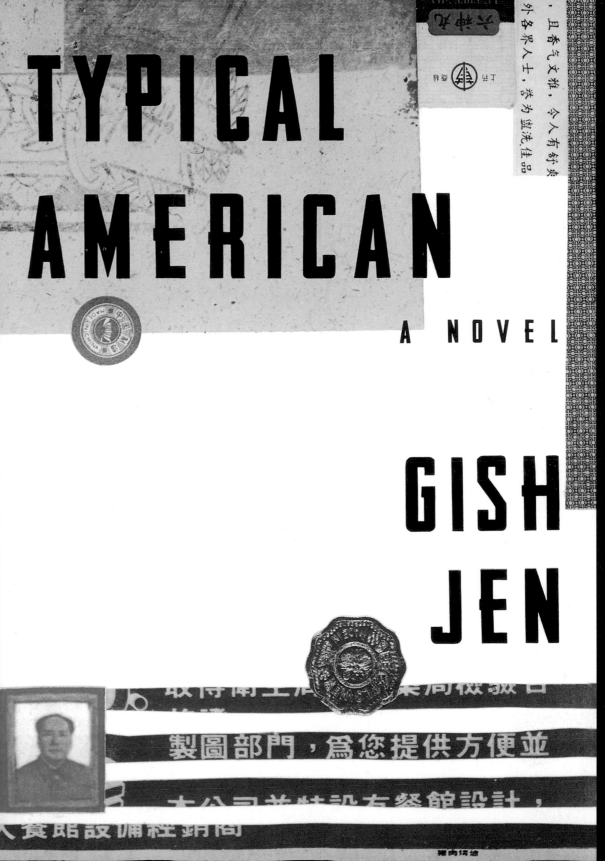

Who's Irish?

Stories

Gish Jen

Knopf

Mona
in the promised land

a novel

GISH JEN

GISH JEN CHRONICLES THE CHINESE-AMERICAN EXPERIENCE with exuberance, warmth, and an unsentimental, no-nonsense view of what it means to embrace a new culture while honoring the old. **PREVIOUS PAGE:** Houghton Mifflin, 1991. I made that collage out of artifacts purchased in Chinatown. **ABOVE:** Knopf, 1999. Photograph by Stephanie Rausser. **RIGHT:** I actually custom-laid each wet noodle on a board to conform with the twists of the image of suburban sprawl. The problem was they didn't really look like noodles any more. They could be ropes, hoses, etc.

A GOOD BABY

A NOVEL BY

LEON ROOKE

running wild

J. G. BALLARD

Criminals

WHAT WE DON'T KNOW ABOUT CHILDREN

A NOVEL

SIMONA VINCI

a novel by Margot Livesey

WHEN I READ 'RUNNING WILD,' J. G. Ballard's gripping story about a group of British teens in a privileged community who one day mysteriously vanish, it was in manuscript form and so cleverly done that I thought it was non-fiction. It's not. One could make a similar mistake with Simona Vinci's *What We Don't Know About Children,* a tale of youthful exploration of sex and violence in a rural Italian village. There is no scene in which the kids actually pull wings off of butterflies, but I got the impression they were the sort who would have eventually gotten around to it. The image, by Eldon Gamet, is perfect because on first glance it's merely pretty and could be mistaken for pot-pourri or dried leaves. Only on closer inspection is the quiet horror of it borne out. **ABOVE:** Knopf, 1990. **ABOVE RIGHT:** FSG, 1989, co-designed with Barbara deWilde. **BOTTOM RIGHT:** Knopf, 1996. **FAR RIGHT:** Knopf, 2000.

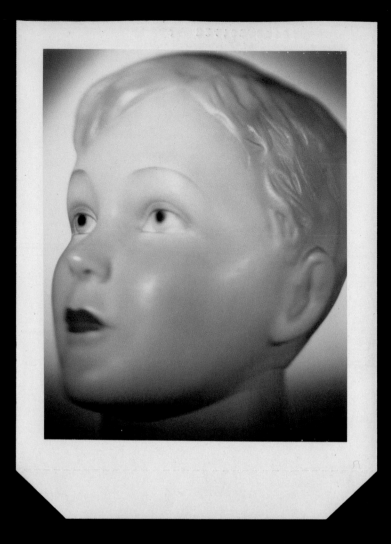

Head shot.

THE DIFFERENCE BETWEEN A GOOD PHOTO AND A GREAT PHOTO usually hinges on knowing when you've got it and when to keep trying. Compare the two images on this page to the one opposite on the left. All three are the same mannequin head, but the contrast is akin to dead vs. alive. I shot the black-and-white one on our stat camera in the office, just as an experiment to see what the possibilities were. Then I took it to Geoff Spear's studio, so he could shoot it in color with his 4" x 5" camera. Geoff always shoots a test color polaroid before we go to film, and the first one for this shoot is shown above. It is okay, but *just* okay, and it's the art director's job to recognize this and go for something better. The three key factors to keep in mind when you're doing a shot like this is angle, focus, and lighting, and it can take a good bit of experimenting to get the right balance. Geoff is a genius at figuring this stuff out, and the result magically glows with an inner life. The use of selective focus on the eyes not only softens the image, it also makes the figure appear to be actually looking at something.

ENGLISH
MUSIC

A NOVEL

PETER ACKROYD

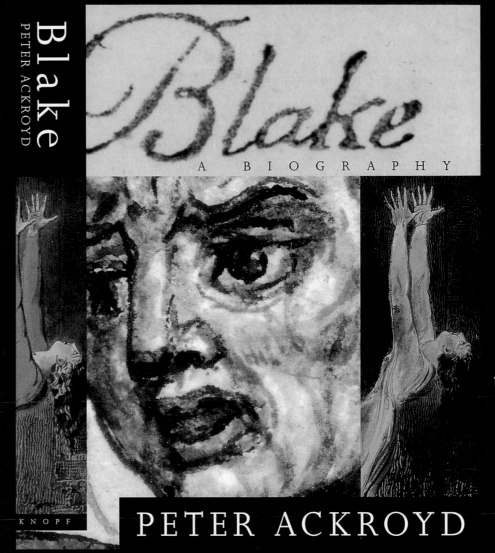

Blake
A BIOGRAPHY

KNOPF

PETER ACKROYD

157

OPPOSITE LEFT: An early experiment on the stat camera using continuous tone paper. I'd found this mannequin head at a flea market in central Pennsylvania. **OPPOSITE RIGHT:** Geoff's first try at lighting and positioning it for the cover of *English Music*, a novel in which a young boy receives strange visions. **LEFT:** Knopf, 1992. The final jacket. **ABOVE:** Knopf, 1995. For this biography of William Blake I used his own signature for the title, and selectively cropped and scaled his drawings. I tried to give it a sense of passionate longing and astonishment, and the use of two different versions of the same female figure also implies ritual and ecstacy. The overwhelming visage of God is simultaneously adoring and ignoring her.

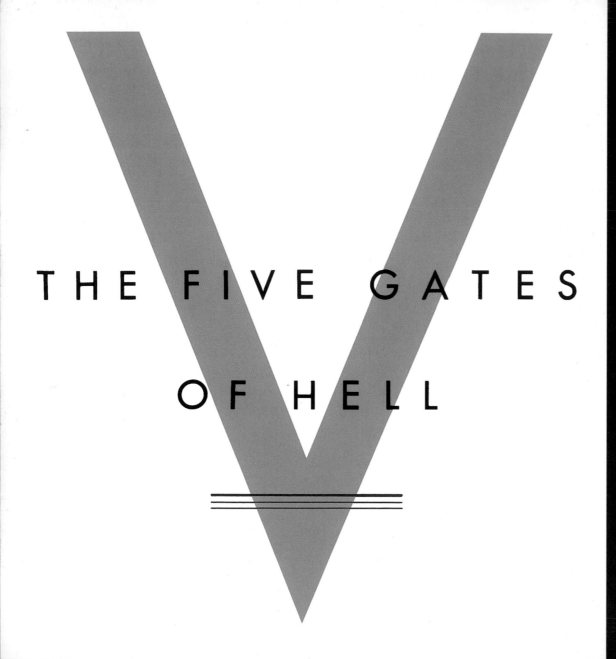

THE FIVE GATES OF HELL

V

A NOVEL BY

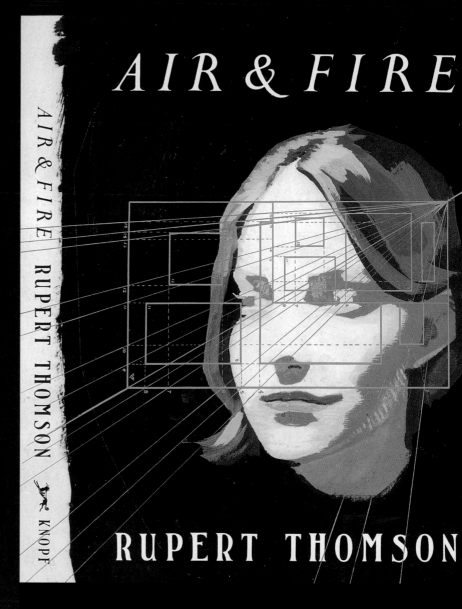

AIR & FIRE

RUPERT THOMSON

LEFT: Knopf, 1991. The title refers to a sexual apparatus, a kind of leather and chrome harness-type thing used by the villain in the story, who is loosely based on that fun-loving ray of sunshine, art dealer Andrew Crispo. I wanted the design to be elegant and not in any way exploitative. It's severe, but it lets the title do the talking. **ABOVE:** Knopf, 1994. Illustration by Kent Bench. *Air and Fire* is a completely different book— a period novel about a 19th-century French couple who travel to Mexico to attend the construction of a pre-fabricated wrought-iron church. The husband is a protegé of

RUPERT THOMSON

London Bridge is . . .

IN 'DIVIDED KINGDOM', ENGLAND IN THE NEAR FUTURE HAS BEEN CORDONED OFF into restricted areas and interaction from one to another is forbidden. While still in the middle of the manuscript I took in a group photography show in Chelsea and came upon the work of Thomas Kellner, whose specialty is "deconstructing" iconic buildings from around the world by shooting parts of them at different angles and putting them back together in patchwork fashion on his contact sheets. The feel of Kellner's work was perfect for the novel. On display were treatments of the Guggenheim Museum and the Coliseum, but nothing in England. So I wondered if he ever had a crack at Big Ben and asked the gallery owner. And blimey, lucky for me he had. **ABOVE:** Knopf, 1998. Photograph by Geoff Spear. This wry satire is about the insanity of marketing strategies in the soft-drink industry. **RIGHT:** Knopf, 2005. Photographic montage by Thomas Kellner.

I SEEM TO GET THE FORMAL SIDE OF CHIP KIDD'S TALENT: graphics only, two colors plus a sash. But I like the austerity he reserves for me. Most importantly, his covers answer the mood of the books.

—Martin Amis

MARTIN AMIS

A NOVEL

TIME'S ARROW

LEFT: A photostat type experiment, pre-computer. The old "under-exposed" trick. Always looks cool. **ABOVE:** Harmony, 1992. This is a sort of design "follow through" from *London Fields*. Geoff Spear actually photographed this, to get the coming-and-going effect. My original idea was to have all the type in reverse, period. Not a chance. **OPPOSITE LEFT:** Harmony, 1991. This was my first jacket for Martin. What was wanted was "a big book look" that also implied there was an edge to it. **OPPOSITE RIGHT:** Harmony, 1994. I color-copied the more appealing parts of my passport for this one.

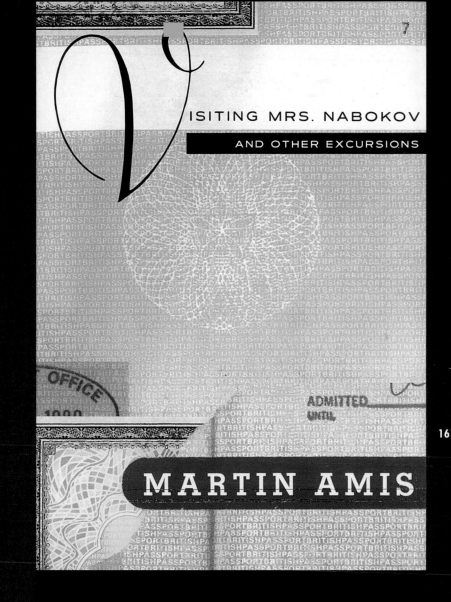

The information bringer.

BULMER ITALIC IS THE PERFECT MARTIN AMIS TYPEFACE. Exactly why is hard to say. Elegence is part of it, but there's nothing about Bulmer itself that hints at the considerable bile lurking underneath the surface of most of Amis's cool characters. So for *London Fields*, in order to "bile-ize it" I reduced it by 25% on a Xerox machine, and then reduced that, and reduced that, etc. Then I blew it all up again and voilà: instant grunge. This is the easiest, most effective trick in the book. The worse the Xerox machine, the better. While Amis was at Harmony I had the pleasure of designing all of his books under the art direction of John Fontana.

THE
INFORMATION

A Novel

•

b y

MARTIN
AMIS

Who let *me* in?

The lovable Maureen O'Brian snapped this for *Publisher's Weekly* at the launch party for *The Information*, fall 1995. To my left: Martin, Michael Herr (author of *Dispatches*, *Walter Winchell*), and uber-agent Andrew Wylie. This could easily be a scene from the book, which skewers some of the more banal aspects of writing and publishing.

LEFT: Harmony, 1995. This was one of the last jackets I did using our photostat machine and continuous tone stat paper. We had just gotten computers in the department, and I typeset the title page in an early version of Quark. Then I inserted it into a book and shot it myself. It's title page as jacket—the idea is that you've entered the book before you've even opened it. **OPPOSITE:** Signed, limited, slipcased edition. Harmony, 1995. My hand, again, also shot on the stat machine. This was especially fun to do, because I could abstract the original idea to an extent that I'd never be able to get away with on the commercial release. They printed an edition of 126.

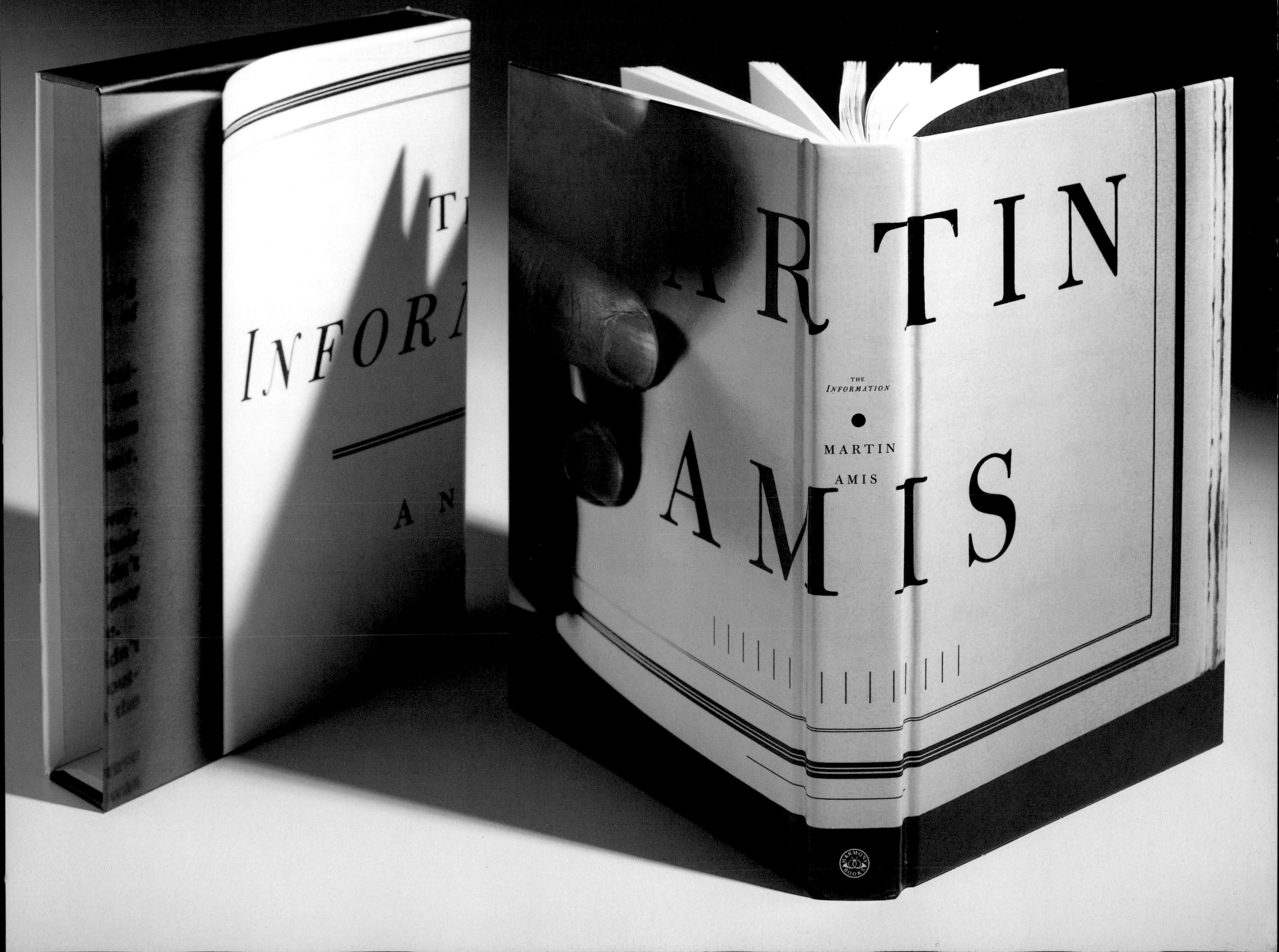
THE
INFORMATION
MARTIN
AMIS
MARTIN
AMIS

THE TAX
INSPECTOR

A NOVEL   PETER CAREY

JACK
MAGGS

A Novel

By the Booker Prize-winning author of *Oscar and Lucinda*

I SAT, ONE EVENING, WITH CHIP AND GARY FISKETJON, looking at the penultimate cover of *Jack Maggs* while Sonny Mehta, like one of those old codgers in a Village chess club, suggested the final visual element that would bring the whole thing snapping into place. As Sonny made his move, Chip nodded his head, and I thought, this is like a jazz band. These guys have been doing this for years.

Everything Chip makes is different from the thing he made before, but *The Unusual Life of Tristan Smith* was the design of his that most surprised and delighted me. *Tristan Smith* is the first-person narrative of a seriously malformed little creature whose appearance brings with it a peculiar set of visual problems. I don't know exactly how many designers have grappled with this, but Chip is the only one in the world to ever really solve it. With one elegant Matissean abstraction he wittily evoked the monstrous face. It was not like any book I had ever seen. Its bold, bright yellow and dangerous purple would stand out in any bookstore in the world. If it was my most commercially disastrous novel, the fault is not Chip's but all those bastards reading Barbara Cartland at the beach.

—Peter Carey

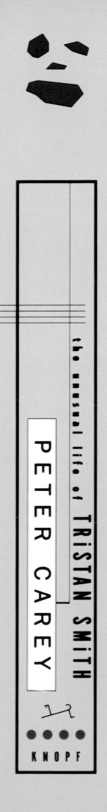

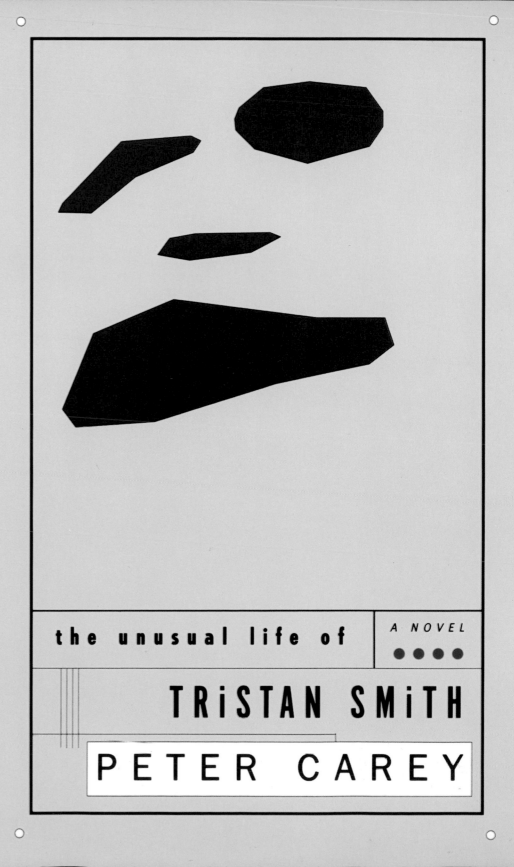

the unusual life of

A NOVEL

TRiSTAN SMiTH

PETER CAREY

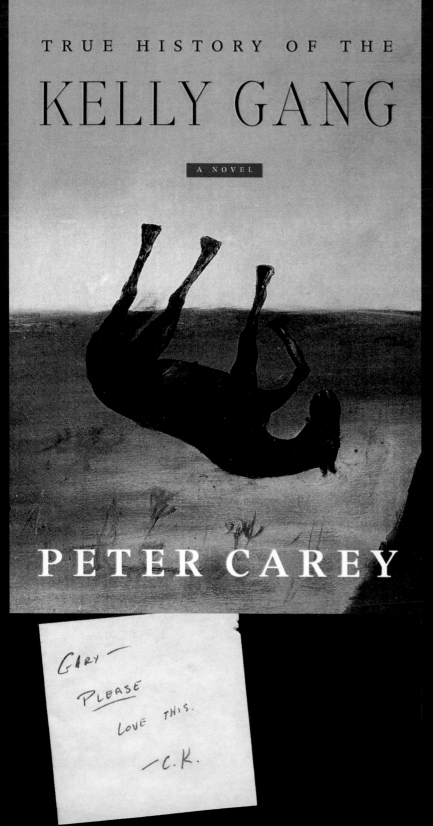

TRUE HISTORY OF THE

KELLY GANG

A NOVEL

PETER CAREY

GARY —
PLEASE
LOVE THIS.
— C.K.

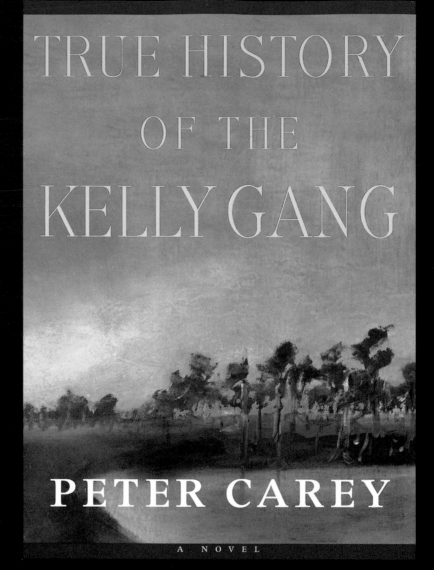

TRUE HISTORY
OF THE
KELLY GANG

PETER CAREY

A NOVEL

¥300

The Carey Gang.

I TRY TO CHALLENGE MYSELF WHEN I DESIGN PETER'S BOOKS AS MUCH as he obviously challenges himself when he writes them. It's the least I can do. He is as fearless as he is talented, whether writing in the voice of an immigrant Irish folk hero from 19th-century Australia, or that of a British lesbian poetry scholar on the run in Malaysia in the 1970s. And then there's that misshapen dwarf from the future and his quasi-Shakespearean acting troupe. With material this rich and varied, it's important that each book have its own visual personality. Over the years I've been proud to call Peter a friend, and I look forward to whatever astonishment he throws at me (and his legions of readers).

LEFT: A pathetic plea to editor Gary Fisketjon, stuck on a sketch using a painting by Sidney Nolan. Nice try. **ABOVE:** Knopf, 2003. The final cover, also using a detail of a Nolan painting. **OPPOSITE LEFT:** An experiment for Peter's travel memoir of bonding with his son through Japanese pop culture. That's Astroboy's eye. Too abstract. **OPPOSITE RIGHT:** Knopf, 2005. The finish, juxtaposing an old samurai trading card (which I found in Jimbocho, Tokyo) with a Gundam robot flight suit.

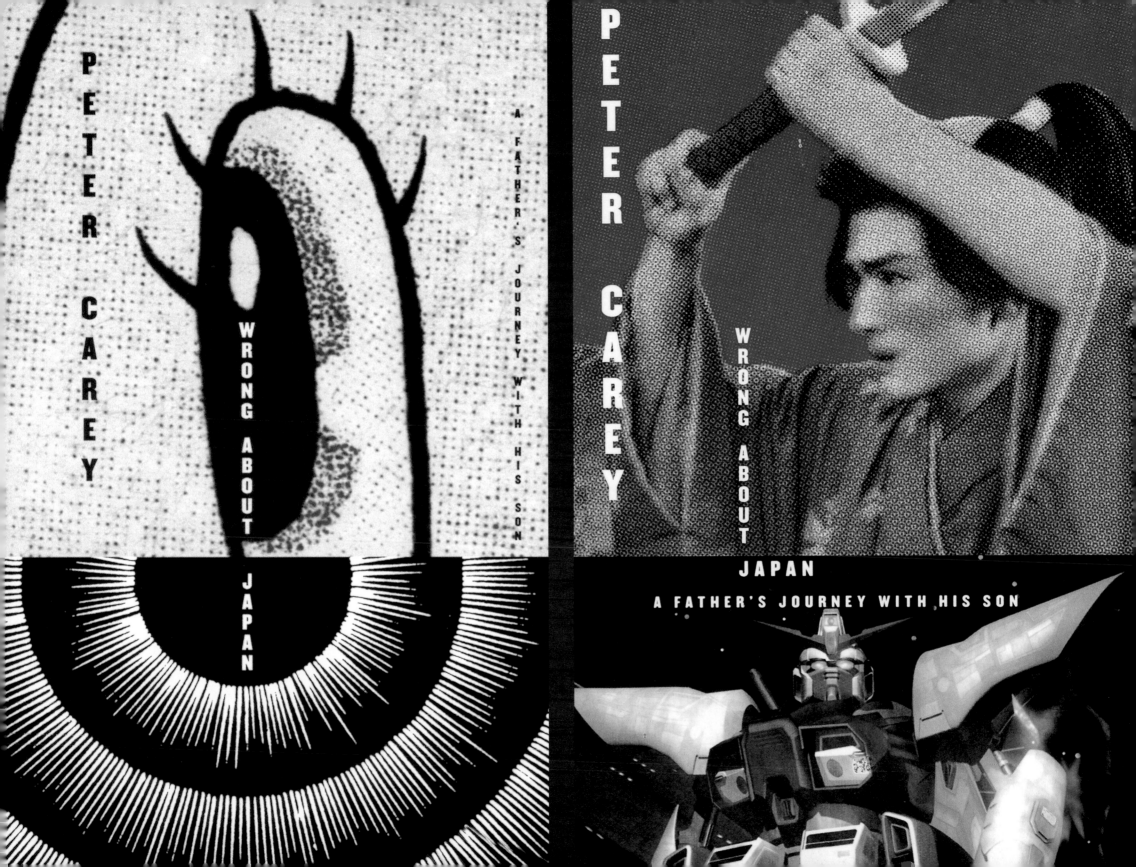

DRAWLET PENS

R. Esterbrook & Co.

Round Nibs

1 — R. ESTERBROOK & CO. Nº 1 DRAWLET PEN
2 — R. ESTERBROOK & CO. Nº 2 DRAWLET PEN
3 — R. ESTERBROOK & CO. DRAWLET PEN
4
5

17

Square Nibs

6 — R. ESTERBROOK & CO. DRAWLET PEN
7 — R. ESTERBROOK & CO. Nº 8 DRAWLET PEN
8 — DRAWLET PEN
9
10

Shading Nibs

11 — R. ESTERBROOK & CO. DRAWLET PEN
12
13
14
15
16

Text Writer Pens

1 — R. ESTERBROOK & CO. TEXT WRITER
1½ — R. ESTERBROOK & CO.
2 — R. ESTERBROOK & CO.
2½ — R. ESTERBROOK & CO.
3 — R. ESTERBROOK & CO. TEXT WRITER
3½ — R. ESTERBROOK & CO. TEXT WRITER
4 — R. ESTERBROOK & CO. TEXT WRITER
4½ — R. ESTERBROOK & CO. TEXT WRITER
5 — R. ESTERBROOK & CO. TEXT WRITER
6 — R. ESTERBROOK & CO. TEXT WRITER

Lithographic Pen

"A pen for every purpose"

Printed in U. S. A. J-313. 2206

PETER CAREY

My Life
as a
FAKE

a novel
by the author of *The True History of the Kelley Gang*

PETER
CAREY

BOOKER PRIZE–WINNING
AUTHOR OF

My
Life
as a
Fake

a novel

OPPOSITE: I got this vintage display card of pen nibs at a flea market in Austin, Texas, and it became the inspiration for the cover of *My Life as a Fake*. **LEFT:** An early sketch that Peter never saw. Gary suggested taking the pen motif on the spine and making that the focal point on the front for this story about a mysterious writer who may or may not exist or just may be a ghost. **ABOVE:** Knopf, 2003. Final jacket.

Glenn Horowitz · Bookseller

141 East 44th Street, Suite 808
New York, NY 10017
212-557-1381
FAX 212-557-2976

87 Newtown Lane
East Hampton, NY 11937
516-324-5511
FAX 516-324-5796

Mr.Chip Kidd
Alfred A. Knopf
NYC

Chipp:

I trust this finds you well. I've given much thought
to the question of an exhibition of book and dust
jacket design in the East Hampton store and I'd like
to talk further with you about it. Are you in East
Hampton this weekend? Give a ring at your convenience.
For now, I am,

Yours sincerely,

Glenn Horowitz

FICTION, NONFICTION

AN EXHIBIT OF USEFUL SPECIMENS BOTH ANCIENT
AND MODERN

FICTION,

AN EXHIBIT OF USEFUL SPECIMENS BOTH ANCIENT
AND MODERN

JUNE 19 THROUGH JULY 5

NONFICTION

Barbara deWilde and Chip Kidd
display their book jacket designs
in a pleasant and effective fashion
at the Glenn Horowitz Bookstore,
87 Newtown Lane
in East Hampton, N.Y.

Hey kids! Let's put on a . . .

IN THE EARLY 1990s I'D BEEN SPENDING MOST WEEKENDS IN EAST HAMPTON, and when an extraordinary antiquarian bookshop suddenly appeared on Newtown Lane, I practically moved in. Glenn Horowitz Bookseller was like nothing I'd ever seen—everything was impeccably selected and displayed, and Glenn's almost supernatural ability to find the impossibly rare (an inscribed *Catcher in the Rye! A Streetcar Named Desire* signed by the entire original cast!) made each trip to the store like a visit to a museum of contemporary literature. In winter 1991 Glenn brought up the idea of doing a gallery exhibition of book jackets, and I coaxed Barbara into making it a two-person show. *Fiction, Nonfiction* was scheduled to open in June 1992, and we spent a good bit of the previous spring putting together a limited-edition catalogue to accompany it, with quotes from the authors. We wanted to do something special but didn't have the time to publish a bound book, so we decided on an archival box of individual postcard-sized versions of the jackets, with accompanying texts on separate pieces of paper. Coral Graphics (which printed most of the jackets in the first place) very generously donated their services, and we hired a professional handmade bookbinder named Sfjord Hofstra to construct the boxes. With this format we thought we were being smart, but we were really in way over our heads—we miscalculated the thickness of the boxes, which had to go into production before we spec'd the text paper stock, and they were way too small for what we originally had in mind. So to make everything fit we had to print on both sides of the text pages using bible-thin tissue. This made collating the whole thing an utter nightmare, and we were literally up for 36 hours assembling enough catalogues for the opening of the show. Which, it must be said, was a hoot. Sonny hired a car and motored all the way out from Manhattan, as did a bunch of other people from Knopf, as well as our families. **OPPOSITE:** Invitation and poster for the show. **LEFT:** Limited to an edition of 300, the monster in a box. **ABOVE:** With

INTERVIEWING MATISSE

OR THE WOMAN WHO DIED STANDING UP

A NOVEL BY LILY TUCK

VAN GOGH'S BAD CAFÉ

a love story

Frederic Tuten

author of *tintin in the new world*

I SUPPOSE IT'S PRACTICALLY BLASHPHEMOUS TO ADMIT, BUT I'VE ALWAYS HATED MATISSE. However, that didn't stop me from cranking out what is hopefully a passable fake one for Lily Tuck's charming novel about two women who, upon receiving the news that a mutual friend has died, spend a night on the phone with each other discussing her life. The entire book is their conversation, and refers constantly to the title interview, which their friend conducted on assignment for a magazine decades earlier. **LEFT:** Knopf, 1991. **ABOVE:** William Morrow, 1997. Frederic Tuten is well connected in the art world and commissioned Eric Fischl to create the painting.

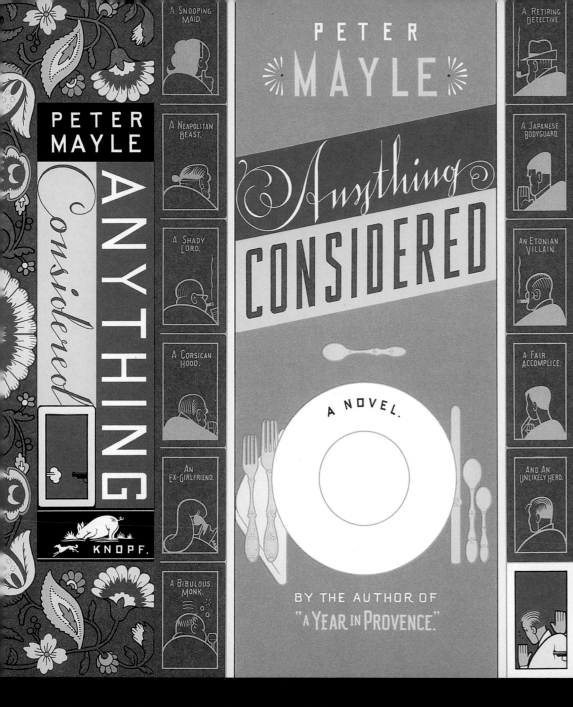

PETER MAYLE IS CERTAINLY ONE OF KNOPF'S MORE ASTONISHING SUCCESS STORIES of the last fifteen years. *A Year in Provence* became a worldwide phenomenon and created a new genre of travel-writing-as-memoir that has since been widely copied. I worked on two of his subsequent novels, enlisting Chris Ware to draw and design *Anything Considered*, a "caper" novel about a renegade truffle hunter. Chris is reluctant to take credit for much of his freelance work and signed this as George Wilson, his nom de plume of choice. More than one of his fans phoned me to complain that this George person was ripping Chris off egregiously and shame on me for using him. **ABOVE:** Knopf, 1996. **RIGHT:** Knopf, 1997. *Chasing Cézanne* is about art forgers on the run. The figure of the dashing man is culled from the logo for a French courier service from the 1930s.

TRICK OF THE EYE

JANE
STANTON
HITCHCOCK

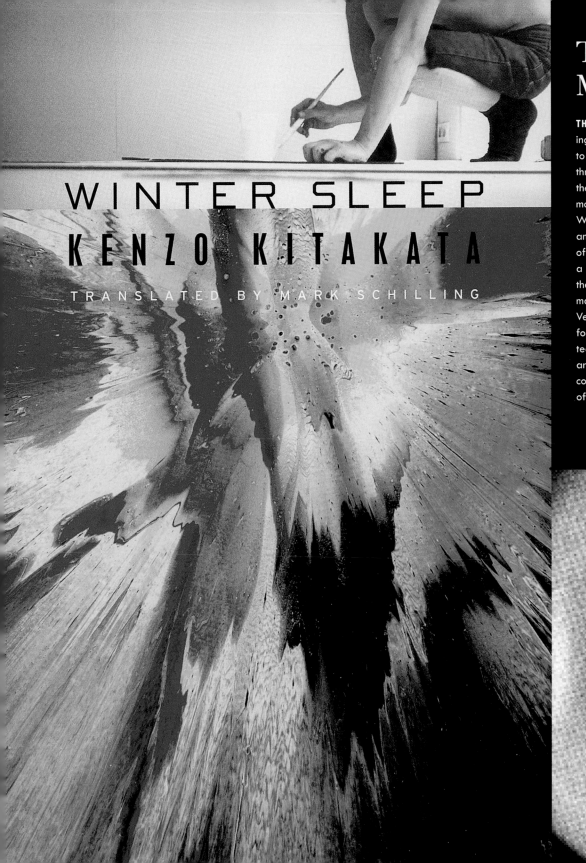

WINTER SLEEP
KENZO KITAKATA
TRANSLATED BY MARK SCHILLING

The Magpie Method.

THAT'S WHAT I CALL THE PRACTICE OF "repurposing" found objects (in the fine art world referred to as "ready-mades"). There are many examples throughout this book, and it could be argued that the magpie method is my modus operandi for most of the archival comics books I've worked on. What's important is to take the thing in question and transform it, so that it's completely taken out of any previous context—a cigar label becomes a Victorian portrait, a "spin art" souvenir from the 1964 World's Fair is turned into an instant masterpiece. **OPPOSITE LEFT:** Dutton, 1992. **LEFT:** Vertical, 2005. Simulating Abstract Expressionism for a novel about an aging painter and his protegés. **RIGHT AND BELOW:** Vertical, 2006. Before and after, for this eerie sci-fi tale of a sentient computer program that literally sucks the life out of her victims.

PARASITE EVE
HIDEAKI SENA

PARASITE EVE
HIDEAKI SENA

By the Pulitzer Prize–winning author of Lonesome Dove

...ASE DO NOT REVEAL THE ENDING...

"What an imagination he has! When it comes to spinning a good yarn, few do it better." —Houston Post

THE LAST PICTURE SHOW

A NOVEL

LARRY McMURTRY

TEXASVILLE

A NOVEL

"*Texasville* shows off Larry McMurtry at his popular storytelling best." —The New York Times

LARRY McMURTRY

THE Pulitzer Prize–winning author of LONESOME DOVE

Lonesome Dovetail.

'DUANE'S DEPRESSED' IS THE THIRD IN LARRY MCMURTRY'S TRILOGY that began with *The Last Picture Show*. It chronicles the post-midlife crisis of Duane Moore and his decision to abandon his car and travel only by foot. In Texas. Which is kind of like trying to explore outer space with a bicycle. I found a typical roadside landscape from the Lone Star State and turned it 90 degrees (right). This jacket was to usher in the redesign of McMurty's entire backlist, à la the revamp I designed for Elmore Leonard (both plans being engineered by agent Andrew Wylie), so I wanted to include a motif that could be carried through to all his other books, regardless of setting or timeframe. I started thinking about Larry's characters—what would they wear? For Duane it would be denim, for the doyenne of *Terms of Endearment* and *Evening Star* striped cotton broad cloth, for the rodeo cowboys of *Moving On* flannel plaid work shirts. These familiar textures give the reader an instant introduction to the mileu of each book, and the "in-close" feel of the swatches of cloth contrasted nicely with the "far away" scale of the photos they accompanied. At first it all seemed to go well. Larry was great to work with and loved what I was doing. What I didn't know was that the higher-ups at Simon & Shuster felt exactly the opposite and were only very grudgingly approving the designs. When it came time to re-work the paperback of *Lonesome Dove*—the Pulitzer Prize–winning and perpetually bestselling crown jewel of Larry's oeuvre—they drew the line and called me in "for a conference." In what I will forever remember as The Nuremberg Meeting, I was hauled unsuspecting before the president of S&S, accused of my crimes, and promptly convicted and sentenced to exile—as Andrew stood alongside and did his best to defend my honor. In vain. And since Larry's entire backlist was tied up at the house he was also essentially powerless to do anything. I designed a few more of his titles and had the pleasure of visiting Archer City, his astonishing town-as-bookstore north of Dallas, but for all intents and purposes that was that. At least we got a few good covers done for some great books, but it was a sobering reminder of how good I had (and have) it at Knopf.

OPPOSITE: Scribner, 1999. Photographs from Photonica and Keith Carter. **RIGHT:** Simon & Schuster, 1999. Photograph by William Huber. **OVERLEAF AND FOLLOWING SPREAD:** Scribner, 1999. Photographs by Dominic Rouse, Heller and Son, and Bastienne Schmidt.

The final volume of THE LAST PICTURE SHOW/TEXASVILLE story

DUANE'S
DEPRESSED

LARRY McMURTRY

Terms of Endearment

LARRY McMURTRY

Pulitzer Prize–winning author of LONESOME DOVE

"McMurtry is one of our best, and *Terms of Endearment* is one of his finest." —*Los Angeles Times*

A NOVEL

The Evening Star

A NOVEL

LARRY McMURTRY

Pulitzer Prize–winning author of LONESOME DOVE

"Works very well....The reader [is] in the hands of a real pro."
—Robert Plunket, *The New York Times Book Review*

Moving On

A NOVEL

LARRY McMURTRY
Pulitzer Prize–winning author of LONESOME DOVE

"A novel of monumental honesty....Attention must be paid."
—John Leonard, *The New York Times*

ZEKE
AND
NED

LARRY McMURTRY
AND
DIANA OSSANA

LEFT: Larry's directions for a trip I took to Texas in 1999. His massive bookstore complex—encompassing four buildings—comprises most of tiny Archer City, which has all of one traffic light and provided the film location for 1969's *The Last Picture Show*. **BELOW LEFT:** The Dairy Queen loometh. I enjoyed a chocolate malted there with Larry and somehow he made it seem profound. **BELOW RIGHT:** Simon & Schuster, 1997. Not my finest work, but all of the type is from period ranch brands. **RIGHT:** Now *that's* roadkill. Beep beep!! Photo by Dirk Anschütz.

STILL WILD

Short Fiction of the American West

edited by

Larry McMURTRY

1950 to the Present

LARRY McMURTRY

Walter Benjamin
at the
Dairy Queen

REFLECTIONS AT SIXTY AND BEYOND

COMANCHE MOON

A NOVEL

THE FINAL VOLUME OF THE
LONESOME DOVE SAGA

LARRY McMURTRY

WINNER OF THE PULITZER PRIZE

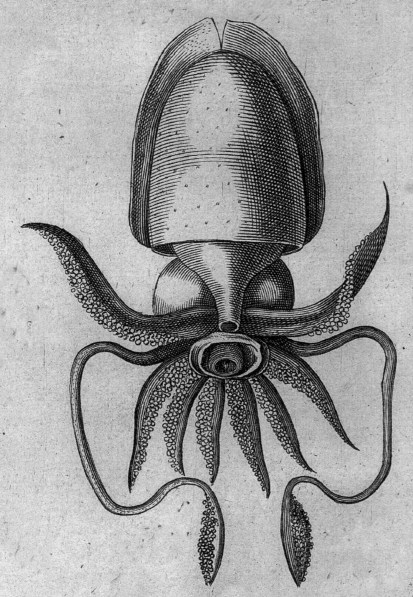

NATIONAL BESTSELLER

AN ANTHROPOLOGIST
ON MARS

OLIVER SACKS

AUTHOR OF

THE MAN WHO MISTOOK HIS WIFE FOR A HAT and AWAKENINGS

THE
ISLAND
OF
THE COLORBLIND

OLIVER SACKS

Author of An Anthropologist on Mars

LEFT: Vintage, 1996. I knew that Oliver had a thing for cuttlefish, so why not? They already look like space beings anyway. **ABOVE:** Knopf, 1997. Ditto cycad trees—not the alien part, the fact that Oliver is obsessed with them. The title is literal, about a remote island in the Pacific on which most of the population is colorblind. **OVER-LEAF AND FOLLOWING SPREAD:** Vintage (left to right), 1996, 1999, 1999, 2000. Who says that science books have to look dull? To redesign Oliver's backlist for trade paperback I plundered his archives and unearthed a wealth of material, such as his old medical ID cards (to use for his name on the front), notes and diagrams, and artwork by patients from the many fascinating cases he chronicled. Considering the vast number of editions of his work that had been previously published, both domestic and foreign, it amazed me that no one had thought to do this before.

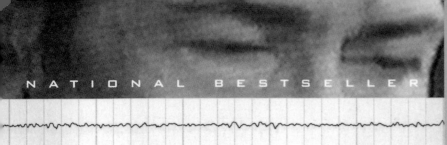

OLIVER SACKS

AWAKENINGS

I EXPRESS MY MOTIONS WITH THAT
I WANT TO TALK WITH GESTURES OF
MY HANDS—THE GESTURES GO WITH WH

"ONE OF
THE MOST
BEAUTIFULLY
COMPOSED
AND MOVING
WORKS OF
OUR TIME."
—THE
WASHINGTON
POST

"BALANCED,
AUTHORITATIVE
. . . BRILLIANT."
—THE
LONDON
TIMES

L-DOPA

TICS, URGES

Oral ✱.
Tongue pulsions, gag
Licking, lapping
Sucking, smacking
Snouting, pouting
Mastication
Lip inversion, &
eversion

MOVEMENT

OLIVER SACKS

MIGRAINE

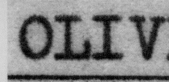

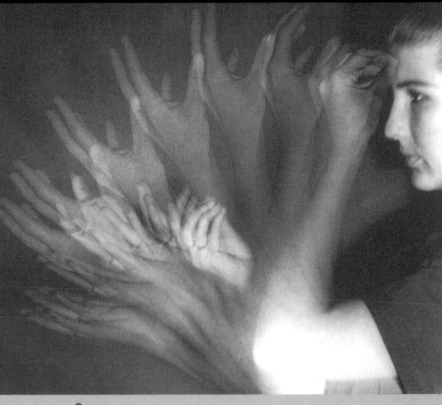

OLIVER SACKS

AUTHOR OF **THE MAN WHO MISTOOK HIS WIFE FOR A HAT**

SEEING VOICES

please   thank you   sorry   why? (confused)   why? (harsh)   why? (rhetorical)

OLIVER SACKS

OLIVER SACKS

BY THE AUTHOR OF **THE MAN WHO MISTOOK HIS WIFE FOR A HAT**
AND **AWAKENINGS**

NATIONAL BESTSELLER

AN
ANTHROPOLOGIST
ON MARS

SEVEN PARADOXICAL TALES

OLIVER
SACKS

UNCLE
TUNGSTEN

KNOPF

OLIVER SACKS

UNCLE TUNGSTEN

by the author of THE MAN WHO MISTOOK HIS WIFE FOR A HAT

MEMORIES OF A CHEMICAL BOYHOOD

IN HIS FIRST COVERS FOR MY BOOKS, CHIP CREATED beautiful individual images: an exquisite cycad (for my "double" book, *The Island of the Colorblind and Cycad Island*) and a delicious, rather Victorian cuttlefish for *An Anthropologist on Mars* (the book had nothing to do with cuttlefish, but I was in love with them, and Chip indulged this odd love—perhaps he felt they looked alien enough to be from Mars).

Subsequently, Chip designed a series of covers that are composites of many images—images taken from the books themselves (as with *Migraine* and *Mars*), or from a variety of other sources. For *Awakenings*, we painstakingly combed through a documentary film of my patients to get just the right frame, and combined this with photographs of the chalkboard notes I often "think" with. To me this cover captures the immediacy and the reality of the experience I write of in the book, which happened, now, more than thirty years ago.

When Chip was asked to design a cover for my "chemical" autobiography, *Uncle Tungsten,* he managed to track down an extraordinary cache of old lightbulb packaging and electrical devices and meters, and put these together in an assemblage that perfectly captures the feeling of the book—not once, but twice.

—Oliver Sacks

RATHER THAN GO THE TRADITIONAL ROUTE (family photos, period lettering) I wanted to make Oliver's account of growing up in a family of brilliant, eccentric scientists and doctors look like a memoir of scientific invention itself—as if electric light were reminiscing about its own origins. Geoff Spear suggested I get in touch with Eli Buk, an antiques dealer in Soho who specializes in turn-of-the-century gizmos from the dawn of electricity. He didn't disappoint. Amidst his mesmerizing curiosity shop of diodes, volt meters, and, for all I knew, Krypto-death-rays, I found more than enough for Geoff to shoot. **LEFT:** Knopf, 2001. Photography by Geoff Spear. Using a light bulb on the jacket of a book about discovering the joy of ideas might seem a little obvious, but the luminosity was too seductive to resist. It turns the viewer into a moth. **OPPOSITE:** Binding for *Uncle Tungsten.* There was no indication (i.e., a die-cut hole) that any of this lay underneath the jacket. The reader just had to get into the spirit of curiosity that enlivens the text.

OLIVER
SACKS

UNCLE
TUNGSTEN

KNOPF

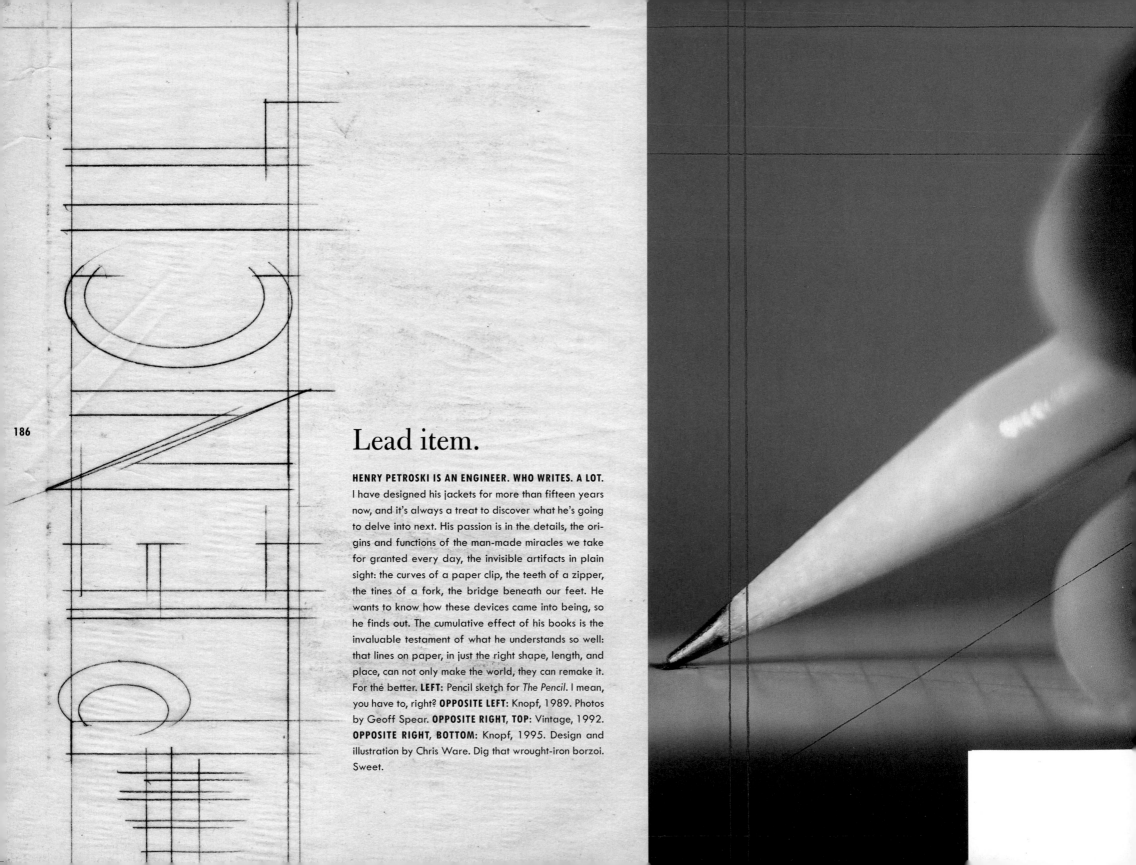

Lead item.

HENRY PETROSKI IS AN ENGINEER. WHO WRITES. A LOT.
I have designed his jackets for more than fifteen years
now, and it's always a treat to discover what he's going
to delve into next. His passion is in the details, the origins and functions of the man-made miracles we take
for granted every day, the invisible artifacts in plain
sight: the curves of a paper clip, the teeth of a zipper,
the tines of a fork, the bridge beneath our feet. He
wants to know how these devices came into being, so
he finds out. The cumulative effect of his books is the
invaluable testament of what he understands so well:
that lines on paper, in just the right shape, length, and
place, can not only make the world, they can remake it.
For the better. **LEFT:** Pencil sketch for *The Pencil.* I mean,
you have to, right? **OPPOSITE LEFT:** Knopf, 1989. Photos
by Geoff Spear. **OPPOSITE RIGHT, TOP:** Vintage, 1992.
OPPOSITE RIGHT, BOTTOM: Knopf, 1995. Design and
illustration by Chris Ware. Dig that wrought-iron borzoi.
Sweet.

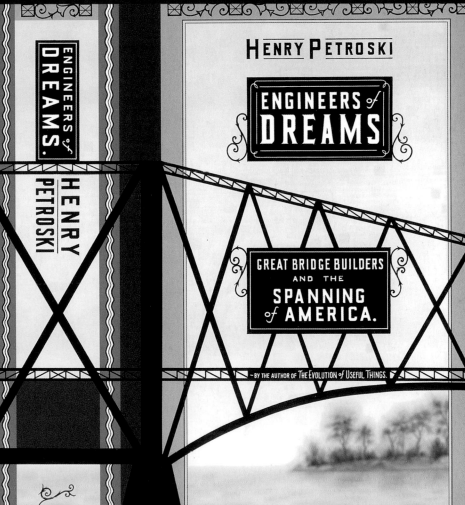

THE EVOLUTION OF
USEFUL THINGS

HOW EVERYDAY ARTIFACTS—FROM FORKS AND PINS TO
PAPER CLIPS AND ZIPPERS—CAME TO BE AS THEY ARE

HENRY PETROSKI

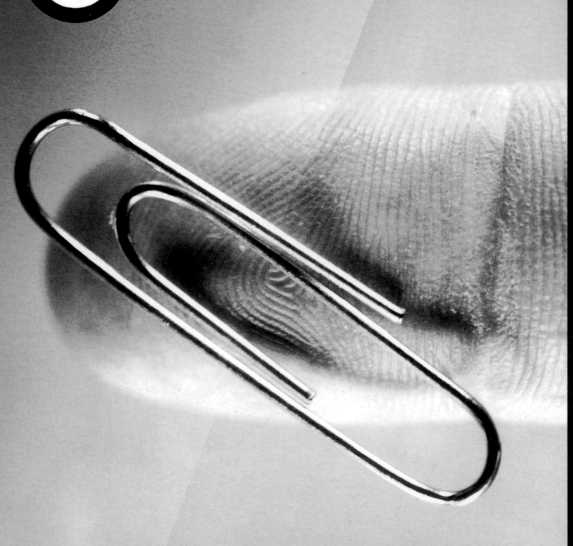

I CONSIDER MY BOOKS FORTUNATE to have dust jackets designed by Chip Kidd. His well-tailored masterpieces of graphic art fit their books perfectly, and like fine clothes they do not fall out of fashion. I still occasionally take down a copy of *The Pencil* to admire the stark brilliance of its getting to the point of the book. The jacket for *The Evolution of Useful Things* is perfectly apt, and it contains two bijoux that never cease to delight me: on the front, the detail of a patent drawing of an early paper clip and, on the spine, the playful treatment of Knopf's colophon as if the borzoi were a patent drawing itself. Kidd's designs reward repeated study, since there are always details to delight the eye and the mind. The wonderful trompe l'oeil jacket on *The Book on the Bookshelf* is a concept that was carried over to foreign translations of the title, demonstrating the broad cultural appeal of the design. The cover of *Remaking the World* is appropriately foxed, in keeping with the book's historical essays. The dust jacket of *Paperboy* is another trompe l'oeil, and on my book tour many an interviewer ran fingers over the raised rubber band, as if checking to see if it were real. The newspaper in which the book is wrapped might have had any page facing out, but Chip Kidd chose carefully a page of want ads, with engineering jobs advertised front and center. In *Small Things Considered*, I returned to putting ordinary things under the microscope of design criticism, and Chip magically magnified a common wooden ruler for the cover. The proof of this design was overnighted to me in London, where I had changed hotels, and I recall my pleasure when I tracked down and opened the envelope to see the jacket concept for the first time. My latest book, *Pushing the Limits*, wears a high-tech variation on the classic engineering graph-paper pattern. Here, Chip literally pushed the design limits with computer graphics that are so apt for the subject matter of the book. Like all of his designs, this one is not a mere apron or facade, for the theme is carried over masterfully to the book's spine and to its back, where critics' comments on my previous books are displayed. As usual, in this and all of Chip's designs, the "small things" and the large equally delight the eye.

—Henry Petroski

KNOPF

REMAKING
THE
WORLD

ADVENTURES
IN
ENGINEERING

HENRY
PETROSKI

KNOPF

REMAKING THE WORLD

ADVENTURES
○
IN
○
ENGINEERING

HENRY
PETROSKI

OPPOSITE: Knopf, 1992. Self-portrait with paper clip. **LEFT:** Knopf, 1997.
I love that those red skyscrapers look like something out of Jules Verne,
but are actually the state-of-the-art Petronas Towers in Malaysia. **ABOVE:**
Knopf, 1999. Photograph by Geoff Spear.

PAPERBOY

CONFESSIONS OF A
FUTURE ENGINEER

HENRY PETROSKI

Author of The Pencil *and* The Evolution of Useful Things

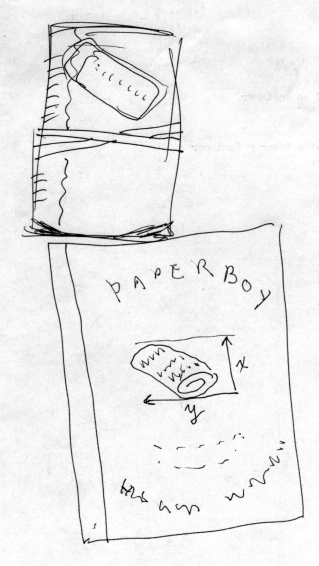

SMALL THINGS CONSIDERED

Why There Is No Perfect Design

Henry Petroski

Knopf

OPPOSITE LEFT: Knopf, 2002. Photograph by Geoff Spear.
OPPOSITE RIGHT: My sketch on the back of manuscript page 236 of *Paperboy*. I returned to the other idea for the paperback edition, one year later. **ABOVE:** Vintage, 2003. The bicycle is Petroski's own that he uses to this day. **RIGHT:** Knopf, 2003. Photograph by Geoff Spear. The ruler is shown actual size. It was actually a prop in the movie *Big*. **OVERLEAF:** Knopf, 2004. A little Photoshop magic. This solution is swiped from an assignment I had in Typography 101: make the type do what it says it's doing.

"A fond but cleareyed glance back at what it was like growing up middle-class and upwardly striving in 1950's New York."
—*The New York Times Book Review*

PAPERBOY

confessions of a future engineer

HENRY PETROSKI

AUTHOR OF *THE EVOLUTION OF USEFUL THINGS*

VINTAGE

HENRY PETROSKI

AUTHOR OF *THE EVOLUTION OF USEFUL THINGS*

PUSHING THE LIMITS

NEW ADVENTURES IN ENGINEERING

Spine

HENRY PETROSKI PUSHING THE LIMITS

KNOPF

SCIENCE/ENGINEERING
ISBN 1-4000-4051-5

52500

9 781400 040513

Nothing if not intimidated.

YES, DESIGNING BOOK JACKETS FOR THE PREMIERE ART CRITIC in the world is LOTS of fun. Well, as a matter of fact, it *is*, but nervous-making in the extreme. How could it not be? As someone who was force-fed Clement Greenberg in college (and spit him out into my napkin whenever no one was looking) I hold Hughes's concise, astute, common-sense-fueled analyses in the highest regard. When it comes to doing work for him what lets me off the hook a bit is that Robert obviously looks at his covers with completely different criteria from what he uses for a painting or sculpture, and I end up being far more critical of myself than he ever is. **LEFT:** Knopf, 1990. I had this canvas custom-stretched for the book by a professional, but I've since regretted not finding an actual painting—this just looks too pristine to me. Photo by Mark Hill.

SOME COVERS ARE SO RIGHT THAT YOU CAN'T IMAGINE THE TEXT WITHOUT THEM, and this [*Nothing If Not Critical*] was one. The simplest visual trope for a collection of art criticism is that of looking at a painting. But any particular painting would have been too specific—it would have made the book seem like a monograph on a particular artist—while a "generic" image would have been merely diffuse and probably vulgar. So Kidd came up with the back of the canvas, complete with an elegantly casual wire. Your instinct, seeing the back of a canvas, is to turn it around. Kidd's design makes this into the impulse to open the cover, turn it back, see the text. It prompts curiosity: *what's inside?* A visual epigram, not a piece of hype. My book was lucky.

—Robert Hughes

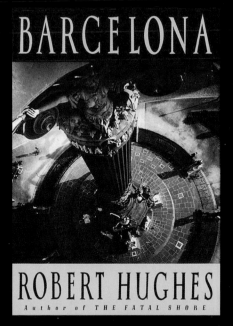

ABOVE LEFT: Knopf, 1992. **ABOVE RIGHT:** Knopf, 1988. Ugh. I'm obviously still new at this. Really just dreadful. And it actually got printed. Fortunately, I had the opportunity to redeem myself with an expanded edition (see following page).

THE SHOCK OF THE NEW

THE HUNDRED-YEAR HISTORY OF MODERN ART—
IT'S RISE, ITS DAZZLING ACHIEVEMENT, ITS FALL

ROBERT HUGHES

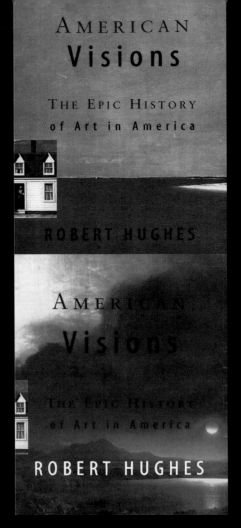

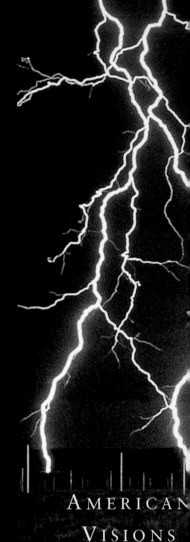

AMERICAN VISIONS

THE EPIC HISTORY OF ART IN AMERICA

ROBERT HUGHES

KNOPF

LEFT: Knopf, 1991. Now this is more like it. I was lucky enough to get another shot at designing *The Shock of the New* three years later for this expanded edition. Can you spot the typo? No one in copyediting did. Oops. My original idea was to allow the pink panel to be peeled back, revealing Anita Ekberg covered in bananas foster, but the people in marketing nixed it. Philistines. **ABOVE:** Unsuccessful stabs at the *American Visions* jacket. For some reason I couldn't get landscapes and Hopper out of my head. I didn't even show these to anyone—they just don't look epic, and I was trying too hard with the type to make it look both classic and modern and achieved neither. I think it was the book's editor, Susan Ralston, who suggested trying Walter De Maria's *The Lightning Field*. It had never occurred to me to use anything other than a painting, but this was totally perfect—vast, dramatic, natural and mystical at the same time. It's a work Robert describes as having "an intensely poetic presence." **RIGHT AND OPPOSITE LEFT:** Knopf, 1997. Photograph by John Clieff.

AMERICAN VISIONS

THE EPIC HISTORY

OF ART IN AMERICA

ROBERT HUGHES

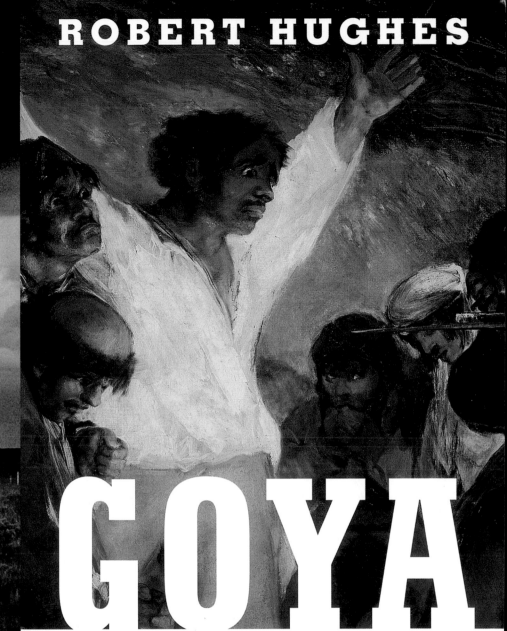

ROBERT HUGHES

GOYA

ABOVE: Knopf, 2003. The second I heard of this project's existence I knew what the image had to be. Robert agreed completely. From the text: "With [*The Third of May*] the modern image of war as anonymous killing is born, and a long tradition of killing as ennobled spectacle comes to its overdue end . . . [it is] the prototype of all modern views of war."

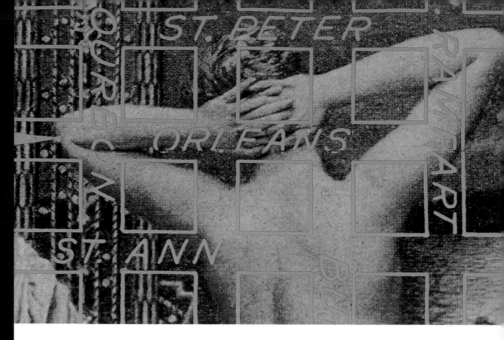

MY PILGRIM'S PROGRESS

GEORGE W. S. TROW

MEDIA STUDIES, 1950-1998

THE MUSE IS ALWAYS HALF-DRESSED

IN NEW ORLEANS

and other essays

ANDREI CODRESCU

As Heard on "All Things Considered"

LEFT: Pantheon, 1998. Print media meets television halfway to form an image of Trow's hero, Ike. **ABOVE:** St. Martin's Press, 1993. **OPPOSITE LEFT, TOP:** Daniel Chester French's *Memory*, 1919, which I re-shot slightly out of focus for *Mystic Chords of Memory*, **OPPOSITE RIGHT**, Vintage, 1991. **OPPOSITE LEFT, BOTTOM:** Knopf, 2000, co-designed with Abby Weintraub.

THE GLOBAL SOUL

JET LAG, SHOPPING MALLS, and the SEARCH for HOME

PICO IYER

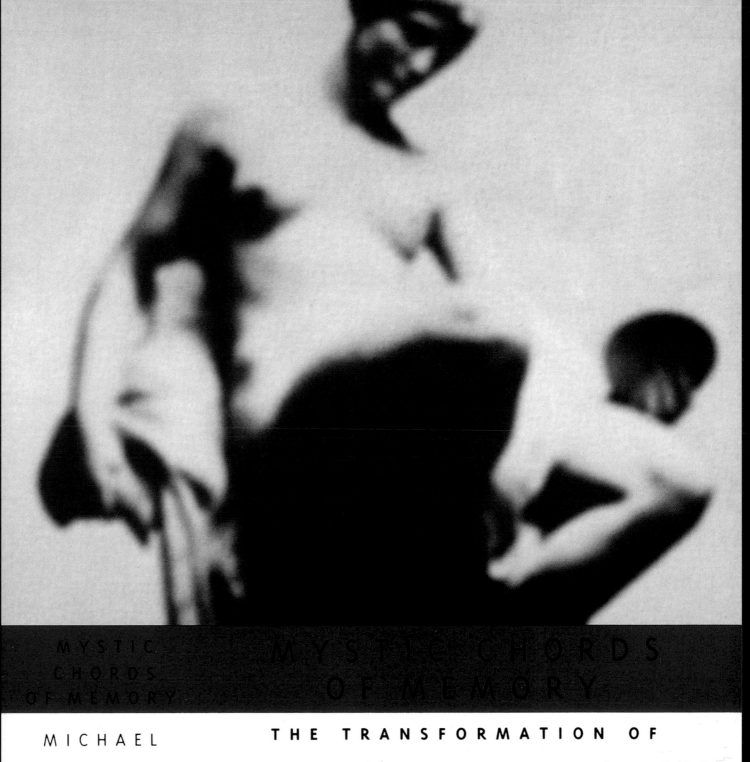

MYSTIC
CHORDS
OF MEMORY

MICHAEL
KAMMEN

VINTAGE

**MYSTIC CHORDS
OF MEMORY**

THE TRANSFORMATION OF
TRADITION IN AMERICAN CULTURE

MICHAEL KAMMEN

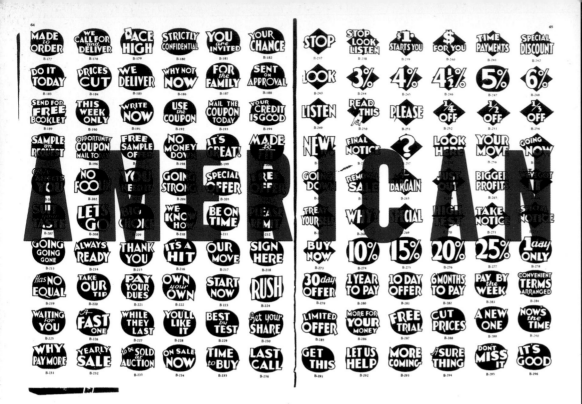

poems by Campbell McGrath

Compounding interest.

A GOOD IDEA IS WORTH REPEATING. Especially when you're totally desperate, as I was here. In this case, for the front page of the *New York Times* "Week in Review" I was asked to produce an illustration for an article on rampant consumer debt. There was, of course, no article to read—just a brief description from the art director, Nicholas Blechmann, of what the editors were thinking. They needed something in a day. So I reached back eleven years to a poetry cover I'd co-designed with Barbara deWilde. I rationalized that not only had its statute of limitations run out, I was cross pollinating from one media form to another. Even I wouldn't be shameless enough to do this on another book cover.

Would I?

I soon found that the advantage to working on this section of the *Times* is that you can work with color (as opposed to the Op-Ed page, which can't accomodate it). This idea could still work in b/w, with "DEBT" ghosted back in grey, but here we can literally have the word running into the red.

LEFT: Ecco Press, 1993. Co-designed with Barbara deWilde. **BELOW:** Illustration for the front page of *The New York Times* "Week in Review" section, December 4, 2004.

Editorial and Op-Ed pages, 12-13
Education Advertising
Careers in Education and
Health Care Employment

The New York Times

Sunday, December 5, 2004

Week in Review

Section 4

'Ka-Ching'

Maybe It's Not All Your Fault

By STEVE LOHR

THE spectacle of American spending always gets a little silly in the holiday season, but shoppers over the next few weeks will be hard-pressed to match the performance last year of Antoinette Millard. She ran up bills of nearly $1 million in Manhat... control spending. After all, the United States economy depends on its citizens' penchant for spending with abandon. Consumer spending accounts for two-thirds of the nation's $11 trillion economy, and the machinery of American advertising, marketing, media and finance all encourage the consumption habit. Many consumers are unable to resist the overpowering mantra: spend, spend, spend.

many American families. The Commerce Department reported last week that the personal savings rate fell near to a record low in October, when American households saved a meager two-tenths of 1 percent of their disposable income. The rate implies that a family with take-home pay of $40,000 saves on average $1.50 a week.

The average American household now spends 13 percent of its after-tax income to pay debts, the highest per-

An economy built on the borrower-industrial complex.

WILD RIDE
BIA LOWE

Earthquakes, Sneezes and Other Thrills

MIXING
MESSAGES

Graphic Design in CONTEMPORARY

CULTURE

ELLEN LUPTON

BIA LOWE'S COLLECTION OF ESSAYS RANGES FROM HER CHILDHOOD FEARS AND FANTASIES, to acute observations of life and nature. Lowe reveals herself to be a keen observer of whatever catches her attention. Meditating on bats, Lowe notes that, like humans, they are long-lived and sexy. The scent of skunk leads her to a discussion of fear, feces and the odor of a lover's infidelity. She writes about blood, dancing school, a lover's surgery, cave art, horses and horror movies. **ABOVE:** HarperCollins, 1995. Photograph by Deborah Sugarman. **RIGHT:** Princeton Architectural Press, 1996. For what amounted to the end-of-the-century graphic design equivalent of the Amory Show at the Cooper-Hewitt Museum, curator Ellen Lupton commissioned me to design the exhibition's catalogue cover. Candy packaging from Chinatown grafted onto patterns by Zuzana Licko contrasts the low with the high.

BRAZZAVILLE
beach

A NOVEL

WILLIAM BOYD

AUTHOR OF

A GOOD MAN IN AFRICA & AN ICE-CREAM WAR

TO HAVE A PREDOMINANTLY YELLOW BOOK when the word "beach" is in the title is one of those apparently obvious ideas that no one can ever think of. But the uncompromising vibrancy of the yellow set against the black band draws the eye with a confidence that would gladden any author's heart. The lettering of "Brazzaville" suggests Africa to me in ways I can't define, and the little touches of the plane and the hint of mathematical formulae are like a private code for initiates and teasingly obscure for those yet to open the book. And the italicized, lowercase "beach" is a masterful touch: a suggestion of reticence? of modernity? ambiguity?

—William Boyd

ABOVE & BELOW: I've never successfully smoked a cigarette in my life, yet here is the research for *Brazzaville Beach*—the undeniably beautiful packaging for smokes from around the world. The heroine in the story is hooked on an African brand called Tuskers, and for the jacket I tried to imagine what a box would look like. Her husband is also a crazed mathematician, and that's what the bit at the top is about. I truly love this book. It's one of my favorite novels, ever. **LEFT:** William Morrow, 1991. This was NOT originally accepted, as the advance copy on the opposite page depicts. Eventually, they came around to the design, but only after a lot of hand-wringing.

LEFT: The Campari label was the inspiration for the cover of *The Blue Afternoon* (**RIGHT:** Knopf, 1995) a co-design with Carol Carson. In this case, it wasn't like the characters were drinking Campari, or even mentioned it. It was just a stylistic starting point. I did the lettering of the title by hand, and Carol provided the fan.

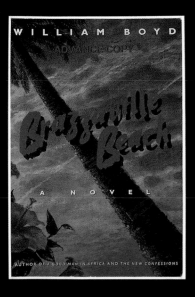

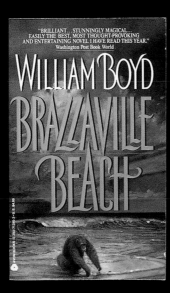

ABOVE LEFT: An advance reader's copy of *Brazzaville Beach*, one that I did NOT design. The art is by Tom Woodruff, whom I also coincidentally worked on for titles by Gabriel García Márquez. **ABOVE RIGHT:** The mass-market version of the cover. Who knows how this sort of thing gets done, but what amused me about it was that I was beseeched on the original not to show any monkeys.

SPORTSMAN'S
PARADISE

NANCY LEMANN

A NOVEL

ALFRED A. KNOPF

CHIP KIDD   6/26/89

DEAR SPY:

    Now that the eighties are practically
depleted, we feel it's finally safe
to unleash this decade-summarizing
toungue twister on a breathless, despairing populace:

SISSY SPACEK'S SPECTACULAR SPACE SHUTTLE
SPORTS AN ESPECIALLY SPACIOUS SUSHI SPICE
RACK.

    Keep repeating it and never look back.

                    yours, yours,yours,

        Chip Kidd and Barbara deWilde

    P.S. Tequila is the devil's urine.

W: (212) 572-2363 or 572-2641

Maximalism.

LEFT: Knopf, 1992. **ABOVE:** In a desperate bid for attention, Barbara and I turned again to *Spy* magazine. This one they didn't print, surprise surprise. **OPPOSITE LEFT:** Doubleday, 1989. This was my first attempt at mimicking supermarket tabloids and it's pretty sloppy. If you're going to do this sort of thing (and how can you not, with this title?) then you've got to be dead on. This is only about 85% there—those hand-drawn lines around "celebrities" are pathetic and totally give it away. **OPPOSITE RIGHT:** FSG, 1994. *Necrofile* magazine said it better than I ever could: "*Going Native* is about the round-the-clock bombardment of inanity and violence that has so thoroughly invaded mundane existence as to render it cartoon-like." Right. So I made it look like a box of laundry detergent. Sue me.

COLIN
McENROE

U.S. $7.95

CANADA $9.95

AUTHOR OF SWIMMING CHICKENS

"UP WITH McENROE!"
—PEOPLE

L O S E
WEIGHT
→ **THROUGH**
GREAT SEX
★★★★ WITH
CELEBRITIES!

(the Elvis way)

Stephen
Wright

GOING NATIVE

A NOVEL!

ONLY IN AMERICA

SOME UNEXPECTED SCENERY

photographs

David Graham

INTRODUCTION BY JANE AND MICHAEL STERN

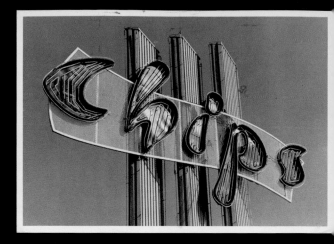

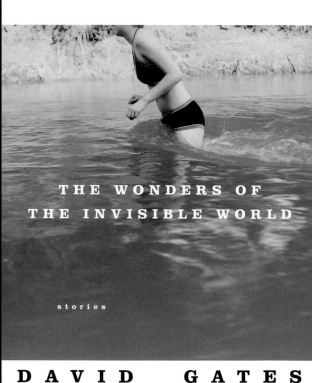

THE WONDERS OF
THE INVISIBLE WORLD

stories

DAVID GATES

author of **Jernigan** and **Preston Falls**

LEFT: Knopf, 1991. I was trying to channel M&Co. on this one. **TOP**
If I had to have my name in lights I could do worse than this
ABOVE: Knopf, 1999, co-designed with John Gall. Photo by the
beautiful and talented Jason Fulford.

MY PARENTS NEVER DISCOURAGED ME FROM PURSUING DESIGN, but they were adamant that I have a "back-up" just in case things didn't work out. International American Realty College of West Virginia gives you the 75 hours of credit you need in order to become a licensed real-estate salesperson. You do not need to be a resident of West Virginia or even a citizen of the United States. You will be able to access the course from any computer worldwide. The course includes all materials, school exam, and free enrollment in a "cram course" exam review weekend at the "pied-à-terre" of one of their handsome or buxom agents. Obtaining a West Virginia Real Estate License does not require expensive and time-consuming real-estate school classroom attendance! You needn't ever even set foot in West Virginia, nor point it out on a map of the southern United States! Call now! They're standing by! **ABOVE:** Somewhere in the heartland, 2001. **RIGHT:** Knopf, 2003. Photo by David Graham, from *Only in America*. Now *that's* synergy.

205

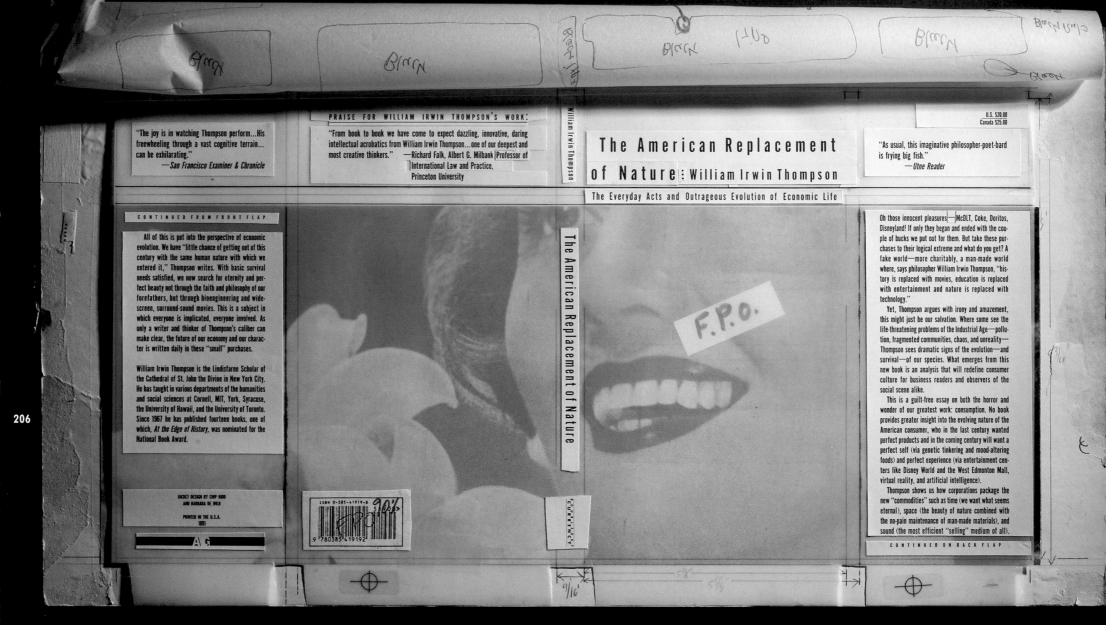

ABOVE: *The American Replacement of Nature* book jacket mechanical.

The computer replacement of mechanicals.

WHILE I DEFINITELY WOULDN'T WANT TO GO BACK, there really was something physically satisfying about designing and doing mechanicals by hand. But boy, was it time consuming. First you'd spec the type, and leave it in the overnight bin for a pick-up. Then you'd get it the next day, on slick stat paper, and it would either look the way it was supposed to, or . . . not. If not, you could phone in a change, but that would take another day. So if you didn't have the time, you'd order in-house stats of it, enlarged or shrunk, as need be, which would take another hour or two, depending on if the technician was backed up (which she usually was). Then you'd either wax it or rubber-cement it to a vellum overlay on the board you'd oh-so-carefully ruled up, according to the specifications provided by the production editor, and then cut and adjust accordingly. If there were images to deal with, you sent out for either a For Position Only c-print, or had a continuous tone stat made by the tech (who was still backed up) and pasted that down where it needed to be. And off it goes for circulation among the editor, copyeditor, etc. Then it comes back, and you make the corrections, and send it off again. Finally, when all the corrections have been made, and everyone has signed off on it, it's ready to go off to the printer when . . . the production editor phones, and says the text-paper weight has changed, and now the spine sizes are completely invalid, and now you have to rule the whole thing up again. And that's just for a jacket—imagine doing boards, one spread at a time, for *an entire book.* **ABOVE:** Ah, the good old days. **OPPOSITE LEFT:** Doubleday Currency, 1991. Co-design with Barbara deWilde. Alex Gottfried, art director. *The American Replacement of Nature* is an anthology of critical essays on the culture of consumption.

The American Replacement

of Nature : William Irwin Thompson

The Everyday Acts and Outrageous Evolution of Economic Life

Oops.

WHEN YOU'VE BEEN AT THIS AS LONG AS I HAVE, you develop a pretty thick skin. In the beginning I was terrified my ideas would get rejected, and of course some of them were. But not all of them, and after a while, I found that if you keep at it you build up enough quality work so that the sting of the occasional turn-down isn't quite so sharp. But every now and then along comes a real heartbreaker, and this was definitely it—especially because I'm such a fan of the author. I think Anthony Lane is the single best movie critic writing today. So when I heard what the title of his collection of reviews was going to be, it was so obvious: make it look like there was a massive screw-up at the bindery and all the jackets were put on wrong. I even figured it out so that the spine worked. I was so psyched. And for naught—this was met with across-the-board blank stares and scratched heads. **BELOW:** Unused idea. Nobody got it.

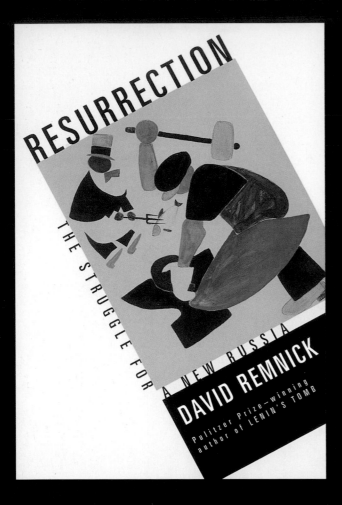

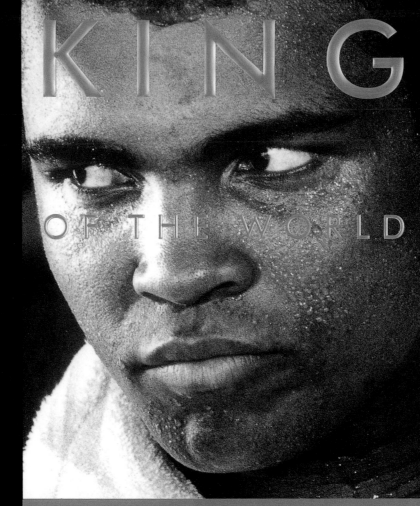

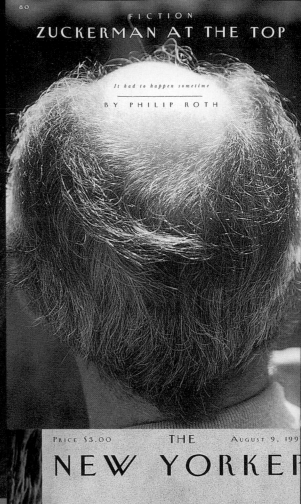

KING OF THE WORLD

DAVID REMNICK

WINNER OF THE PULITZER PRIZE

ZUCKERMAN AT THE TOP

It had to happen sometime

BY PHILIP ROTH

PRICE $3.00   THE   AUGUST 9, 199

NEW YORKER

I WAS STANDING IN LINE AT THE BOOK PARTY FOR 'KING OF THE WORLD', waiting for David Remnick to sign my copy. As I drew closer, I saw someone was sitting next to him, and then I recognized . . . Muhammad Ali himself. Although he is still a regal and commanding presence, the heavy toll from years of blows to the head and Parkinson's was nonetheless undeniable. When I got to the front of the line, David kindly pointed out to him that I designed the cover. Then, the Great Ali motioned for me to draw near and whispered, slowly, into my ear: "You're not as dumb as you look." And I grinned, thankful. Yep, he was still in there. **ABOVE LEFT:** Random House, 1997. **NEAR RIGHT:** Random House went to press proof with this jacket, then asked me to rework it, using the same photo. **ABOVE RIGHT:** Random House, 1998. Art director, Andy Carpenter.

IN 1998 DAVID APPROACHED ME ABOUT A POSSIBLE REDESIGN OF 'THE NEW YORKER'. Of course I was keen, but it was tricky: SI Newhouse had just sold Random House and there was a strict "no-raiding" clause. But doing it freelance was kosher, and I excitedly worked up a bunch of ideas. That led to my art directing the special double-length Fiction Issue of Summer 1999—one of the most thrilling jobs of my life. I still can't believe it: to go from almost no magazine experience to overseeing an entire issue of the country's most venerated periodical. **FAR RIGHT:** Elements from my proposed redesign of the *The New Yorker*, including allegorical images to illustrate the fiction and the introduction of photography on the front. The former idea stuck and is used to this day, the latter was too much of a leap. **OPPOSITE PAGE:** Excerpts from the Summer 1999 Fiction Issue, which featured 20 stories by writers under 40. It remains the only issue of the magazine to use full-bleed art. On the front cover, illustrated by Chris Ware, I pulled the first sentence from each story and ran them across the "sky," marking the first time text from the interior was featured on the cover.

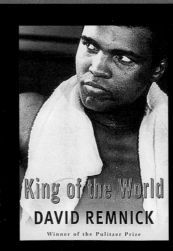

King of the World
DAVID REMNICK
Winner of the Pulitzer Prize

Price $3.95
THE NEW YORKER
June 21 & 28, 1999
1. Being a Spokane Indian, I only pick up Indian hitchhikers. I learned this particular ceremony from my fathe
2. Lee Strasberg, a founder of the Group Theatre and the great teacher of the American Method, famously advi
3. The autumn I was seventeen Richard Nixon made a visit to our town, at the western edge of Cape Cod, and
4. Josef Kavalier's determination to storm the exclusive Hofzinser Club of Prague took full form over breakfast
5. My father is gone. I am slouched in a cast-aluminum chair across from two men, one the manager of the hote
6. He sits on the mattress, the fat spread of his ass popping my fitted sheets from their corners. His clothes are st
7. Jim and Uncle Al did not set out on their journey until after supper, when the heat of the day had broken at l
8. Allen Fein is on his way to Port Authority when he stubs his toe and scuffs his shoe—puts a nick in a five-hu
9. Skulls make better pillows than you think. Dr. Peter Luce (the famous sexologist) rests his cheek on the varn
10. Down the long concourse they came unsteadily, Enid favoring her damaged hip, Alfred paddling at the air wit
11. You couldn't tell anymore that they had separate desks. For fifteen years, Roselva and Helen had worked tog
12. on a raft in water. Floating. Every day when she comes home from school, she puts on her bikini
13. ppy East Coast resort island in the middle of summer, we just flew in for the wedding of my i
14. with a certificate in commerce and the equivalent, in those days, of ten dollars to my name
15. man, I didn't seek out the pleasure of women. At least not like my comrades in arms, wl
16. reamers, by the bathhouse entrance. Tuna on shish kebab and pineapple slices i
17. l Emily. She caught her breath. Everything was striking her in the solar pl
18. letter of 23 Feb., which accompanied the I CAN SPEAK!™ you returned, m
19. -haired, pale-faced, slender idealist, tells itself with a grim brevity, in keep
20. t as a asset like that would you. But it's the arm. You want to see it? You
THE FUTURE OF AMERICAN FICTION

COVER *20 Writers for the 21st Century, by Chip Kidd and Chris Ware*

il the October Rev-
her am-
nya Ka-
termined
n Russia
nination.
e Krup-
l equally
was kept
of the
ths, un-
d M. F.
herself to death to
prisonment. Embar-

$3.50? THAT'S EXPENSIVE!

to have resembled the letter
a sort of O that
it rejoins its start
and sports a tin
top, which bride
as a precious stor
add that this ch
the mystical alph
bolizes both help
Who knows t
those shining cir
ring that Krupska
upon Lenin's finger was n
again. As for the one he slid

ad eighty-five degrees. "It's
be a hot one," Jim
oud, for no reason
to make himself
all he knew, a hobo
or a ghost was hid-
the building. There
ression on. Mama
ssion made people
tiptoed to the build-
window, sucked his
l of courage, and
ough the glass. Inside was a
ade of rough lumber, and a

plantation did not seem to
where they belong
Al knocked at the
doors of the house
time. Jim was glad
one answered.
Back at the m
Uncle Al turned
toward a collection
and farm buildin
distance. The ca
passed on the w
main barn seemed locked up
though a dog slept on the po

200

THE THIRD AND FINAL CONTINENT

JHUMPA LAHIRI

I LEFT India in 1964 with a certificate in commerce and the equivalent, in those days, of ten dollars to my name. For three weeks I sailed on the S.S. Roma, an Italian cargo vessel, in a cabin next to the ship's engine, across the Arabian Sea, the Red Sea, the Mediterranean, and finally to England. I lived in London, in Finsbury Park, in a house occupied entirely by penniless Bengali bachelors like myself, at least a dozen and sometimes more, all struggling to educate and establish ourselves abroad.

I attended lectures at L.S.E. and worked at the university library to get by. We lived three or four to a room, shared a single, icy toilet, and took turns cooking pots of egg curry, which we ate with our hands on a table covered with newspapers. Apart from our jobs we had few responsibilities. On weekends we lounged barefoot in drawstring pajamas, drinking tea and smoking Rothmans, or set out to watch cricket at Lord's. Some weekends the house was crammed with still more Bengalis, to whom we had introduced ourselves at the greengrocer, or on the Tube, and we made yet more egg curry, and played Mukesh on a Grundig reel-to-reel, and soaked our dirty dishes in the bathtub. Every now and then someone in the house moved out, to live with a woman whom his family back in Calcutta had determined he was to wed. In 1969, when I was thirty-six years old, my own marriage was arranged. Around the same time, I was offered a full-time job in America, in the processing department of a library at M.I.T. The salary was generous enough to support a wife, and I was honored to be hired by a world-famous university, and so I obtained a green card, and prepared to travel farther still.

LEFT: DETAIL FROM MARGO HOFF, "MURDER MYSTERY" (1945)/© ART INSTITUTE OF CHICAGO

By then I had enough money to go by plane. I flew first to Calcutta, to attend my wedding, and a week later to Boston, to begin my new job. During the flight I read "The Student Guide to North America," for although I was no longer a student, I was on a budget all the same. I learned that Americans drove on the right side of the road, not the left, and that they called a lift an elevator and an engaged phone busy. "The pace of life in North America is different from Britain, as you will soon discover," the guidebook informed me. "Everybody feels he must get to the top. Don't expect an English cup of tea." As the plane began its descent over Boston Harbor, the pilot announced the weather and the time, and that President Nixon had declared a national holiday: two American men had landed on the moon. Several passengers cheered. "God bless America!" one of them hollered. Across the aisle, I saw a woman praying.

I spent my first night at the Y.M.C.A. in Central Square, Cambridge, an inexpensive accommodation recommended by my guidebook which was within walking distance of M.I.T. The room contained a cot, a desk, and a small wooden cross on one wall. A sign on the door said that cooking was strictly forbidden. A bare window overlooked Massachusetts Avenue. Car horns, shrill and prolonged, blared one after another. Sirens and flashing lights heralded endless emergencies, and a succession of buses rumbled past, their doors opening and closing with a powerful hiss, throughout the night. The noise was constantly distracting, at times suffocating. I felt it deep in my ribs, just as I had felt the furious drone of the engine on the S.S. Roma. But there was no ship's deck to escape to, no glittering ocean to thrill my soul, no breeze to cool my face, no one to talk to. I was too tired to pace the gloomy corridors of the Y.M.C.A. in my pajamas. Instead I sat at the desk and stared out the window. In the morning I reported to my job at the Dewey Library, a beige fortlike building by Memorial Drive. I also opened a bank account, rented a post-office box, and bought a plastic bowl and a spoon. I went to a supermarket called Purity Supreme, wandering up and down the aisles, comparing prices with those in England. In the end I bought a carton of milk and a box of cornflakes. This was my first meal in America. Even the simple chore of buying milk was new to me; in London we'd had bottles delivered each morning to our door.

IN a week I had adjusted, more or less. I ate cornflakes and milk morning and night, and bought some bananas for variety, slicing them into the bowl with the edge of my spoon. I left my carton of milk on the shaded part of the windowsill, as I had seen other residents at the Y.M.C.A. do. To pass the time in the evenings I read the Boston *Glob* downstairs, in a spacious room with stained-glass windows. I read every articl and advertisement, so that I would grow familiar with things, and when my eye grew tired I slept. Only I did not slee well. Each night I had to keep the window wide open; it was the only source o air in the stifling room, and the noise wa intolerable. I would lie on the cot with my fingers pressed into my ears, but whe I drifted off to sleep my hands fell away and the noise of the traffic would wak me up again. Pigeon feathers drifted ont the windowsill, and one evening, when I poured milk over my cornflakes, I sav that it had soured. Nevertheless I resolve to stay at the Y.M.C.A. for six weeks until my wife's passport and green car were ready. Once she arrived I woul have to rent a proper apartment, an from time to time I studied the classifie section of the newspaper, or stopped in a the housing office at M.I.T. during m lunch break to see what was available. I was in this manner that I discovered room for immediate occupancy, in house on a quiet street, the listing sai for eight dollars per week. I dialled th number from a pay telephone, sortin through the coins, with which I was sti unfamiliar, smaller and lighter than shil lings, heavier and brighter than paisas

"Who is speaking?" a woma demanded. Her voice was bold an clamorous.

"Yes, good afternoon, Madam. I an calling about the room for rent."

"Harvard or Tech?"

"I beg your pardon?"

"Are you from Harvard or Tech?

Gathering that Tech referred t the Massachusetts Institute of Technology, I re plied, "I wor at Dewey Li brary," addin tentatively, "a Tech."

"I only ren

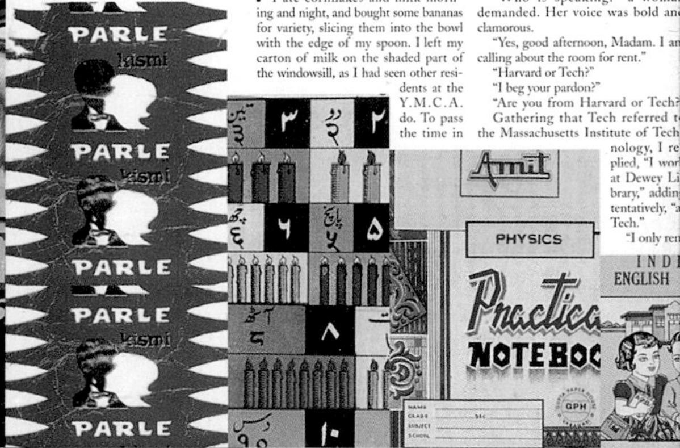

PARLE
kismi
PARLE
kismi
PARLE
PARLE
kismi
PARLE
Amit
PHYSICS

防諜

THE VOLUNTEERS

CHANG-RAE LEE

15

WHEN I was a young man, I didn't seek out the pleasure of women. At least not like my comrades in arms, who in their every spare moment seemed ravenous for any part of a woman, in any form, whether in photographs or songs or recounted stories, and, of course, whenever possible, in the flesh. Pictures were most favored, being easy. I remember a corporal who kept illicit photographs of disrobed maidens in his radio codebook, a sheaf of images he had salvaged from a bombed-out colonial mansion in Indonesia. Whenever I walked by the communications tent, he would call out in a most proper voice, "Lieutenant Kurohata, sir, may I receive an opinion from you, please?"

The women in his pictures were Western, I think French or Dutch, and had been caught by the camera in compromising positions—bending over to pick up a dropped book, for example, or being attended in the bath by another nude woman. Corporal Endo had perhaps a score of these, each featuring a different scene, and he shuffled through them with an unswerving awe and reverence that made me think he might be a Christian. Of course, I shouldn't have allowed him to address me so familiarly, as I was superior to him in rank, but we were from the same province and home town, and he was exuberantly innocent and youthful and he never called to me if others were within earshot. I knew that he had never been with a woman, but in going through his photos he seemed to have become privy to the secrets of lovemaking.

I myself, at that time, had been initiated only once, but, unlike the Corporal, I found little of interest in the hand-size tableaux. They held for me none of the drama that he clearly savored in them. Instead, they smacked of the excess and privilege of a sclerotic, purulent culture—the very forces that our nation's people were struggling against, from Papua New Guinea and Indonesia to the densely forested foothills of old Burma, where we were posted, approximately a hundred and twenty-five kilometres from the outskirts of Rangoon. The women in the photo cards were full figured, and no longer really young, though several of them were attractive in an exotic manner.

The image I preferred was the one of the bath, and although Corporal Endo offered several times to give me that particular card, I didn't want the worry of keeping it among my few persona things. Should I be killed, those items along with my ashen remains, would b tendered to my family in Japan, as wa customary. In most cases, the officer i charge of such transferrals checked th package to make sure that it containe only the most necessary (and honorable effects, but one heard of embarrassing in stances when grieving elders were force to confront awkward last notions of thei dead. I feared it would be especiall shaming in my circumstance. When was a young boy, I had left the narrow existence of my birth family and ou ghetto of hide tanners and renderers—most of us were ethnic Koreans, though we spoke and lived as Japanese, if ones i twilight—to live with a Japanese couple well-to-do and childless, who treated m as if I were their son. I believed that a adoptive parents they might shoulder th burden of my vices even more heavil than if I had been born to them, blood o their blood, as there would be no excus but their raising of me. Indeed, I wante to prove myself in the crucible of the bat tlefield, and to prove to anyone wh might suspect otherwise the worthines of raising me away from the lowly quar ters of my kin. Still, being twenty-thre years old and having been with only on woman, a prostitute, during my first post ing, in Singapore, I was periodically give to the enticements of such base things and unable to stop myself from steppin into the radio tent whenever the Corpo ral addressed me.

"Have I shown you this new series sir?" he said one sweltering afternoon reaching into the back flap of his code book. His eyes seemed bright, almos feral. "I traded some of mine to a fellow in munitions. He had these. He said h was tired of them, sir."

There were several photograph pasted into a small journal which de picted women and men together, patentl engaging in sexual intercourse. I ha never seen such pictures before. The styl of the photography was documentary, al most clinical, as though the overexpose frames were meant for a textbook o human coitus. To my mind, there wa nothing remotely titillating in them, sav perhaps the shocking idea that peopl had willingly performed the acts whil someone else had photographed them.

The Corporal took more than a cus

LIVING TO BE

100

STORIES BY

ROBERT BOSWELL

author of MYSTERY RIDE

101

Presidents Who Aim High

Chip Kidd

ANDERSEN KURT KURT ANDERSEN THE CENTURY TURN OF THE TURN OF CENTURY RANDOM HOUSE

Count on it.

ALONG WITH MANY OTHERS, I FIRST BECAME AWARE of the work of Kurt Andersen with the appearance of *Spy* magazine in the fall of 1986, though I didn't realize it was his writing. His op-ed pieces were anonymous but brilliantly constucted riffs on the absudities of celebrity and political culture in the city. In some ways, *Spy* was my introduction to the city itself, and I felt an instant connection to it not only because it was so smart and funny, but also because we both arrived in the great metropolis at the same time.

Since then, in articles for *Time* and *New York* magazines, Kurt has been one of my staunchest supporters in the media, so I welcomed the opportunity to return the favor with the design of his monumental novel *Turn of the Century*. An epic story of one family's stuggle to survive in the heart of the world's greatest city at this most symbolic of eras, I knew that it had to convey the sense of one grand epoch ending and giving way into the next. The result is both familiar and futuristic, and was ultimately selected for inclusion of the 4th edition of Phillip Meggs's *History of Graphic Design*.

LEFT: Knopf, 1994. **ABOVE:** April 29, 2001, Op-Ed, *The New York Times*. **OPPOSITE LEFT:** Random House, 1999. There was never any question about the legibility, for which I was most grateful to editor Ann Godoff. **OPPOSITE RIGHT:** Rejected *New York Times* Op-Art for December 31, 1999. This almost went to print, but the hysteria of Y2K (especially concerning the possible of a disaster in Times Square) rose to such a fever pitch that the editors felt they couldn't "risk it."

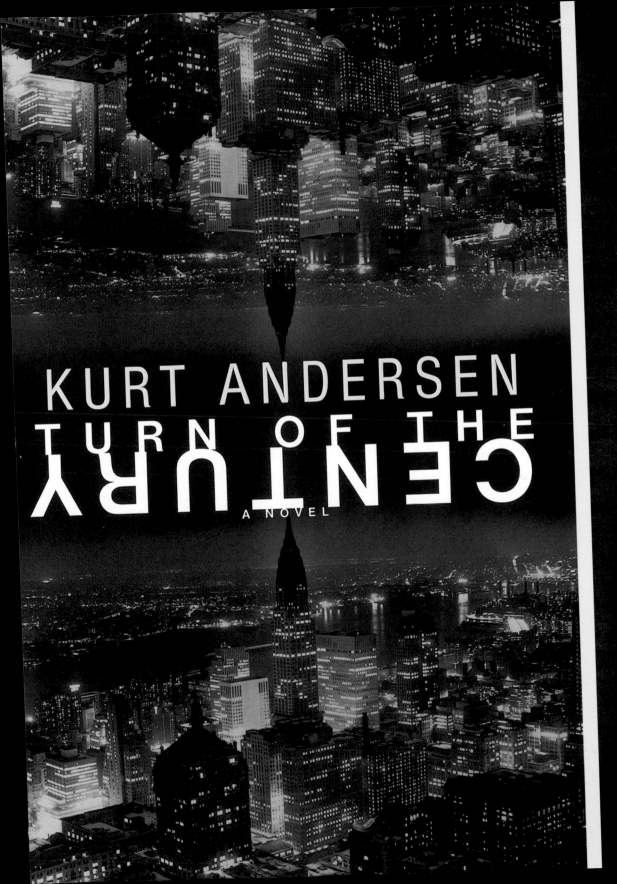

-kled in the ballroom, aswhirl with the city's *beau monde*. It all felt like the center of the Universe. At the first of the twelve bells, the band launched into Auld Lang Syne, and Chip took Sandy in his arms—lifting her like a prize, his joy almost beyond bearing. Still in love, after all they'd been through--the decade, the century, the millenium, that unpleasantness in the Hamptons.

"Happy New Year, darling!" They kissed. Sandy never felt so *alive*.

"And to you, my dearest! To the Future!"

"My goodness. Did you feel that? Say, what's that noi--"

The End

THE
PARIS
REVIEW

133

INTERVIEWS
WITH
CHINUA
ACHEBE
AND
CZESLAW
MILOSZ

FICTION BY
A.S. BYATT

POETRY BY
EDWARD
HIRSCH
AND
DAVID
WAGONER

WINTER
1994-
1995

THE PARIS REVIEW

$10.00   133 $14 IN CANADA

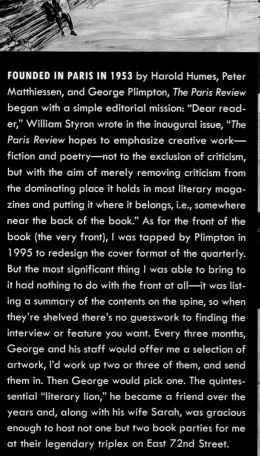

FOUNDED IN PARIS IN 1953 by Harold Humes, Peter Matthiessen, and George Plimpton, *The Paris Review* began with a simple editorial mission: "Dear reader," William Styron wrote in the inaugural issue, "*The Paris Review* hopes to emphasize creative work— fiction and poetry—not to the exclusion of criticism, but with the aim of merely removing criticism from the dominating place it holds in most literary magazines and putting it where it belongs, i.e., somewhere near the back of the book." As for the front of the book (the very front), I was tapped by Plimpton in 1995 to redesign the cover format of the quarterly. But the most significant thing I was able to bring to it had nothing to do with the front at all—it was listing a summary of the contents on the spine, so when they're shelved there's no guesswork to finding the interview or feature you want. Every three months, George and his staff would offer me a selection of artwork, I'd work up two or three of them, and send them in. Then George would pick one. The quintessential "literary lion," he became a friend over the years and, along with his wife Sarah, was gracious enough to host not one but two book parties for me at their legendary triplex on East 72nd Street.

THE PARIS REVIEW

$10.00   134 $14 IN CANADA

DETOUR

THE PARIS REVIEW

$10.00   141 $14 IN CANADA

THE PARIS REVIEW

$10.00   144 $14 IN CANADA

THE PARIS REVIEW

$10.00   146 $14 IN CANADA

THE PARIS REVIE

$10.00   148 $14 IN CANADA

THE PARIS REVIE

$10.00   149 $14 IN CANADA

$12.00   165 $16 IN CANADA

50TH ANNIVERSARY YEAR

ABOVE: The Last Party in New York. The evening of September 10, 2001. Left to right: Paul, Billy, George, & Ringo. Thank heavens for photographer Star Black, who was working the party and caught the moment I met Paul McCartney. **BELOW:** My account of the evening for *The New York Observer*, December 17, 2001.

$12.00   169 $16 IN CANADA

THE PARIS REVIEW

$12.00   159 $16 IN CANADA

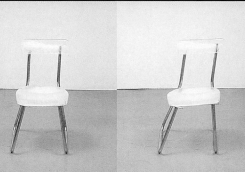

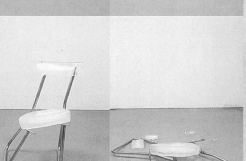

THE NEW YORK OBSERVER   DECEMBER 17, 2001

September 10: Day of Famy

I would have remembered Monday, Sept. 10, forever anyway.

First, there was that fresh-off-the-presses full-page photograph in *New York* magazine of me sucking a lollipop. Knowing dam well when my profile was due to appear, I picked a copy up on the way to work. Eek!—I'm no stranger to sucking (ask *Entertainment Weekly*)—but candy? Did I really do that? Of course I did; I had a book to sell. The novel I'd worked on for six-plus years was finally going to appear in less than a month, and if going down on a cherry Blow Pop at the orders of a heavily caffeinated photographer with loose ideas and a tight deadline would put books into people's hands, then by God, change my name to Hoover. I'd already dubbed 2001 "The Year of Saying Yes." At least they didn't run the shot with the necklace made of Sweet Tarts.

And I'd be remiss if I didn't admit: The three-page article that accompanied it was a first novelist's wet dream. Nothing mitigating or snarky about it. Sure, it made me sound like an alcoholic homosexual superhero-fetishist who's well into his fourth childhood and has a taste for men old enough to be his naughty uncles, but all of that's true. What really mattered was they showed the book, spelled the title correctly and apparently couldn't get anyone who hates me on the phone.

On to the office.

I had a presentation to give the next morning to the Pantheon sales force about a new book of comics I was editing, so I worked on that while fielding calls from my editor and my agent, both congratulating me that the reporter from *New York* magazine couldn't get anyone who hates me on the phone.

In the afternoon, I was visited by a young photographer who showed me a picture of an albino man in his early 20's, nude and standing in someone's backyard at night, holding a live chicken tightly to his chest. I made a color Xerox of it, just in case Katherine Dunn ever gets over her writer's block.

But that wasn't what made the day a keeper. I had an invitation that night for a book party at George Plimpton's in honor of the poet Billy Collins. I didn't really want to take the time to go; I had an impending month-and-a-half book tour set to start in three weeks, and I was already in a panic about getting my ducks in a row. What I really needed was a night at my desk.

Couldn't, though—George was going to host *my* book party in the very same space in early October, and I just *had* to appear and say hello. I'm always afraid he's going to forget who I am, and if that happened to me at my own book party, it would force me to become *sad*.

The event was from 6 to 8. At 7:25, I tore myself away from a jacket I was designing for Thomas McGuane and headed for the subway.

At 7:50, I was still two blocks away, practically running and cursing myself for forgetting what a long walk it was from the subway stop.

People streaming out when I got there, I swam against the tide up the steps. Only a few at the bar—no George in sight.

Highball in hand, I made the rounds—through the living room, past the steamed vegetables on the pool table, attended by a gaggle of last spring's bright young things from Smith munching limp carrots.

Back in George's study, a small group, maybe five or six, chatting.

Could hear George there, and I gingerly made my way up. Our host was speaking to someone with his back to me, a middle-aged man in a smart black suit, the guest of honor to his left. George eventually noticed me (yay!) and introduced me to the fellow he was talking to.

Chip Kidd

It was Paul McCartney.

Who shook my hand.

As a graphic designer, this was like meeting the logo for Coca-Cola. I'd only met one other person in my life with that level of fame, and then as now, I just couldn't accept that he was real. He left soon after.

An hour later, I walked home (only four blocks away), and I did what I always do: stripped to my underwear, pulled out a manuscript, played some music and drank myself to sleep. You would have thought I put on the Beatles, but I'd just gotten an advance bootleg CD of the new album by my very faves, New Order. Their first new album in 13 years, and anyone who cared about it was skeptical.

What a happy surprise: It was terrific. They were really back to their old form—orchestral rather than techno. Swirling and full, spinning me back to my sophomore year. I thought the best song was one called "Primitive Notion." The chorus was just killer. It's nothing without the sound, but:

I've done it before, and I'll do it again.
I'm charged with a light that will burn till the end.

And I was, too. Incredible day. And oh, the album had such a fucking great title. It was addressed to me, to everyone I wanted to read my book, to the world:
Get Ready.

—*Chip Kidd, graphic designer and author of* The Cheese Monkeys.

THE CONSCIENCE OF THE EYE

The Design and Social Life of Cities

RICHARD SENNETT

I ♥ N.Y.

Call me crazy.

STILL IN A STATE OF SHOCK FROM THE EVENTS OF SEPTEMBER 11TH, in November I was asked to illustrate an editorial in *The New York Times* about the resilience of the city. Milton Glaser had already amended his ubiquitous "I ♥ NY" for the cause by adding "More Than Ever," and I wanted to take it a step further. **ABOVE:** My reinterpretation was not meant to be funny or as a satire in any way—what I was trying to say was that after all the smoke clears, we still love the city and always will, no matter what happens. The Op-Ed editors understood, but thought it was too graphic and could be perceived as saying we'd all been burned to a crisp. Art director Peter Buchanan-Smith saved the day when he suggested turning it into a handbill that could be placed in the context of the street. This got the point across perfectly while also heartbreakingly calling to mind the countless "Missing" posters that instantly sprung up everywhere, desperate for information about loved ones who would likely never be seen again. **LEFT:** Knopf, 1991. **OPPOSITE LEFT:** *The New York Times*, November 22, 2001. Peter Buchanan-Smith, art director and photographer.

DANIEL LIBESKIND

BREAKING

GROUND

ADVENTURES IN LIFE

AND ARCHITECTURE

Just Crazy About the Place

By Roger Rosenblatt

A homeless man known to me as Charlie, who was only a little crazier than the rest of us, decided to set up a living room a few years ago on the sidewalk outside the church at 86th and Amsterdam. He had scavenged and found a spotted sofa, two end tables, a Barcalounger stuck in the recline position, a rug that had probably been orange in the 1960's and a standing lamp that plugged into nothing. It was a pretty nice-looking place, and since I knew Charlie from the neighborhood, I sat down in his outdoor room to talk. After a while, it was clear that I was boring him. "Well, Roger," he said through his four remaining teeth. "I've enjoyed this chat. But I'm expecting guests."

Let us now praise famous cities, but not for the wrong reasons. Since Sept. , many elegant pitchmen, from the mayor on down, have been selling this city to tourists as a warm and welcoming town, soaring with resilience and dreams. New York is some of those things, sometimes, but that is not why millions of us are especially grateful to it this Thanksgiving. The reason we love this city is that it is difficult to live here. Come visit New York and observe a strange grace born of a hard and crazy life.

Welcoming? On the first night my grandparents arrived at St. Mark's Place via Ellis Island, they were welcomed by robbers who stole every little thing they had. Young people who come to the city these days are welcomed just as lavishly, with unaffordable apartments and ungettable jobs. They come, nonetheless, because whether they know it or not, they are looking for trouble — trouble

If you'r up at sou in New you their you kno work. Po desperate them kn thing."

There': city at t there's weather lines of meal, or help get week or 1

Germa pick up at a food the Chu drew on Side. The Side Cam

"This i Barahon Sept. 11. that work fell she l

Edwin pantry, w 3-year-ol to make never ca

He sai working heart att the food sum up inevitable he casua sometime train so I for my g

There kitchens and they

Chip Kidd

world. I always thought that George Washington moved the nation's capital from New York southward because he saw that New York would be

Gratitude for

War Stories.

THE WORD "NAPALM" IMMEDIATELY brings to mind the famous 1972 photograph by Huynh Cong Ut of a young Vietnamese girl, naked, shrieking and running for her life from South Vietnamese troops and toward the camera. For Bruce Weigl's ironically titled book of Vietnam War–themed poems, *Song of Napalm*, I researched the chemical itself and discovered, not surprisingly, that in addition to setting things afire it acts as an extreme form of tear gas and attacks the unprotected eyes and nose. So I placed the type accordingly. **FAR RIGHT:** Atlantic Monthly Books, 1988. Robbin Schiff, art director. **ABOVE:** There were four steps to creating the artwork—1. My pencil sketch on tissue, 2. A high-contrast Xerox copy, to strengthen the darks, 3. A continuous tone photostat of the Xerox, which was then 4., Hand-colored with water-based dyes. **RIGHT:** Unused idea for Weigl's follow-up collection. Whatever saves us, it didn't here.

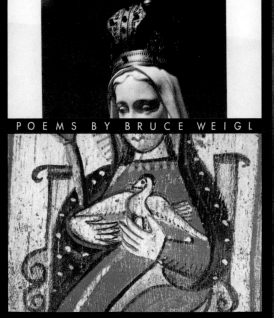

WHAT SAVES US

POEMS BY BRUCE WEIGL

SONG OF

NAPALM

INTRODUCTION BY ROBERT STONE

MOST OF ESTEEMED, PULITZER PRIZE–WINNING poet Anthony Hecht's earlier books featured elegant, typographical covers by longtime Knopf editor and designer Harry Ford. After Ford's death, Hecht (who with his wife Helen had since become a good friend) asked that I design the cover for *The Darkness and the Light*, using a painting by Tiepolo of Abraham about to sacrifice his son Isaac. Given the dichotomy of the title, I wanted to add a contrasting image—something to highlight the unique creative tension in the poet's style, which often juxtaposes classical textures with violent subjects. The stark realism of trench warfare seems to assault and complement the painter's elegant modeling, while eerily echoing his composition. **RIGHT:** Knopf, 2001.

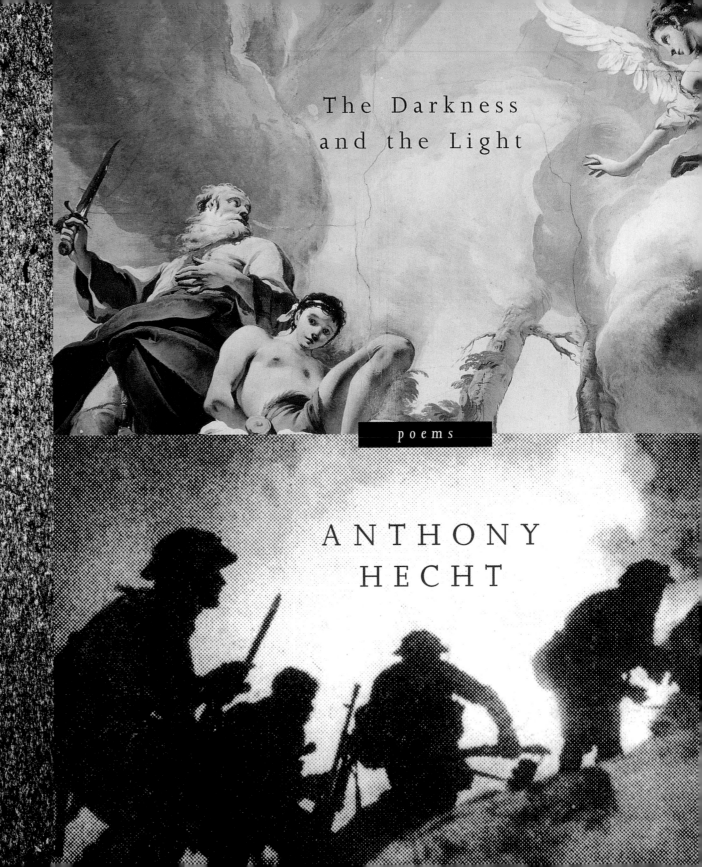

The Darkness
and the Light

poems

ANTHONY
HECHT

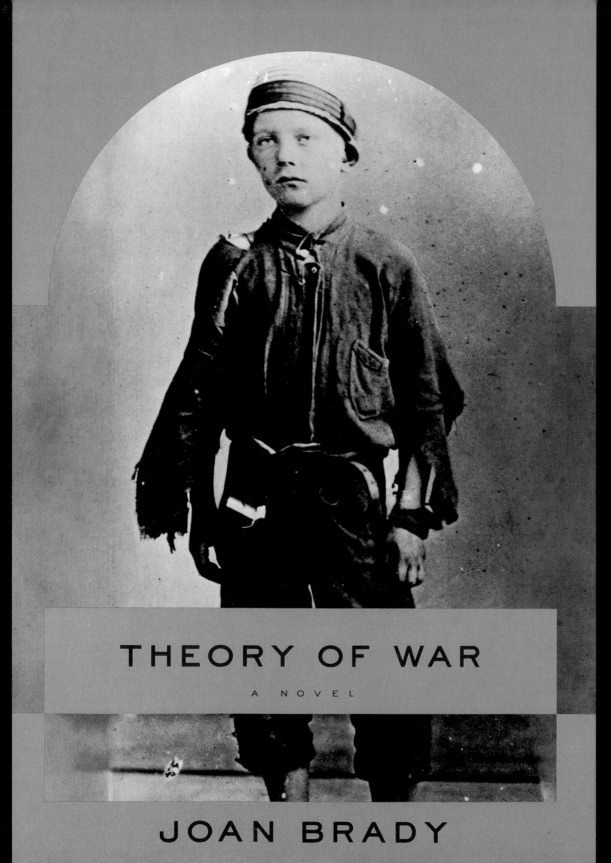

THEORY OF WAR

A NOVEL

JOAN BRADY

AMERICAN HERO

A NOVEL

LARRY BEINHART

MALLORY CARRICK, THE NARRATOR OF 'THEORY OF WAR', is the granddaughter of a white slave, Jonathan Carrick, who was "bound out" to a farmer as a boy in 1865. Though Jonathan escaped at age 16, and died years before Mallory was even born, his enslavement instilled a fury into Mallory that she's desparate to understand. She flies from her home in England to Washington state, where her great-uncle recounts the story of Jonathan's life: his horrific boyhood, his years as a railroad brakeman, his conflict as a fundamentalist minister who doubted what he preached, his war against the imperious son of his owner. **LEFT:** Knopf, 1993. **ABOVE:** Pantheon, 1993. Illustration by Stephen Kroninger. The book is a fantastic political satire of the Machiavellian machinations behind Operation Desert Storm and is the basis for the movie *Wag the Dog.* **OPPOSITE LEFT, TOP:** Knopf, 1994. **OPPOSITE LEFT, BOTTOM:** *The New York Times* Op-Ed page, April 9, 1999. **OPPOSITE RIGHT:** Counterpoint, 1997.

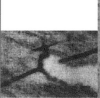
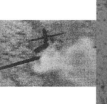

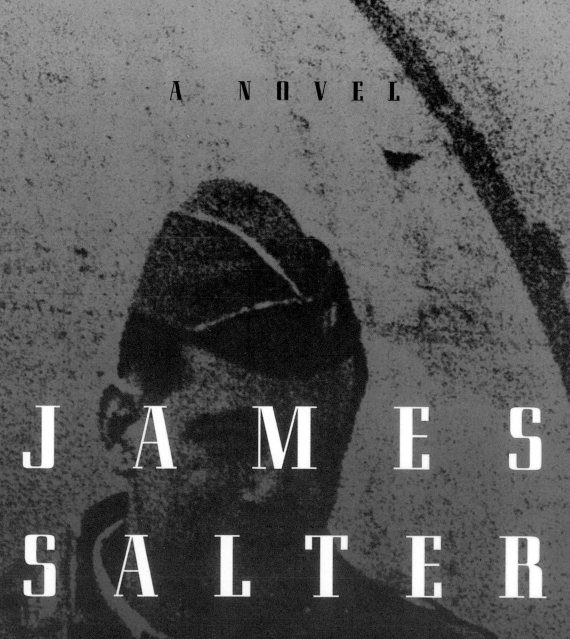

THE PRESIDENCY

Below the Beltway.

A 'NEW YORK TIMES' OP-ED PAGE COMMISSION IS THE CLOSEST THING YOU CAN GET to a graphic design pop quiz. At Penn State Lanny Sommese used to give us surprise "twenty-minute assignments," which were exactly that—less than a half hour to contemplate the problem, devise a solution, and then face a critique. We used to complain that such a thing would never happen in the "real world" but Lanny promised us that indeed it would, and a *Times* Op-Ed can come darn close. Here's the drill: the art director phones and asks if you have time to do it, which is really asking if you can drop everything for the rest of the afternoon. If you can, he tells you what the story—which usually isn't written yet—is going to be about. My rule is that if I don't have an idea for a solution by the time he's done summing it up, then I probably shouldn't take it on. But I almost always do anyway, and we're off to the races. As with so much else, it was a *lot* harder before we had computers, and more than once I literally ran across town to the *Times* offices to deliver my piece by five o'clock. But now with e-mail of course you can send just about anything with the click of a mouse, and spend more time on the concept. I think the most successful solutions act in the same way good book jackets do—they communicate instantly the nature of what the writer is trying to say. The responsibility for these pages has to be one of the most stressful art directorships in the city, as he or she is forever at the mercy of a volatile, 24-hour news cycle. I don't know how anyone does it.

OPPOSITE LEFT: Knopf, 1998. Below the book is an excerpt of a letter from George H. W. Bush to his editor, Ashbel Green, 1998. I pretty much designed this in my sleep and forgot all about it until the presidential race heated up in the summer of 2004, when a mass e-mail started circulating with a truly damning passage from the book quoted word-for-word, regarding Iraq and why Bush chose not to invade it after Desert Storm. It ran contrary to everything his son was doing at the time. I was outraged and just for my own sanity redesigned the cover with the quote front and center. Then I tried to get it published as an Op-Art (a self-contained visual opinion piece). Unfortunately, the editors felt I was too late because John Kerry had cited the quote in the first presidential debate just a few days before, and that made it old news. **OPPOSITE RIGHT:** Op-Art attempt, 2004. Brian Rea, art director. **TOP RIGHT:** *The New York Times*, September 25, 1998. Op-Arts are both easier and harder than merely illustrating an Op-Ed piece. Easier because you don't have to follow someone else's text, and harder because you have to come up with the whole thing yourself—the design equivalent of political cartooning. But when *The Starr Report* was released, commenting on it visually was a no-brainer. Nicholas Blechman, art director. **BOTTOM RIGHT:** *The New York Times*, January 21, 1999. This is as timely as ever, unfortunately. Just substitute the name of the president. Nicholas Blechman, art director. **ABOVE:** Unpublished Op-Art idea conceived during the height of the Clinton impeachment hearings (then "re-purposed" for Augusten Burroughs's *Dry*, p. 282).

220

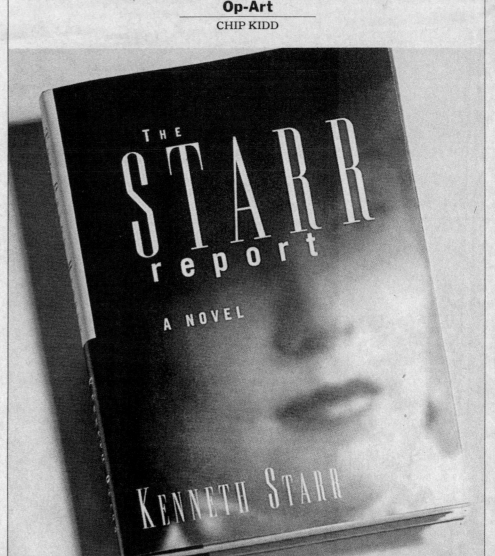

Op-Art

CHIP KIDD

THE STARR report

A NOVEL

KENNETH STARR

THE NEW YORK TIMES OP-ED THURSDAY, JANUARY 21, 1999   A23

SOCIAL SECURITY

Clinton Is Right to Go Slow on Pension Investments

A WORLD TRANSFORMED

THE COLLAPSE OF THE SOVIET EMPIRE

THE UNIFICATION OF GERMANY

TIANANMEN SQUARE • THE GULF WAR

GEORGE BUSH

AND

BRENT SCOWCROFT

I am so pleased with the book's cover. I love the clean look and I love having my name shown exactly as Brent's name appears. For years he was the behind the scenes guy, never sitting at the head table, always quietly and effectively doing his job. The Cabinet officers were out front. Brent was not. But now, given this book, he appears the way he should appear- my peer, my friend.

Sincerely, Gy Bush

A Cover Transformed

Amidst the blizzard of political chain-mails that have become the stuff of our in-boxes these days, one I got a few weeks ago in particular struck a personal chord. It pointed out a paragraph from George H. W. Bush's 1998 presidential memoir, A World Transformed, in which he eerily foreshadows that everything his son has been doing in the past year and a half regarding Iraq is a big mistake. At first I was just stunned by how damning it is, but then I remembered--I'd designed the jacket of the book. Which, I'll be the first to admit, was nothing special. So, in light of this I decided to give it another go. If the book were to be re-issued today, here's the jacket I would do. Usually, as a designer I loathe putting long quotes on the fronts of books--it's too distracting. Not this time.---

A WORLD TRANSFORMED

BY GEORGE H. W. BUSH

FROM PAGE 489, on the aftermath of Desert Storm: "Trying to eliminate Saddam...would have incurred incalculable human and political costs. Apprehending him was probably impossible...We would have been forced to occupy Baghdad and, in effect, rule Iraq...There was no viable "exit strategy" we could see, violating another of our principles. Furthermore, we had been consciously trying to set a pattern for handling aggression in the post-Cold War world. Going in and occupying Iraq, thus unilaterally exceeding the United Nations' mandate, would have destroyed the precedent of international response to aggression that we hoped to establish. Had we gone the invasion route, the United States could conceivably still be an occupying power in a bitterly hostile land."—GHWB, 1998

SEE PAGE 489.

A WORLD TRANSFORMED

GEORGE H.W. BUSH

Knopf

221

THIS
IS THE LIFE

A NOVEL

JOSEPH O'NEILL

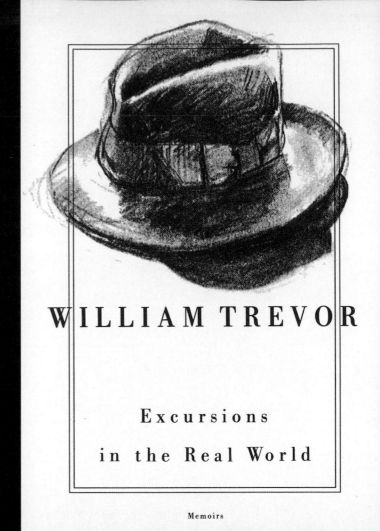

WILLIAM TREVOR

Excursions

in the Real World

Memoirs

"Plastics."

THIRTY YEARS AFTER DUSTIN HOFFMAN WAS TOLD in the 1967 movie *The Graduate* that plastics were the future, not even its forward-thinking screen-writer Buck Henry could have predicted that polymers would show up in as many places under the automotive hood as they do today. Although the development of underhood plastics began five years before Mr. Hoffman and Simon & Garfunkel made Mrs. Robinson famous, plastics suppliers and molders still have a sales job to do when introducing new applications for engine-compartment components. "With each application, people's confidence grows," says Mark Schuchardt, a technician at DuPont Automotive.

LEFT: FSG, 1991. Photo by the Douglas Brothers. **ABOVE:** Knopf, 1994. Illustration by Lucy Willis. **OPPOSITE LEFT:** TCG, 1996. Photo by Geoff Spear. **OPPOSITE RIGHT:** Knopf, 1997. Photo by John Scully.

drinks before dinner

a play by
E. L. Doctorow

Barney's Version

A NOVEL

Mordecai Richler

MOLDING PLASTIC INTO ONE PART REPLACING SEVERAL METAL PIECES and the weight savings associated with plastics are the principal drivers in bringing more plastics under the hood. Other benefits include lower assembly costs and a reduction in manufacturing cost, because there is rarely any machining or painting necessary. Plastics started appearing under hoods as fan shrouds and liquid reservoirs in the late '70s. It wasn't until the late '80s that they became sufficiently heat-resistant to be placed directly on the engine.

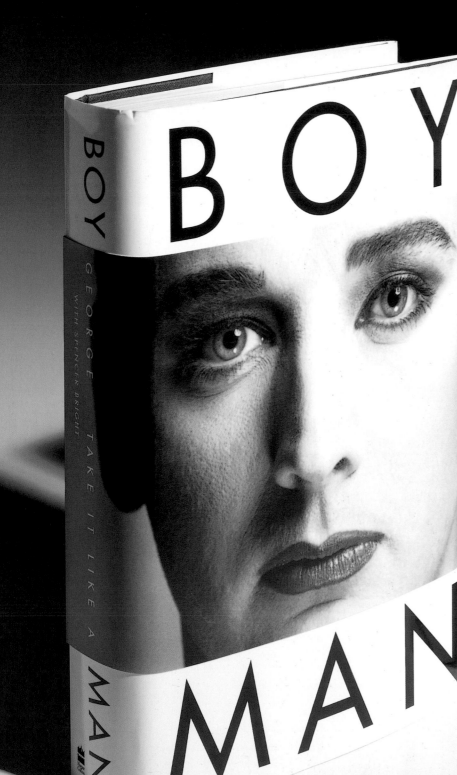

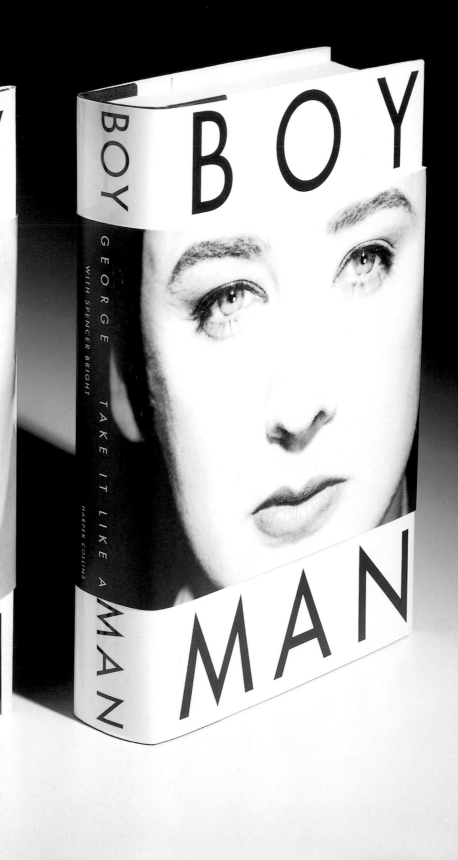

BOY

GEORGE

WITH SPENCER BRIGHT

THE AUTOBIOGRAPHY OF BOY GEORGE

TAKE IT LIKE A

MAN

You come and go.

THE MOMENT I HEARD THE TITLE OF GEORGE O'DOWD'S MEMOIR I KNEW what to do. It was so obvious: somewhere between a boy and a man was Boy George. The idea was that his face would be on a separate wrapper, obscuring the rest of the type so only the two most important words are shown. I felt his image was iconic enough to carry the message. The art director, Joseph Montebello, totally got it and championed it at HarperCollins, which in turn produced an advance reader's edition in hardcover to show how the design would work (oh, those were the days).

And then His Boyness weighed in. Ahem.

I had chosen a Mary Ellen Mark photograph (opposite, left) that had originally run in *Rolling Stone* (we did not have the budget to do a new shoot). I thought it was absolutely right—he was perfectly recognizable, but also clearly beyond his days as a geisha girl for Culture Club. The shot (which I cropped in on tightly) has a poignant dignity and frankness that the book actually does too. Well, George didn't agree (this via his agent—he certainly didn't deign to meet or speak with me). I suspect it was the bags under the eyes that sealed its fate, but that's what makes it such a great picture. You look at it and think "This guy's really been through it." Anyway, somehow a replacement photo magically appeared, by Uli Weber (opposite, right). And that's what they went with. Now, it's not terrible, but in light of the first one it's a damn shame. The gloss and posed sheen belie what he's trying to do in the text, which is come across as an actual person.

OPPOSITE: HarperCollins, 1995. Before and after the author stamped his high heels. **LEFT:** Jacket, with bellyband removed.

EDMUND WHITE
THE BEAUTIFUL ROOM IS
EMPTY
a novel
EDMUND WHITE

In a White room . . .

TO ME THE WORK OF EDMUND WHITE REPRESENTS A BYGONE ERA of meaningful curiosity both intellectual and sexual—a union of the two. *The Beautiful Room Is Empty* is the sequel to *A Boy's Own Story* and satisfies as a successor to that acclaimed 1982 novel, taking the narrator through the 1950s and '60s as he matures as a gay man at the University of Michigan and later in New York. White's discursive style—a modified stream of consciousness that leans luxuriantly and effectively on metaphor and simile—aptly suits this book of memory, never too tightly plotted, but always revelatory of character and milieu as a wise narrator dissects his past and the web of his relationships with family, lovers, and friends. Life in the novel is life as it is remembered, and the two books form the lyrical but politically pointed fictional autobiography of a homosexual recalling his youth, the last years of self-loathing, and the first sweet years of liberation. White's gift for dialogue, anecdote, and a melancholic elegance (often at odds with the narrator's spiteful tone) persuade the reader to reserve judgment as the author suspends time, moving with the protagonist back and forth between past and deeper past—delving deeper inside the soul of a man whose spiritual and sexual odysseys chart his development and joyfully confirm the existence of the elusive notion of what exactly constitutes a "gay sensibility." White's work soars above the genre that has been labeled Gay Fiction. It's great writing, period. **OPPOSITE:** Unused art for *The Beautiful Room Is Empty*. I was still trying to pass myself off as an illustrator-collagist. **RIGHT:** Knopf, 1988. Photo by Christine Rodin. **BELOW:** Promotional postcards.

THE BEAUTiFUL ROOM IS EMPTY

a novel

By the author of A BOY'S OWN STORY

EDMUND WHITE

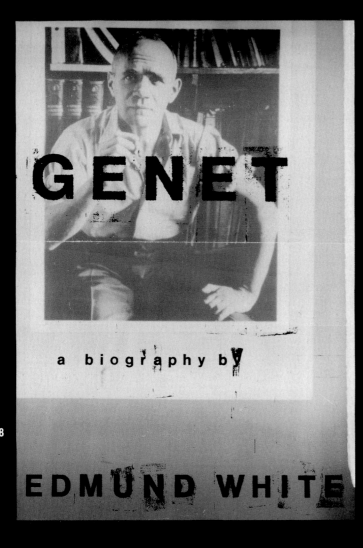

MY FAVORITE CHIP KIDD COVER FOR ONE OF MY BOOKS IS 'GENET'. Kidd apparently saw a very good copy of the Brassaï photo of Genet (taken in the late '40s when Genet was a dandy—notice the monogrammed shirt—after he earned the first real money in his life from his play, *The Maids*) and bought it in a shop in the Hamptons. It was shipped, and when it arrived the glass over it was cracked. It was Kidd's genius to see that the fracture is a perfect echo of Genet's theory that the origin of beauty is always the "blessure," the wound or imperfection that breaks down the obsidian surface of art and allows humanity to come forth.

In St. Paul Minnesota a young man told me that he had bought several of my books. When I thanked him he said, "Oh, it has nothing to do with you. I collect Chip Kidd covers".

—Edmund White

ABOVE: Early, later abandoned, comp. I was trying to do something different with a very familiar image of Genet. **RIGHT:** Knopf, 1993. God bless faulty packing material. Photo of photo by Geoff Spear.

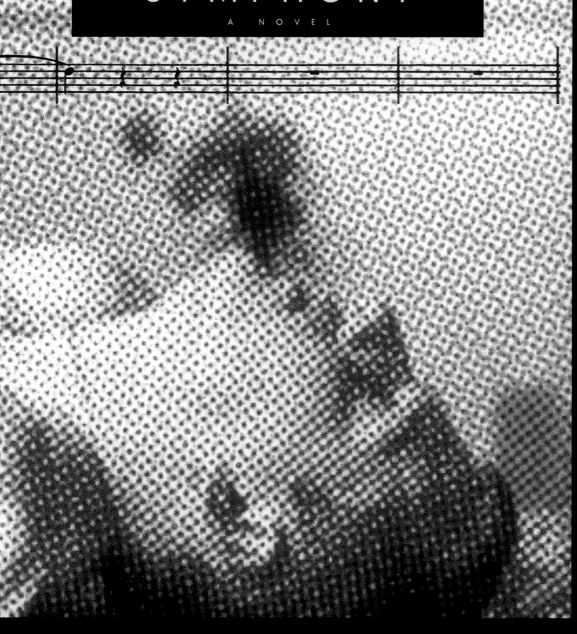

THE FAREWELL SYMPHONY

A NOVEL

EDMUND WHITE

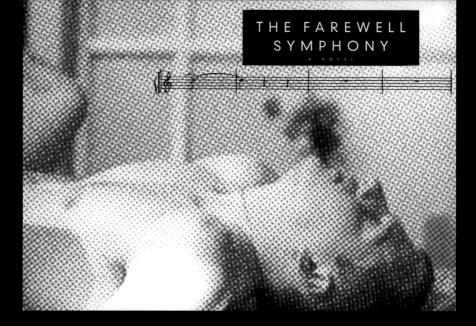

ANOTHER OUTSTANDING COVER KIDD DID FOR ME was the one for *The Farewell Symphony*, a novel that is elegaic (before and after AIDS), highly sexual, and titled after the Haydn symphony in which all the musicians tiptoe off the stage leaving just two violins playing. That's how I thought of outliving all my friends—except in my case it was just a single soloist left playing.

Kidd took a still from a porno film of the past (a pretty blond guy with his legs lifted) and made sure that this sexy image was visible only on the back cover. On the front cover is the boy's head thrown back in profile but reproduced with coarse Benday dots—a cross between pointillism and an over-enlarged photo. Above his head—is he dead? in ecstasy?—are red blotches that could be flowers but are probably blood (that fatal infected blood always associated with AIDS). Finally, four bars of music are reproduced, from a hand-written manuscript. The last two bars are scored but silent, and the first two bars give us just two notes in a treble register. With a few simple symbols Kidd was able to capture all the crucial elements of this extremely complex novel.

—Edmund White

229

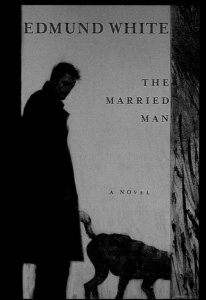

FAR LEFT & ABOVE: Knopf, 1997.
LEFT: Knopf, 2000.

CHRISTOPHER ISHERWOOD

DIARIES

Volume One   1939 – 1960

EDITED AND INTRODUCED BY KATHERINE BUCKNELL

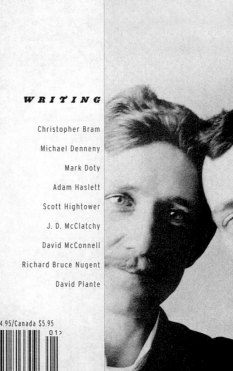

The James White Review

VOL. 16 · NO. 1 · WINTER 1999

WRITING

Christopher Bram

Michael Denneny

Mark Doty

Adam Haslett

Scott Hightower

J. D. McClatchy

David McConnell

Richard Bruce Nugent

David Plante

ART

Barbara Confino

Philip Friedman

Nina Jorgenson

George Platt Lynes

Eric Rhein

Patrick Webb

USA $4.95/Canada $5.95

0 74470 81330 9   01>

AS WITH ANY OTHER GENRE, AVOIDING CLICHÉS FOR GAY-THEMED BOOKS is tricky but mandatory. Partial off-limits list: unnaturally sculpted hairless abs, pecs, and butts; gauzy pastel shots of doe-eyed shirtless youths; Tom of Finland or any drawing remotely evoking his work; rough trade leaning against seedy streetlamps; bandanas dangling from either rear pocket of a stuffed pair of jeans; and (shudder) angels. **LEFT:** HarperCollins, 1996. The clear-eyed immediacy and transparency of Isherwood's diaries is reflected in his radiant gaze. He is the image of a man with nothing to hide. **ABOVE:** Lambda Literary Foundation, 1999. When Patrick Merla assumed the editorship of *The James White Review,* a gay literary magazine of distinction, he asked me to redesign the cover format. A quick scan tells you exactly what you're getting. **OPPOSITE LEFT:** Beacon Press, 2004. When does pornography become something else? In this case, when you crop out the naughty bits. **OPPOSITE RIGHT:** Four Walls, Eight Windows, 1999. Self-portrait supplied by the author. Rick Whitaker had been a colleague at Knopf for years, and when he later asked me to design the cover for his book, he hesitated to tell me what it was about. Imagine my surprise when I read the manuscript and learned of his double life. No wonder he seemed so *tired* all the time.

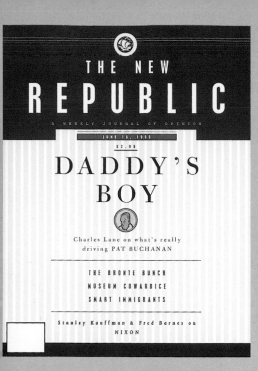

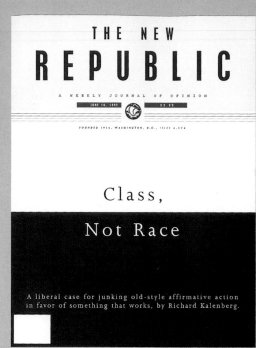

THE NEW REPUBLIC
A WEEKLY JOURNAL OF OPINION
JUNE 16, 1995
$2.95

DADDY'S BOY

Charles Lane on what's really driving PAT BUCHANAN

THE BRONTE BUNCH
MUSEUM COWARDICE
SMART IMMIGRANTS

Stanley Kauffman & Fred Barnes on NIXON

THE NEW REPUBLIC
A WEEKLY JOURNAL OF OPINION
JUNE 16, 1995 $2.95
FOUNDED 1914, WASHINGTON, D.C., ISSUE 4,174

Class, Not Race

A liberal case for junking old-style affirmative action in favor of something that works, by Richard Kalenberg.

Virtually NORMAL

AN ARGUMENT

ABOUT HOMOSEXUALITY

ANDREW SULLIVAN

Your log cabin or mine?

ANDREW SULLIVAN IS AMONG THAT MOST CURIOUS OF SPECIES, a gay conservative. Not to mention a devout Catholic AIDS activist. And a disciple of The Pet Shop Boys (at least *that* makes sense). But he's also one of the smartest people I know and writes about these and other contradictions in his life with such brilliantly argued analysis it ultimately doesn't seem strange at all. As the youngest editor in the history of *The New Republic*, he took that venerable institution of beltway opinion into uncharted territory and made it vital to the national conversation in ways it hadn't been in years. On one of my only two real forays into magazine design (see *The New Yorker*, page 208), I did several covers for him, and was then asked to overhaul the entire weekly itself. The proposal had gone all the way to the final approval stage when Andrew abruptly stepped down from the exhausting rigors of running the magazine and the redesign went with him, alas. I was able to adapt it, how- ever, for the cover of his book *Virtually Normal*, which he wanted to look "like Thomas Paine's *Common Sense* if it were being published today." **OPPOSITE LEFT:** various covers for *The New Republic*. **OPPOSITE RIGHT:** Vintage, 1997. This may not be the strongest cover I've ever designed, but for this subject one just *cannot* show two plastic grooms together on the top of a cake anymore. The Cliché Police have declared that a Class One Felony for the rest of eternity. **ABOVE:** Proposed redesign for *The New Republic*, ultimately adapted into a book jacket, **RIGHT:** Knopf, 1995.

LEFT: Knopf, 1998. **ABOVE:** *The New Republic,* December 20, 1993. I used an actual Batman panel from the 1950s and substituted Robin for Batwoman. I was worried it could cause copyright trouble, but Sullivan LOVED it and ran it without a second thought. I will say this about Andrew: the man is fearless. DC Comics didn't like it at all, surprise surprise, but didn't take any action. After all, they do publish *MAD* magazine. **OPPOSITE:** *The New York Times Magazine,* 1996. This cover for Andrew's story about the hope of the new AIDS drugs accompanied a spread in the inside about how it was conceived, with an interview by art director Janet Froelich. It was unusually great exposure for a graphic designer and all Janet's idea.

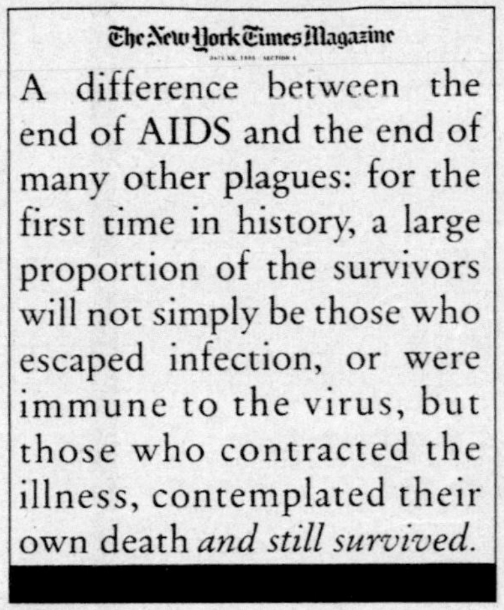

'A difference between the end of AIDS and the end of many other plagues: for the first time in history, a large proportion of the survivors will not simply be those who escaped infection, or were immune to the virus, but those who contracted the illness, contemplated their own death *and still survived*.'

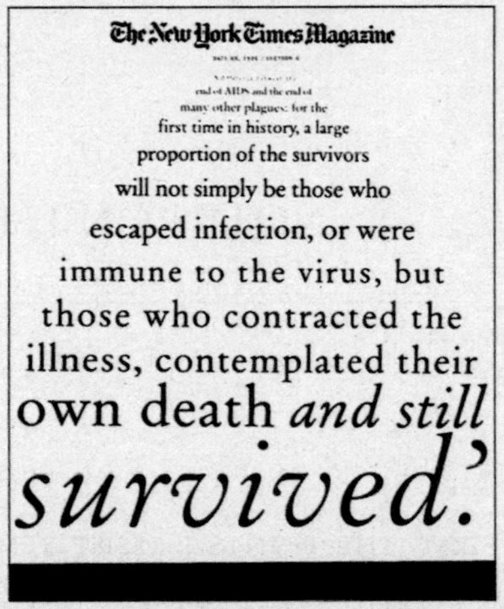

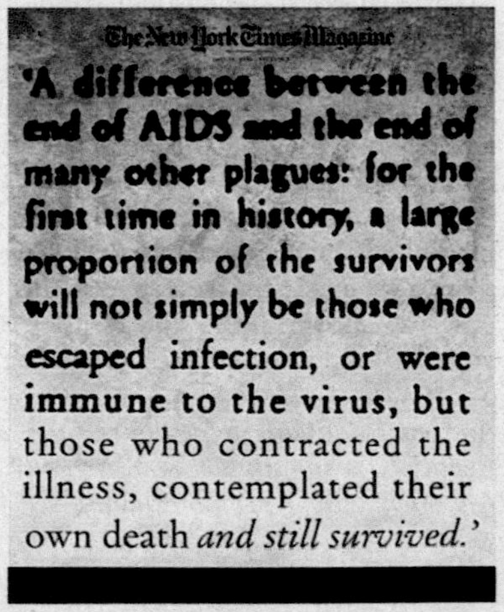

A hopeful solution:
Kidd arrived at the design for this week's cover after two drafts. "The prose was so strong that it became a key. Then it was just a matter of trying to give the text an allegorical vision. It became like a Type 101 solution — make the type do what the type is saying. I thought, What if the type started out sick and then got well?"

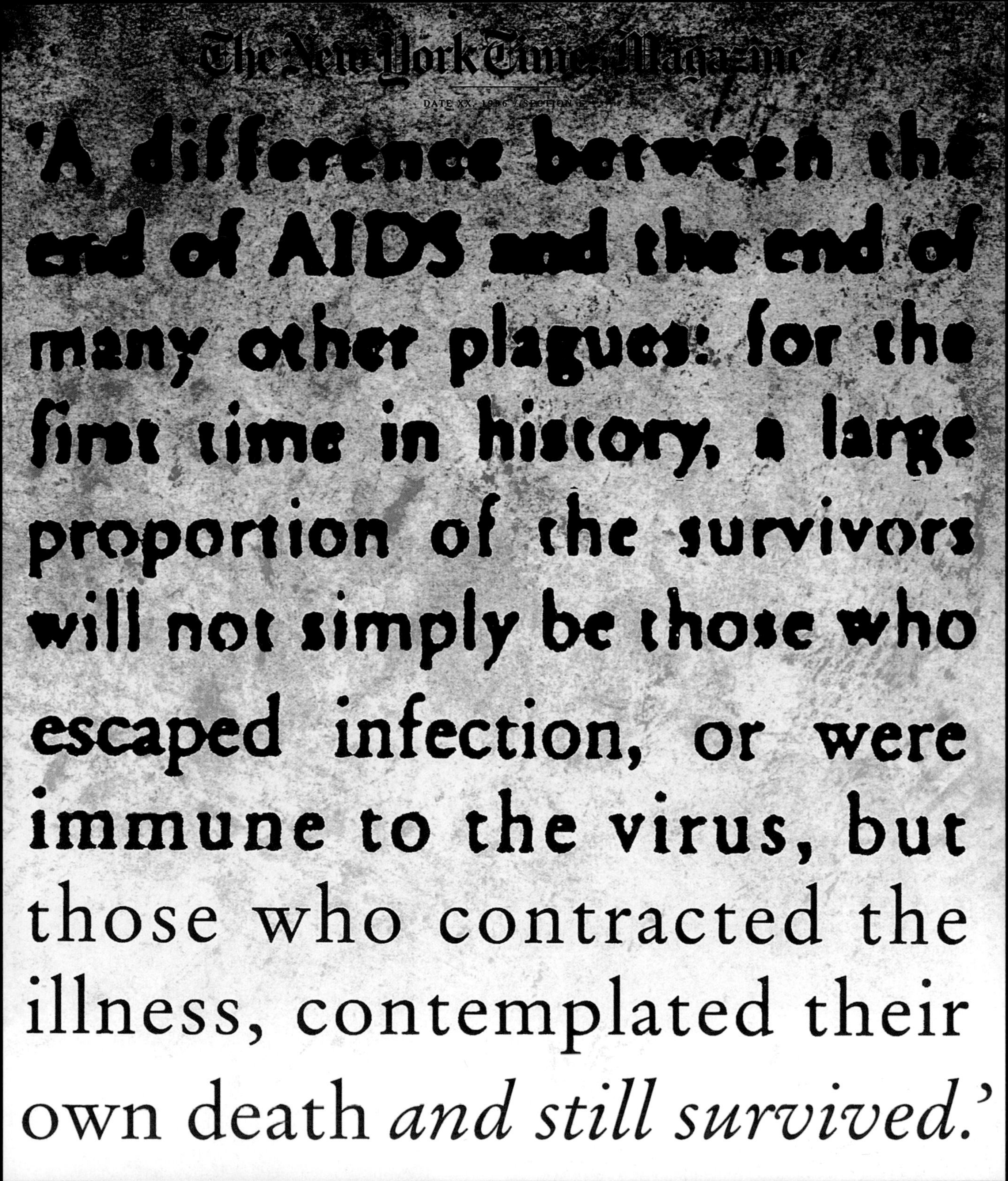

235

THE BEGINNING OF THE END OF AIDS by ANDREW SULLIVAN

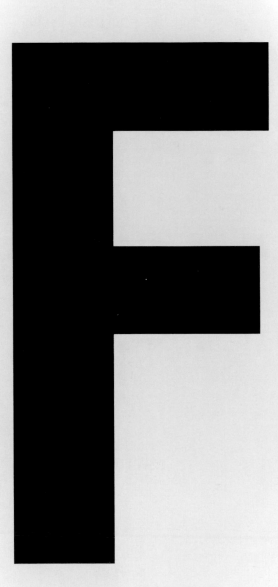

The

F

Word

Edited by Jesse Sheidlower

WITH A FOREWORD BY ROY BLOUNT, JR.

@#&¢$?!

FULLY FOLLOWING INTO THE FLORID FESTOONING FUNCTIONS OF PHONETIC FACULTY, Jesse Sheidlower has made the archaeology of American slang into an art—an unending quest to officially document the evolution of popular speech. A former Knopf editorial assistant, Jesse is the closest thing to a celebrity in the world of popular linguistics, and his efforts to specifically define such terms as "bitch-slap" and "knot-top" allow us to understand just how much the way we talk has changed, for better and worse. Inspiration for my first sketches for his book *The F Word* (an exhaustive compilation of every conceivable permutation of our favorite and feared expletive) came from cigarette ads, which have been regulated to the point of surreality and can't show anyone smoking—or even cigarettes. So I applied the same restrictions here: if you can't say the word, you can show its effect on people, right? Fuck yeah! **ABOVE AND OPPOSITE LEFT:** Unused ideas for *The F Word.* Jesse's name is set in the style of the Surgeon General's warning you find on a box of smokes. These sketches cracked everyone up but were never really taken seriously. The book itself, however, is more than just a novelty—it's culled in part from the *Random House Historical Dictionary of American Slang.* **LEFT:** Random House Reference, 1995. Rather tame considering its content, but it lets you know in no uncertain terms what you're in for, without wearing any of the inherent vulgarity on its sleeve. **OPPOSITE RIGHT:** Granta, 1995. Photograph by Tina Barney.

THE F WORD

EDITED BY: Jesse Sheidlower

The

The

The GRANTA

GRANTA

book of the

book

book

of

of

the

the

Family

Family

GRANTA BOOKS

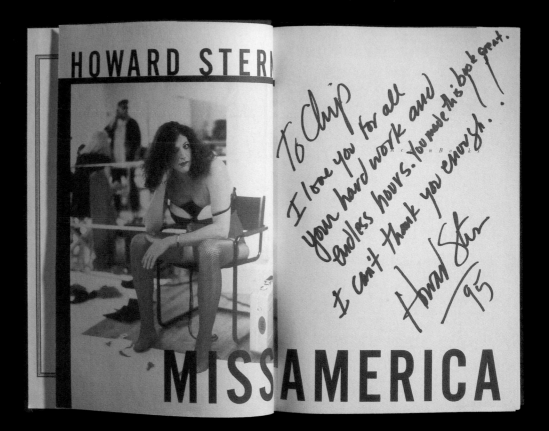

I AM AN AVID HOWARD STERN FAN, AND HAD BEEN FOR YEARS when I was listening in August 1995 as he suddenly announced he was writing a second book, to be published by ReganBooks/HarperCollins—that fall, no less. So I phoned Joseph Montebello and said I'd love to do the cover, if there was any interest. He promised he'd pass that on. A couple of weeks later he called back and said that not only did they want me to do the cover, they wanted me to design the entire book. Whoa. I couldn't—I was just getting to the layout stage for *Batman Collected* and didn't have time to take on an interior of such huge scope. But thanks for asking. Cut to: me in a conference room with Howard and Judith Regan, as they pledged the entire Harper art department at my disposal for the project. This book absolutely HAD to get finished in five weeks, and I was the only one who could do it. WHAT?!! Good GOD. It would take any sane person at least six months to do it properly. Luckily, none of us were sane. Also luckily, it was exactly an 8-minute walk from my office at Knopf to Harper's. So three times a day I made the trip, and for the next month and a half I got about three hours of sleep a night, including weekends. I still don't know how we did it. I figured out the typographic conceit fairly early on—highlighting certain phrases I thought were especially funny or outrageous and setting them in larger bold or italic fonts, so the text read in your head the way Howard sounded on the radio (sans any censorship, by the way). Howard was great to work with, but also constantly rewriting the text as I was designing it, which then meant a lot of redesigning. Nina Gaskin and the rest of the staff at Harper assisted me with expert diligence, and in the mornings we'd sit toiling away while listening to Howard on the radio talk about the fact that we were toiling away on it—totally surreal, and by the end we were all up for 48 hours straight. Ironically, I didn't end up designing the jacket, just the binding (left). Brilliantly and weirdly titled, *Miss America* became one of the bestselling books of all time. And yes, all the Judith Regan stories are true. She MUST be stopped.

THE NEW YORK TIMES BOOK REVIEW

Best Sellers

	This Week	Fiction	Last Week	Weeks On List	This Week	Nonfiction	Last Week	Weeks On List
	1	**THE LOST WORLD,** by Michael Crichton. (Knopf, $25.95.) Scientists visit a Costa Rican jungle that is the breeding ground of dinosaurs; a sequel to "Jurassic Park."	1	8	1	**MISS AMERICA,** by Howard Stern. (Regan Books, $27.50.) Anecdotes and fulminations from the radio talk show host.		

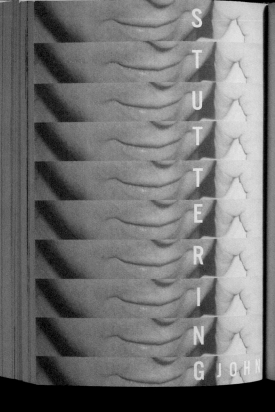

CHAPTER 10

I LOVE STUTTERING JOHN. Who else could take so much abuse from us in the studio and then go out into the real world and get harassed ten times worse? To me, John has *the scariest job imaginable*. He has to approach celebrities and, armed only with a microphone and a list of cleverly engineered questions that we write, **verbally terrorize them** into revealing their true essence to the world.

Twenty years of flapping his tongue and machine-gunning his words is nothing compared to the humiliation John experiences at the hands of the handlers, publicists, security guards, and assorted hangers-on whose very jobs are to preserve the aura of *IMPORTANCE* and *DIGNITY* around the celebrities who are John's prey. **HE'S BEEN SCREAMED AT, PUNCHED, PUSHED, SHOVED, ELBOWED, SPIT ON, SLAPPED IN THE FACE, PICKED UP, THROWN OUT, AND PUSHED DOWN A FLIGHT OF STAIRS.** Yet, like a stammering Energizer bunny, he comes back for more, and more, and more. This year, Stuttering John celebrates his seventh year as our celebrity interviewer. Here are some of his latest achievements.

359

My mother was no King Solomon. That was a shitty solution. A ten-year-old girl and a six-year-old boy don't watch the same shows. Hell, the first thing I did when I had kids was put a TV in each of their rooms. I did that before I got medical insurance. Life's too short. I don't need to teach my kids to watch TV together. Shit, to this day I can't even watch TV with my wife. I want it quiet and I don't want to be hassled during my special shows. *Beverly Hills, 90210* is meant to be viewed alone. In fact, it gives me an opportunity to pretend I'm one of the 90210 gang.

So my mother laid down the law. She said I could have control of the TV for one day and then my sister would have control of the TV for the next day. Every other day I would have to watch love movies instead of Yogi Bear. That was the deal. Okay, sounded fair. So I went downstairs to watch Yogi the next morning, and it was my sisters day, but I wanted to watch my bear cartoons. I begged my sister.

"Please let me watch my fucking bear cartoons," I cried.

"No," my selfish sister said, "it's my day."

So I whined some more and finally she said. "Okay, you can watch your RETARDED cartoon today if you let me watch whatever I want for a year."

Now, I was six years old and I was not the swift negotiator I am today. So I agreed. I had no idea what a year was. Of course I gave my tricky sister a year of TV so I could watch Yogi that day, because I thought a year was like two days. I was six years old!

Six months went by. I got fed up with the arrangement and I blew my stack. I hadn't seen Yogi in ages. I ran up to my mother crying and whining and I told her that my sister tricked me. I explained the whole situation to her. I defended myself like a professional attorney. I was a regular F. U. Bailey.

"Ma," I whined. "I'm only six. I didn't know what a year was. She tricked me." You know what my mother said to me? My mother said, "Howard, you made a deal and you can't go back on your word. You have to watch whatever your sister wants."

My mother must have been **SMOKING HEROIN** because she made as much sense as Courtney Love backstage at the MTV Awards. If she'd been thinking clearly, she would have

hauled my sister's ass upstairs and told her that fooling a six-year-old was a dirty, rotten trick. It was dishonest for my sister to take advantage of a baby. But my mother made a dumb-ass decision. Just like that. There was no court of appeals. No arbitration. Boom. A dopey, illogical decision with no recourse. By the time I got to see Yogi again I was too old to enjoy him. This is what I call getting a good ass fucking by a wiseguy. *My sister and my mother fucked me in the ass.*

So, what's my point? I don't know. I knew I had a point; I just don't remember it. I'll go eat something and see if I remember my point.

Okay, I'm back. I just ate diet pizza. My wife bought a vegetable pizza with no cheese and whole wheat dough. Fucking yuppie pizza. No cheese, just tomato sauce and a bunch of vegetables. It tasted good, damnit! If it tastes good, it must be bad for you. Now I'm all freaked out that I ate something FATTENING. I'm obsessing on how I shouldn't have eaten it, Fuck it. So I'll be fat. **It's not like I have to look good for anybody. I'm married.**

Anyway, halfway through this New Age pizza I remembered my point. The point is I'm still getting fucked in the ass, but this time it's by five guys I don't even know. I can't even tell you their names or what they look like. I'M GETTING GANG RAPED BY FIVE OLD MEN and their dicks are going in dry and *my bunghole is bleeding.* I'm getting the worst ass fucking in history. It's happening in front of the world and no one will help me.

Everyone knows about my stupid rape. In fact, they report about it on TV and in the newspaper. I'M TALKING ABOUT THESE SHITHEADS ON THE FCC. Five of the worst human beings Satan has ever created. Five pricks who insist on *ending my livelihood* because . . . because, I have no idea why. Maybe it's because they can't stand that their jobs are boring, dull, and meaningless. These guys were probably the dweebs who dreamt of stardom way back in college radio but failed. By fining me, they'd see their names in print, a last shot at doing something that would

432   433

ALL INTERIOR SPREADS: ReganBooks/HarperCollins, 1995. **OPPOSITE BOTTOM RIGHT:** *The New York Times* Best-Sellers List, November 26, 1995. The first and only time this ever happened—titles I've worked on, fiction and non-fiction, both at #1. **BELOW:** *The New York Times Book Review*, December 10, 1995. Design historian Steven Heller reviewed it not as a celebrity book, but as typographic experimentation.

RICHARD JOHNSON   NEAL TRAVIS   LIZ SM...

...day: New York's best gossip columnists every day in The P...

NEW YORK POST

LATE CITY FINAL

...DAY, SEPTEMBER 3, 1995 / Sunny and pleasant both days, 75-80 / Details, Page 22 ••

HOWARD PAYS $1.7M

Howard Stern

Shock jock's boss settles FCC indecency charges for cash

See Page 3

EXTORTION

HOW THE U.S. GOVERNMENT

FUCKS

YOU AND ME

MAKE IT IN UNMARKED BILLS IN A PLAIN PAPER BAG PLACED IN A TRASH CAN OUTSIDE 1919 M STREET, WASHINGTON, D.C.

You ever get fucked in the ass by a wiseguy? I don't mean literally. Well, if you *did* literally get fucked in the ass, I'd be interested in hearing about it because I need to learn more about this amazing phenomenon. No way that LITTLE EXIT should be able to handle *a big, full cock* and yet it does. That kind of butt fucking is interesting, and maybe in my next book I'll devote a chapter to it. In this particular instance I'm talking about a different kind of butt fuck. I'm asking you, has anyone ever screwed with you real bad when you were 100 percent in the right and you still couldn't win? When you were absolutely 100 percent not guilty and **you lost anyway?**

I'll give you an example of what I'm talking about: I have a friend who's been going through a divorce for two years. They are arguing over child custody and money. She hired lawyers and private detectives but her husband keeps hiring more lawyers and outspending her and then she has to turn around and hire more lawyers and more private detectives. Her legal bill is now

429

Many people already know everything there is to know about the contents of Howard Stern's **MISS AMERICA (Regan Books, $27.50),** the cover of which shows Mr. Stern in drag on the front and in a tuxedo hobnobbing with O. J. Simpson on the back. Inside, the jacket tells us, you'll find details of Mr. Stern's secret meeting with Michael Jackson and his pact with Adolf Hitler, as well as 40 pictures of naked breasts, so there is little point in discussing the literary merits here. But what readers may take for granted is the book's design, a complex mélange of typographic hierarchies. It is a remarkable display of deconstructive, post-structural, post-modern experimentation — or to put it simply for the layman, words explode across the page. The text and binding were designed by Chip Kidd and Nina Gaskin; the jacket and the inserted color section were designed by Jack Heller (no relation) and Ralph Cirella. Each of the 482 pages is a distinct design experience. But this kind of expressive typography is not new. In 1918 Guillaume Apollinaire published an antiwar poem, "Il Pleut," with lines of type falling down the page simulating a rainstorm; in 1914 F. T. Marinetti wrote and designed the Futurist book "Zang Tumb Tuuuum," using discordant typefaces designed to visually approximate the sounds that he described in words; and in 1967 Quentin Fiore gave a visual voice to Marshall McLuhan's "Medium Is the Massage" through a rebuslike integration of word and image complemented by shifts in typographic size and weight. In 1970 Mr. Fiore brought the same kinetic type and page design to Jerry Rubin's book "Do It!," to which "Miss America" owes a distinct debt. Unfortunately, "Miss America" really doesn't go as far as some of these books. While the design shouts and screams, by the standards of other 20th-century books it is actually pretty timid.

STEVEN HELLER

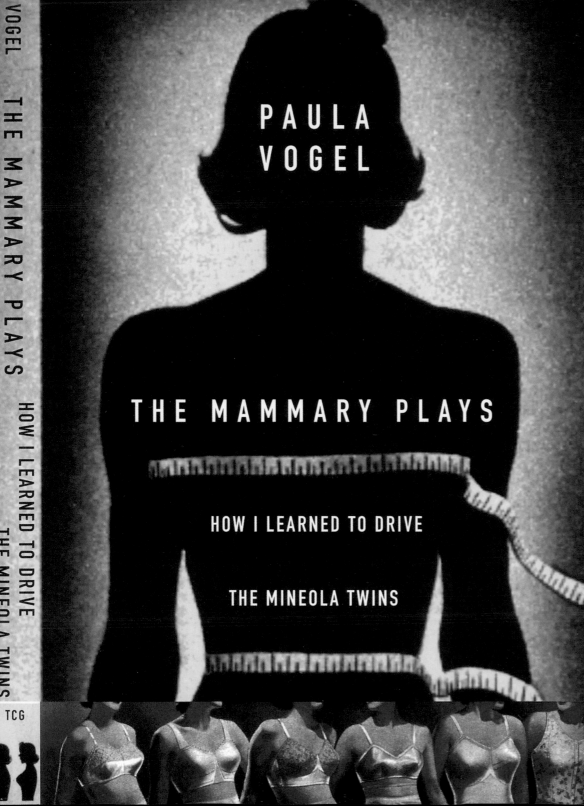

PAULA
VOGEL

THE MAMMARY PLAYS

HOW I LEARNED TO DRIVE

THE MINEOLA TWINS

MEASURE

It's
S A

Are You Short, Averag

We consider you SHORT if you are 5 feet 2 inche
feet 3 inches to 5 feet 6 inches; TALL if you are ov
height without shoes. You will note in the descriptio
down. To determ

$1.00 VALUES
FOR
69¢
Any Two
for $1.35

SKINNER PURE DYE SILK SATIN BRA ↑
Beautifully made, perfect fitting Bandeau . . . designed for the average size bust. You'd pay
$1.00 or more elsewhere. Molds sleekly to the fig-
ure; gives proper uplift; accents youthful lines.
Light weight and comfortable, it's all fine quality
Pure Dye Skinner Satin and net lined lace. Adjust-
able straps. Hooks back.

BIAS CUT BARGAIN ↑
Fine Cotton Faille, cut on
the bias to raise and mold
your bust. Correct for small
and average size bust. Elastic front insert. Tapered self-
material shoulder straps.
Hooks back.

EXQUISITE LACE ↑
Perfect fitting, nicely shaped
Bra for average size bust.
Rich pure Dye Skinner Satin
diaphragm band and back—
net lined bust section. Hooks
in back.

EVENING GLAMOUR!
Bias cut Bandeau of Skinner
Silk Satin, for small to average bust. Grand for day or
night wear with low back
dresses. Elastic band goes
round body, fastens in front.

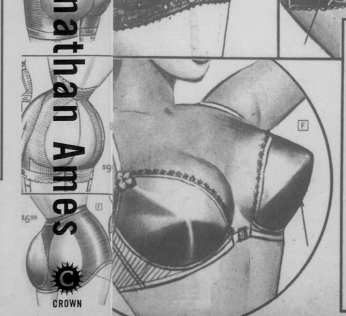

WHAT'S NOT TO LOVE?

By the author of THE EXTRA MAN

Jonathan Ames

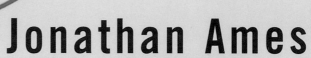

241

WHAT'S NOT TO LOVE? Jonathan Ames

The
Adventures
of a
Mildly
Perverted
Young
Writer

CROWN

C. I. K. & T. + A.

ALL RIGHT, SO A NICE SET OF MILKBAGS IS NOT EXACTLY MY THING, but as a professional graphic designer it's my duty to serve the subject matter, and sometimes that means getting yer ya-yas out, as the Stones used to say. For the projects on these pages, the only obscenity would be to deny their carnal origins. And there *is* a way to do it without raising the ire of the FCC. At least for now. One approach is to play up the absurdity of America's often contradictory attitudes toward sex. **OPPOSITE LEFT:** TCG, 1998. Source material: Sears catalogue circa the 1940s. Check out the tiny "Before and After" at the base of the spine. *How I Learned to Drive*, by the way, won the Pulitzer Prize and was one of the best plays I saw in the 1990s. **RIGHT:** Crown, 2000. I've often concluded that Jonathan Ames is me if I were straight. You'll have to read the book to understand what exactly that means. God knows I'm not going into it here.

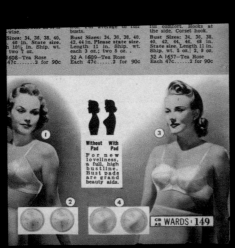

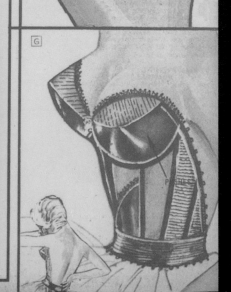

MY MOTHER: DEMONOLOGY, a novel
by KATHY ACKER

Sexual Slang

A COMPENDIUM OF OFFBEAT WORDS
AND COLORFUL PHRASES
FROM SHAKESPEARE TO TODAY

Alan Richter, Ph.D.

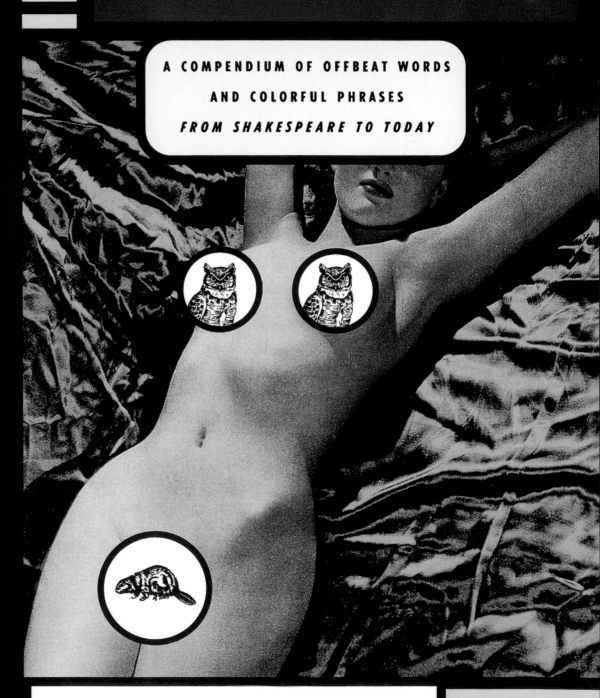

Sexual Slang

A COMPENDIUM OF OFFBEAT WORDS
AND COLORFUL PHRASES
FROM SHAKESPEARE TO TODAY

Roye, England, ca. 1940

Alan Richter, Ph.D.

Hooters and *what*?

SEX, SEX, SEX. THAT'S ALL ANYONE THINKS ABOUT. Let's talk about annuities. An annuity is a contract sold by an insurance company designed to provide payments to the holder at specified intervals, usually after retirement. The holder is taxed only when they start taking distributions or if they withdraw funds from the account. All annuities are tax-deferred, meaning that the earnings from investments in these accounts grow tax-deferred until withdrawal. Annuity earnings are also tax-deferred so they cannot be withdrawn without penalty until a certain specified age. Fixed annuities guarantee a certain payment amount, while variable annuities do not, but do have the potential for greater returns. Both are relatively safe, low-yielding investments. An annuity has a death benefit equivalent to the higher of the current value of the annuity or the amount the buyer has paid into it. If the owner dies during the accumulation phase, his or her heirs will receive the accumulated amount in the annuity. This money is subject to ordinary income taxes in addition to estate taxes. In the mood yet? **OPPOSITE LEFT:** Pantheon, 1993, co-designed with Barbara deWilde. Marjorie Anderson, art director. Watch where you step. **OPPOSITE RIGHT AND RIGHT:** HarperCollins, 1995. Joseph Montebello, art director. My idea was a cover for each sex, and the publisher proofed both, but finally went to press with only the female version. The male freaked out the sales force—which only proves Maggie Paley's point (overleaf): penises, even when only hinted at, are the last taboo! **ABOVE:** My original source material, which was returned by the Coral Graphics's scanning department after seven years.

PRAISE

Andrew McGahan

PRAISE

"The most sexually explicit book to win
The Australian/Vogel Literary Award." — *Elle*

Andrew
McGahan

Carroll
& Graf

THE
BOOK
OF THE
PENIS

Maggie
Paley

ABOVE: Carroll & Graf, 1993. I took the photograph myself, of an empty pair of jeans (thank you very much) using continuous-tone paper on our trusty—and long-retired—stat camera. **RIGHT:** Grove Press, 1999. Confession: this is actually an ivy leaf plucked from my terrace. Even in Manhattan, fig leaves are in staggeringly short supply. Hey, it's not like anyone noticed, or complained.

You're an animal, Viskovitz

a novel

Alessandro Boffa

Father's Day

A NOVEL BY

PHILIP GALANES

You're an ANIMAL, Viskovitz!

ALESSANDRO BOFFA

TRANSLATED BY JOHN CASEY

ABOVE: Fun in the wild kingdom! Where's Marlon Perkins when you need him? These initial ideas for Alessandro Boffa's whimsical yet biologically accurate stories about mating rituals among animals horrified all who saw them. And so . . . **LEFT:** Knopf, 2002. Illustration by Roz Chast. The Goddess of *New Yorker* cartooning to the rescue! She was great to work with and totally came through. **RIGHT:** Knopf, 2004. Photo by Geoff Spear. This absorbing novel of a gay man's reckoning with his father's suicide features the covert purchase of a yellow cashmere cable-knit sweater. Which gave me a great excuse to buy one. So then I did a little research and found an outfit in the midwest that did custom label-making. No sooner had I faxed in my order than a very sweet but concerned sales rep frantically called and said: "We make labels for sweaters, not novels. You realize that, don't you?" I said, "Not in this case, ma'am," and explained. Then she said "All right, you can have it in six weeks." A month and a half? Yikes! Me: "Isn't there a way to get it faster?" "Yes, but it will cost you." "How much?" A beat. "Well, let's see . . . ," she demurred, as I waited for five figures, "uh . . . five dollars." I said, "Hmmm, I think we can swing that."

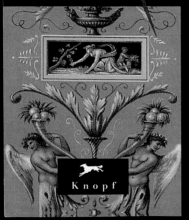

The
Marquis
de Sade

A LIFE

Neil Schaeffer

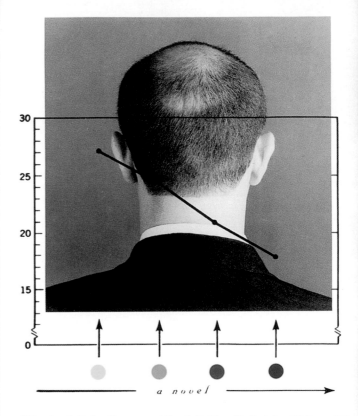

a novel

"Equal parts Kafka, Burgess, and *Brazil*, Matthew Stadler's beautifully morbid novel...smoothly weaves in and out of grandiosity, fantasy, and sentiment with rare grace and cleverness." — *Village Voice*

Matthew Stadler

THE DISSOLUTION
OF NICHOLAS DEE

Matthew Stadler

author of THE SEX OFFENDER

"If this apocalyptic and darkly humorous work is any indication Stadler looks to be a Pynchon-in-the-making."
— *L.A. Weekly*

THE HEART WANTS WHAT THE HEART WANTS. And then there's the rest of the anatomy. Books about sexual deviance have to be dealt with carefully or they'll just look like porn. Not that there's anything wrong with porn, but this is, ahem, *literature* we're talking about. **OPPOSITE LEFT:** Knopf, 1999. The slashes were debossed—subtlety is all. **OPPOSITE RIGHT, TOP:** HarperCollins, 1994. This is the un-mug shot, which gives the title character a sense of humanity as well as mystique. **OPPOSITE RIGHT, BOTTOM:** HarperCollins, 1995. **BELOW:** Knopf, 2003. Houellebecq is notorious in France and throughout Europe, less so here. My favorite line from *Platform:* "Our genitals exist as a source of permanent, accessible pleasure." Yay!! Photo by Arno Rafael Minkkinen. **RIGHT:** Knopf, 2000. The eyes belong to the author himself.

PLATFORM

A NOVEL

MICHEL
HOUELLEBECQ

THE
E
LEMENTARY
PARTICLES

MICHEL

HOUELLEBECQ

KNOPF

MICHEL HOUELLEBECQ

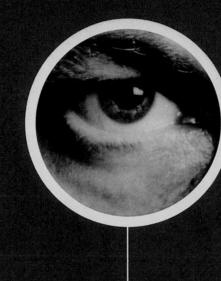

A NOVEL

THE ELEMENTARY
PARTICLES

THE SPECTACLE OF THE BODY

NOY HOLLAND

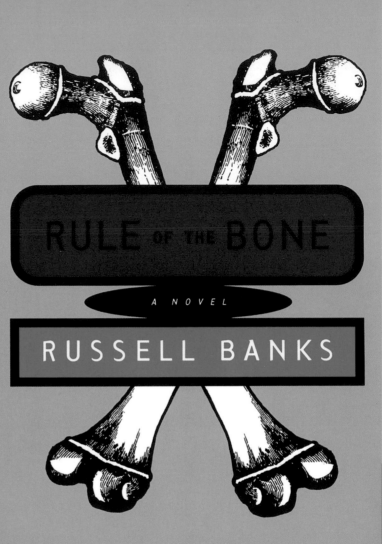

RULE OF THE BONE

A NOVEL

RUSSELL BANKS

Birds - Finch

The gist of the titles.

SOMETIMES CERTAIN KINDS OF BOOK TITLES GRAB THE ZEITGEIST and don't let go. I remember we once published books called *The Heart of the World* and *In the Heart of the Whole World*, both in the same year. One was fiction and one was not, so it wasn't considered a conflict. But sometimes it can be, and then something's got to give. This can even happen at the last minute—no title is set in stone, and of course subtitles change *all* the time and can derail many a carefully constructed typographic scheme. It's almost shocking when it doesn't happen. **LEFT:** Knopf, 1994. Art by James Fish. I added the peg board. **ABOVE LEFT:** HarperCollins, 1995. *Rule of the Bone* certainly captured the spirit of mid-'90s America: its self-destructive yet emotionally vulnerable (and, yes, tatooed) 14-year-old narrator slacked onto the scene shortly after Kurt Cobain's suicide and the overall pessimism following the economic recession of the early '90s. **ABOVE RIGHT:** Source material from The New York Public Library. **OPPOSITE LEFT:** Knopf, 1994. This amazing chronicle of evolution in our time won the Pulitzer Prize.

THE **BEAK**
OF THE **FINCH**

A STORY OF EVOLUTION
IN OUR TIME

JONATHAN WEINER

CAROLINE BLACKWOOD'S STORY OF THE LAST DAYS of the Duchess of Windsor (right) isn't really about Wallace Warfield Simpson Windsor at all. It's about deception. In 1980 the *Sunday Times* asked Blackwood to pen a feature on the most famous divorcée of the 20th century. She tried for months to gain access to the reportedly ailing, bedridden duchess and was road-blocked every time by Maître Suzanne Blum, the formidable and creepily controlling lawyer who was Simpson's legal guardian. Blum's bizarre claims that the duchess was "in the pink of health," made it all the more frustrating. As the result of this aristocratic *Whatever Happened to Baby Jane* scenario, Blackwood, who never did get an audience with her intended subject, ultimately concluded that Blum was holding the duchess more or less prisoner in her own palatial home in the Bois de Boulogne. For the jacket I blurred the portrait of Simpson so she is recognizable but remote, and placed a sliver of Blum's face on the spine, as if she's opened a slot in a locked door and is hissing at you to go away. **RIGHT:** Pantheon, 1995.

PANTHEON

CAROLINE BLACKWOOD

The Last of the Duchess

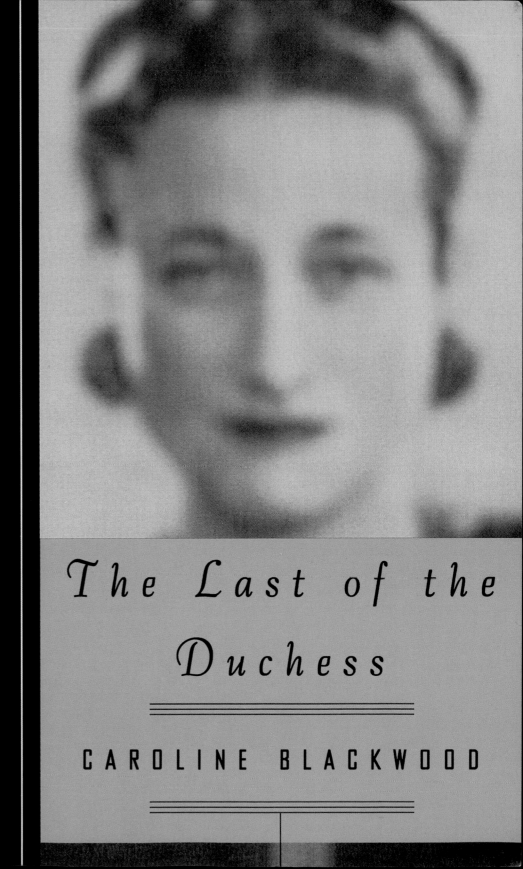

The Last of the

Duchess

CAROLINE BLACKWOOD

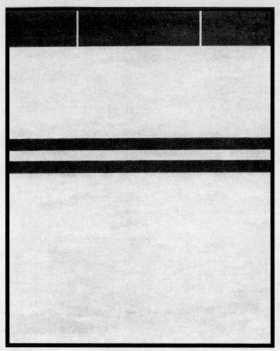

Cobweb Gray No. 8820

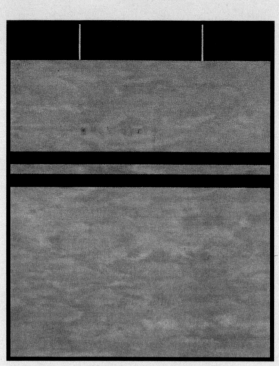

Elfin Green No. 8821

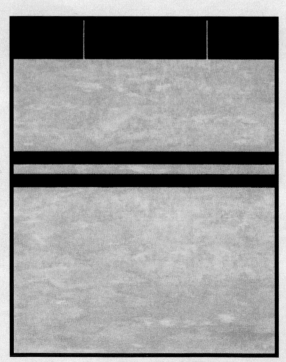

Daisy Yellow No. 8822

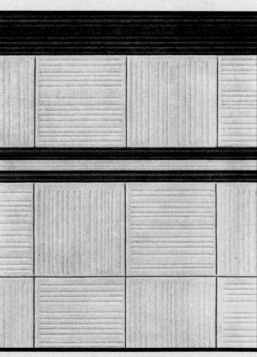

Gray No. 8842

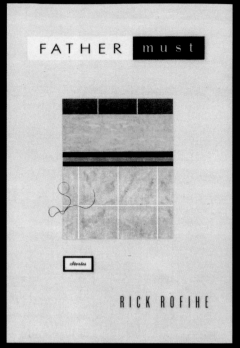

Recycling begins at home.

AT SOME POINT IT OCCURRED TO ME—LINOLEUM PATTERNS were book jackets waiting to happen, and a freelance job from FSG for a collection of stories called *Father Must* seemed the perfect opportunity to test the theory. I created an amalgam of patterns and set it among a pristinely ordered layout of serif, sans serif, and script type. Then I violated the entire thing with a nasty, curly hair (this symbolized some sort of indiscretion described in the story—I can't for the life of me remember what). So I sent it in with high hopes. Well, it was not "a wow," as art director Doris Janowitz used to say. Which meant bill a kill fee. Oh well. And then another collection of stories came along at Knopf, a Gordon Lish book (surprise surprise) called *City of Boys*. I read it and thought "Hmm. The linoleum-and-hair thing could work for this. What's the harm?" So with no one the wiser I copied *Father Must* inch for inch, with the difference that I substituted a piece of hair that looked like it came from someone's head rather than . . . somewhere else. Gordon loved it. Of *course* he did—it was really weird. I got the approval on this early enough to take on the interior design of the book too and follow the whole thing through. **LEFT:** Source material, from a 1950s Armstrong linoleum catalogue. **ABOVE LEFT:** Origin of the idea, for a freelance job at FSG. Rejected. **ABOVE RIGHT:** Proposed 1993 redesign for *ID* magazine (designed with Barbara deWilde) featuring linoleum on the front. We didn't get the job, and I was starting to wonder if linoleum was cursed. **OPPOSITE LEFT:** Knopf, 1992. Success! It was fun watching people trying to rub the hair off. **OPPOSITE RIGHT:** Knopf, 1997. Photograph by Kristine Larsen. Behind this cover lies the most uncanny story: I had the *Live Girls* manuscript for all of two weeks when a promotional postcard with this photograph magically appeared in my mailbox. Just add author's name and "a novel." Done! The design gods have smiled on us!

CITY of boys

Stories

BETH NUGENT

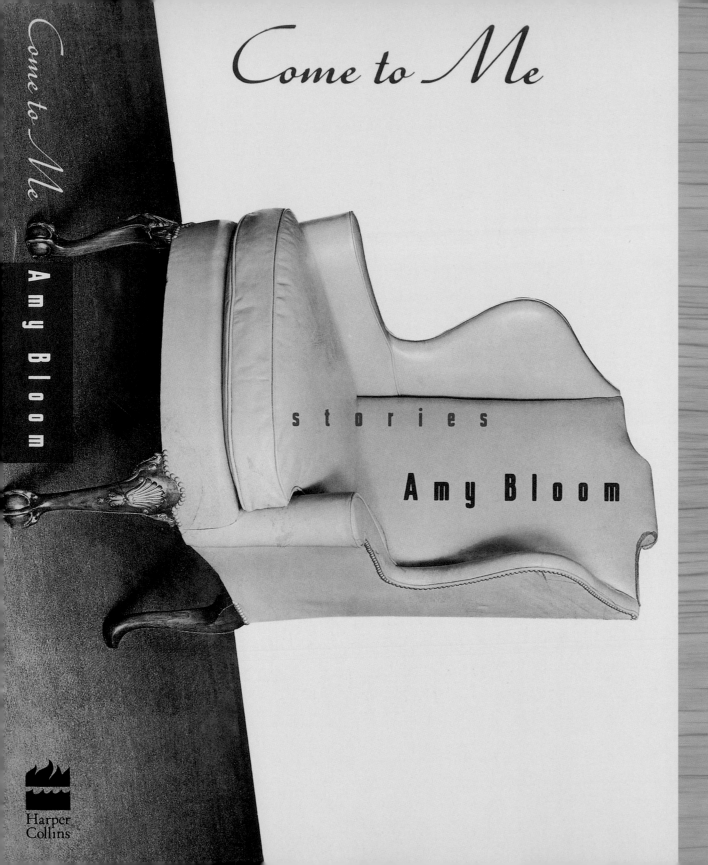

Come to Me

Come to Me

Come to Me

Amy Bloom

s t o r i e s

Amy Bloom

Harper Collins

Harper Collins

I HAD NEVER HAD A COVER BEFORE. I HAD NEVER HAD A BOOK BEFORE.
I didn't even give a damn about book covers until I had one of my own.
Then it was like pregnancy or marriage or infidelity; if it's on your screen,
you see it everywhere.

The first two times I read my work aloud, I was surprised when people
asked if my having been a psychotherapist had influenced my fiction. I
didn't know why they asked. I said that there was no connection. I went
around saying that there was no connection for a while, and then I looked
at my book jacket. The chair on the cover was the exact replica of the
two in my office: a beige wingback armchair, set at just that angle to the
wall, as on the cover. But on the cover, the chair is sideways, which star-
tled everyone but me. And scattered on the cover are mysterious pencil
marks, signs of things erased, signals half-understood, notations either
just coming or just going. I don't understand the connection any better
than I did, but I don't say there isn't any anymore.

—**Amy Bloom**

I FOUND THE IMAGE FOR AMY BLOOM'S 'COME TO ME' in a dumpster on
the street in the East Village in the late 1980s. Someone had thrown
out a whole stack of 1930s-vintage product shots of stuffed furniture.
Fabulous. That sort of thing just doesn't happen much any more—not
only is there a dearth of good stuff as time goes on, but once you turn
30, dumpster diving becomes kind of sad, like finishing the drinks of
strangers left behind in restaurants and banquets when no one is looking. Anyway, this is the first time I tried tilting an image at 90° to produce a disorienting effect (and it would not be the last). I agree with
Amy—it *does* look perfectly natural. It's certainly worthy of analysis.

Sandra Bernhard loved the contrast between jackets for two collections
of her humor essays ("Like night and day!" or something like that). You
have to give her credit for allowing me to crop her image so severely
on *May I Kiss You on the Lips, Miss Sandra?* and downplay the title. But
even she understood: who else could it be?

LEFT: HarperCollins, 1993. **OPPOSITE LEFT, TOP:** I sit calmly by while
Sandra shrieks at someone during the party for *May I Kiss You on the
Lips, Miss Sandra?*, at Mercer Kitchen in Soho, 1998. **OPPOSITE LEFT,
BOTTOM:** HarperCollins, 1993. Photo by Melanie Acevedo. **OPPOSITE
RIGHT:** Rob Weisbach Books, 1998. Photo by Moshe Brakha.

May I kiss you on the lips, Miss Sandra?

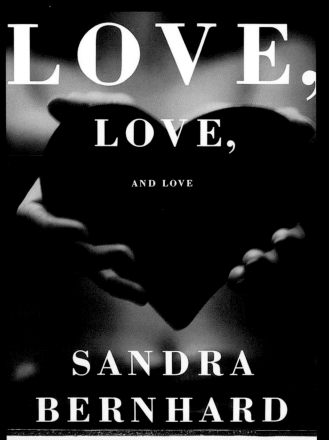

LOVE,
LOVE,
AND LOVE

SANDRA
BERNHARD

AUTHOR OF *CONFESSIONS OF A PRETTY LADY*

Sandra Bernhard

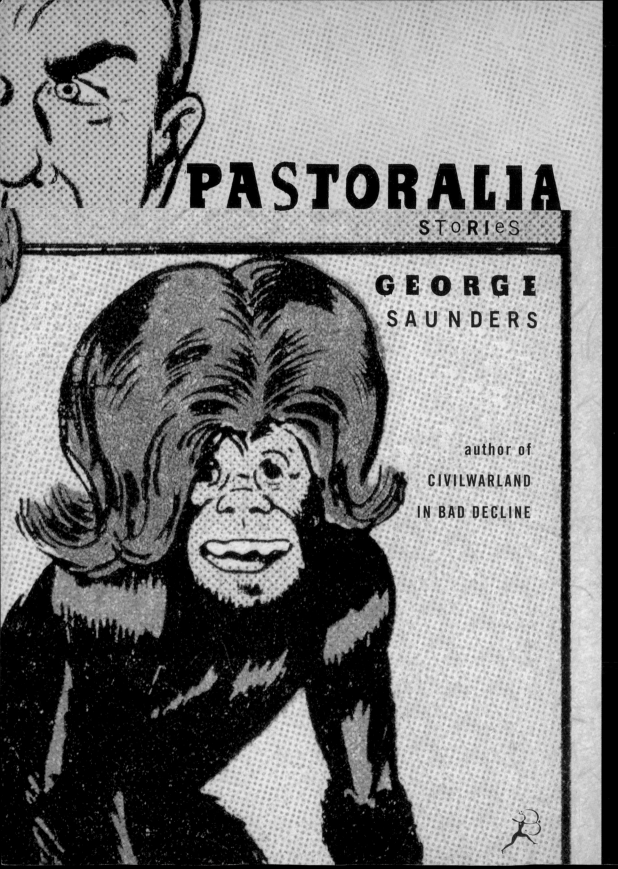

PASTORALIA

STORIES

GEORGE SAUNDERS

author of
CIVILWARLAND
IN BAD DECLINE

LEFT: Bloomsbury (UK), 2000. I first read the title story from *Pastoralia* when it was under consideration for *The New Yorker*'s Summer 1999 Fiction Issue, which I art directed (see p. 209). Deftly combining hilarity and abject dispair, the story weaves the tale of a prehistoric theme park as seen from the eyes of two of its denizens: a pair of down-at-heel strangers who in order to survive are forced to take on the roles of caveman and cavewife for the amusement of tourists. One of the art researchers at the magazine suggested these drawings (both, below) from an old *Daktari* book. Reconfigured, I thought they would be perfect. Unfortunately, a shorter piece by Saunders was selected for the issue because of limited space. But I'd filed the images away in my memory, and a

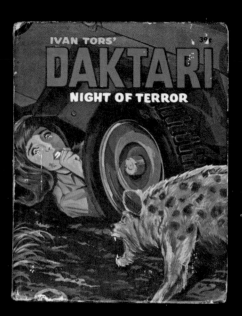

year later when George called out of the blue and asked me to design the jacket for the collection, I knew what the solution was before the phone hit the cradle. I went online, found the book on eBay, won it for pennies, had a ball putting the design together, sent it to George, and he loved it. A happy ending, right?

WRONG. THE PUBLISHER HATED IT, and fought George like a stuck mastodon. When he enlisted the aid of his agent, she sided with the publisher. They hired someone else, and we were defeated. A crappy ending, right? Not quite. In a very neat end-run trick, George then proposed the cover directly to his UK publisher for their edition, and it was saved. Let it forever be said: Bloomsbury knows a good monkey in a scarlet wig when they see one.

60   DAKTARI

with rage. "*That* does it! I'm going to lock you up in a cage until Doctor Tracy gets back!"

Laughter died on the chimp's lips and, pawing awkwardly at the wig, she backed away from the screen door. No one was going to lock *her* in a cage!

"Paula!" shouted Jack as he brushed the dust from his trousers. "Help me corner this confounded pet of yours!"

Paula, sudsing a baby elephant in a nearby pen, put down her

A Redheaded Chimp

SLACKJAW

S
L
A
C
K
J
A
W

NIPFEL

SLACK JAW

JIM KNIPFEL

RCHER
UTNAM

AT FIRST I DIDN'T KNOW WHAT TO MAKE OF THE FACT that people usually had more to say about the covers of my books than about anything that was actually written inside. "I picked it up off the shelf because of the cover," they'll tell me, or "It caught my eye from across the store," or "What the hell's that cover all about?" I've even read reviews that spent more time analyzing the cover art than the prose.

Over time I've come to accept it, and even breathe the occasional sigh of relief when it happens. If they're raving about the cover, that means they're not saying mean things about the clunky writing or incoherent storyline. This can be a very nasty business, and I'm perfectly willing to take what I can get. People, after all, do judge books by their covers (and, I'm tempted to believe, are often absolutely justified in doing so). You can put a brilliant cover on an awful book and sell millions. Likewise, put a lousy cover on a brilliant book and it'll be on the remainder table faster than you can spit.

Consider this: how many book covers have you seen over the past several years featuring a watercolor or blurry photograph of a bunch of pine trees around a lake? A lot of them, right? And how many of those books have you felt compelled to read? Not too many of them, certainly. Why? Because it's clear that any book with blurry pine trees and a lake on the cover is boring crap. Yet for some reason, publishers continue to release books with that same damn image on the cover. That should tell you something. When my first book was coming together, I told my editor, "I don't care what's on the cover, so long as it's not pine trees and a lake." (It wasn't, and as it happens Chip's design for that book won awards.)

See, for better or for worse, book covers are the masks (one of several, but certainly the most obvious) that we authors hide behind. Like masks, they can hide the true identity, misdirect the unwary, or, in the case of the best masks, they can be so revealing, so true to the spirit of the words inside that you might never recognize it until you've finished reading.

Not to blow sunshine here, but that's the trick which has always made Chip's cover designs so masterful. Potential readers can look at the covers he's done for some of my books (for instance) and ask "Why is that monkey wearing a hat and smoking a cigar?" Or "Why is there a fire-breathing lizard next to a map of Alaska and a guy in a fedora?" But then if they actually bother to sit down and read the damn thing, they'll be able to go back to the cover and say, "Oh"—realizing only too late that they'd been told everything they need to know about the book long before reading the first sentence.

—Jim Knipfel

LEFT: Tarcher Putnam, 1999. Photo by Marc Yankus. The jacket for this memoir by a writer who is slowly and steadily losing his eyesight is blind-stamped with the legend "You better start learning Braille now." I know that seems mean, but at least Jim will always be able to read the cover one way or another.

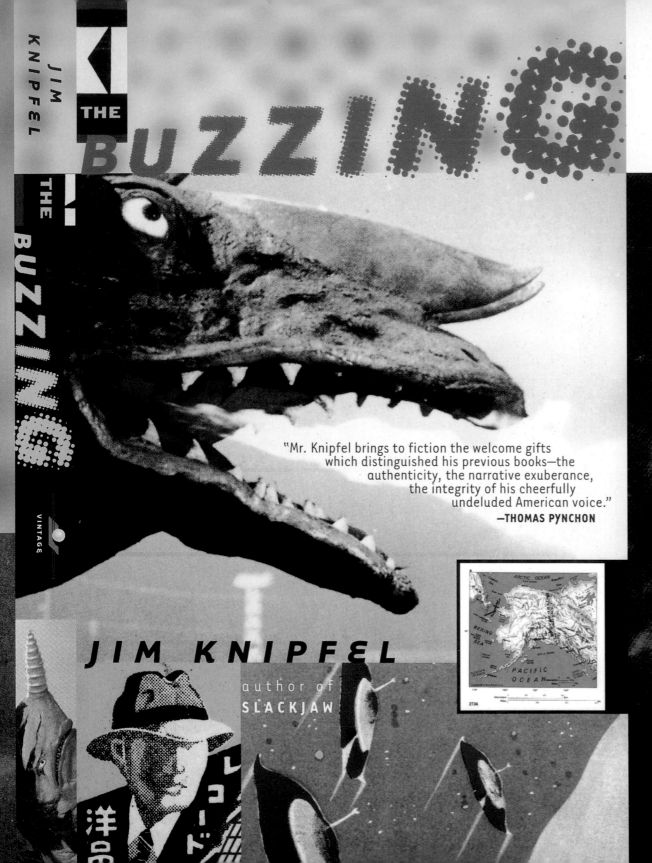

THE BUZZING

JIM KNIPFEL

"Mr. Knipfel brings to fiction the welcome gifts which distinguished his previous books—the authenticity, the narrative exuberance, the integrity of his cheerfully undeluded American voice."
—THOMAS PYNCHON

VINTAGE

JIM KNIPFEL

AUTHOR OF SLACKJAW

JIM KNIPFEL

AUTHOR OF SLACKJAW

QUITTING THE NAIROBI TRIO

A MEMOIR

LEFT: Vintage, 2003. The title refers to Jim's habit of using a fork to find electrical outlets. It also refers to the narrator's belief in the existence of Godzilla, although exactly how remains a mystery. Another mystery is how Knipfel seems to be the only writer alive who regularly gets blurbs from Thomas Pynchon. **ABOVE:** Tarcher Putnam, 2000. Jim's memoir about his stint in a ward for the mentally unbalanced, where he sought refuge in reruns of *The Ernie Kovacs Show*. He was eventually released, so on some level it must have worked.

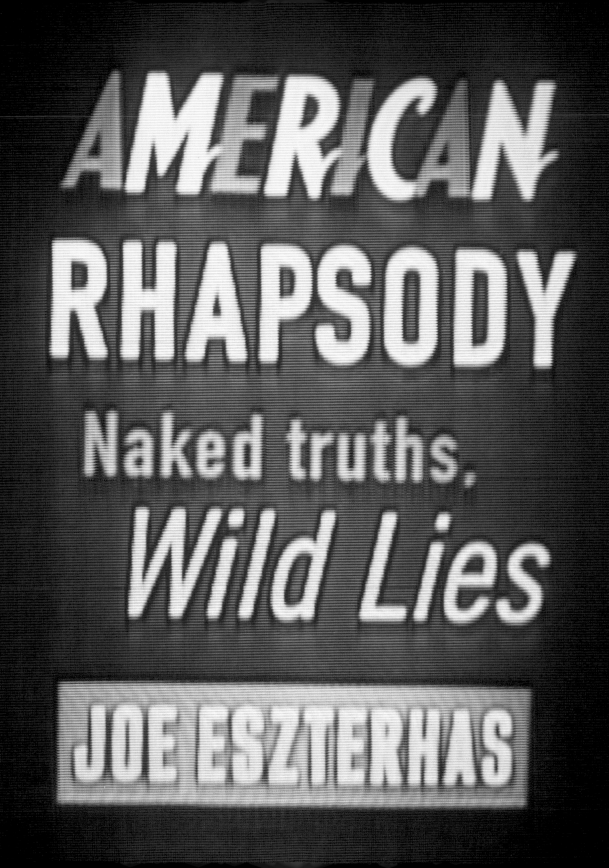

On a stage, against a crimson background, we see a rock and roll band. Hillary is at a mike with Monica and Gennifer Flowers, singing backup. Kenneth W. Starr is at the keyboards. George W. Bush, bare-chested, is at the drums. Al Gore is on bass guitar, John McCain on rhythm guitar. James Carville is on a <u>Deliverance</u>-type banjo. Lucianne Goldberg and Linda Tripp beat tambourines. Peeking out from behind the amps are Richard Nixon, Barry Goldwater, and Bob Dole.

At center stage, the star of the show, wailing on a gleaming sax, under the big spotlight, is a thin and very cool-looking Bill Clinton, looking us right in the eye with a sexy smile.

Only after we take a closer look do we see that his fly is open ... and something ... what is that? ... oh, it's a shirttail! ... is sticking out.

I look forward to seeing Peter next week and going over the manuscript page by page.

Best,

Pucker up.

THE PROSPECT OF WORKING ON A JOE ESZTERHAS BOOK was more than a little intimidating, given his reputation for controversy as a screenwriter. I needn't have worried—he was good-natured, supportive, and hilarious to talk to. But *American Rhapsody* was still a challenge to work on—a novelistic reporting of the Clinton/Lewinsky affair that was also a cunningly scathing portrait of the Washington that spawned it. This simply could not look like any other book on the subject.

I first tried a sketch using a close-up of Monica Lewinsky's actual mouth, but that was too nervous-making and legally dubious. Then Geoff and I simulated the experience of seeing a news item about the book on TV (see left). I set up a type solution, and he sent it through a video monitor and shot it off of that. This proved to be too subtle. Then Sonny said something brilliant, if a little out of character: "Why don't we just give everyone a big kiss?" Indeed. So I went to the CSA Plastock archives and found some lips. Of course the result owes a lot to *The Rocky Horror Picture Show*, but without the blood and fangs. Joe loved it. Especially the embossing.

LEFT: Early comp for *American Rhapsody*, when it had a rather lively subtitle. I don't think Joe ever saw this. **ABOVE:** A cover concept from Joe. This is a hoot, but it would have been almost impossible to pull off with any kind of graphic impact. **FOLLOWING PAGE, LEFT:** Knopf, 2000. Photo from Charles Spencer Anderson's Plastock archives.

AMERICAN
RHAPSODY

JOE ESZTERHAS

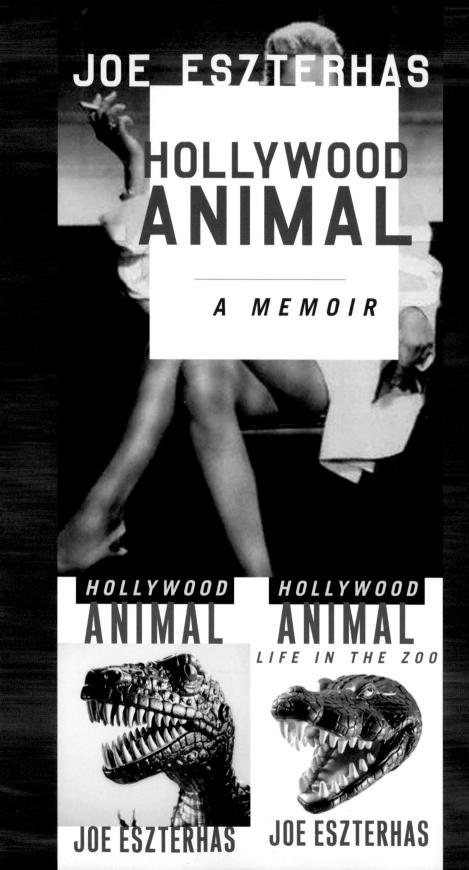

JOE ESZTERHAS

HOLLYWOOD
ANIMAL

A MEMOIR

HOLLYWOOD
ANIMAL

HOLLYWOOD
ANIMAL
LIFE IN THE ZOO

JOE ESZTERHAS

JOE ESZTERHAS

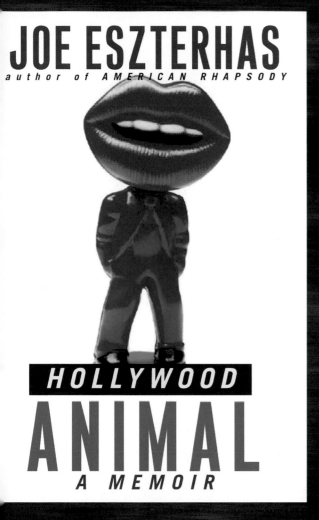

'HOLLYWOOD ANIMAL' WAS EVEN HARDER TO WORK ON THAN 'AMERICAN RHAPSODY'—it's a much more complex book, a memoir that spans Joe's experiences in Hollywood as well as his family history and his complicated relationship with his father. As with the earlier book, a jacket was needed before there was a finished manuscript, which always makes for a more intuitive situation. At first I thought it should be visually linked to *Rhapsody* so I went back to Plastock and chose an image of the lips again, now embodied (above, left). This was thought to be *too* similar, so I tried animals, comically ravenous dinosaurs and alligators meant to represent ruthless denizens of the movie biz. Sonny wanted to take things in a different direction, so I tried a shot from the infamous interrogation scene from *Basic Instinct*. Joe didn't want to go there, and suggested instead a shot of his eyes taken by his wife, Naomi. Even reduced to less than a square inch, the image is more than a little intimidating. **OPPOSITE RIGHT AND ABOVE LEFT:** First ideas for *Hollywood Animal*. **ABOVE RIGHT:** A mock-up by Naomi. While only intended to show placement and scale, I used her hand-written type as is on the final cover. The looseness and primacy of it suit the title and give it a personalized stamp. **RIGHT:** Knopf, 2004.

WAS

A NOVEL

GEOFF RYMAN

Twisted.

DOROTHY GAEL, AN ORPHAN CHURNING WITH RAGE, is sexually abused by her Uncle Henry on their Kansas farm. Aunty Em, who dislikes Toto, looks the other way. Rewriting the Oz story as a gothic fantasy rich in period detail, Ryman casts Baum as a substitute teacher who rescues Dorothy from life as a prostitute on the 1880s Kansas frontier. But Dorothy ends up in a mental institution where she will be discovered in 1956 by Bill Davison, a caring attendant. In a parallel story set in the 1980s, Jonathan, a Canadian-born horror-film actor dying of AIDS, enters therapy with Bill, now a Los Angeles psychiatrist, who asks him to visualize he's in Oz to reenact a childhood obsession. Desperately seeking home, various characters follow the yellow brick roads of their desires and converge in Kansas. Was combines a stunning portrayal of child abuse, Oz lore, and a meditation on the burden of the past. **ABOVE:** The original jacket concept had Geoff photographing a set of Oz figurines and throwing them out of focus. Everyone liked it, except the legal department. While L. Frank Baum's story is in the public domain, the 1939 MGM movie version of it is emphatically not, and even out of focus, this is still obviously Judy & Co. Curses! I'll get you my pretty . . . **LEFT:** Knopf, 1992. The answer lay in a solution I realized was much better—deadpan stock images of what the characters actually are, which is far more appropriate for the realistic approach of the novel. When the pictures are combined with the title you get just enough of a hint as to what it's all about. **OPPOSITE LEFT, TOP:** Washington Square Press, 1990. **OPPOSITE LEFT, BOTTOM:** Knopf, 2001. **OPPOSITE RIGHT:** Knopf, 2001.

MACHINE DREAMS

JAYNE ANNE PHILLIPS

"A BEAUTIFULLY PATTERNED NOVEL. . . . AN ENDURING LITERARY ACHIEVEMENT. . . .
ASTONISHING. . . ." —The New York Times

CONVERSATIONS
with WILDER

CAMERON CROWE

Celluloid Skyline
NEW YORK AND THE MOVIES

JAMES SANDERS

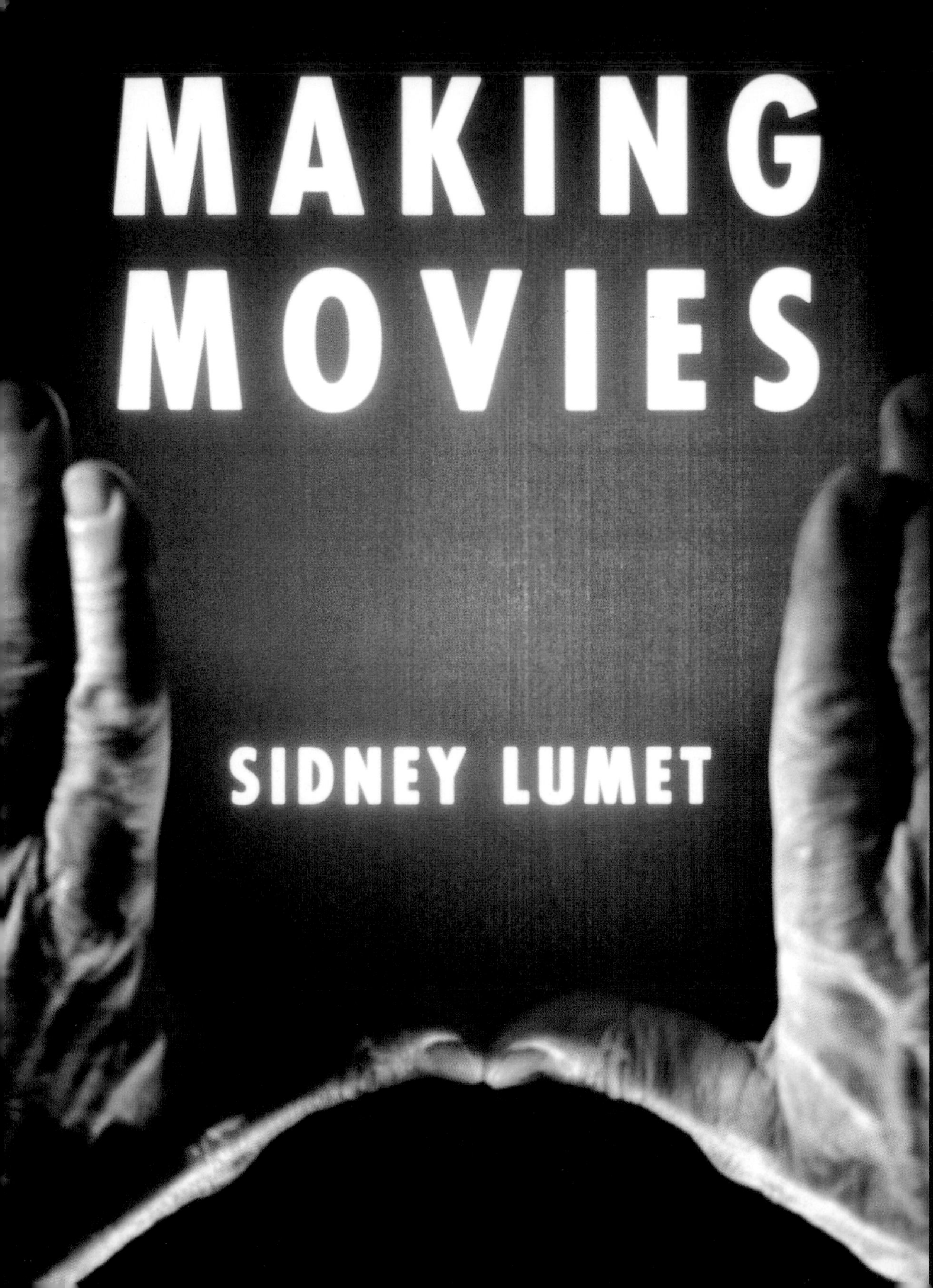

MAKING MOVIES

SIDNEY LUMET

Joan Didion

SLOUCHING
TOWARDS
BETHLEHEM

Essays by

A rich display of some of the best prose written today in this country.

—*The New York Times Book Review*

LEFT: Knopf, 1995. Photograph by Geoff Spear. I was afraid Sidney Lumet would think this was the corniest idea in the world, but he was all for it, saying, "Directors do that all the time." As this was just before the onset of computers, Geoff had to achieve the glowing type effect by rear projection from a slide onto a blank sheet of paper.

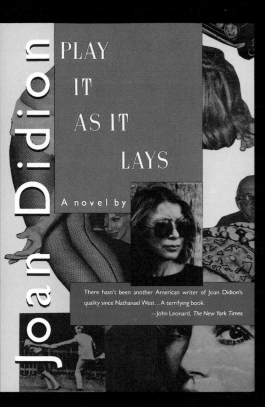

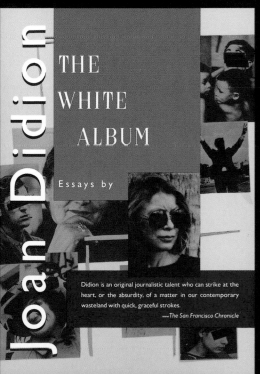

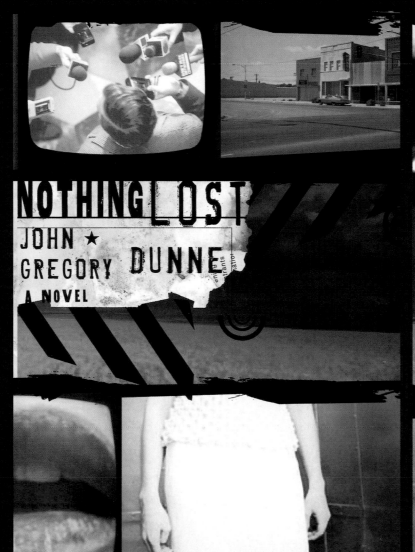

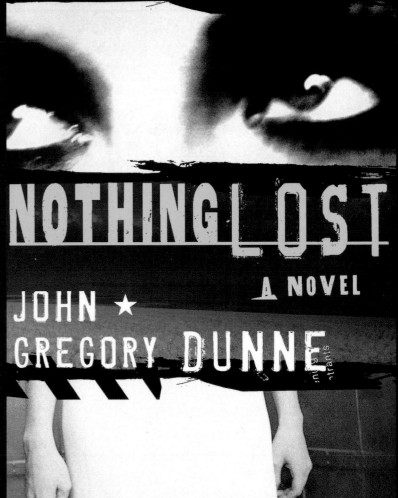

FOR A FIRST COMMISSION TO DESIGN A BOOK COVER SERIES ONE COULD DO A LOT WORSE THAN JOAN DIDION. One of the best journalists working for the last thirty years, Didion's been turning her keen eye and keener mind on the political and cultural landscape with groundbreaking results. Barbara and I worked on this series together, assembling background collages relevant to the subject matter, and my favorite aspect is the idea of essentially replacing Joan's name with her photo. **LEFT AND OPPOSITE RIGHT:** Series design for FSG, 1990, co-designed with Barbara deWilde. **ABOVE LEFT:** Original design for *Nothing Lost*, a novel by Joan's husband, John Gregory Dunne. **ABOVE RIGHT:** Knopf, 2004. Collage by Charles Wilkins/Automatic Art and Design. This is a classic case of the sales force wanting the book to look "bigger." I think we maintained the spirit of the original, but I also didn't think it was necessary to alter it. Sadly, John saw and approved the design, but died suddenly several months before publication.

PAUL ROBESON

BY MARTIN BAUML DUBERMAN

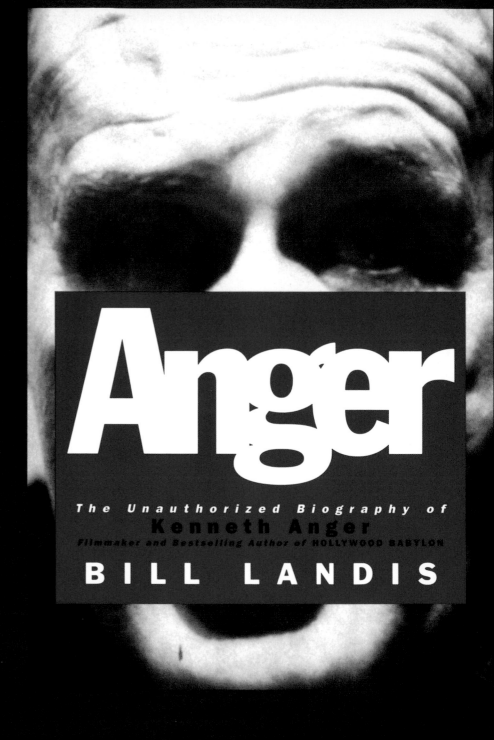

Anger

The Unauthorized Biography of
Kenneth Anger
Filmmaker and Bestselling Author of **HOLLYWOOD BABYLON**

BILL LANDIS

On the spine (vertical):

TRAMP

THE LIFE OF CHARLIE CHAPLIN

JOYCE MILTON

HarperCollins

On the cover:

TRAMP

THE LIFE OF CHARLIE CHAPLIN

JOYCE MILTON

BALL OF FIRE

THE TUMULTUOUS LIFE AND COMIC ART OF

LUCILLE BALL

BY STEFAN KANFER

AUTHOR OF GROUCHO

265

THE CHALLENGE OF A BIOGRAPHY JACKET is to try to do more than just use a picture of the subject and spell his or her name correctly. Sometimes that's simply all you can do, but there's almost always a specific personality trait to tap into and use for insipiration. **OPPOSITE LEFT:** Knopf, 1989. This image was made by accident—it is a dark photocopy I made of a much more brightly lit picture—but it was perfect for the drama and passion of Paul Robeson's life. **OPPOSITE RIGHT:** HarperCollins, 1995. Kenneth Anger is a notorious recluse who hates to have his picture shown. Design-wise, I'm dangerously close to ripping off Barbara Kruger here. **LEFT:** HarperCollins, 1996. Chaplin is a case of such well-worn territory that liberties can be taken, such as a typographic doodle. The one on the spine is better. **ABOVE:** Knopf, 2003. I thought the only way to bring anything new to this was to shoot the image from an actual show off a TV screen. But there were legal problems with that. We were lucky to get the rights to run this as it was. At least we got the whites of those eyeballs.

The Illustrated
Woody Allen Reader

BY WOODY ALLEN AND LINDA SUNSHINE

Woody Allen

A BIOGRAPHY

Eric Lax

LEFT: I can't remember if this design was ever sent to Woody Allen or not. If so, he obviously didn't like it. I thought it was kind of cute—in an angsty, despairing, Nietzschean sort of way. Call me crazy. **RIGHT:** Knopf, 1993. Enlarging his trademark name and reducing all the rest of the type to practically an afterthought was the answer—who else could it possibly be about? Black and white, of course. **ABOVE:** Knopf, 1991. In what would soon become a distant era in the subject's life, this photo was taken by . . . Mia Farrow. Who did a pretty great job, I must say.

The

Illustrated

Woody

Allen

Reader

BY WOODY ALLEN AND LINDA SUNSHINE

CLINT EASTWOOD

a biography by

RICHARD SCHICKEL

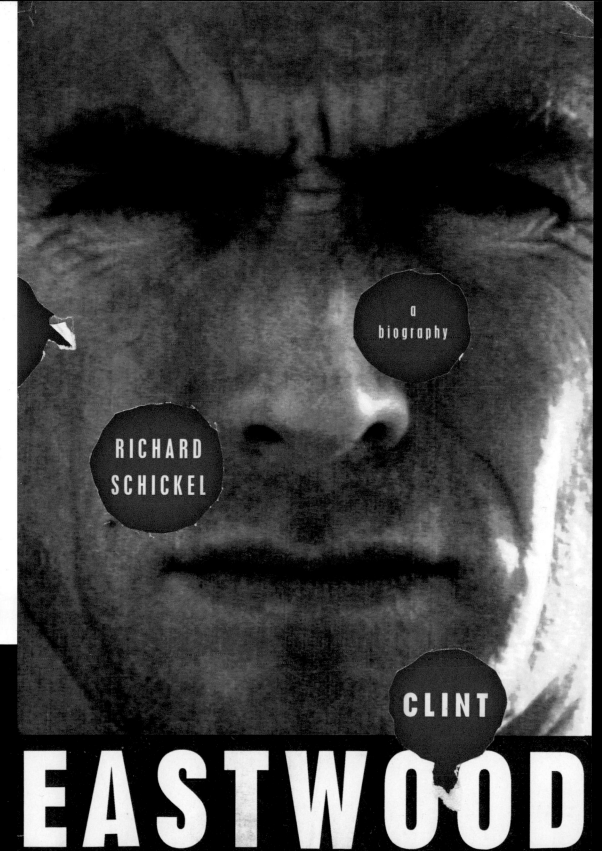

a
biography

RICHARD
SCHICKEL

CLINT

EASTWOOD

RIGHT: When this die-cut comp I made was sent to Richard Schickel he hated it so much he wrote a scathing letter to his editor, saying something to the effect that it was disrespectful and an abberation. That was certainly not my intent—I just liked the idea of some thug firing at the book and having no real effect on it other than just pissing off "Dirty Harry" even more. **ABOVE:** Knopf, 1998. For the revised jacket a stunning portrait by the photographer Albert Watson came to the rescue. Upon publication it was a treat when Eastwood himself came into the office to do a signing for staff with Schickel. When I introduced myself Richard thanked me profusely for the jacket that was "so much better than what that other person did."

Me

Stories of My Life

Katharine Hepburn

Tell and show.

THE DIAMETRICALLY OPPOSITE APPROACHES TO THESE TWO JACKETS reflect the disparity of the actresses themselves: you *listen* to Hepburn, you *look* at Dietrich. One talks, the other poses. That might be over-simplifying it (certainly Hepburn wasn't hard to look at, and Dietrich would quote Goethe to anyone within earshot at the slightest provocation), but often book jackets *are* a simplification—a distillation of a personality or an idea, especially in the service of a celebrity memoir. The Hepburn was much harder to figure out than the Dietrich. There was a lot of trial and error, as Carol and I struggled with which image to choose from Hepburn's life-long career to represent her: *Bringing up Baby? Stage Door? The Philadelphia Story? Guess Who's Coming to Dinner? On Golden Pond?* Just one of these seemed inadequate, and a montage was out of the question—no graphic impact. At some point it just dawned on us: type. Straightforward, not fancy, no-nonsense, free of glitz, how Hepburnian. In retrospect it's just so obvious, but at the time it was a radical idea for such an extremely high-profile book for which Knopf paid a ton of money. Sonny bravely championed it, convincing Hepburn herself it was the way to go, putting everything on the line in the process. The book's enormous success makes this seem like a no-brainer, but it was actually a huge risk.

THE DIETRICH WAS MUCH MORE OF A FOREGONE conclusion; no one involved ever really seriously questioned the idea. Her face is a trademark, and unlike Hepburn, her looks never radically evolved, so a classic image worked fine to represent her entire life. In bookstores when this was literally displayed face out it stole your eyes from anything else around it, just like her.

I realize that we didn't entirely invent the two visual strategies, but not long after these titles were published suddenly celebrity books that either had no type or no image seemed to spring up like bit players for lunch at the studio commissary. It's a tricky prospect to try and mess with. For these ideas to work you need iconic stars, intense public interest, and as always—a terrifically written book.

OPPOSITE LEFT: Knopf, 1991, co-designed with Carol Devine Carson. We tried a version with a cream-colored background and it just didn't work—too warm. Once the design was in place our foreign-rights maven Carol Janeway had to go back and renegotiate with a veritable U.N. of foreign publishers who were contractually obligated to use our cover and now had "no face to sell with." While American audiences were obviously ready for it, some of the overseas markets balked. Though I remember with amusement a Spanish-language edition that just had the word 'Yo' on the front. **OPPOSITE RIGHT:** From inside the book—Hepburn with George Cukor, Joseph L. Mankiewicz, and George Stevens. Someone in copyediting pointed out that in this particular shot Mankiewicz bears an uncanny resemblance to yours truly. How Zelig. **RIGHT:** Knopf, 1993. Co-designed with Carol Devine Carson, photo by Josef von Sternberg.

MARLENE DIETRICH

MARIA RIVA

KNOPF

TRUCK STOP

RAINBOWS

A ROAD NOVEL

THE LIGHT

ries by

MICHEL

Iva Pekárková

**THIEF
OF LIGHT**

**DAVID
RAMUS**

The light brigade.

BOOK JACKETS DO NOT SELL BOOKS. If everyone understood that it would make the job so much easier. There
are many, many factors in the success (or failure) of a
book, and the jacket is just a small part of it. Flap copy,
review attention, advertising, media coverage, and the
all-important word of mouth all play an integral role.
But the jacket is literally the face of the project, so it
gets the credit for making or breaking the chances of the
title. I think the best a jacket can do is act as a name tag
at a singles' party—it can introduce you to the wearer,
and then after that the book is on its own. You'll either
like its personality and take it home, or decide it's not
your type and move on. **OPPOSITE LEFT:** Knopf, 1991.
Photograph by Harry Callahan. **OPPOSITE RIGHT:** FSG,
1992. **RIGHT:** HarperCollins, 1995. Joseph Montebello,
art director. The house had high hopes for this book and
it didn't perform to expectations. So naturally the jacket
was blamed. And yet a similar approach worked well
for Dean Koontz's *Intensity*. Does that mean geometric
abstraction is risky? No, it means you're probably better
off publishing Dean Koontz.

Harper
Collins

THIEF OF LIGHT

A NOVEL

DAVID RAMUS

Strike a pose.

TO SAY THAT MARION ETTLINGER TAKES AUTHOR PHOTOS is to say that Billie Holliday sings songs, or Julia Child bakes cakes, or that Frank Lloyd Wright has put up a shack or two. My Marion axiom: if you aren't even remotely attractive then she will somehow make you look date-able; if you *are* remotely attractive then she will make you look like spouse material; and if you're actually beautiful to begin with, well, she will make you look capable of destroying any relationship unlucky enough to get in your way. Now, there are many photographers to whom this could apply, but Marion uniquely seems to achieve it through pure alchemy: no makeup, no assistants, no stylists, no special filters, no re-touching, all natural light. It is just her and her camera and you, having a threesome. Upon arrival at her modest but cunningly bohemian studio in Chelsea, out comes the wine, on goes the Bill Evans record, off pops the lens cap, and in a click the afternoon disappears. And on the hazy morning after, you wake to the image of a familiar, mesmerizing stranger.

Marion's range of subjects reads like a *Who's Who* of contemporary literature, and as her body of work continues to grow and enters its third decade, it has evolved from the status of merely Ravishing to that of Invaluable Historical Document. From Raymond Carver to Andre Dubus to Lucy Grealy, Marion can lay claim to the most elegant pictures (and in some cases the only professional ones, period) of these departed artists ever captured. She took what was thought to be a dull niche medium (if it was thought of at all) and developed it, shot by shot, into an art form.

LEFT: Simon & Schuster, 2003. On the cover of her monograph collection of writers' portraits, Marion the-sorceress-of-the-lens somehow makes Truman Capote's other two chins disappear. **NEAR RIGHT:** This jacket verso was originally intended as the front of *Author Photo*. Marion loved it, but her editor thought it was too subtle and insisted on Capote. He was probably right, the bastard. **OPPOSITE RIGHT:** Marion desperately tries to make a silk purse out of a simian's ear for the hapless author of *The Cheese Monkeys*. Spring 2001.

AUTHOR PHOTO
MARION ETTLINGER
portraits, 1983-2002
FOREWORD BY RICHARD FORD

PHOTOGRAPH

9 780743 227345
ISBN 0-743

AUTHOR PHOTO

MARION ETTLINGER

portraits, 1983-2002

the informers

BRET EASTON ELLIS

We'll slide down the surface of things . . .

FOR GLAMORAMA, BRET EASTON ELLIS WANTED "THE NEW SERGEANT PEPPER" cover, and that's what I aimed for. The key to it was photographer Patrick McMullen, who makes a cameo appearance as himself early on in the book. Patrick is quite a hoot, and was more than willing to help with his spectacular catalogue of celebrity photos. I had all their heads sihouetted and arranged in a kaleidescope pattern (see opposite page). The idea was for a jacket riddled with holes that would reveal the famous faces, as if someone were literally shooting at them. What our production department found was that the holes could not be die-cut all in one run through the press (it took three) because the resulting "confetti" would clog things up. This was ironic, considering that confetti is a motif referred to throughout the book.

ABOVE: Knopf, 1994. My first Bret cover, for a collection of short stories. This jacket has the distinction—dubious or not—of being the first that I designed using a computer. The black area was spot-varnished in gloss, meant to present the reader with, gulp, a "dark mirror" (my pretentious idea and no one else's). **RIGHT:** Knopf, 1998. Die-cut holes provide a honeycomb of windows for the characters to peer out of. **OPPOSITE:** Case design for *Glamorama*—a galaxy of stars. Since all of the celebrities were actually mentioned in the text it was deemed fair use to show their faces without having to get model releases, which would have been a logistical nightmare.

ABOVE: East Hampton, Summer 1994. I am annoying Bret.
Tremendously. Photo by Geoff Spear.

BRET
EASTON
ELLIS

LUNAR
PARK

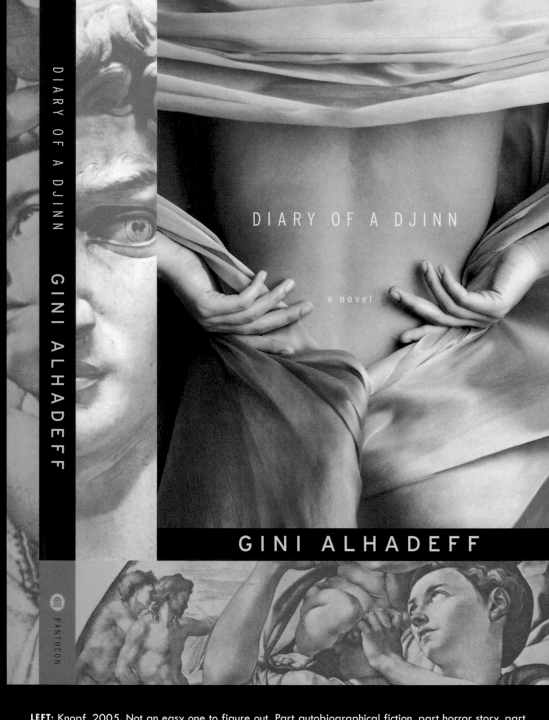

DIARY OF A DJINN

GINI ALHADEFF

DIARY OF A DJINN

a novel

GINI ALHADEFF

PANTHEON

LEFT: Knopf, 2005. Not an easy one to figure out. Part autobiographical fiction, part horror story, part meditation on fathers and sons, and all Bret. I touched on two motifs in the text. The first is a device in which the main character (Bret, basically) keeps noticing that when he is alone and walking across the upstairs corridor of his house, the sconces that line the wall mysteriously turn on and then off as he passes them, almost as if he is being luminously "followed." The second is Bret's son (in the book) and his implicit fascination with the moon. He never talks about it, but he has a moonscape painted across the ceiling of his bedroom, and the title of the book is referred to several times. Though it is never explained.

MODEL
Behavior

a novel and 7 stories

Jay
McInerney

ISBN 0-679-42846-1 FICTION
52400

9 780679 428466

MODEL BEHAVIOR • JAY McINERNEY • KNOPF

THE
GOOD LIFE
A NOVEL
JAY
McINERNEY

OPPOSITE RIGHT: Pantheon, 2003. *Diary of a Djinn* is a novel about the travails of a young woman as she braves the fashion business in Milan. What I liked most about the photo (by Lisa Spindler) is the sense of vulnerability—in a back-stabbing business this is not a good position to be in. Michelangelo's *David* and a figure from the Sistine Chapel seem to agree and are watching over her from the margins. **ABOVE LEFT:** Knopf, 1998.

In order to make this jacket look like a Vogue cover, I put the barcode on the front (which no one noticed until I pointed it out). I also mimicked the magazine's curiously deadpan spine. **ABOVE RIGHT:** Knopf, 2006. For this story of upper-class New Yorkers haunted by the attack on the World Trade Center, I used images of everyday items covered in the ashes of the collapsed towers.

THE MEMORY BOOK OF STARR FAITHFULL

a novel

GLORIA VANDERBILT

THE MEMORY BOOK OF STARR FAITHFULL

a novel

GLORIA VANDERBILT

THE MEMORY BOOK OF STARR FAITHFULL

A MOTHER'S STORY

GLORIA VANDERBILT

The survivor.

GLORIA VANDERBILT HAS BEEN THROUGH IT ALL. From the crucible of unwanted international attention as a child-pawn heiress in the 1930s to the suicide of her beloved son Carter in 1988, she has endured the gamut of celebrity and suffering. She could have easily shared the fate of the debutante Brenda Frazier before her—defeated obscurity. But she didn't. Instead she created a new life for herself in the arts. Part of that has included writing, and the first jacket I did for her was *The Memory Book of Starr Faithfull*, a fictionalized true story of a jazz baby in the 1920s who got in way over her head and whose body was found washed up on the shores of Long Island at the tender age of twenty-three. The rumor was she kept a diary, and Gloria, based on meticulous research, imagined what it might tell. One can't help but suspect that the author related all too well to her subject. **LEFT:** Knopf, 1994. **ABOVE:** Unused design. I don't think Gloria saw this—It needed a face. **RIGHT:** Knopf, 1996. Gloria's heartbreaking memoir of loss. Photograph of Carter Cooper by the author.

INTENSE
YELLOW

MAGENTA—
LIPSTICK
RED

t at the Time

noir

oilt

VAN HEFLIN

TRUMAN CAPOTE

PASQUALE DeCicco

HOWARD HUGHES

GEOFF

LEOPOLD STOKOWSKI

RUSSELL HURD
PAINTING
BILL PALEY

MARLON BRANDO

RENÉ BOUCHÉ
FRANK SINATRA
ACTING
LAWRENCE TIERNEY

GORDON PARKS
FRANCHOT TONE

R. CHICAGO
SIDNEY LUMET
DESIGNING
WYATT COOPER

THE MAJOR

THE FASHION BUSINESS
DAVID BEGELMAN
ROALD DAHL.

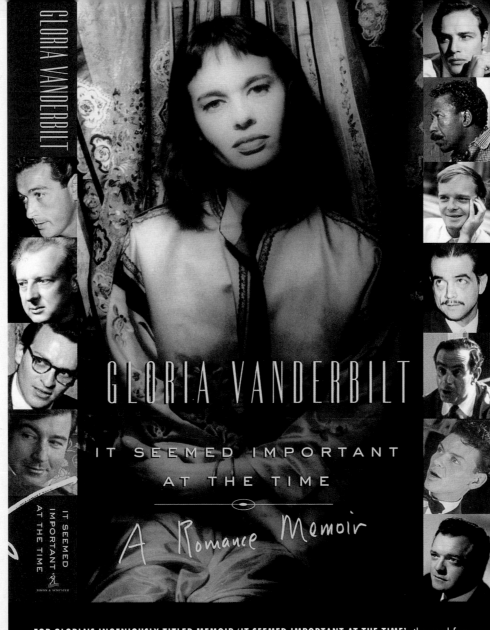

GLORIA VANDERBILT

IT SEEMED IMPORTANT

AT THE TIME

A Romance Memoir

SIMON & SCHUSTER

(spine) GLORIA VANDERBILT — IT SEEMED IMPORTANT AT THE TIME

gvc designs
gloria vanderbilt studio

Chip— for Abrams book

Leaping Lizards — what a thrill
as I wait to see what Chip
comes up with for my book
jackets. Then when I do
I'm blown away by the magic
he's created which brings another
dimension to what I've created
and reveals it in a way I
hadn't thought of before. I
love ya, Kid !

FOR GLORIA'S INGENIOUSLY TITLED MEMOIR 'IT SEEMED IMPORTANT AT THE TIME', the real fun was sifting through her extraordinary personal collection of photographs. She's sat for all the best, but one 1940s shot by Carl Van Vechten stood out—not only is she stunning (duh) but also radiates a captivating combination of defiance and vulnerability. **LEFT:** As I made my way through the manuscript I kept track of the men in Vanderbilt's life, for reference (and almost ran out of ink!). **ABOVE:** Simon & Schuster, 2004. Photo of Gloria by Carl Van Vechten. Ogling her to the right is a phalanx of her suitors and confidantes: Marlon Brando, Gordon Parks, Truman Capote, Howard Hughes, René Bouché, Frank Sinatra and Van Heflin. To the left—on the spine—are her husbands, in order, from top to bottom: Pat De Cicco, Leopold Stokowski, Sidney Lumet, and Wyatt Cooper. They are all gazing at a close-up of the author on the back cover. **ABOVE RIGHT:** With Gloria at the party for *The Cheese Monkeys*. A great friend through the years, she's been especially sweet to my family and is as down-to-earth as a style icon can get. Which is very. But she's more than that—she's proof that where there's hope, there's life.

A. M. HOMES

IN A COUNTRY

OF MOTHERS

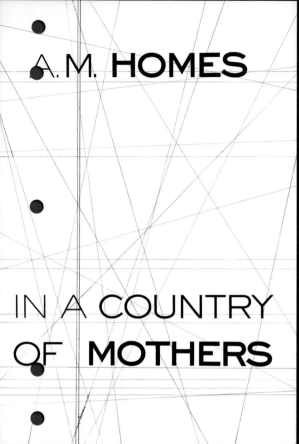

A. M. HOMES

IN A COUNTRY
OF MOTHERS

THE LETTERS OF RACHEL CARSON
AND DOROTHY FREEMAN,
1952-1964

An Intimate Portrait of a Remarkable Friendship

EDITED BY MARTHA FREEMAN

Always,
Rachel

Rules are rules.

NOTHING QUITE SAYS "WRITING" LIKE BRIGHT BLUE HORIZONTAL LINES, though in these examples I tried to vary the usual standard format of notebook paper, to suggest something out of the ordinary. **LEFT:** Knopf, 1993. For this story about a therapist who becomes systematically unhinged and obsessed with her patient, I tried to imagine what she'd be writing on her notepad during a session—or, more accurately, scribbling. The sperm theme is undeniable, but just as unintended (analyze that!). **ABOVE LEFT:** An early sketch. Too geometric. Not sure what I was thinking here—that the doctor took notes with a ruler? Ridiculous. I do like the way the "A" is pierced by the die-cut hole, though. I should have carried that over to the finish. **ABOVE RIGHT:** Beacon Press, 1995. Sara Eisenman, art director. **OPPOSITE LEFT:** Knopf, 1999. Partly obscuring the face suggests someone who was unknowable—a theme of the book. **OPPOSITE RIGHT:** Knopf, 1990. Photo by Joyce Ravid.

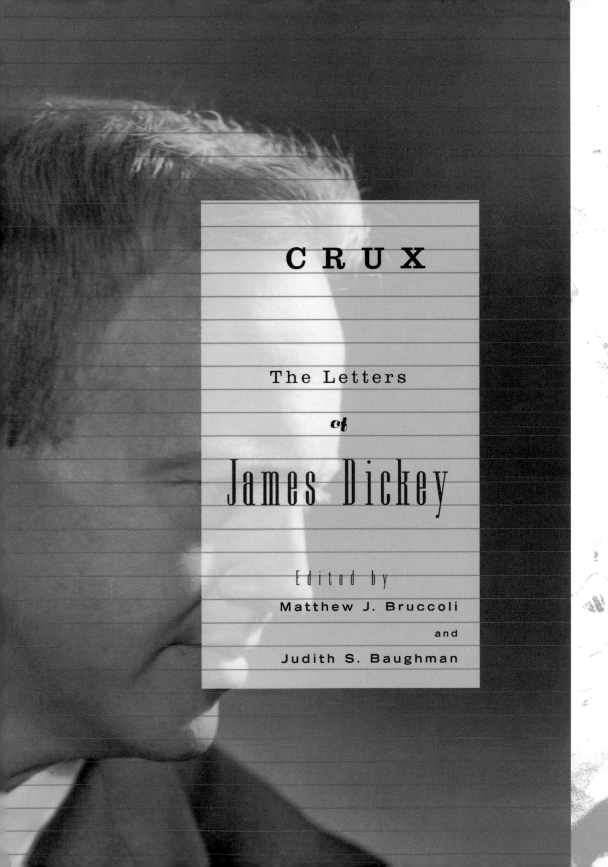

CRUX

The Letters

of

James Dickey

Edited by

Matthew J. Bruccoli

and

Judith S. Baughman

MIRACLES
IN
AMERICA

STORIES BY

SHEILA KOHLER

Dry.

A memoir.

Augusten Burroughs.

Author of *Running with Scissors*

Picador.

Typography in denial.

THAT WAS THE IDEA FOR AUGUSTEN BURROUGH'S HILARIOUS AND HARROWING account of his bout with, and recovery from, alcoholism. I couldn't imagine doing anything else. It was not the most original idea in the world (see Barbara's jacket for Nathan Englander's *For the Relief of Unbearable Urges*), but I did think the execution made it unique. Augusten agreed. Unfortunately, higher-ups at St. Martin's didn't and thought it looked like a horror story (which it pretty much is, by the way), and they wanted to play up the humor. So they went with a sardine in a martini glass instead. Picador, the publisher of the paperback edition, was more sympathetic, and in an extremely rare move rescued the design six months later from the memory hole. This only happened to me one other time (see George Saunders's *Pastoralia*).

Magical Thinking, however, was a real stumper. The title refers to a form of mild psychosis in which one believes he has control over events that he definitely does not. I tried a bunch of goofy stuff until Steve Snider, the art director, sighed with exasperation into the phone: "Why don't you just have a faucet turned on with the water pouring up?" Thanks, Steve. But not a faucet: Geoff and I introduced a human element, which suits the definition better. I also like the oblique visual connection to *Dry*.

LEFT: Picador, 2004. Originally I wanted to hollow the thing out and put a flask of scotch inside. Kidding. **BELOW & OPPOSITE LEFT:** Killed comps. **OPPOSITE RIGHT:** St. Martins, 2004. It took forever to get the water to pour up.

I WAS TOURING FOR THE PAPERBACK OF 'DRY'. And I was in an airport bookstore, looking for something to read on the plane. I noticed that the store had only one copy of *Dry* on the table, and I thought, that's probably a good sign. And as I was standing there, a woman picked up the book, looked it over, and brought it up to the clerk. She said, "Excuse me? But do you have another copy of this book? This one looks like it got all wet." The clerk said, "No, I'm sorry. All of them were wet like that." So the woman PUT THE BOOK BACK and left the store, frowning. I felt so smug and satisfied. The cover had screened out an inappropriate reader and saved me from future hate mail.

—Augusten Burroughs

THE WIVES OF BATH

THE WIVES OF BATH

SUSAN SWAN

KNOPF

SUSAN SWAN

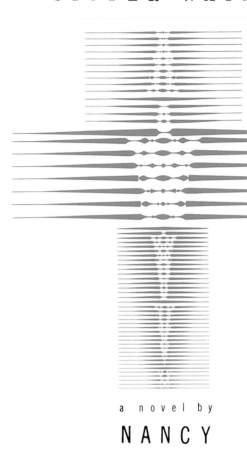

SISTER WATER

a novel by

NANCY

WILLARD

THE WIVES OF BATH

SUSAN SWAN

Soak it up.

FAR LEFT: Knopf, 1993. I love to think that she just remembered she left the tap running. **LEFT:** Rejected sketch. Photographs by Alicia Exum. Girls wrestling. Too scary, I guess. **ABOVE:** Unused idea, 1993. Decorative typographic rules arranged to evoke the shimmer of light on a lake, the ocean, etc. Too abstract for the editor.

ZERO 3 BRAVO

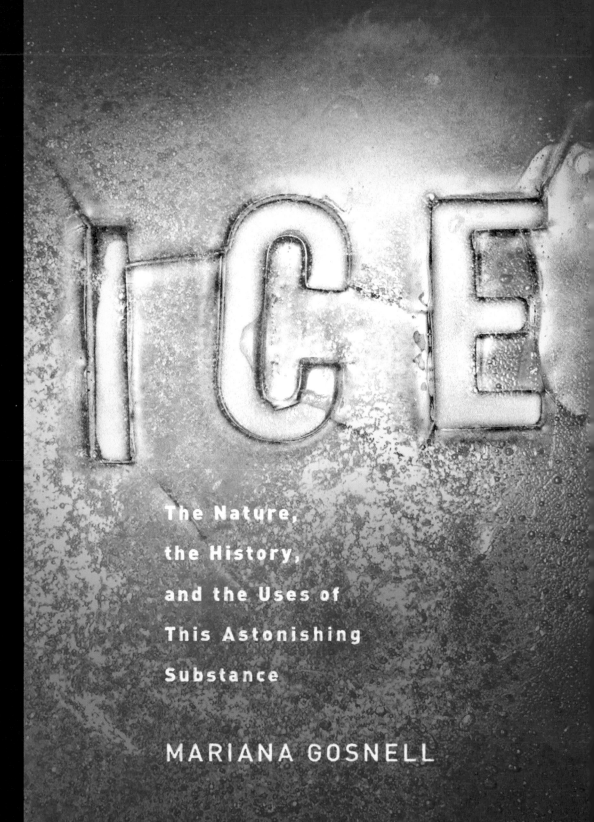

SOLO ACROSS AMERICA IN A SMALL PLANE

MARIANA GOSNELL

ABOVE: Knopf, 1993. Quite possibly the happiest-looking plane I ever saw. You'd be smiling too if the earth always looked to you like a patch of ragged corduroy. **RIGHT:** Knopf, 2005. Photo by Geoff Spear. Geoff froze the letters of the title in a shallow pan, popped them out, and lit it from behind with a blue filter. Really cool (sorry).

ICE

The Nature,

the History,

and the Uses of

This Astonishing

Substance

MARIANA GOSNELL

MAR • 63

OFF KECK ROAD

a novella

Mona Simpson

author of

ANYWHERE BUT HERE

AS WE ALL KNOW, BOOKS, NO MATTER HOW FANTASTICALLY MADE UP, are deeply personal, and we all have our own ways of weaving messages, in code, to our loved ones, to memory.

I had small polaroids I sent Chip Kidd with *Off Keck Road*, a picture of my grandmother's house and a huge tree covered in snow, neither of which exists anymore, and a house somewhere else that still does. The snow seemed almost drawn.

Chip came up with a cover and a binding and a typeface that are each and all together perfect. I love the physical book. It expresses things I wanted it to be that I couldn't describe in words.

Since then, as I write the new book, I've been collecting talismans for Chip, hidden pulses of this book's life for me: a small painting of an orange I found at a flea market, dark red candles made with huge cookie cutters in the shape of a man and a woman, sold outside a particular church outside Manila. This time I want to write the title in my own hand. I can't wait to see what Chip will do with all these mute offerings, which to anyone else would seem like junk.

—Mona Simpson

July 15, 2002

Dear Mr. Kidd,

I'm feeling very lucky just now, as I look for the 50th time at the cover you've created for *Lost in America*. You've captured the essence of my book and even, I think, of my life. That word — "brilliant"— is tossed around too freely, but not in this case. It's precisely the adjective to describe what you've accomplished. Anyone reading the book, or knowing its author, will agree.

I apologize for the quality of this photo, but it was taken with the 1955 equivalent of a box camera. Here's the original, of Meyer and me on my day of graduation from medical school. We're alongside the dorm in which I lived as a senior. Because I was the proctor, my rent was free. My duties consisted of answering the phone (when I was there) and seeing that the communal refrigerator stayed less than roach-infested. In theory, I was supposed to set a mature, Yale-type tone as well, but I doubt that I did.

I hope the photo can be sent back when it's no longer needed.

Again, my deepest thanks,

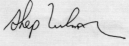

Lost *in* America

A JOURNEY WITH MY FATHER

Sherwin B. Nuland

AUTHOR OF HOW WE DIE

Lost *in* America · A JOURNEY WITH MY FATHER · Sherwin B. Nuland

KNOPF

THE VINTAGE BOOK OF CONTEMPORARY AMERICAN POETRY

Second Edition

EDITED BY J. D. McCLATCHY

SEVENTY-FIVE OUTSTANDING POETS, INCLUDING

Sylvia Plath
Robert Lowell
James Merrill
Amy Clampitt
Louise Glück
Denis Johnson
W. S. Merwin
Charles Simic
Alice Fulton
Frank O'Hara
Elizabeth Bishop
Anne Sexton
John Ashbery
Robert Creeley
Adrienne Rich
Sharon Olds
Mary Oliver
Robert Pinsky
Mark Strand
Denise Levertov
Richard Wilbur
May Swenson
Michael Palmer
Robert Duncan
Robert Hass
Mark Doty
Yusef Komunyakaa

OPPOSITE LEFT: Knopf, 2000. Photograph from the collection of the author. **LEFT:** Knopf, 2003. Photograph of the author and his father, from the author's collection. **ABOVE:** Vintage, 2003. Photograph by Jeffrey Prant.

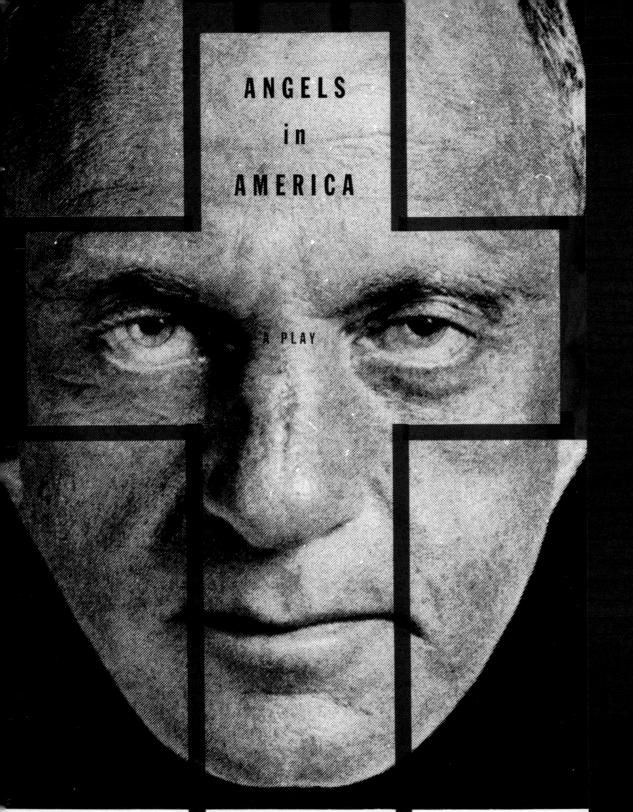

ANGELS in AMERICA

A PLAY

TONY KUSHNER

WE MUST LOVE ONE ANOTHER OR DIE

Edited by LAWRENCE D. MASS

CHRISTOPHER BRAM • JOHN M. CLUM • ALFRED CORN • JOHN D'EMILIO • MICHAEL DENNENY • ANTHONY S. FAUCI
ANDREW HOLLERAN • ARNIE KANTROWITZ • TONY KUSHNER • LAWRENCE D. MASS • RODGER McFARLANE
PATRICK MERLA • MARK MERLIS • MICHAEL PALLER • GAIL MERRIFIELD PAPP • CANAAN PARKER • GABRIEL ROTELLO
DOUGLAS SADOWNICK • MICHELANGELO SIGNORILE • CALVIN TRILLIN • SARAH TRILLIN • DAVID WILLINGER • MAXINE WOLFE

The life and legacies of
LARRY KRAMER

LEFT: A rejected sketch for the cover of *Angels In America*, featuring an eerie portrait of Roy Cohn (clipped from a magazine). This was done months before I ever actually saw the play, and the cover was not a success—all it did was scare anyone who saw it. I soon lost this commission to Milton Glaser, who did a much better job than I ever could. **ABOVE:** St. Martin's Press, 1998. Larry's a friend. I adore him, and am heartened by his role in confronting the AIDS crisis. **OPPOSITE LEFT:** Stanford University Press, 1999. **OPPOSITE RIGHT:** *The New York Times* Op-Ed page, October 16, 1998.

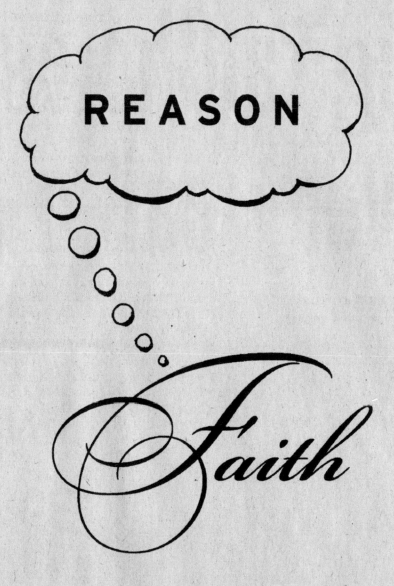

REASON

Faith

Chip Kidd

participated in a conversation about the meaning of our brief lives. Unless we stultify our minds, we are not

I? What should I do? Our most radical drive is the drive to raise questions. Before these personal but uni-

today's rationale is very differ that relativism is the only safe ' dation'' for tolerance. That, say

A commitment to relativism that reason is ultimately irrel that there is only preference. In

DANTE'S
Testaments

Essays

in

Scriptural IMAGINATION

PETER S. HAWKINS

FIGURAE: READING MEDIEVAL CULTURE

STANFORD UNIVERSITY PRESS

BLASPHEMY

LEONARD W. LEVY

KNOPF

...SE AGAINST THE SACRED... ...S TO SALMAN RUSHDIE...

D'

I DESIGNED 'BLASPHEMY' WITH ANDRES SERRANO'S *Piss Christ* years before I used his work for *The New Testament*. When the author wrote to say how much he loved the jacket (below), the implication was that he was reacting to it on a purely visceral level and may not have understood what he was actually looking at. The work was clearly credited on the back flap, so I assume he eventually figured it out. **LEFT:** Knopf, 1993. In its own way, the spine is blasphemous too: the title runs upwards, instead of the conventional opposite, so when it's on the shelf, it's defying the convention of all the rest of the titles alongside it. **OPPOSITE LEFT:** On the revival of the *memento mori* in contemporary design, *The New York Times*, October 9, 1997.

April 6, 1993

Jane Garrett
Middlebury VT 05753

and

FAX to Paul Schnee, Knopf Editorial, 22fl

Dear Jane and Paul,

I now have what Paul slightingly refers to as the "sketch" of the dustjacket for <u>Blasphemy.</u> It is a masterpiece, a work of art, the best jacket I have ever seen.

I am ready now, without further ado, to award the jacket designer with a medal for the finest jacket not only of the year or decade but of the century.

My wife and my daughter and my son-in-law all agree. Each thinks it is the best dustjacket he or she has ever seen. Even my four year old grandson said "Wow!" Never have I seen a jacket as striking, handsome, vivid, dramatic, and colorful.

I am going to frame my copy and hang it in my study.

I am delighted that the designer not only caught the obvious fact that the blasphemy trial of Jesus was the most famous trial of its kind, but that devout believers were usually the victims.

The yellowy dots make me think of a burning fire, sort of combining a crucifixion scene with burning at the stake. I thought not only of Jesus but of Servetus.

Don't change one iota.

You will have to increase the pressrun by several thousand copies. Send a copy to the BMOC.

I cannot understand how you two could play it so cool, never having mentioned the design or your reactions to it. It is great, sensational, glorious. As I said before, a work of art. We all love it. Thanks. My congratulations to the artist. I hope he/she gets credit somewhere on the jacket.

Appreciatively,

Leonard

Leonard W. Levy

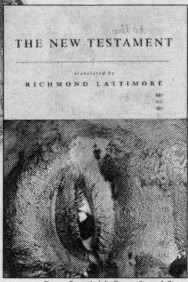

Energy Records, left; Farrar, Straus & Giroux

the memento mori.

r floor. "There was an incredible high
-f life in New York at the time," he
r-d said, but scratch its surface and one
g found "the whole violent and insane
o-e side of New York, which always was
e and will remain a part of the city."
Graphic design projects can range
from the sacred to the profane. One
of the most notorious: a cover design
by the renowned book designer Chip
-f Kidd for the Richmond Lattimore
p translation of the New Testament,
n-d published last year by Farrar,
-r Straus & Giroux. It featured a Serra-
ny- no photograph of a dead man's face
l — all glazed eyes and blood-stained
-s skin. "It's horrifying, but also kind of
ny-e serenely beautiful," said Mr. Kidd,
s who was told to think of the transla-
-e tion as a literary novel. "The cover
-s was startling and fresh and true,"
s noted Laurie Brown, vice president
-s of marketing at Farrar, Straus &
s Giroux. "But we had quite a strong
negative reaction from buyers at
Waldenbooks and Barnes & Noble."
She pointed out that the forthcoming
paperback will offer a more traditional image of Christ on the cross.
Mr. Kidd's current design for Edmund White's novel "The Farewell

Amen.

THE IRONY OF THE DESIGN FOR RICHMOND LATTIMORE'S *The New Testament* is that I owe its existence to Michael Ian Kaye, who has been cited more than once as my "greatest rival" in the "world of book jackets." No such rivalry exists, and when Michael was art director at Farrar, Straus & Giroux he gave me the commission of a lifetime. I had said in *Interview* magazine that the one jacket I always wanted to design was for the bible, and now here was my chance. I was told that this was not a text for churches but for readers, and to treat it like a novel. When I came upon Andres Serrano's *The Morgue (Hacked to Death II)* in the pages of *Colors* magazine (Tibor Kalman's last issue as art director), I knew it was perfect: here was a face looking at and reflecting death and life simultaneously. It was horrifying and beautiful, compelling and repulsive. I also knew it would be considered far too shocking and never get approved in a million years. But I had to try, and to my amazement the editors not only got it, but with Michael's encouragement they championed it.

Then all hell broke loose.

Once the book was published with this image, no religious bookstore would carry it, and neither would any of the national chains. I can only presume this was due to the "guilt by association" with Serrano's *Piss Christ* (see the cover of *Blasphemy*), which is completely insane. And a disaster for the publisher. With no place to sell the book, it naturally didn't sell. There was publicity, but none of it good. The only one to benefit from the whole thing was me—the jacket won every design competition extant. But where I may have triumphed aesthetically, as a practical advocate for the book itself I completely failed.

For the paperback, the publisher went with a very tame and pretty shot of a crucifix. I can't say that I blame them. It was an object lesson in "It's not what you show, it's how you show it." And, perhaps, *who* shows it. Certainly years later Mel Gibson depicted far more graphic imagery to make the same point on film, but because his intent was perceived as sincere it was embraced by a mass audience. Serrano's intent in all his work, by the way, is no less heartfelt and devout.

Neither is mine. If I had to pick one single jacket I'm the most proud of, it would be this one. I never saw it as "getting away with something." It was about serving an extemely difficult subject (to say the least) in the most truthful manner I could—visually, and yes, spiritually. **RIGHT:** FSG, 1996.

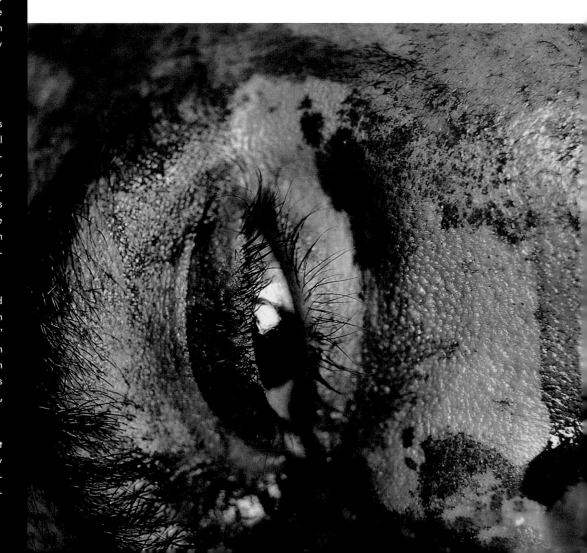

THE NEW TESTAMENT

translated by

RICHMOND LATTIMORE

"PEOPLE NEVER NOTICE ANYTHING."

— *Gordon Lish*

X - L I B R I S : C.K.; B. dW.

High and low.

WHAT IF KURT SCHWITTERS ACTUALLY HAD A sense of humor? And what if he didn't have to cut up originals or send out for c-prints? With the introduction of the color Xerox machine into the Knopf/Random House art department in the early 1990s, these two questions hovered high in my mind. Here was a new way to make and manipulate images, and a harbinger of the computer age yet to come. When David Byrne approached me to work on the design of his second solo album, *Uh-Oh*, one of the ideas he wanted me to pursue (among many) was combining imagery of clowns and God. And our new Canon laser copier would be the ideal means. **OPPOSITE:** Collage studies for fun (top, the "Mona-graphs"), and also (bottom) for David Byrne's *Uh-Oh*. **FAR LEFT:** The most successful of the experiments—it completely transforms the source material (left) to make a new, unique image. I thought for sure this would be perfect for the album cover, but to my surprise and frustration David demurred and asked me to keep working on it and try something else. I soon withdrew from the project and took my Jesus-clown with me. It wouldn't be long until I found another place for him . . .

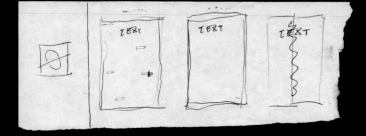

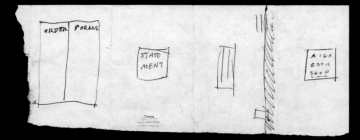

Ex-communication libris.

IN 1991 I WAS INVITED TO CHAIR THE ANNUAL BOOK SHOW of the American Institute of Graphic Arts (AIGA), the most prestigious book design competition in the country. I was extremely honored, not only because of the post but also because I was the youngest person ever tapped to take it on. Among my duties was designing the Call for Entries poster/brochure to be sent out to prospective participants. This was going to be fun, but also extremely intimidating—every graphic designer in the country worth his or her salt was going to see it. I decided to give it a book-like form, with a front cover sporting a re-imagining of the organization's logo, opening up into a spread with a faux bookplate and endpaper on the left and copy on the right set to look like the page of a textbook. Interspersed within the body of the instructions was an extended quote about interpretation by Gordon Lish, from his book *Mourner at the Door*. For the bookplate itself, I used another quote from Gordon, my and Barbara's initials, and . . . you guessed it. There were, of course, some complaints from a few of the more conservative chapters—I would have been amazed if there hadn't been. But everyone at the organization headquarters was extremely supportive. It was also my responsibility to get the printing donated, and for that I was lucky to have Frank Capo and his always reliable Coral Graphics (the printer for the majority of our jackets at Knopf), who graciously took this on. **ABOVE:** My sketches for the brochure, original size, which betray both my lack of skill at making such sketches and my loathing at having to take the time to do so. **RIGHT:** AIGA Bookshow 1991 Call for Entries. I made an amalgam of the group's initials by directly overprinting "a," "i," "g," and "a," in black, red, and gold. **OPPOSITE:** The "X-Libris" plate is hinged at the top and folds up, asking its own question.

AIGA BOOKSHOW 1991

"PEOPLE NEVER NOTICE ANYTHING."

Gordon Lish

X - L I B R I S : C . K . : B . d W .

Eligibility: Please re
bookstores or, in th
have originated and
between January 19
should be entered in
category, we will pl
them to their best a
panel of jurors with
accepted up to Febr
any book if you will
acceptance. *It is rep*
"Tell them that I ha
Books for booksto
books, craft and h
bookstore distributi
books. Limited Edit
Format Books: Colle
all books in which t
mentation is deeme
Books: All books us
and high school te
including encyclope
niles: Books publis
Paperbacks: All pa
mass market. Pape
Museum Publicatio
logues and books (h
or university presse
returned. If you fee
of the book, submit
additional copies

What?

[19]

B O O K S H O W

[91]

"Nope, they don't, do they? So Lish is right, isn't he? Well, what people

sort of do is glance at the surface of something maybe. But, no, they

do not really look at it, do they? Oh, yes, it is infinitely safer just to

gaze. Which is why our job is to turn up the light. To bring the object

forward. To light the object all the way up. And even, if need be, to

color it strange. So that the actuality—the power—of the thing itself

has a chance of its being noticed, of its being revealed, of its being

disclosed."   —*Chip Kidd,* C H A I R M A N

A I G A B O O K

Eligibility: Please re
bookstores or, in th
have originated and
between January 19
should be entered in
category, we will pl
them to their best a
panel of jurors with
accepted up to Febr
any book if you will
acceptance. *It is rep*
"Tell them that I ha
Books for bookstor
books, craft and h
bookstore distributi
books. Limited Edit
Format Books: Colle
all books in which t
mentation is deeme
Books: All books us
and high school te
including encyclope
niles: Books publis
Paperbacks: All pa
mass market. Pape
Museum Publicatio
logues and books (h
or university presse
returned. If you fee
of the book, submit
additional copies

How did the male sex of God affect Israelite men? In order to find a place in the marriage analogy commonly used to describe the relationship between God and Israel, men had to imagine themselves as wives to God. To avoid the homoerotic implications of these images, they were feminized. Eilberg-Schwartz outlines biblical and rabbinic stories in which this feminization occurs, through the threat of castration, death, or more subtle forms of gender reversal.

In the last chapter, Eilberg-Schwartz offers a way to reincorporate embodied, fatherly images of God into contemporary Judaism. By embracing loving masculine images of God along with powerful feminine images, both men and women can relate more intimately to the divine.

Howard Eilberg-Schwartz is assistant professor of religious studies at Stanford University and an ordained rabbi. He is author of *The Savage in Judaism*, winner of the 1991 American Academy of Religion Award for Excellence, and other books.

Jacket design by Chip Kidd
Author photo by Carolyn Clebsch

"In this absorbing and provocative exploration of the problems raised when men worship a male god (while trying to avoid the sexual implications of that worship at the same time), Howard Eilberg-Schwartz uncovers many of the tensions and contradictions that bedevil conceptions of masculinity and male bonding to this day."
—Susan Faludi, author of *Backlash: The Undeclared War against American Women*

"*God's Phallus* is one of the most exciting and original projects I have encountered in some time. I have little doubt that the book could become a classic."
—David Biale, author of *Eros and the Jews: From Biblical Israel to Contemporary America*

"In the context of feminist discussion of the psychological and social effects of a father God, Eilberg-Schwartz explores the tensions created by the symbol for conceptions of masculinity. This provocative book will stimulate and complexify discussion of the psychological effects of images of God."
—Margaret Miles, author of *Carnal Knowing: Female Nakedness and Religious Meaning in the Christian West*

"From its beginnings, feminist theology has called on male theologians and scholars of religion to understand their work as gendered rather than as speaking from a disembodied, universal perspective. Taking this critique seriously, this exciting new book explores the dilemmas the image of a male God poses for men and masculinity and, in doing so, deepens and extends the feminist critique of male God-language. *God's Phallus* is an important and mind-expanding book that challenges readers to reexamine many received ideas about Jewish monotheism."
—Judith Plaskow, author of *Standing Again at Sinai: Judaism from a Feminist Perspective*

"An original and provocative work that returns the missing phallus to God the Father and promises to end the circumcision of the sons."
—Sam Keen, author of *Fire in the Belly: On Being a Man*

GOD'S PHALLUS

HOWARD EILBERG-SCHWARTZ

GOD'S PHALLUS

AND OTHER PROBLEMS

FOR MEN AND MONOTHEISM

HOWARD

EILBERG-SCHWARTZ

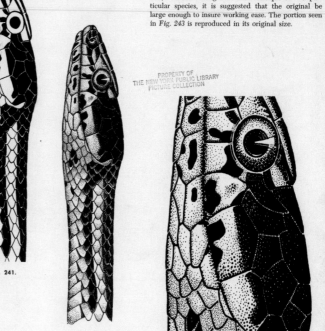

With a fine pointed scalpel (after the ink is thoroughly dry) start to shade the dark scales. On the white scales, use pen and ink for the dotted shadings (*Fig. 242*). When working with this technique on this particular species, it is suggested that the original be large enough to insure working ease. The portion seen in *Fig. 243* is reproduced in its original size.

Fig. 241.

Fig. 242.

Fig. 243.

The scratch board method of drawing is laborious and slow when drawing reptiles. Its greatest advantage, however, is that you may use dots and lines for indicating tones of color and shading. The first step, as you have been instructed many times, is to sketch your outline on tracing paper first and then transfer it to the scratch board. Ink in the completed outline and cover the dark scales with ink and a brush (*Fig. 241*).

An instrument of God.

NOW THIS WAS MY KIND OF JOB: it was my first freelance gig for Sara Eisenman once she became the art director of Beacon Press in Boston. My initial solution was an upside-down cross (right), which was deemed too abstract. They were right. Then I remembered the old joke about the "one-eyed trouser snake" and couldn't resist the biblical implications. The best part was that I was able to extend (sorry) the idea across the entire jacket, flaps and all.

ABOVE: Original source material. From the picture collection of the New York Public Library. **LEFT:** Beacon Press, 1994.

GOD'S PHALLUS

AND OTHER PROBLEMS FOR MEN AND MONOTHEISM

HOWARD EILBERG-SCHWARTZ

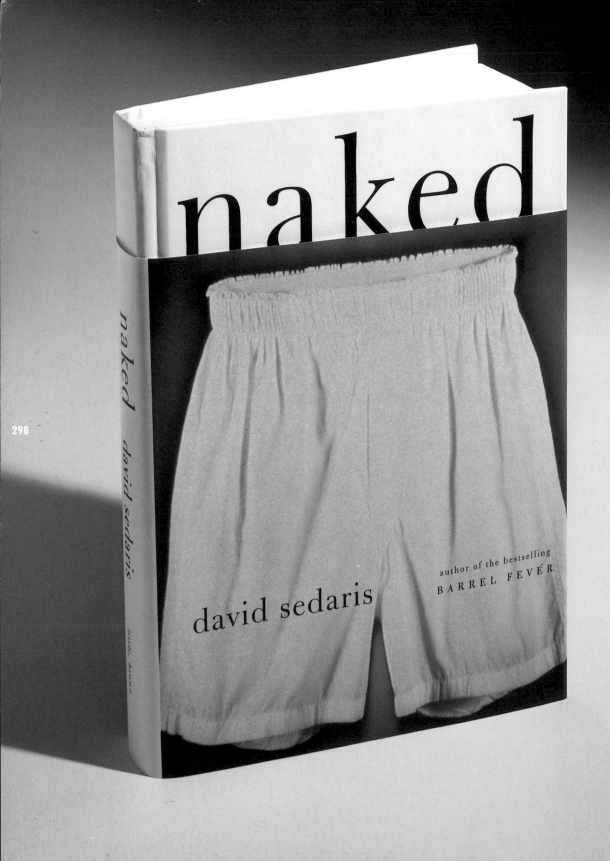

Shorts story.

I THINK THE HARDEST THING TO DO is make a book look Funny. Scary is a close second. But Funny (*truly* Funny), for me, is the greatest challenge. If you don't handle it just right you end up with Silly, or Goofy, or Undignified, or just plain Dumb. And dumb David Sedaris is not. His writing is as sharp as it is hilarious, and I had been a fan long before I was asked to design *Naked*, his second book of essays.

So back to Funny. It's not the same as Witty. Witty, you smile. Funny, you laugh. That's about as much as I can offer to define it, but as any humorist will tell you, if you only come off as *trying* to be funny you have failed miserably. So I think the best design approach is not to try. Instead you let the images, the type, and the concept do it for you. If it works, it will seem to have done so by accident.

After reading the title essay, which is about David's experience at a nudist colony, I felt the concept of nudity he was exploring was not about skin but about what was underneath, as in the soul and ... baring it. I couldn't show that exactly, but I thought I could try to replicate the idea. This demanded an attention to surfaces. Somehow, the reader needs a cue to "pull the pants off" of the book, and they get it from the fact that the jacket doesn't fully cover it. Why doesn't it? And what's under there? When they remove it and look, they usually laugh because what they see is not what they're expecting. But then they also laugh because now they've gone too far.

As for the typography, I ususally hate the conceit of rendering people's entire names in lower case—it usually looks too cute. But here I thought it worked for several reasons: 1) The title is all lower case too, which it needs to be in order to appear more vulnerable—it looks awkward and uncomfortable, and literally not covered by the jacket. 2) David writes in a very conversational style—you really feel like he's sitting there next to you, and it's tremendously endearing. So it's like he's speaking it, and when we speak we don't capitalize anything. Does that sound crazy?

Also, please note how relatively small his name is on the front, which certainly didn't stop anyone from buying it.

LEFT AND OPPOSITE LEFT: Little, Brown, 1997. David told me that at signings he enjoys taking off the jacket and drawing a penis with magic marker on the binding, right where it belongs. Wish I'd thought of that.

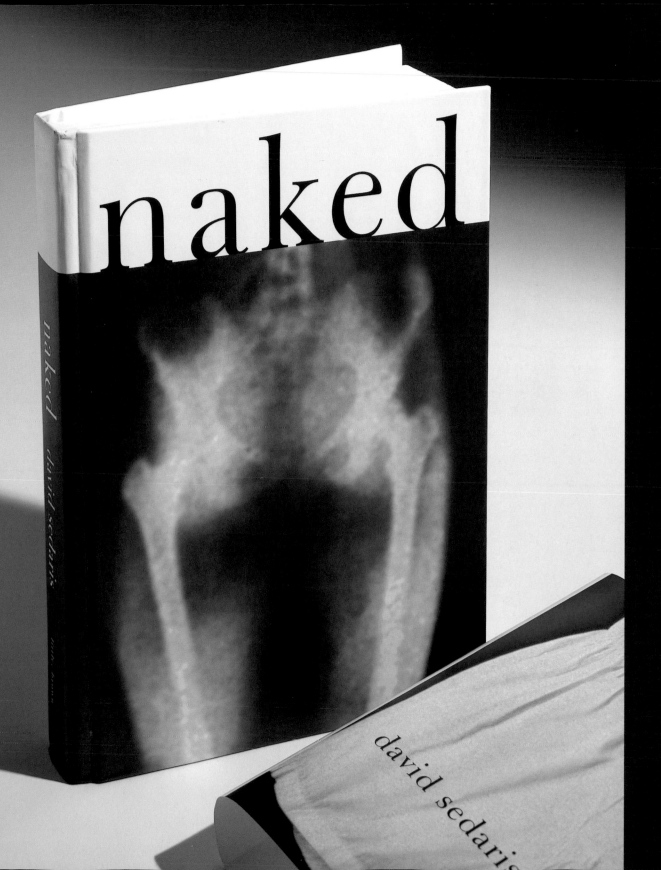

299

ABOVE: All too brief (sorry). Rejected comp for the paperback edition of *Naked*. As a logical progression from the hardcover this made perfect sense to me, but it was deemed too sexual. What is it about briefs that does that? I will always treasure the memory of meeting David for lunch in midtown and walking away from it with a plain brown bag containing his skivvies to use for the shoot. No, he did not shed them in the Men's—he very nicely brought a pair separately as per my request. I wanted authenticity. For the final cover, the hardcover design was adapted with the background color changed to red.

Process.

THE ONION: What's your process like?

CHIP KIDD: It's extremely organic. The stock answer is that every book is different, or at least reasonably different, so the process is going to change from book to book, depending on what they are. Sometimes you hit it right away, sometimes you have to do eight different things, sometimes the publisher or the author or the agent will wear you down to the point where you want it to be over with, and what you end up with is kind of a mess. You just accept it and move on. The most tiring—and yet the most rewarding—experiences are when you have to keep redoing it again and again, but what you end up with is actually the best thing. A perfect example of that is something I just did for the new David Sedaris book, *Dress Your Family in Corduroy and Denim.* I gave three ideas, and those didn't cut it, and then I gave two more, and I heard nothing, and I started doing photo research for a different job. Luckily, my design gene was secreting, and I just happened upon an image that I thought would be perfect. It was great. Those moments are worth everything.

—Reprinted from *The Onion,* June 2, 2004

RIGHT: Assorted attempts. None of these inspire, and while the Swahili one is funny, it is only funny if you know the source material, which of course the reader would not. The little blue guy, by the way, is a perfectly healthy human fetus at six weeks old. **OPPOSITE RIGHT:** Little, Brown, 2004. Photo by Oote Boe. Bingo. This works on many levels—graphically, conceptually, emotionally, with just enough humor. The thematic link to *Naked,* while not overt, is there.

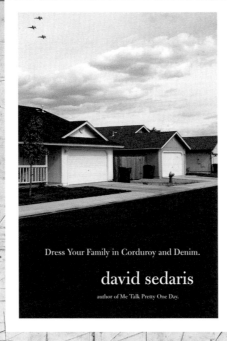

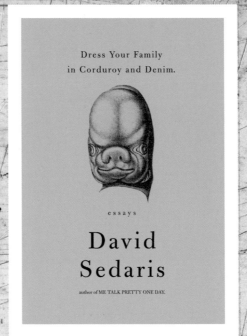

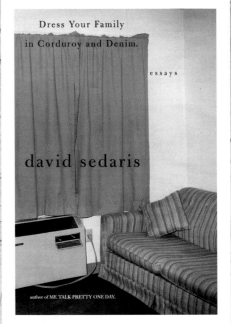

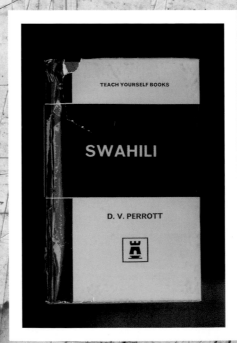

April 6
Dear Chip,

Thank you for putting so much work into my various book covers. I kept meaning to call you and talk discuss them, but I was never quite sure what to say. I have no vocabulary when it comes to design, and it seemed wrong to make suggestions based upon what usually amounted to a whim.

Each of the covers left me with a different feeling, but because I had no real understanding of the book, it was hard to tell which one best conveyed the contents. I liked the loneliness of the first cover, the one with the row of textured houses. The second cover appealed to me as well, the one modeled on a Swahili textbook. If I saw someone carrying it I think I'd feel a little sorry for him. It seemed like a book a person was being forced to read. This was exactly what I'd wanted, but when I saw it realized I understood that it might present a problem.

I also liked the cover picturing what looked like a head drawn onto a thumb. It was mysterious, this ugly face on a Tiffany blue background. I could have chosen any of the above, but couldn't seem to make up my mind. Then came the doll cover and the choice was even harder. I like that it widens the definition of family. I'd been thinking brother, parents, etc., but this suggests that a person can make his own family, out of people or toys or whatever is at hand. Were the entire doll pictured I'd look instinctively at the head, so I like that it's cropped, and I notice instead the impossible waist, and the simple joints for moving the legs. It's curious and I can easily see myself picking it up.

Now that I have the cover and the galleys you'd think I might have some concept of the book, but I don't. It's completely abstract to me, like the idea of a book I haven't yet written. I'm sorry that my failure of imagination had to affect you, and I apologize for not writing earlier. I chose a book title that made no sense, and you were the one who had to pay a price for it. I love the book cover, and thank you again for being so patient.
Sincerely
David Sedaris

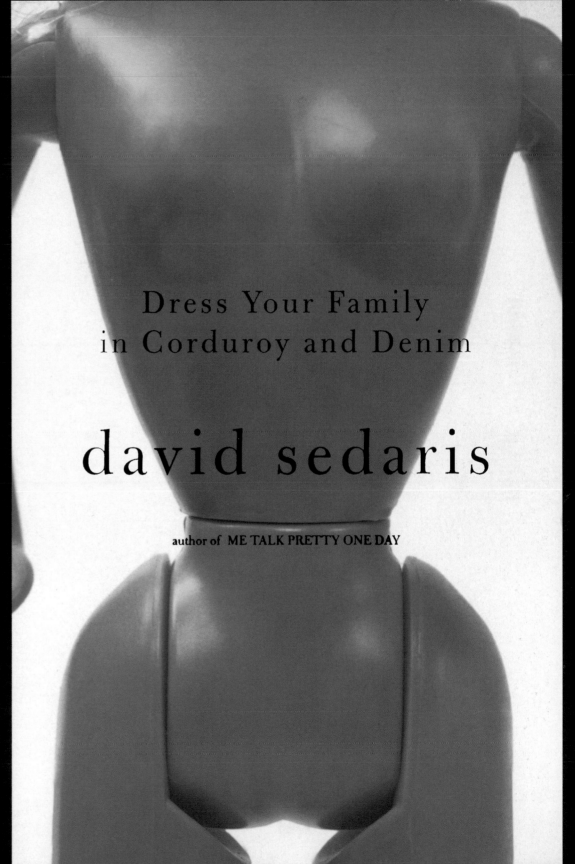

Dress Your Family
in Corduroy and Denim

david sedaris

author of ME TALK PRETTY ONE DAY

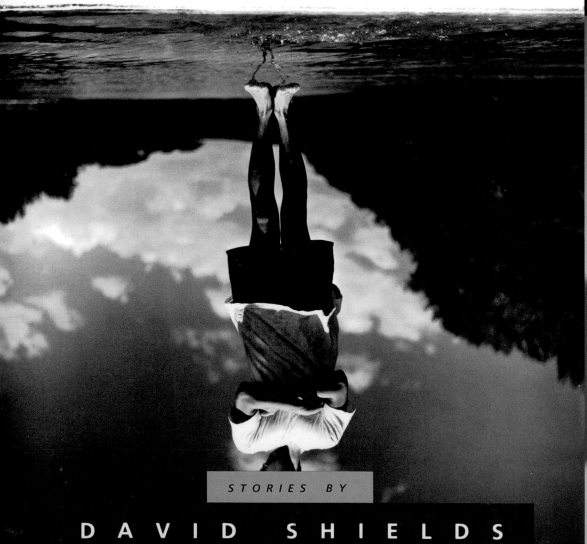

A

H A N D B O O K

F O R

D R O W N I N G

STORIES BY

DAVID SHIELDS

A HANDBOOK FOR DROWNING IS A KIND OF IMPOSSIBILITY (for whom would such a manual be intended? who would bother to compose such a gloomy guide?), as is the photograph: unreadable, paradoxical, is he sinking or ascending or, somehow, perhaps, doing both simultaneously?

Browsers often can't abide the endlessly falling figure and need to turn the book "right side up"—upside down—but any such resurrection reveals the method of its contrivance.

The isolation of the widely spaced sans serif characters; the boy's blocked-out eyes; the blue, black, white, and gray of the sea; the water spilling over into clean white space: every detail is gorgeously, sneakily metaphorical.

—David Shields

LEFT: Knopf, 1991. Co-designed with Barbara deWilde. Photograph by David Barry. **BELOW** (case) **AND OPPOSITE LEFT** (jacket): Knopf, 1996. With a title like that, what else could the design possibly be?

re-

mote

Knopf

DAVID
SHIELDS

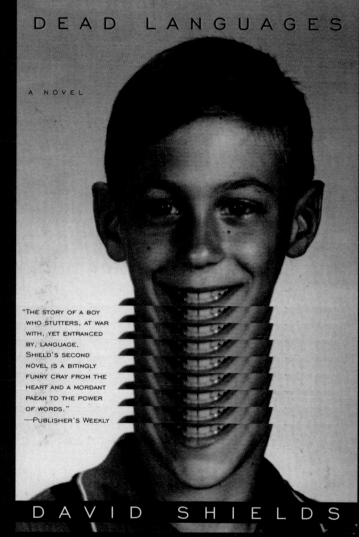

DEAD LANGUAGES

A NOVEL

"THE STORY OF A BOY
WHO STUTTERS, AT WAR
WITH, YET ENTRANCED
BY, LANGUAGE,
SHIELD'S SECOND
NOVEL IS A BITINGLY
FUNNY CRAY FROM THE
HEART AND A MORDANT
PAEAN TO THE POWER
OF WORDS."
—PUBLISHER'S WEEKLY

DAVID SHIELDS

303

ABOVE: A killed comp; the project was eventually handed to another
designer. Although seemingly conceived solely for this job, I actually bor-
rowed the solution from another design of mine, an interior spread about
Stuttering John, for *Miss America*, by Howard Stern. That spread, as well
as others for the Stern book, can be seen on page 238.

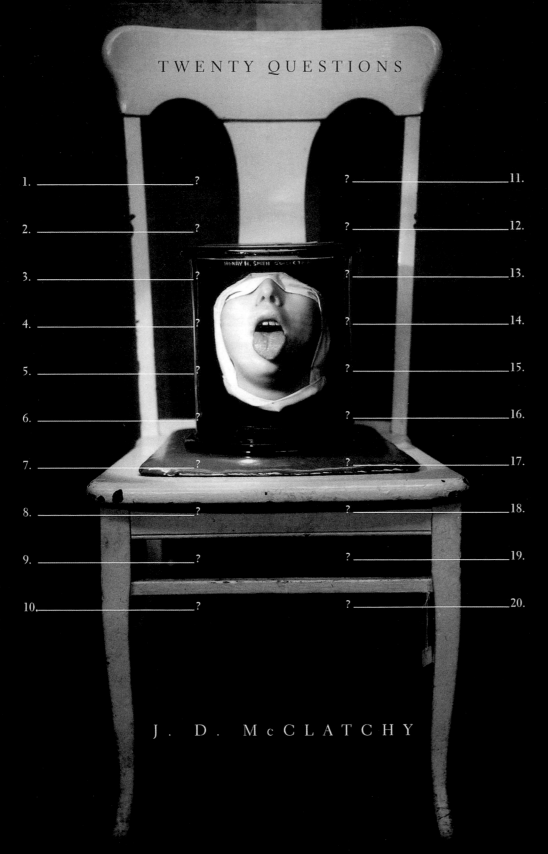

TWENTY

QUESTIONS

J. D.
McCLATCHY

COLUMBIA
UNIVERSITY
PRESS

The author who loves you.

COUPLES WORKING TOGETHER CAN DEFINITELY get into trouble—look at what happened to Bonnie and Clyde, Leopold and Loeb, Julius and Ethel Rosenberg, Sonny and Cher, etc. Even after ten years of our living together, I tacitly refer to every new project I take on with J. D. (Sandy) McClatchy as The Latest Test of Our Relationship. It's gotten easier with time, but at first there were sparks—he thought I was too weird and I thought he was too stuffy. I mean, really: how can you *not* use a perfectly good photograph of a disembodied diseased mouth in a jar lying on a rickety old chair for your collection of scholarly essays? Loosen up! Seriously though, I've been lucky enough to know two true geniuses in my life, and Sandy is the one who stole my heart. But he's done more than that—he's given me a day-to-day example of what it means to work with intellectual panache, unstinting energy, and an eloquent moral authority. **LEFT:** Columbia University Press, 1998. Photograph by Max Aguilera-Helwig. **ABOVE:** Photograph by Marion Ettlinger, 1996. **OPPOSITE LEFT, BOTTOM:** Redesign for *The Yale Review*, 1999. **OPPOSITE RIGHT:** Vintage, 1996.

THE VOICE OF THE POET

SYLVIA PLATH

*Includes never-before released recordings
read by the author*

companion book contains the text of the poems
and a commentary by J. D. McClatchy

THE VOICE OF THE POET

W. H. AUDEN

*Includes never-before released recordings
read by the author*

A companion book contains the text of the poems
and a commentary by J. D. McClatchy

YR

THE YALE REVIEW

OCTOBER 1999

Volume 87
No. 4

IT HAS BEEN SAID THAT A POEM IS "A MOMENT'S MONUMENT." So is a photograph. Most collections of poems have had—no, continue to have—decorous High Art or typographical cover "solutions," reinforcing with a yawn the aloof nature of the book's contents. Chip's eye searches instead for images that embody not the matter but the intention of a book. The photograph's realism grounds the book, yes, but the haunting composition of his cropping and brilliant placement of type give an eerily iconic look to the jacket. This is design at work in the way poetry is meant to affect its readers: by creating in them new alignments of feeling.

—J. D. McClatchy

ABOVE: Random House Audio, 2003. Series of poets reading their own work, produced by Jane Garmey. The great part about the Plath tape is that on Side A she's still married to Ted Hughes—and has a relatively confident, comfortable tone. Side B is recordings after he left her—right before she baked her own head—and she sounds like she's trying to simultaneously squirt blood from her eyes. As a piece of unintended conceptual performance art *alone* it's astounding. Run, don't walk.

THE VINTAGE BOOK OF CONTEMPORARY WORLD POETRY

EDITED BY J.D. McCLATCHY

EIGHTY OUTSTANDING POETS, INCLUDING:

PABLO NERUDA

PIER PAOLO PASOLINI

PAUL CELAN

DEREK WALCOTT

JOSEPH BRODSKY

CZESŁAW MIŁOSZ

OCTAVIO PAZ

BEI DAO

NÂZIM HIKMET

ODYSSEUS ELYTIS

ZBIGNIEW HERBERT

INGEBORG BACHMANN

WOLE SOYINKA

YEHUDA AMICHAI

WISŁAWA SZYMBORSKA

ROBERTO JUARROZ

YANNIS RITSOS

YVES BONNEFOY

hazmat

J. D. McClatchy

J. D. McClatchy

Ten Commandments

J. D. McCLATCHY

1.
2.
3.
4.
5.
6.
7.
8.
9.
10.

COMMANDMENTS

POEMS

Knopf

KNOPF

'EMMELINE' IS THE OEDIPAL TRUE STORY OF A WOMAN IN RURAL, CIVIL WAR–ERA MASSACHUSETTS who unwittingly marries her own son. Sandy wrote the libretto for this ideal stuff of opera. Frustrated that I couldn't design the poster for its City Opera performance at Lincoln Center, I was at least able to do the album package. **ABOVE:** Albany Records, 1998. Design assistance by Chin-Yee Lai. A two-CD set, I wanted the discs to look like they wanted each other. **OPPOSITE:** Knopf, 1998. Photograph by David Graham. **LEFT:** Knopf, 2002. Photograph by Erika Larsen.

ANTONIETTA

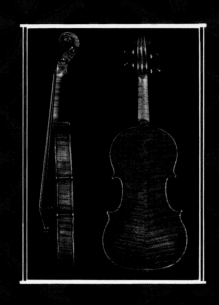

a novel

EVERY SO OFTEN EVEN A FULLY APPROVED DESIGN HITS A SNAG. For John Hersey's story of a violin handed down through the ages I originally used a background pattern by the legendary W. A. Dwiggins, who designed more than 300 books for Knopf beginning in the 1920s. Unfortunately, Dwiggins died in 1956, and his widow denied us the right to reproduce the pattern. While I was able to find a substitute (above), nothing could match the Dwiggins. **THIS PAGE:** (clockwise from above) Knopf, 1991; Knopf, 1990; Knopf, 1990; Carroll & Graf, 1996; Carroll & Graf, 1997.

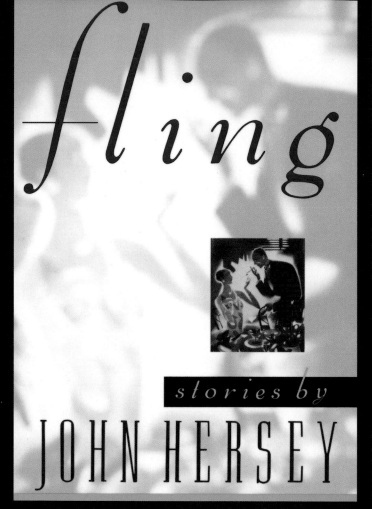

fling

stories by

JOHN HERSEY

April 11, 1991

Dear Chip Kidd:

The <u>Antonietta</u> jacket is stunning!
Many thanks. I'd love to know one day
what got into Dwiggins's widow to make
her refuse permission to use that
pattern. But the new one, subdued as it
is, turned out very nicely.

Sincerely yours,

John Hersey

PIETRO CITATI

KAFKA

ANTHONY BURGESS

A DEAD MAN IN DEPTFORD
[A NOVEL]

BYRNE

Anthony Burgess

BUDDENBROOKS

THE DECLINE OF A FAMILY

A new translation from
the German by John E. Woods

THOMAS MANN

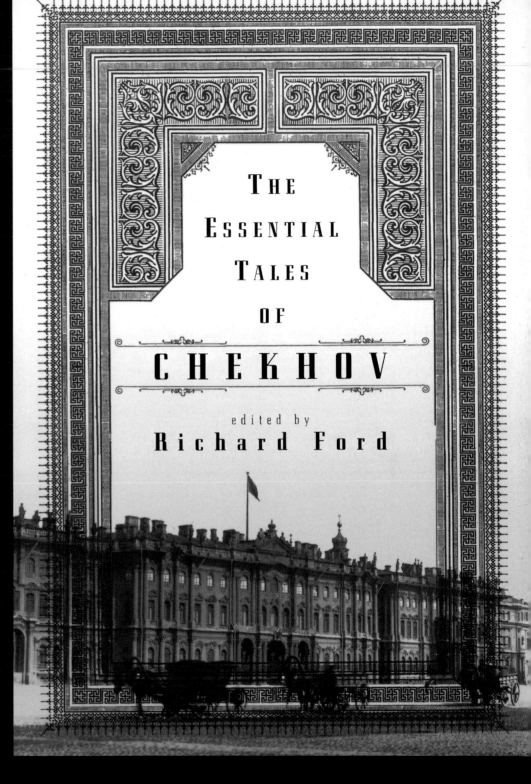

THE
ESSENTIAL
TALES
OF
CHEKHOV

edited by
Richard Ford

LEFT: Knopf, 1993. I had the classic binding of the original Knopf edition of Thomas Mann's *Buddenbrooks* photographed for use on the jacket of a new translation. **ABOVE:** Ecco, 1998.

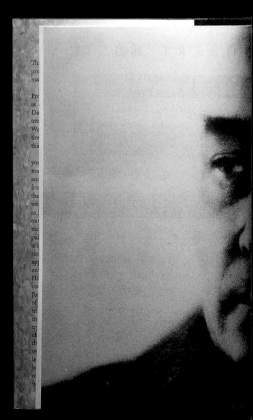

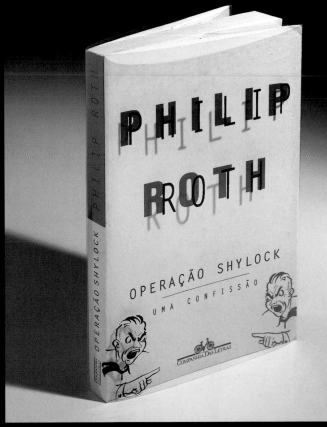

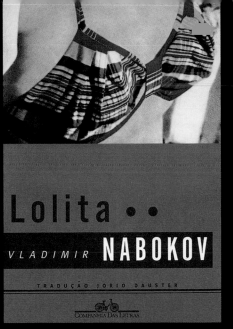

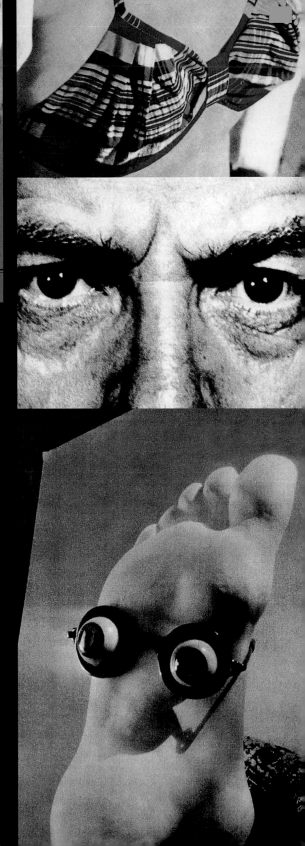

ROBERT MUSIL

INTO THE MILLENNIUM

TRANSLATED FROM THE GERMAN BY
SOPHIE WILKINS
EDITORIAL CONSULTANT: **BURTON PIKE**

FROM THE POSTHUMOUS PAPERS

TRANSLATED FROM THE GERMAN BY
BURTON PIKE

THE MAN

WITHOUT

QUALITIES

ALFRED A. KNOPF ✦ NEW YORK 1995

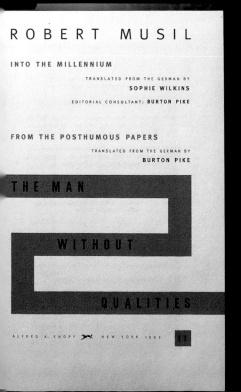

Qual-lit.

ROBERT MUSIL'S MASSIVE UNFINISHED NOVEL, which he began in the early 1920s (he died in 1942), has often been compared to the work of Proust and is set on the verge of World War I. It revolves around the efforts of Ulrich, the man without qualities, to find meaning in a society in which convention stifles a new era struggling to emerge. Experimental in form, the book eschews plot, relying on character studies and essayistic passages. We all knew this was going to be a major literary event, and the design had to be something very striking. Since this was the first major project we worked out on the computer, Barbara and I ran into many technical snags, but the spines-as-portrait-of-the-author idea was an immediate hit and subsequently has been widely copied. I remember with amusement when the question of flap copy came up: it was a shrink-wrapped boxed set—how on earth would a bookstore browser be expected to read it? But old habits die hard and intrepid editor Carol Janeway spent weeks writing it anyway. Brilliantly, as usual. **OPPOSITE PAGE:** Knopf, 1995. Co-designed with Barbara deWilde. Knopf has a long tradition of boxed sets of books, but this is the first one that's notched at the top, so the volumes are easier to remove. **LEFT:** Title page spreads of volume one and two.

My one steady foreign client is Companhia Das Letras in Sao Paolo, Brazil, for whom I designed a series of peek-a-boo covers for Vladimir Nabokov, one of my favorite authors. It's an opportunity I've never had in the U.S. They don't publish in hardcover, but are otherwise willing to go the extra mile with unusual approaches. **ABOVE LEFT:** 1997. *Operation Shylock*, by Philip Roth, is about the author and his doppelganger. **ABOVE AND BELOW:** (series), 1997. Try to sneak a look at Lolita's you-know-what and you get a faceful of Humbert Humbert.

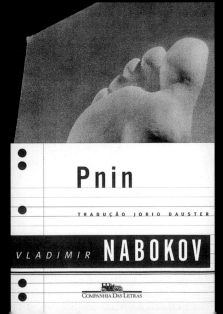

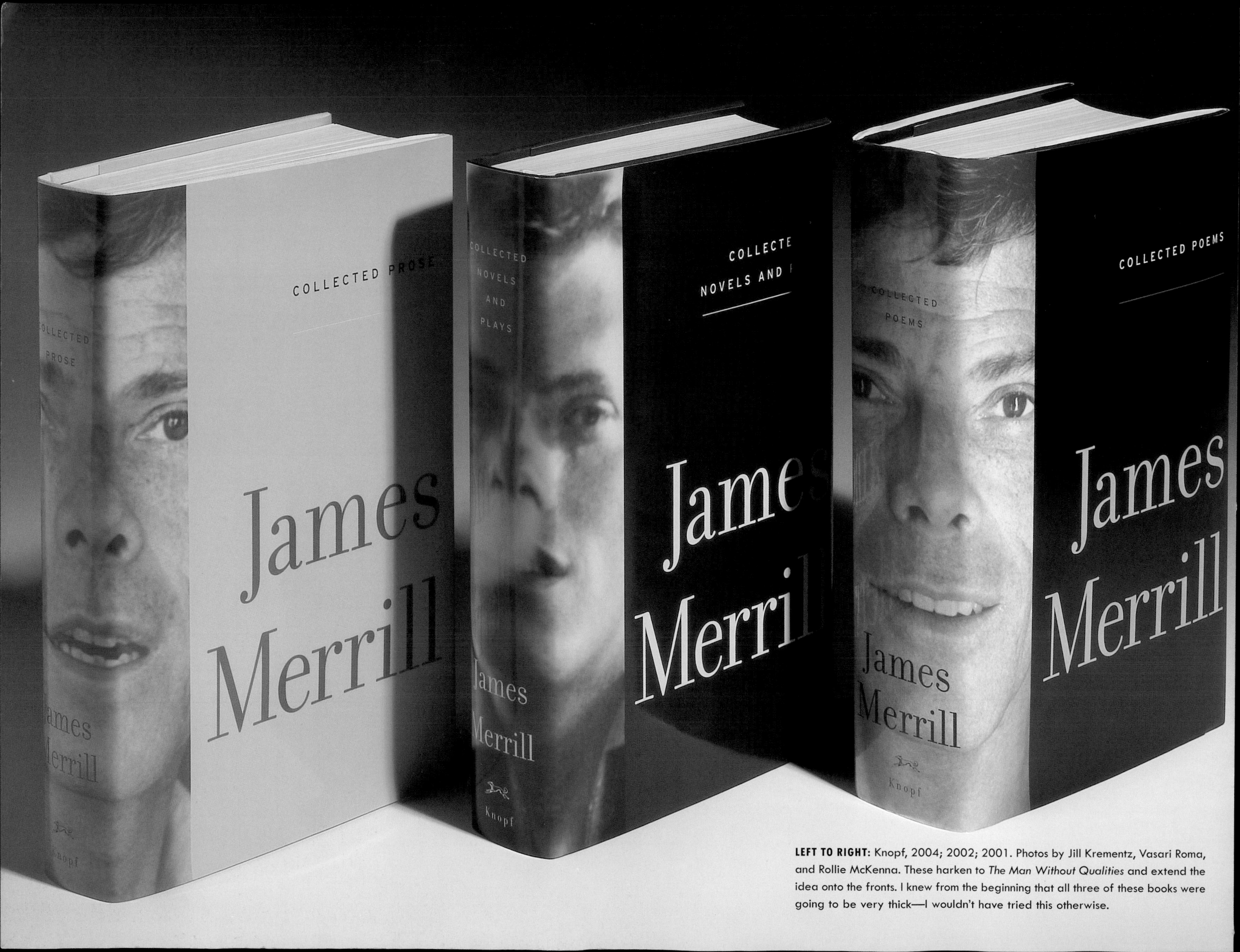

LEFT TO RIGHT: Knopf, 2004; 2002; 2001. Photos by Jill Krementz, Vasari Roma, and Rollie McKenna. These harken to *The Man Without Qualities* and extend the idea onto the fronts. I knew from the beginning that all three of these books were going to be very thick—I wouldn't have tried this otherwise.

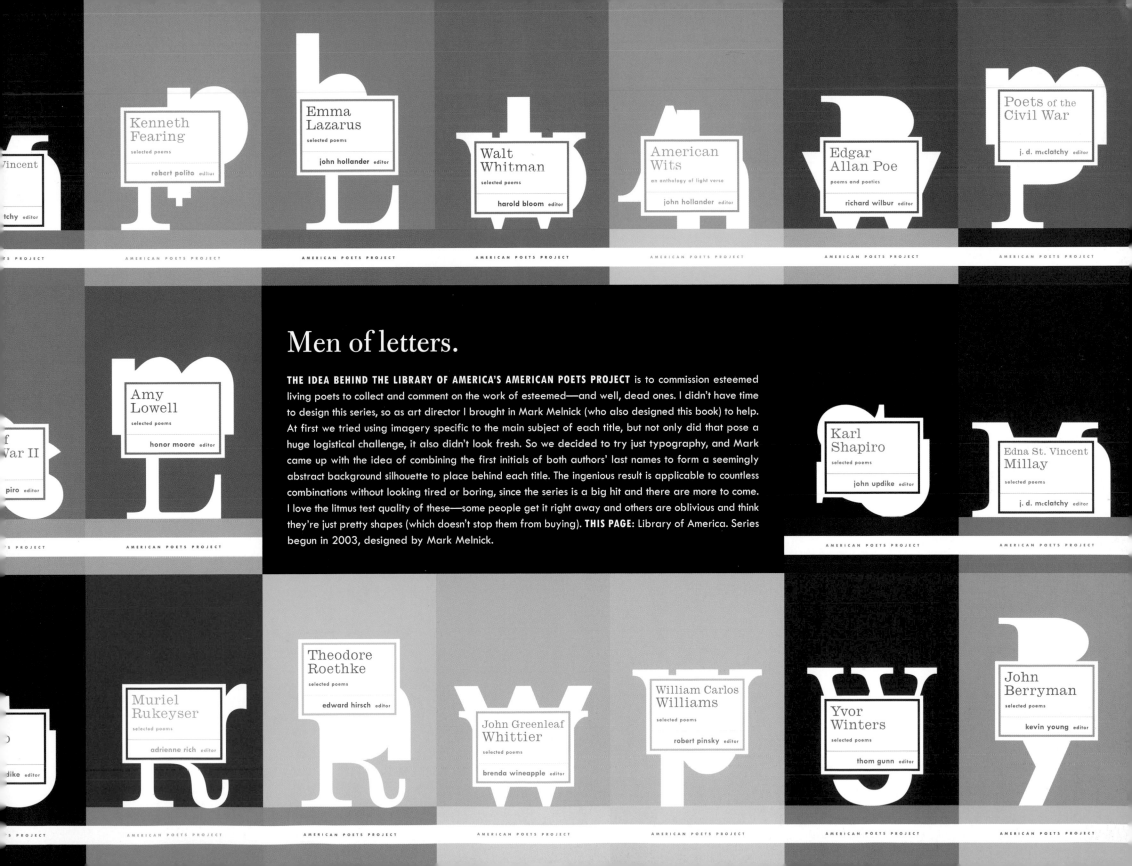

Men of letters.

THE IDEA BEHIND THE LIBRARY OF AMERICA'S AMERICAN POETS PROJECT is to commission esteemed living poets to collect and comment on the work of esteemed—and well, dead ones. I didn't have time to design this series, so as art director I brought in Mark Melnick (who also designed this book) to help. At first we tried using imagery specific to the main subject of each title, but not only did that pose a huge logistical challenge, it also didn't look fresh. So we decided to try just typography, and Mark came up with the idea of combining the first initials of both authors' last names to form a seemingly abstract background silhouette to place behind each title. The ingenious result is applicable to countless combinations without looking tired or boring, since the series is a big hit and there are more to come. I love the litmus test quality of these—some people get it right away and others are oblivious and think they're just pretty shapes (which doesn't stop them from buying). **THIS PAGE:** Library of America. Series begun in 2003, designed by Mark Melnick.

Vincent

tchy editor

Kenneth
Fearing

selected poems

robert polito editor

Emma
Lazarus

selected poems

john hollander editor

Walt
Whitman

selected poems

harold bloom editor

American
Wits

an anthology of light verse

john hollander editor

Edgar
Allan Poe

poems and poetics

richard wilbur editor

Poets of the
Civil War

j. d. mcclatchy editor

f
War II

piro editor

Amy
Lowell

selected poems

honor moore editor

Karl
Shapiro

selected poems

john updike editor

Edna St. Vincent
Millay

selected poems

j. d. mcclatchy editor

dike editor

Muriel
Rukeyser

selected poems

adrienne rich editor

Theodore
Roethke

selected poems

edward hirsch editor

John Greenleaf
Whittier

selected poems

brenda wineapple editor

William Carlos
Williams

selected poems

robert pinsky editor

Yvor
Winters

selected poems

thom gunn editor

John
Berryman

selected poems

kevin young editor

DOLDER *HOTEL*

u n d   V e r w a l t u n g s - A G

(*vormals* **Dolderbahn-Aktiengesellschaft**)

GESCHÄFTSBERICHT   1993

✠

1 8 9 4 - 1 9 9 4

Our spies are everywhere.

VERY EARLY INTO READING THE MANUSCRIPT OF *The Night Manager* I made an intriguing discovery: I recognized that the luxury hotel outside of Zurich that employs the title character was based on none other than the Dolder Grand Hotel. This in and of itself wouldn't have been that big a deal, except that at the time the owner of said establishment and I were a couple. So I phoned Andreas in Switzerland and asked him if David Cornwell (LeCarré's real name) had stayed there. Well, not only had he stayed there, he was a well-regarded annual customer. So I had Andreas send me all of the paper ephemera connected with the hotel: stationary, business cards, matchbooks, pamphlets, etc. Then Carol and I commissioned Bruce Licher to produce cards in his letterpress shop that had the elegant look and feel of the Dolder material. The final step was to have Geoff shoot the cards with lighting that played up the engraving and made it look nocturnal and slightly ominous.

When we did our presentation for David, it was in Sonny's office at the end of the day. Scotch was poured, cigarettes lit, calls put on hold, eyes eager. I was probably a little more pleased with myself than was necessary when I announced that before we showed him the jacket we wanted to show him where it came from. And with that I laid out the Dolder reference on Sonny's desk. Cornwell's jaw hit the floor, with a "How the hell did you know?" look on his face. Then he asked the question. I replied "Well, *everyone* knows the Dolder Grand Hotel." Then I 'fessed up. What really caught him off guard was that he hadn't told anyone at the Dolder about the book yet—particularly the night manager himself—and he was worried that there could be a problem. We assured him it would be fine, that the owner was delighted. He was relieved, for more reason than one, that we hadn't blown his cover . . .

LEFT: Annual report cover for the Dolder Grand Hotel, commemorating its one hundredth anniversary. At the time I was in thrall to the twisted classicism of the typography created for the Quay Brothers' film titles, and that's what I'm trying to mimic here. **OPPOSITE TOP LEFT:** Letterpress card, shown actual size. Printed by Bruce Licher at Independent Projects Press. **OPPOSITE LOWER LEFT:** A polaroid by Geoff testing various lighting effects to enhance the look of embossed paper. **OPPOSITE RIGHT:** Knopf, 1993. Co-design with Carol Devine Carson. I'm not a big fan of foil stamping, but in this case the little jewel of the canon (representing an insignia for a military regiment that figures in the plot) adds the perfect touch.

I THINK THE JACKET DESIGN FOR *The Night Manager* quite masterly: moody, stylish, delightfully unostentatious, backing elegantly into the limelight.

—John LeCarré

JOHN
LeCARRÉ

THE NIGHT
MANAGER

· A NOVEL ·

JOHN
LeCARRÉ

THE NIGHT
MANAGER

· A NOVEL ·

10 SEC.

Chip says you can judge these books by his covers

▶ *Continued from Page F-1*

Gabriel Garcia Marquez, shows a photograph of a shadowy woman dressed in turn-of-the-century garb overlaid on a snippet of mystical background.

A new biography of newsman Walter Winchell by Michael Herr features a silhouette of a man wearing a slouchy hat hunched over a microphone. The cover model, as it turns out, is Kidd himself.

Kidd also designed the cover for John Updike's recent book of art criticism, which pictures the Shillington native browsing in a museum.

"**Updike has** very specific ideas about what the cover should look like," Kidd said, noting that the author designed the covers for all of his "Rabbit" books.

"I wouldn't feel comfortable trying to design those," admitted Kidd, pulling his fingers through his lank brown hair. "Those books are like an icon."

He added, however, that "Updike doesn't design the way I would."

Despite his growing reputation among graphic artists, Kidd is acutely aware how quickly one can fall from favor in the highly competitive publishing industry.

"You're only as good as your last jacket," he said, during a brief a visit with his parents, Thomas and Ann Kidd of Lincoln Park.

Kidd, who developed a flair for graphic design while he was a student at Wilson High School, took off for New York five years ago, armed only with determination, a degree in design from Pennsylvania State University and a portfolio of his work as a student.

Kidd moved in with a friend who lived in an old factory in Brooklyn. The neighborhood consisted primarily of Hasidic Jews, who dressed in dark clothing and long earlocks. They made Kidd feel oddly at home.

"They reminded me of the Amish living in the middle of a big city," he said. "Living there was fun and romantic."

Every day, Kidd made the rounds of the publishing houses. Within six weeks, Knopf offered him a full-time job in the two-person art department.

Kidd was ecstatic.

Then they told him that his starting salary would be $15,500.

Kidd was stunned. This was supposed to be the big time.

"At least I didn't want to be an editorial assistant," he said. "They get $13,500."

Kidd soon discovered, however, that the job has other compensations. He sets his own hours, wears whatever he wants to work, and is allowed to do free-lance assignments to supplement his salary, which has risen somewhat over the years. Best of all, he puts his name on the back inner flap of every book jacket he designs.

In addition, Kidd has met many of the famous authors whose book jackets he designs. Some, he said, are gracious and professional, such as Marquez, Anne Rice and Anne Tyler.

Others bang through the publishing house with their elephantine egos.

"**First-time novelists** go berserk," Kidd said. "If you're not so uptight and insecure, you're not going to be as obsessive."

Shere Hite, author of a nationwide sex survey called "The Hite Report," was a dragon lady, he said.

"Nothing was ever right," Kidd recalled. "She drove everyone crazy."

Novelist Thomas Tryon was even worse.

"He was a nightmare," the artist said, his eyes widening behind round, wire-rimmed spectacles. "The book I worked on was awful; the cover was awful.

"He was mean-spirited and evil."

Kidd said he reads each book before he designs the cover, and sometimes an idea for an illustration springs on him immediately. Other times, inspiration simmers slowly.

"Sometimes I get an idea I think is perfect and no one else thinks so," he said.

Kidd, who condemns much of the cover art he sees as "awful, tacky and ugly," said he designs with the idea that the books, along with his covers, will be around for many years.

"They have to look good for a long, long time, so you want your work to age well," he said.

Kidd seems content with the direction of his burgeoning career and is uncertain about what his next step will be, although he admits to having an itch to write a book of his own.

"What do I want? What do I want?" Kidd mused, pondering his future. "I want a big ice cream sundae."

JUST
LOOKING

essays on art

JOHN
UPDIKE

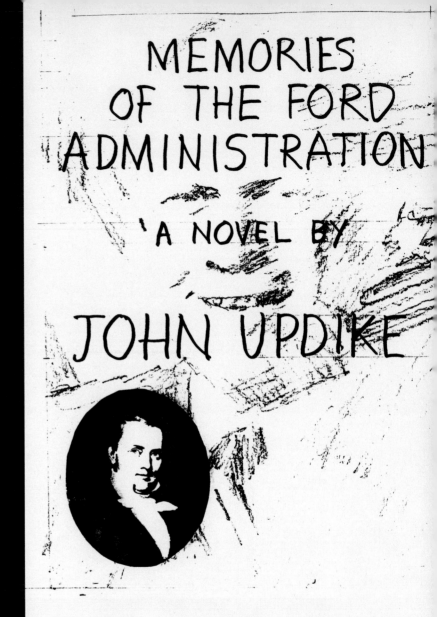

MEMORIES
OF THE FORD
ADMINISTRATION

'A NOVEL BY

JOHN UPDIKE

December 18, 1991

Many points, many goodies.

Here is my vision of the jacket. I like it rather more than I thought I would -- the letters fall nicely across Ford's features, it seems to me. To get the full impression you should hold it up to the light, so you see him come through. The photo I took this photocopy from was itself flipped, I think -- at least a smaller reproduction of the same portrait faces left in the encyclopedia. A good glossy print should be obtainable from the Library of Congress, and as I said the Eicholz portrait is a the Smithsonian. This oval is from the *Buchanan Dying* front flap; I don't know who made it oval, but it works well here, no? The type I think should be sans, to keep the busy-ness down. A nice no-nonsense sans, thick enough to read will black on gray. The toning of the Ford background would have to be done artfully as Carol and Chip can no doubt do it. Shades of gray, ghostly but not invisible. It's a complicated jacket but does go with the book. As I note, Buchanan could be in color.

Dear John.

JOHN UPDIKE IS THE ONLY AUTHOR I'VE EVER WORKED WITH WHO SUPPLIES HIS OWN SKETCHES. He also might be the only one qualified to do so, having studied both drawing and typography in college. So when he asks for the phrase "a novel" to be set in 19-point Albertus Medium, that is exactly what he means. Sometimes though, he lets me (or Carol Carson, who also designs many of the prolific author's titles) do my own thing and let him react to it. **ABOVE LEFT:** *The Reading Eagle*, 1991. My first interview for our local paper, and I sound every bit the snot-nosed punk that I am. (Althought the indiscreet bits about Shere Hite and Tom Tryon were totally true). **ABOVE RIGHT:** Knopf, 1989. Photograph by Benno Friedman, shot on location in the Florence May Schoenborn Gallery in The Museum of Modern Art. **RIGHT:** A memo from John along with his original sketch. **OPPOSITE PAGE:** Knopf, 1992, co-designed with Carol Carson. This was a big departure for John, as he says. I can't quite remember how we talked him into it, but he definitely gets credit for taking the risk. His statement opposite was originally written for the limited edtion *Fiction, Nonfiction* catalogue (p. 170).

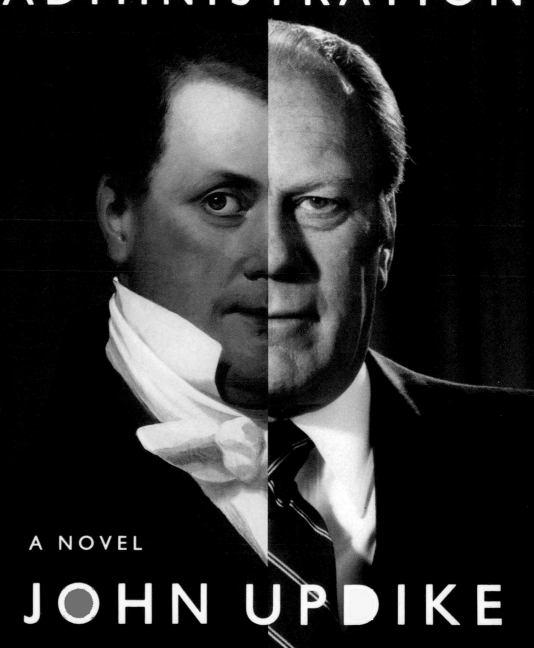

OF THE FORD ADMINISTRATION

WHEN I FIRST SAW A PASTED-UP VERSION OF THIS JACKET by Chip Kidd and Carol Carson, I thought it so monstrously ugly it must be a joke. I had offered a quite detailed sketch—which the art department quite ignored—presenting a much less violent conflation of the images of James Buchanan and Gerald Ford. But gradually I came to see the advantage of this one, as establishing, by its very weirdness, that my oddly titled book was not a political memoir by, say, a staid member of Ford's Cabinet but something more fanciful and wild, a novel. And so the jacket, approved, inched forward into production. The fit seemed better on the first trial than ever afterward; the shock and laughter must come with an initial impression of a single staring presence.

Nevertheless, this Buchanord splicing has some charm, owed largely to the rosy brick tones of the Buchanan portrait by Jacob Eichholtz on the left side. It is not a flattering photograph of Ford and not the one I had chosen. I think the jacket slightly misled those reviewers and readers who pedantically searched the novel for parallels between the Ford and Buchanan administrations. No strict parallel was intended, and the ways in which the two Presidents figure in my text are very different. The book is, in more than half its pages, about Buchanan, as a young aspiring lawyer, a middle-aged politician, and as an old President saddled with the Secession Crisis of the late 1860s. It is not at all about Gerald Ford: my narrator repeatedly admits he can remember almost nothing of Ford's years, except his own personal predicament and erotic adventures. In my proposed jacket, a halftone of Ford was muted to soft grays to serve as a background behind the print and a small, inset, oval, full-color reproduction of the Eichholtz portrait of Buchanan, almost like a badge Ford was wearing. However unsensational an image it may have projected, this design embodied my own sense of the novel and its internal balances.

However, a jacket exists on the borderline where an author's legitimate control gives out, and the realm of the bookseller begins. Yet *Memories* did not sell very well, as it turned out, and I wonder how many prospective buyers were scared off by this alarming apparition.

—John Updike

A NOVEL

JOHN UPDIKE

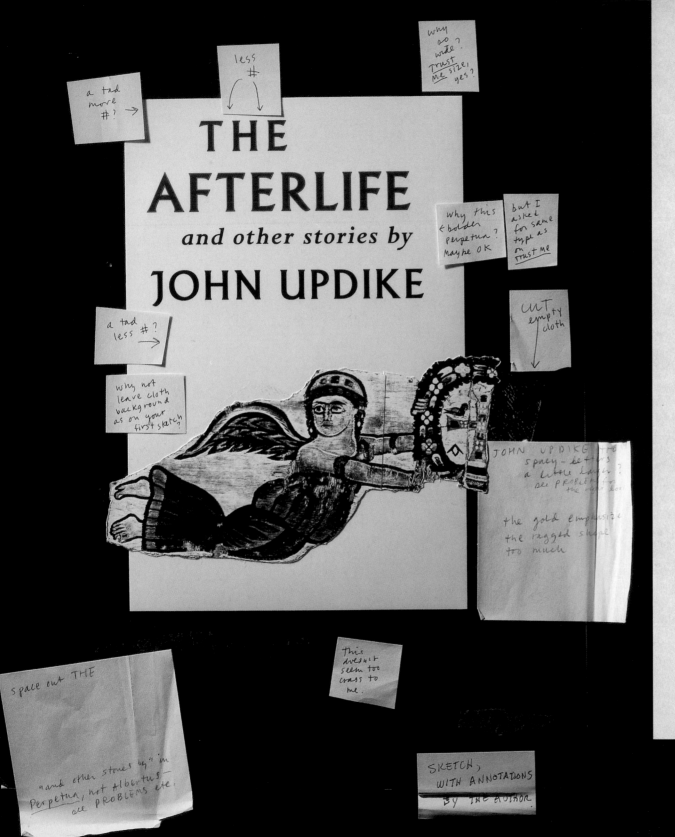

THE
AFTERLIFE
and other stories by
JOHN UPDIKE

a tad more #? →

less #

why so wide? trust me size, yes?

why this bolder perpetua? maybe OK

but I asked for same type as on trust me

a tad less #? →

CUT empty cloth

why not leave cloth background as on your first sketch?

JOHN UPDIKE too spacy — letters a little lower? see PROBLEMS for the next book

the gold emphasizes the ragged shape too much

space out THE

"and other stories by" in Perpetua, not Albertus ALL PROBLEMS etc.

This doesn't seem too crass to me.

SKETCH, WITH ANNOTATIONS BY THE AUTHOR

GERTRUDE
AND
CLAUDIUS

A NOVEL BY

JOHN UPDIKE

LEFT: John is nothing if not thorough. While some designers' hearts might sink at such instruction, I thought the attention to detail was touching and got a real kick out of it. At least he cares. 1994. **ABOVE:** Knopf, 2000. John found the illustration, and I constructed the type out of 19th-century playbills.

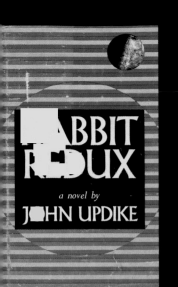

RABBIT REDUX

a novel by

JOHN UPDIKE

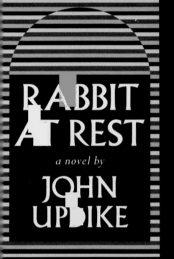

RABBIT AT REST

a novel by

JOHN UPDIKE

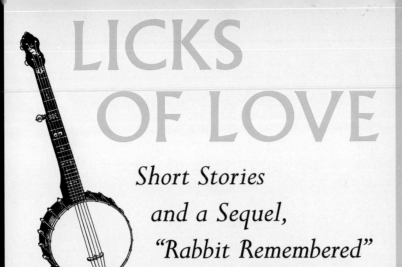

LICKS OF LOVE

*Short Stories
and a Sequel,
"Rabbit Remembered"*

JOHN UPDIKE

I NEVER THOUGHT I'D HAVE THE CHANCE TO WORK on a "Rabbit" title, the last of which presumably was *Rabbit at Rest*, in 1990. But lo and behold, along came *Licks of Love*, which contained a coda to Rabbit's life called *Rabbit Remembered*, and John wanted it designed in the style of the others. Best of all, he also wanted a drawing of a banjo on it—an assignment Chris Ware was born to take on because it combined two of his favorite things in the world: banjos and John's writing. **ABOVE LEFT:** Earlier "Rabbit" novels, designed by Updike based on earlier jackets by Harry Ford. **ABOVE RIGHT:** Knopf, 2001. Drawing by Chris Ware. **FAR RIGHT:** Knopf, 2001, incorporating John's suggestions (right). Photo by Geoff Spear.

November 18, 2000

Dear Chip:

First of all, thanks for the swift and obliging way you turned my tiny sketch into an arresting jacket. The pale blue, with a little more punch, makes a subtle and lyrical background. I do prefer the new title face, though I wonder if there isn't a third face somewhere that might be better yet. How would it look if you took the same face my name is printed in, using it in red?

Also, there seems to be too much envelope, and I'm slightly troubled by the bent right edge, with its bit of black. What I would like to see you try is: take an inch off the bottom and distribute the space in the top half, mostly between my name and the envelope. Maybe move the envelope over a half-inch, to avoid a knifelike wedge of blue on the right.

I would hesitate to make these tentative suggestions, but I imagine that computer magic makes such adjustments nothing like the hassle they used to be.

All best,

John

AMERICANA

AND OTHER POEMS

JOHN UPDIKE

John Updike

Seek My Face

A NOVEL

'SEEK MY FACE' IS THE STORY OF HOPE CHAFETZ, AND IS THEREFORE the story of postwar contemporary art in America. Hope is loosely based on Lee Krasner, so Jackson Pollack is the model for her first husband. After his death, Hope's second husband is depicted as an amalgam of Andy Warhol, Roy Lichtenstein, Claes Oldenburg, and Wayne Thiebaud. Set in the form of a day-long interview toward the end of her life, the novel deftly examines the mores and cultural politics of the art world. LEFT: Knopf, 2002. I wanted to show an abstracted painting of a face that was only recognizable from about ten or so feet away. John gave me free reign on this one. ABOVE: The jacket art (uncropped), by Nicholas Raynolds, which is in turn based on a portrait of Polyxena Stasova by Ilya Repin. Shown here just slightly larger than actual size.

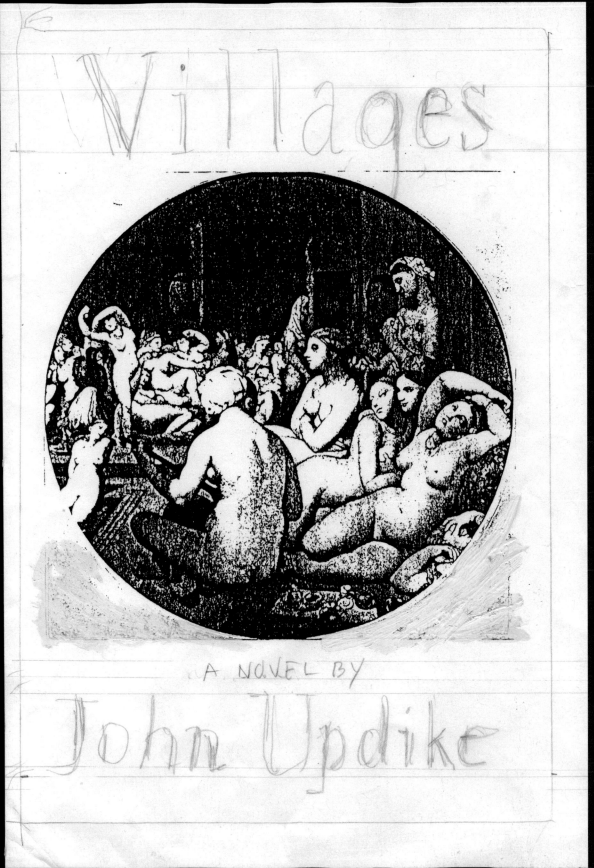

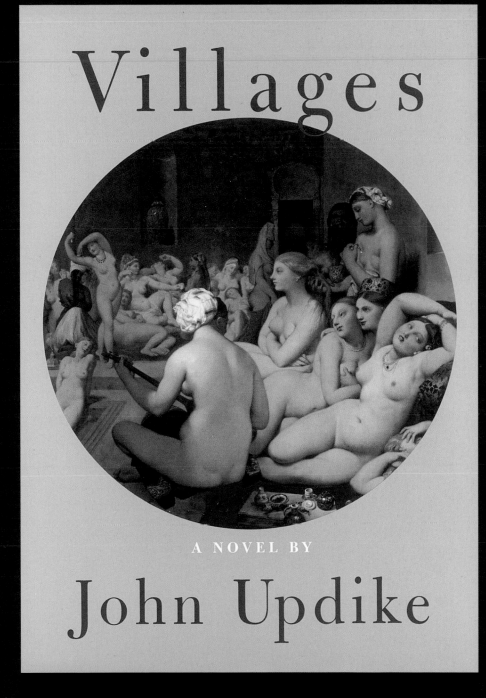

Villages

A NOVEL BY

John Updike

321

IN THIS 21ST NOVEL BY ONE OF THE PREMIERE CHRONICLERS OF AMERICAN LIFE, a man recalls a lifetime spent in three northeastern communities and the women who have beguiled him. Owen Mackenzie, now in his 70s and living in the small village of Haskell's Crossing, Connecticut, with his second wife, Julia, spends his days immersed in the daily routines of retirement while reminiscing about his childhood town of Willow, Pennsylvania (yay, Shillington!), and the village where he spent his adulthood, Middle Falls, Connecticut.
LEFT: John's rough sketch. **ABOVE:** Knopf, 2004. Art by Ingres.

All the Pretty Horses

Cormac McCarthy

LEFT: Slipcased promotional bound galley, which has since become a favorite of rare book dealers. **RIGHT AND OPPOSITE:** (left to right) Knopf, 1992; 1994; 1998. Photographs by David Katzenstein, Melanie Acevedo, and Larry Schwarm. True confessions: David's photo isn't actually a horse—it's a burro. No one ever guessed. And Larry's photo is not one of destruction but of an agriculture process by which the stubble of wheat fields is set afire to help recycle nutrients in the soil.

McCarthyism.

ONE OF MY FAVORITE STORIES ABOUT CORMAC UNFOLDED WHEN HE CAME TO KNOPF in the early 1990s, to 201 East 50th Street, before we published any of his books. He was either early for his appointment or completely unrecognized by the receptionist—so he just sat in the waiting area, unassumingly biding his time for at least an hour before someone figured out who he was and apologetically ushered him into editor Gary Fisketjon's office. He wasn't put off by it in the slightest. I was privileged to meet him twice—both times in Sonny's office, hanging out after hours and shooting the breeze, while I swooned and tried not to drool. He has since garnered a reputation as a recluse, but I found him to be articulate and charming.

It took some time for everyone to come around to the idea of a totally black and white scheme for *All The Pretty Horses.* Even after I showed the sketch, Gary kept regularly asking me: had I thought at all about color? Of course I had, and if I got my way there wasn't going to be any. The animal's mane in David Katzenstein's mesmerizing photograph was so inviting and tactile I didn't want to distract from it. I also wanted to keep it black and white because we knew from the start it was the first of a trilogy, and I wanted the jackets to form a triptych that would build visually to a climax. So *The Crossing* is duotone sepia, and *Cities of the Plain* erupts into full flaming red.

The divided-through-the-horizon-line design approach is one I've come to rely upon (perhaps to excess), but it represents not only my great belief in separation of type and image, but also suggests a theme of the stories. These books make up *The Border Trilogy,* which is not a metaphoric name. In each, the characters cross the border from Texas into Mexico, where they meet their various fates. And so, the eye starts at the top and reads the type and then crosses the border south to find the image.

The Crossing

Cormac McCarthy

Cities of the Plain

Cormac McCarthy

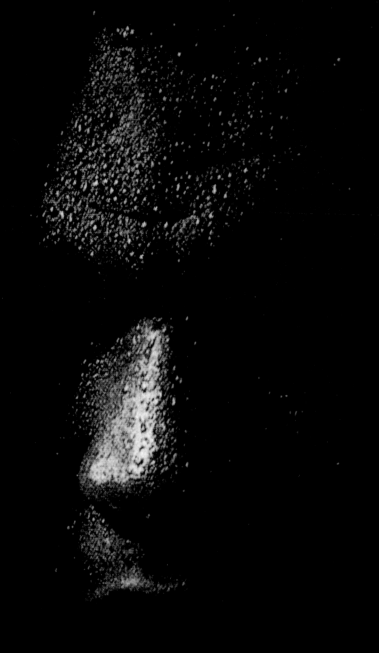

CORMAC McCARTHY

THE STONEMASON

A PLAY IN FIVE ACTS

NO COUNTRY FOR OLD MEN

CORMAC McCARTHY

the n*o*rmals

a novel

David Gilbert

author of *Remote Feed*

THE GREAT FIRES

poems *1982—1992*

JACK GILBERT

OPPOSITE LEFT: Ecco, 1994. **OPPOSITE RIGHT:** Knopf, 2005. Photograph by Matt Lindsay/Nonstock. **ABOVE:** Bloomsbury, 2004. For this novel about a psychotic drug test control group (the "normals" of the experiment), I thought this picture of scientists watching a top-secret A-bomb test made a compelling visual allegory. And of course the "o" of the title isn't quite right, which clues you in to the very abnormality of the proceedings. Photograph courtesy of Michael Light, from *100 Suns*, a collection of postwar nuclear test photos. **RIGHT:** Knopf, 1994. Yet another stat camera shot, this time ultra-high contrast. Note: authors on this page are not related.

LOVE IN THE TIME OF CHOLERA

a novel by

Gabriel

García Márquez

THE FIRST BIG "EVENT" BOOK I WORKED ON, with Carol Carson, was *Love in the Time of Cholera* by Gabriel García Márquez. Again, being the relative ignoramus I was, I had never heard of Márquez or *One Hundred Years of Solitude* before, and I remember secretly wondering why everyone was getting so worked up about this title at the pre-sales meeting. (Duh!) That changed very quickly. What a thrill to read this book in manuscript. **LEFT:** Knopf, 1988. Designed with Carol Devine Carson, photograph by Edward Steichen. **RIGHT:** My media breakout in *The Reading Eagle*, my hometown newspaper, in 1988. I'm sitting behind a large folded binding-type poster version of the jacket produced by our promotional department. I'm incorrectly referred to as an illustrator, which happens frequently, even now. **BELOW:** Knopf, 1990. Designed with Carol Devine Carson, painting by Thomas Woodruff. **BELOW RIGHT:** Early sketch. **OPPOSITE LEFT:** The Advance Reader's Copy for *Of Love and Other Demons* had a die-cut sleeve over a text-free version of the final art. **OPPOSITE RIGHT:** Knopf, 1995. Designed with Carol Devine Carson, painting by Thomas Woodruff.

Illustrator Chip Kidd holds the cover he designed for "Love in the Time of Cholera."

The General in His Labyrinth

Gabriel García Márquez

TRANSLATED BY EDITH GROSSMAN

OF LOVE
and
OTHER DEMONS

a novel

GABRIEL
GARCÍA MÁRQUEZ

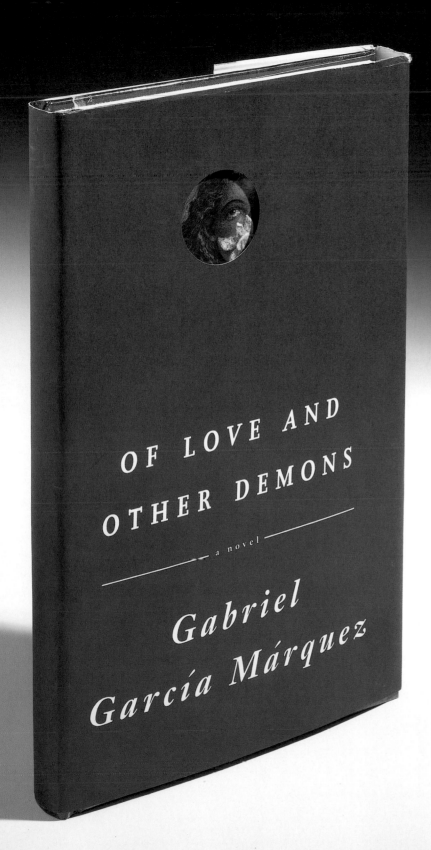

OF LOVE AND
OTHER DEMONS

a novel

Gabriel
García Márquez

TRANSLATED BY EDITH GROSSMAN

NINE NOTES ON BOOK COVERS
(translated by Maureen Freely)

- If a novelist can finish a book without dreaming of its cover, he is wise, well rounded, and fully adult, but he has also lost the innocence that once made him dream of writing novels.
- We cannot recall the books we most love without also recalling their covers.
- We would all like to see more readers buying books for their covers and more critics not despising books written with those same readers in mind.
- Detailed depictions of heroes on book covers insult not just the author's imagination but also his reader's.
- When designers decide that *The Red and the Black* deserves a red and black jacket, or when they decorate books entitled *Blue House* or *Chateau* with illustrations of blue houses and chateaux, they do not leave us thinking they've been faithful to the text but wondering if they've even read it.
- If, years after reading a book, we catch a glance of its cover, it returns us at once to that long-ago day when we curled up in a corner with that book to enter the world hidden inside.
- Book covers serve as conduits, spiriting us away from the ordinary world in which we live, ushering us to the world of the book.
- A bookshop owes its allure not to its books but to the variety of their covers.
- Book titles are like people's names: they help us distinguish a book from the million others it resembles. But book covers are like people's faces: either they remind us of a lost happiness or they promise a blissful world we have yet to explore. That is why we gaze at book covers as passionately as we do faces.

—Orhan Pamuk

'MY NAME IS RED' AND 'SNOW' COULDN'T BE MORE DIFFERENT BOOKS, requiring radically disparate visual approaches for works by the same author. *Red* is a murder mystery involving 15th-century Turkish court painters, and *Snow* is a contemporary existential romance that takes place in a small Turkish town called Kars. **LEFT:** Knopf, 2001. Deconstructed period paintings suggest a narrative of deception, lethal treachery, and illicit love. Making the title blue, for me, was a given (see point #5, above). **OPPOSITE LEFT:** Knopf, 2004. Orhan very handily had all the shots taken for this jacket, and that's the author himself on the front. I blurred it in Photoshop, not only to obscure his identity but also to provide a sense of mystery—otherwise, it could have appeared to be non-fiction. **OPPOSITE UPPER RIGHT:** Knopf, 2005. Orhan also provided the photo for this historical memoir. Actually, he provided what seemed like at least a hundred pictures, and I selected this one. The red border suggests the Turkish flag.

Orhan Pamuk

author of MY NAME IS RED

Snow

Orhan
Pamuk

Knopf

Snow

a

novel

ISTANBUL

Memories and the City

ORHAN PAMUK

Author of MY NAME IS RED and SNOW

Snow

a novel

Orhan Pamuk

RIGHT: Unused idea for *Snow*, shot by Geoff Spear. Orhan never saw it. The consensus within the house was that it was too creepy. I thought it was . . . cool.

THE ENGLISH PATIENT

PATIENT

Michael Ondaatje

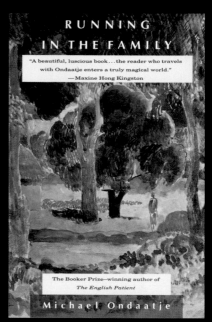

THE ENGLISH PATIENT

Michael Ondaatje

KNOPF

I GREW UP WITH SMALL PRESSES AND SO I AM A WRITER who gets totally involved with the production of a book. The final stage of any novel or book of poems for me is the clothing it will wear in public. And while most writers ignore this last stage, I immerse myself in it—typefaces, paper stock, spacing, cover design—I drive everyone crazy.

So it was a delight when I saw Kidd's work that Knopf used on the cover of my book. I love the startling sliver of Italian mural laid onto the desert landscape—the memory of one world a talisman in the other. And also the emerging of the man and desert tent out of the texture of grain and sand.

I am a writer who also loves the book as object. I know that any book is a gift, the best thing we can do and make for a reason.

—Michael Ondaatje

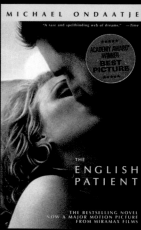

IT'S NOT EVERY DAY YOU GET THE NOTION to pair the work of Cecil Beaton and Hieronymus Bosch, but *The English Patient* seemed to demand it. We had just published a book on Bosch, so he was fresh in my mind as I read the manuscript. The descriptions of the frescoes in the dilapidated villa where the title character is being treated is evoked by the eccentric fifteenth-century painter's lush use of color, and Beaton's ghostly image of a nomad in a sandstorm perfectly evoked the scene of Count de Almasy emerging from a desert plane wreck. Their contrasts in color and texture let them play off each other beautifully. **LEFT:** Knopf, 1992. Photograph by Cecil Beaton. **ABOVE LEFT:** Vintage, 1992. **ABOVE RIGHT:** Dreadful movie tie-in version, Vintage, 1993. Independent booksellers actually complained about it and demanded the original be restored, which it eventually was.

LEFT: Knopf, 2005. **RIGHT:** Knopf, 2003. Both jackets resulted from extensive conversations with Linn. Her most unintentionally intimidating piece of advice on how to preceed visually was "Think of Bergman." As in Ingmar. As in her father, who was certain to see them. Gulp.

HAVE SEEN SO MANY DUST JACKETS ATTEMPTING TO LIMIT A BOOK, so many designers not being able go with the book's movement. The good ones, the really good ones, are able to go with the flow and thereby expand the book's universe rather than limit it. Being a writer and a woman, I sometimes get the feeling that almost every designer and publishing house wants to put a glamorized photo of a young female on the cover, no matter the content, no matter who is the narrator, no matter what the story is.

When Chip Kidd created the dust jacket for my second novel, *Stella Descending*, he not only captured the many different voices speaking in the book—he also, and this is almost magical, captured the speed and the feel and the fear of falling that the book is built upon and around.

Right now, my third novel, *Grace*, has just been published in the USA, and though I am far away from American bookstores, I feel very close to the American edition—partly because the jacket is exactly what I wanted, as if I had dreamt it or imagined it. And even though I wasn't able to convey to Chip exactly what this dream was all about, he captured it and made it real. I wanted something red, I said (or rather wrote in an e-mail). And he gave me red. The book is red like blood, red like wild strawberries, red like a coward's heart and a crying man's eyes, red like the fire of shame and the fire of love. It is as red as love until death do us apart.

Chip's dust jackets are brilliant, mysterious, daunting, and perceptive. He has always had my admiration. (Years ago picking up a novel by Orhan Pamuk and saying to myself: "One day I want to work with this guy. This Chip Kidd!") Now he has my thanks. When he visits Oslo I will make him a fabulous home-cooked meal! And serve him a bottle of Norwegian Aquavit to go with it.

—Linn Ullmann

WITTGENSTEIN'S

NEPHEW

a novel

THOMAS BERNHARD

THE LOSER

A NOVEL

THOMAS BERNHARD

EXTINCTION

A NOVEL

EXTINCTION

THOMAS BERNHARD

EXTINCTION THOMAS BERNHARD

Better off dead.

OKAY, I ADMIT IT: I would never had taken the time to read Thomas Bernhard had I not been assigned his books. This of course is my failing, not his. Hypnotic in their portraits of existential despair, Bernhard's fictions are austere and haunting. *The Loser* is about an aspiring piano player who is excellent but has the misfortune of having Glenn Gould as a fellow student. Gould's genius drives the narrator to give up music forever. The design just hints at the visual cue of piano keys without literally depicting them. What matters here is the human story—a man whose hands simply won't do what he needs them to.

OPPOSITE LEFT: Knopf, 1989. I hand-lettered the author's name myself, badly. **OPPOSITE RIGHT:** Knopf, 1991. Geoff Spear took the photograph, a black-and-white Polaroid. **RIGHT:** Knopf, 1995. An early Photoshop job. Someone—I can't remember who—voiced the inevitable worry that the title would be read as *"A Novel Extinction."* Luckily, intrepid editor Carol Janeway put any such fears to rest.

Mr.
COGITO

poems

Zbigniew Herbert

When we were Jungian.

ANYONE WHO WANTS TO UNDERSTAND THE HUMAN PSYCHE will learn next to nothing from experimental psychology. He would be better advised to abandon exact science, put away his scholar's gown, bid farewell to his study, and wander with human heart throughout the world. There in the horrors of prisons, lunatic asylums and hospitals, in drab suburban pubs, in brothels and gambling halls, in the salons of the elegant, the Stock Exchanges, socialist meetings, churches, revivalist gatherings and ecstatic sects, through love and hate, through the experience of passion in every form in his own body, he would reap richer stores of knowledge than textbooks a foot thick could give him, and he will know how to doctor the sick with a real knowledge of the human soul. Because as far as we can discern, the sole purpose of human existence is to kindle a light of meaning in the darkness of mere being. Everything that irritates us about others can lead us to an understanding of ourselves. Nobody, as long as he moves about among the chaotic currents of life, is without trouble.

I'm sorry, I zoned out there for a second. Was I saying something? It's these cholesterol pills I'm on. Just ignore me. **LEFT:** Ecco, 1993. **OPPOSITE LEFT:** Clarkson Potter, 1993. Photo courtesy of the author. **OPPOSITE RIGHT:** Carroll & Graf, 1994.

Kafka
was the rage
A Greenwich Village Memoir

ANATOLE BROYARD

¿eating
Pavlova

a novel

D.M.
THOMAS

AUTHOR OF THE WHITE HOTEL

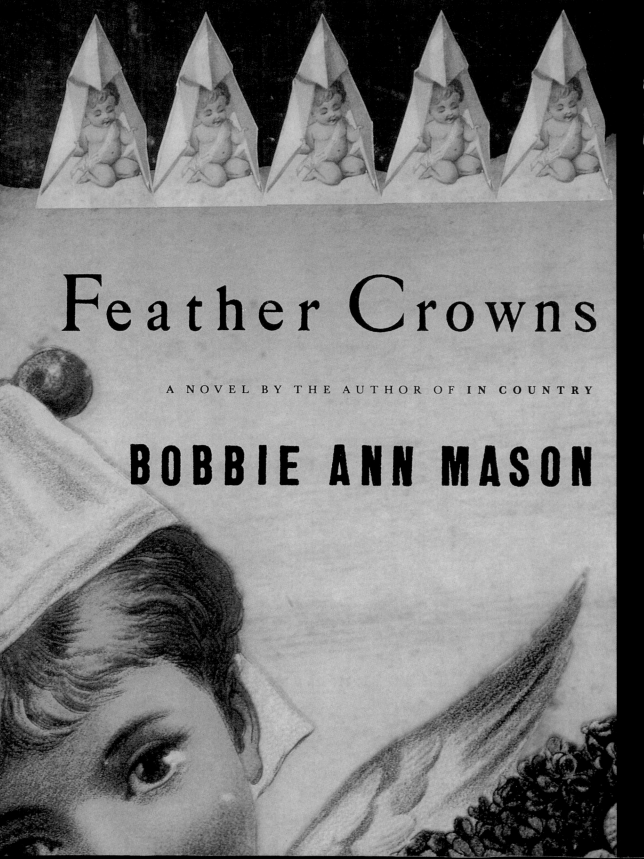

Feather Crowns

A NOVEL BY THE AUTHOR OF IN COUNTRY

BOBBIE ANN MASON

Rough around the edges.

SCRAPBOOKS WERE THE GAMEBOYS OF THE LATE NINETEENTH AND EARLY TWENTIETH centuries—a means for children to entertain themselves in the long-ago age before Pokémon and Grand Theft Auto. I've collected them for close to two decades now, and to find a good one (usually at a flea market or paper dealer) is to enter the mind of its maker. Scrapbooks can also provide great source material if the project is right. Bobbie Ann Mason's *Feather Crowns* is a novel about the first recorded American birth of quintuplets, in 1900, which is regarded as both a miracle and a freak show. By repeating the image of the baby in the tent-like blanket (above), both the quints and a crown are represented. **LEFT:** HarperCollins, 1994. **OPPOSITE:** (both) HarperCollins, 1994. Carrying through the approach to Mason's backlist. **ABOVE:** All of the images on the three covers came from the the same scrapbook.

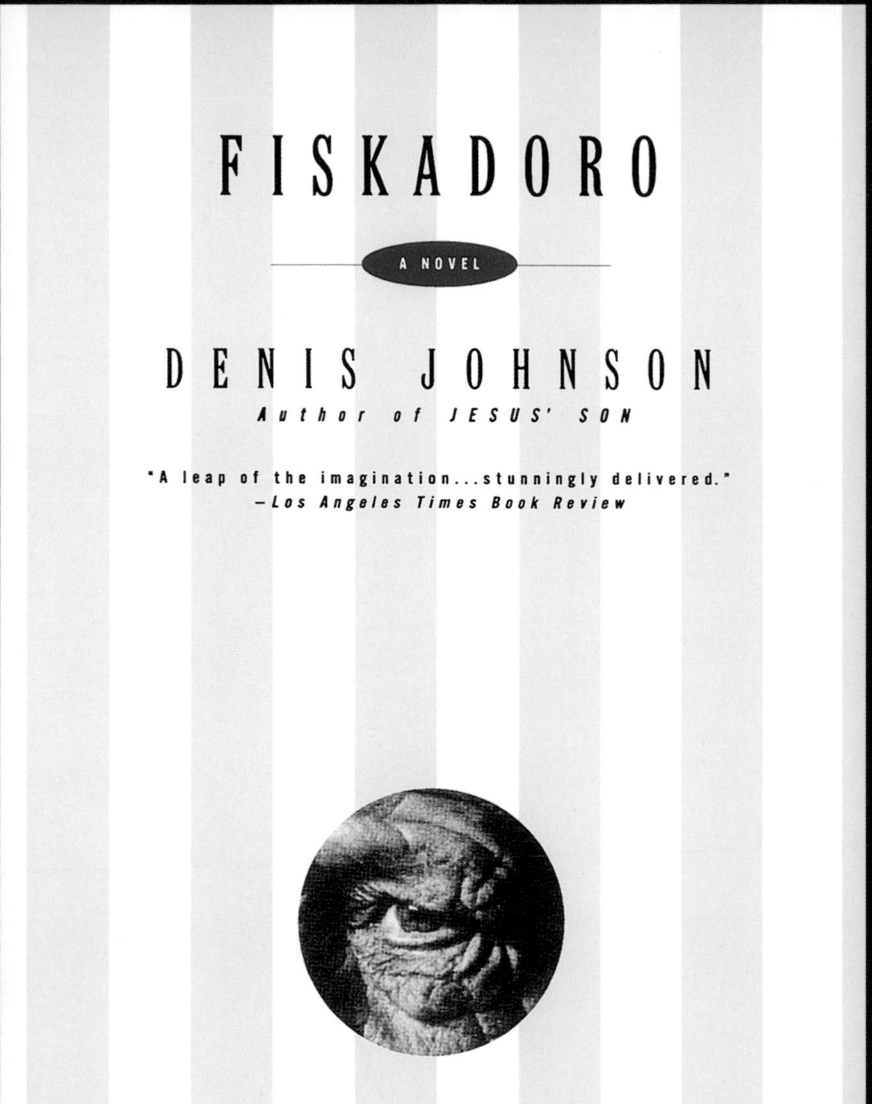

FISKADORO

A NOVEL

DENIS JOHNSON

Author of JESUS' SON

"A leap of the imagination...stunningly delivered."
—Los Angeles Times Book Review

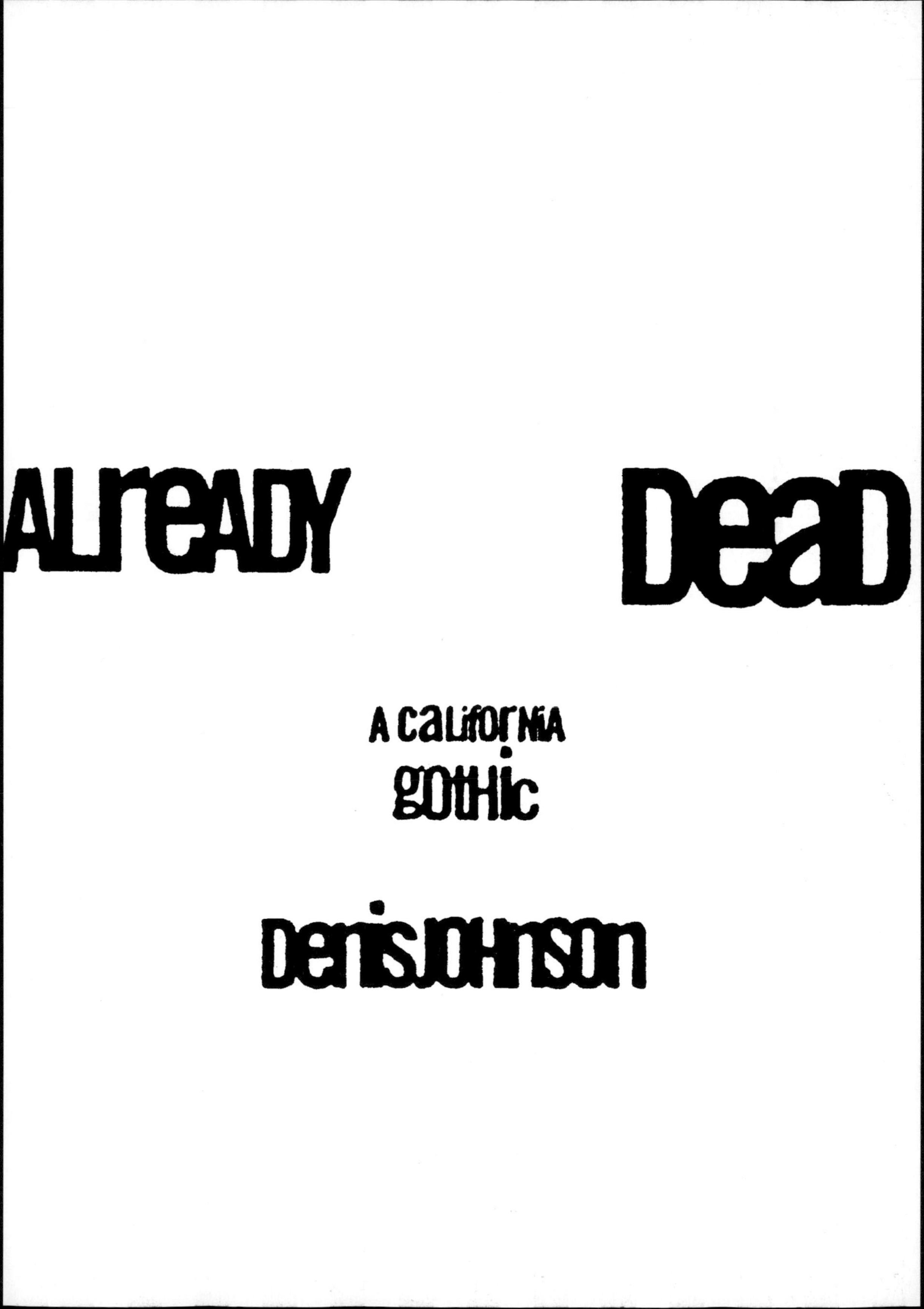

ALREADY DEAD

A California
gothic

Denis JOHNSON

MICHAEL
malone

time's witness

"GRIPPING . . .
AS RESONANT AS
TO KILL A
MOCKINGBIRD."
—BOOKLIST

A JUSTIN &
CUDDY NOVEL

MICHAEL
malone

uncivil seasons

A JUSTIN & CUDDY NOVEL

"EXCELLENT...VIVID...BEAUTIFULLY RENDERED...COMPELLING."
—THE NEW YORK TIMES BOOK REVIEW

MICHAEL
malone

handling sin

"PHENOMENAL...A HILARIOUS SUCCESS."
—THE NEW YORK TIMES BOOK REVIEW

CHIP KIDD WORKS ON ASSIGNMENT. SO DID HOLBEIN, BACH, AND MUCHA. And just as it is impossible to imagine Tudor portraiture without Holbein, or Art Nouveau theatrical posters without Mucha, so one cannot conceive of contemporary book illustration without imagining a Chip Kidd cover. There is a quality of Kidd in all of the book jackets he has designed. They are bold, vivid, smart, sui generis. And as he is a stylish, kind, and quickly witty man, these talents are always in his art as well. But there is also in Chip's work a responsiveness to the different qualities of very different books. The response is specific to that particular work, and it is quite remarkable. As a writer with the luck to have Chip design covers for many of my novels, I am struck by, and grateful for, his gift for finding that local habitation. He sees the fictional landscape shared by my novels, including a sense of place that he embodies with a strip of road map at the lower edge of their covers. Then, within that world, he gives readers the narrative tone of each individual book. The covers for Handling Sin, Foolscap, and The Killing Club tell you what those novels will be like to read. The romantic garden statue of "gentleman with hunting dogs" is perfectly right for the narrator of Uncivil Seasons; the blunt juxtaposition of electric chair and the capped profile of a modern young ethnic male is perfectly right for Time's Witness. All the covers are perfectly Chip Kidd.

—**Michael Malone**

ABOVE: Sourcebooks, 2000. All photos by Martin Parr.
OPPOSITE LEFT: Hyperion, 2005. A mystery within a book within a storyline within a TV screen, a project like The Killing Club doesn't come along every day. Or should I say daytime? Michael was the head writer on ABC's "One Life to Live" when he concocted the idea of having one of the characters on the show write a novel. Then he wrote me into the script as doing the jacket. Then he wrote the book. Then Hyperion, the publishing wing of ABC/Disney, published the book. Then they staged a book party for the book on the show, for author Marcie Walsh, who didn't actually write it. Confused? You won't be after today's sixth gin and tonic. Sorry, I meant episode. **OPPOSITE RIGHT:** Marcie (Kathy Brier) makes a miraculous recovery from her mysterious car accident to appear at her publication party, which aired 2/10/05. Celebrating on camera along with me are Hyperion editor Gretchen Young and editor-in-chief Bob Miller. Set photos by Steve Fenn. The

THE KILLING CLUB

A MYSTERY

MARCIE WALSH with **MICHAEL MALONE**

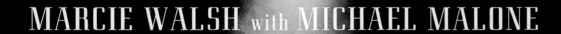

(CUT TO: ACT FIVE D: PALACE RESTAURANT. [AFTERNOON] MARCIE IS AT THE TABLE, SIGNING BOOKS, AS GUESTS LEAVE THE LUNCHEON. MICHAEL, JEN AND RILEY ARE NEARBY WITH CHARLIE, RON AND ERIC, ALL LOOKING ON PROUDLY. CHIP KIDD APPROACHES MARCIE WITH GRETCHEN YOUNG AND BOB MILLER)

    BOB MILLER
Marcie, Michael Malone was upset he couldn't make it here today, but he wanted you to know that though you may not have believed it, he always knew this day would come.

    MARCIE
Only because of everything I learned from him. (TURNS TO CHIP) And you -- do you know how excited I was when I saw you put my name on that beautiful cover?

    CHIP KIDD
Thank you.

    GRETCHEN YOUNG
Congratulations.

    BOB MILLER
We're proud to have you in the Hyperion family.

    MARCIE
Thank you so much. (REX APPROACHES WITH A BOOK)

GOOD AND PLAIN AS GOOD,
PLAIN WHITE People,
my thanks,
Alan
CHIP MY COVER IS AS

WHITE PEOPLE

stories and novellas by

ALLAN GURGANUS

author of

LDEST LIVING CONFEDERATE WIDOW TELLS ALL

THE PRACTICAL HEART

f o u r   n o v e l l a s

ALLAN GURGANUS

AUTHOR OF

OLDEST LIVING
CONFEDERATE WIDOW
TELLS ALL

Plays well with practical white people.

ALAN GURGANUS IS A CHAMPION STORYTELLER in the tradition of Flannery O'Connor on amphetamines—which isn't a traditional tradition, I know, but it works. I've done all of his covers since 1991's *White People*, and he's been a delight to get to know over the years. His readings are spellbinding, thunderous affairs, like Baptist revival meetings as conducted by Oscar Wilde. **LEFT:** Knopf, 1991. No sex for us please, we're caucasians. This kind of deadpan approach works well in a crowded bookstore, but you have to use it very, very sparingly, as it were—there's a fine line between effective minimalism and boring reduction. In this case it's the title that really takes advantage of the monotone and makes it funny. **ABOVE:** Knopf, 2001. Art by John Singer Sargent (courtesy of Christie's), who figures prominently in the title story of this collection of four novellas. **OPPOSITE LEFT:** Knopf, 1997. Poko-chan, Japan's Milky Candy mascot looks very, very naughty, for this novel about a young man's coming of age in New York during the height of the AIDS crisis. **OPPOSITE RIGHT, TOP:** Alan is a terrific penman and calligrapher—here's a pack of his penis-powered borzois, from a letter dated 1996.

PLAYS WELL WITH OTHERS

A NOVEL

ALLAN GURGANUS

author of *OLDEST LIVING CONFEDERATE WIDOW TELLS ALL*

"ONLY SUPERFICIAL PEOPLE DON'T JUDGE BY APPEARANCES." Oscar Wilde, the prophet, might've been praising Chip Kidd. Nobody finds more value-drama in juxtaposed surfaces: school photos, faux alligator, hardware tin. Now his work harkens to Kurt Schwitters, now to marbleized lava-lamps, next we get a tony touch of the Eameses parked alongside Walker Evans drunk on circus posters' tattered grandeur. Kidd remains a prodigy at forty since his way of seeing is like Huckleberry Finn's—mischief forever adrift and therefore always on course.

One secret of Kidd's wizardry? He reads the books. This might seem logical and usual. And yet, in our present Mad Hatter age, such genuflecting service to literature, such love, grows daily rarer. Bush-league shortcuts abound now: jacket designers read just the jacket copy then start.

But when you, as a novelist, receive Chip's jacket for your book, you are likely holding the smartest (and kindest) literary criticism your work will ever receive. The joy of having one's narrative sent out to seek its fortune whilst clothed in Kiddness! His sandwich-board wrapping constitutes a sort of body armor, a rental tux for life, some chain-mail warding-off of harm that every anxious mother wishes for. Galoshes, a halo— the fairest representation of one's true contents. My publishing contract now contains a "Chip Kidd" clause. "I am ready for my . . . cover, Mr. DeMille."

The first Chip Kidd book design I saw magnetized me. Talk about superpowers. Kidd had used dappled pony fur, plus metal slug letters found at some flea-market in his native Pennsylvania. I felt compelled to pick up the book in order to learn if each copy had not taken a goodly bite out of some child's unlucky pony. Turns out, the pony had simply been sat upon some open Xerox machine. But Kidd's trope yielded intimacy, my need to touch, hold, then adopt this work of art. Seduction achieved.

My own fiction has benefited from Chip Kidd's clarion reading and sly wit. For *White People*, a collection of stories concerning WASPs' politeness even while self-destructing (especially during that weekly rite), Chip placed undersized formal white letters on a deep black glossy field. The impact is like a wedding invitation from Hell. For the cover of a novel set during Manhattan's awful first wave of the AIDS pandemic, Chip found a Japanese candy wrapper. Its brand name, sounding mistranslated if sweetly, is "MILKY!" Our designer used this candy bar's mascot, a grinning pug-nosed cartooned little boy, to stand for all that Age's lost innocents. So *Plays Well with Others* arrived improbably bound in colors of heraldic ribaldry. It evinced the sadness of a newly made flag already flown half-staff. *The Practical Heart*, my book of four novellas, contains one tale of a spinster's quest to get herself painted by John Singer Sargent. Kidd found the only Sargent portrait I had never seen before. Like some stage magician, he then cut its lady-subject in half, then quarters. He turned all her segments away from each other. Our eye rushes to reassemble the seg- mented gentlewoman; and, as if by accident, in doing so, said eye describes the book's four separate but equal novellas.

One could write a metaphysical tract about each of Kidd's covers. (The Japanese, I understand, are doing precisely that.) What's clear: he has revitalized a snoozy occupation, has re-interested it in itself. And, as someone who has set forth bound and furred and armored in Kidd's deep certainty of surface, I feel warmer, larger, and oddly always more myself.

—Allan Gurganus

Yes, but what does it *mean*?

GOOD QUESTION. IT'S A METAPHOR ON OVERDRIVE, a child of bizarre serendipity. Once I started to read the manuscript of *The Abomination* I became instantly mesmerized by the gorgeous prose and the author's searing command of it. This was a writer of tremendous power, telling the story of a gay man looking back on his fucked-up childhood and musing on the way it shaped who he has come to be—which he frankly admits is someone he doesn't like, at all. How did it happen? The answer is as fascinating as it is disturbing.

The very day after finishing it our department received a promotional don't-forget-me postcard in the mail: a stuffed bunny doing a headstand, from Lars Klove, a wonderful photographer. And presto, one of those rare moments bloomed in my head: *I don't know why, but . . . this IS the book. It's crazy, and completely unexplainable. Am I out of what's left of my mind? Will anyone else get this?*

And the initial answer is always: you won't ever know until you try. So I put it together and marched up to Sonny's office, and presented it. He took it in, he squinted, he glanced at his e-mail, he asked me to leave it with him. Which is rarely a good sign. But here's the brilliant thing: he just left it on his desk, face up, amidst everything else that had washed up. And day by day, meeting by meeting, as people descended upon him as they regularly did and do, at some point during their business, they stopped and noticed it. The rabbit. And they would say, *Sorry . . . but, what the hell is this?*

That was all he needed. He knew it was right.

Then the fun started.

The sketch was sent to the agent, who HATED IT. As in, refused even to show it to the author. He thought it was insulting and an affront to the integrity of the book, etc., etc. So Sonny did something very smart (surprise surprise), which was, nothing. We all had other things to do, and we had time on this one, so he took it. The book was scheduled to come out in England first (with a jacket designed by the author, and not a bad one, I must admit), a full season ahead of our publication. But when it did, things hit the fan—because even though it was a novel, the book purported that there were sexually inappropriate relations between faculty and students at a very posh and poorly disguised boy's school in London. The British tabloids had a field day. Fingers were pointed, reputations ruined. Alas, notoriety does not always guarantee sales, and definitely didn't this time. Eventually it was decided that the book needed a fresh start in the States, and the agent finally relented and sent our design to Mr. Golding. Well. We got the most ecstatic fax I'd ever seen (see opposite). His thoughtful appreciation and rhapsodic understanding was what every designer dreams of. He not only completely, totally, got it—he articulated it. Better than I ever could.

RIGHT: Promotional postcard that our department received from photographer Lars Klove, which I turned into *The Abomination* (**OPPOSITE LEFT:** Knopf, 2000), one of my favorite covers ever for an astonishing book. **OPPOSITE RIGHT:** The author's analysis. This victory was particularly sweet.

Random House
201 East 50th Street
New York, NY 10022

Lars Klove

Photo Service

212 989 9643

315 7th Avenue, #10B, New York, NY 10001

aul Golding

the abomination

a novel

Paul Golding

nopf

LONDON SW3 2LA

Gillon Aitken Esq.,
London SW10 0TG

27th April 2000

Dear Gillon,

Thank you for letting me see the sample jacket proposed by America. I think that Mr. Mehta's people have triumphed. The image may not carry the beautiful classical innocence of our British cover, but England is much less developed in visual matters than the States.

The reason why I think that Knopf's suggestion works so well is this: the bunny rabbit, though obviously emblematic of childhood, is almost immaterial here. It could have been a teddy bear, or a jelly baby, or a rag doll, or an animated character - because, with this sort of treatment, the result isn't funny: it's full of poignant, slightly brutal aesthetic irony. The proportions are so stunted, and the body-parts so naïve and blunt, that the inversion of the animal can only add to this impression.

What Knopf's art department has produced is a very high-quality, almost surreal, still-life. Smart, sophisticated; both intelligent and classy. The fact that the photograph is in black and white makes the whole thing appear peculiarly traditional, nostalgic rather than kitsch, almost Thirties in feel; and the sharp, diagonal, downward light against which the toy is shot makes the eye, at first view, fly up toward the top part of the picture. There is something beefily phallic about it, adult and virile. I can't explain, but if you observe the jacket at a distance (as the design plainly intends) it evokes male genitals in profile. Fantastically clever, and technically difficult to achieve.

The result is neither squeaky-clean nor grubby, yet it remains powerfully textured: the fur is worn and very alive, almost damp. The spine, of course, could not be more dramatic if it tried. And as for the business of my name: nothing, as you know, could please me more than seeing it printed in blood. Please say Yes to them, and thank them on my behalf. Somebody has really thought about this, and I find it very heartening.

All best wishes.

Yours,

Paul Golding.

THE ELEPHANT VANISHES

—Haruki Murakami—

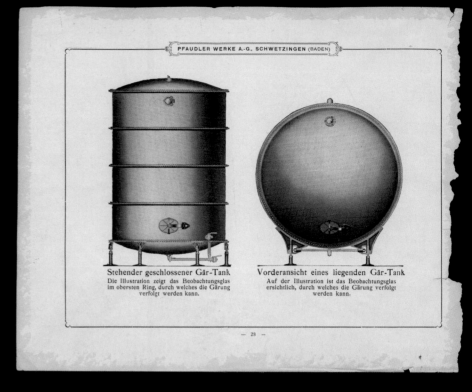

PFAUDLER WERKE A.-G., SCHWETZINGEN (BADEN)

Stehender geschlossener Gär-Tank
Die Illustration zeigt das Beobachtungsglas im obersten Ring, durch welches die Gärung verfolgt werden kann.

Vorderansicht eines liegenden Gär-Tank
Auf der Illustration ist das Beobachtungsglas ersichtlich, durch welches die Gärung verfolgt werden kann.

— 23 —

LEFT: Knopf, 1993. **ABOVE AND LOWER LEFT:** Source material I used for the jacket collage.
LOWER RIGHT: A novel reuse of the art, for a Brazilian publisher, Companhia Das Letras.

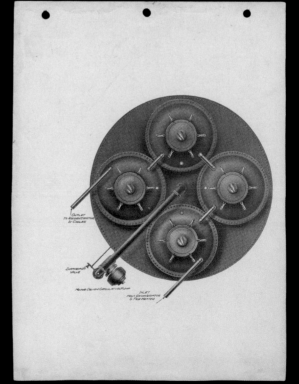

A MECÂNICA DAS ÁGUAS

E.L. DOCTOROW

43c

Watch Gobbling Goose Peck Away

Goose all dressed up in his suit lithographed in bright colors on his body. Waddles along on his web feet, swaying his head up and down pecking at the ground. Durable metal and equipped with good spring. Measures, 9 inches long and 4½ in. high. Shpg. wt., 1 lb.
49J5712—.................................**43c**

Duck Waddles.

Handsomely colored metal. Spring motor, runs over floor or carpet, wabbling from side to side. Size, 6¼x4¼ in. Shipping wt., 6 oz.
49F5757—Price, each.................**39c**

Rooster and Duck.

Very naturally colored. Comical struggle for possession of frog. Runs around floor in a very funny manner. One of our best toys. Size, 11 inches long. Shipping weight, 12 ounces.
49F5778—Price.................**59c**

Hopping Bird.

A full size bird, metal, lithographed in six colors. Wind up and he hops away in very realistic manner. Length over all, 7 inches; 3¾ inches high. Shipping weight, 10 ounces.
49K5756—Price.................**39c**

SEARS.

Peacock With Voice.

Nicely enameled in colors. Very lifelike. Walks around floor, squawking as it walks. Size, 9¼x6¾ inches. Shipping weight, 14 ounces.
49F5771—Price, special at.................**89c**

Mechanical Goose With Movable Wings.

When wound goose darts across the floor on wheels flapping its wings in a very natural manner and at the same time quacking. Made of metal and painted in natural looking colors. Good spring motor and well made throughout. A toy that every child will enjoy. Shipping weight, 1 pound.
49F5797—Price.................**39c**

This Goose Lays Golden Color Eggs

Plenty of Pep and Lots of Fun

Repeats action when rewound and eggs inserted. Just wind the strong spring and watch it hop along bobbing its head up and down in the most realistic manner; at the same time laying golden colored wooden eggs as it hops along. Goose made of metal beautifully lithographed in gold with red and black details. Size about 9 inches long by 5 inches high.
49D5712—Postpaid.................**45c**

THE FIRST TIME I WORKED WITH CHIP KIDD was when my short story collection, *The Elephant Vanishes*, was published by Knopf in 1993. When I first laid eyes on the cover Chip designed for that book, I was frankly a bit taken aback. The elephant depicted on the cover looked like some nineteenth-century steam engine. Like one of those gloomy-looking machines that appear from time to time in David Lynch's film *The Elephant Man*. Or like part of the enigmatic Gothic landscape of Gotham city in the film *Batman*.

When most people draw an elephant, they follow the standard image of an elephant. They depict the two large ears, the long trunk, the two curved white tusks, in order to emphasize the enormity of this living being. Because that's the shared perception we all have of what makes up an elephant. It's all quite clear cut—so much so that it's hard to know if it's the elephant that creates the shared perception, or the shared perception that creates the elephant.

But the elephant Chip designed wasn't like this at all. Chip's elephant was one that emerged from his own world, an elephant found only in the world according to Chip Kidd. An elephant constructed of steel, bolted down, with countless gears meshed together, the whole contraption most likely operated by steam power. In Chip's world it's a given that that's how elephants run, through mechanical means. In other words, Chip employed the shared perception of an elephant to come up with an image that isn't shared. And as far as I'm concerned, that's one of the indispensible qualities of an original artist.

Since that first book, Chip has designed the covers for all the books I've published with Knopf. Every one of these covers is fantastic, and tremendously original. He carefully reads the text, lets the contents become part of him, and then weaves his own unique designs. And these aren't, as is so often the case, egocentric creations. The scenes and objects Chip creates collaborate, in a wonderfully natural way, with the scenes and objects in the books. His designs are always novel, but they never interfere with the structure of the books. Cover design and book work together. That's what always impresses me about his art.

Every time I publish a book in the US, I really look forward to getting a sample of the cover, and seeing what design Chip has come up with. What sort of object will emerge now, I always wonder, from Chip Kidd's world and make its way over to our own? I'm constantly surprised by what I see, and invariably delighted. His designs will continue to be an essential part of my own novelistic world.

—Haruki Murakami

(translated by Philip Gabriel)

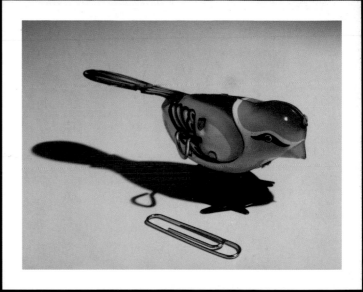

FAR LEFT: Where it all began, source-wise, for The *Wind-Up Bird Chronicle*. **CENTER:** Wind-up bird box. **ABOVE:** Polaroid by Geoff Spear showing the scale of the toy. **BELOW:** Philip Weiss waxes rhapsodic in *The New York Observer*, December 22, 1997.

THE NEW YORK OBSERVER

PHILIP WEISS

Forget DeLillo, Pynchon— Murakami Is My Man!

CONTINUED FROM PAGE 1
ki Murakami, came out in October with high hopes. The Japanese author had lately been profiled in *The New Yorker*. *New York* magazine put its full weight behind the book. Mr. Murakami has partisans in such literary lights as Bret Easton Ellis, Robert Gottlieb and the poet Tess Gallagher, and the crack team of editor Gary Fisketjon and designer Chip Kidd helped make *The Wind-Up Bird Chronicle* the most elegant object a novel could ever be (only halfway through did I notice that the page numbers were traveling). Knopf hoped that it would at last break the 48-year-old author out of a cult American following "into the vast audience that he already

a Mongol shepherd.

"The man started by slitting [...] mamoto's shoulder and proceed [...] off the skin of his right arm fro [...] down—slowly, carefully, almos [...] As the Russian officer had said, it [...] thing like a work of art. One wo [...] have imagined there was any pai [...] if it weren't for the screams."

Mamiya survives the night, to [...] by the Mongolians (and pissed on [...] tom of a deep well. Until Honda [...] some days later, he is in complete d [...] for moments when the sun sudde [...] straight down.

"I feel as if, in the intense light [...] for a mere 10 or 15 seconds a day [...]

'THE WIND-UP BIRD CHRONICLE' WAS THE MOST AMBITIOUS AND INTRICATE DESIGN for a work of fiction I'd ever attempted and is probably only matched in complexity by *The Cheese Monkeys*. In this sweeping novel of both contemporary and wartime Japan, the narrator is constantly haunted by the sound of what he imagines to be a wind-up bird, which he never sees. While I'm usually loathe to go so literal with title and imagery, the idea was to make the device on the jacket so relatively large that it can't be perceived as a whole when wrapped around the book and so becomes completely abstracted. I took on the interior design as well, and the folios (not pictured) very gradually revolve clockwise around the pages and can best be viewed by rapidly shuffling the pages like a flip book. I was ably assisted on these and other aspects of the text by Misha Beletsky, who also helped me on Ben Katchor's *The Jew of New York*. **ABOVE:** Knopf, 1997. Photograph by Geoff Spear. Chris Ware's astonishingly imagined rendering of the interior workings of the wind-up bird were surprinted over Geoff's photograph with a hi-gloss spot-laminate that contained tiny bits of flaked metal to help give it that extra glint (Andy Hughes's idea, of course). It should also be said that all of these bells and whistles added a tremendous amount to the per-book costs, which Sonny very generously approved—a testament to Knopf's commitment to the book, and to the author. **RIGHT:** Printed case for the binding. Illustration by Chris Ware, based on Geoff's photograph. **OVERLEAF:** (left to right) Unused idea, later recycled for the Vertical book *Sayonara Gangsters* (p. 357). Knopf, 1999. Knopf, 2001. Unused idea for *After the Quake*. The final is on the following page.

THE WIND-UP BIRD CHRONICLE

HARUKI MURAKAMI

THE WIND-UP BIRD CHRONICLE

HARUKI MURAKAMI

KNOPF

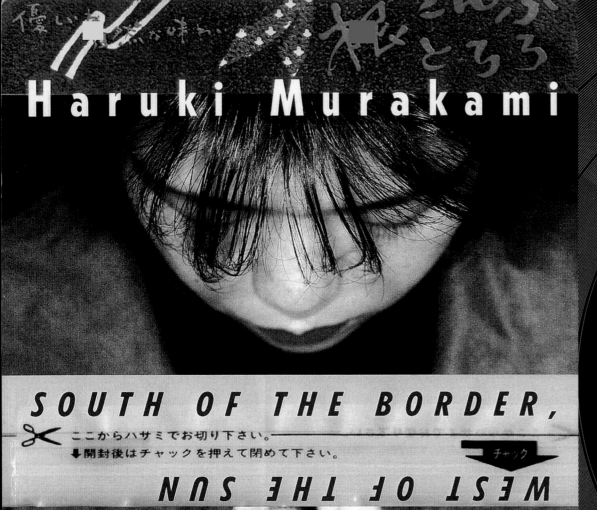

Haruki Murakami

SOUTH OF THE BORDER,

WEST OF THE SUN

by the author of THE WIND-UP BIRD CHRONICLE

South
of the Border,

author of THE WIND-UP BIRD CHRONICLE

HARUKI MURAKAMI

West of the Sun.

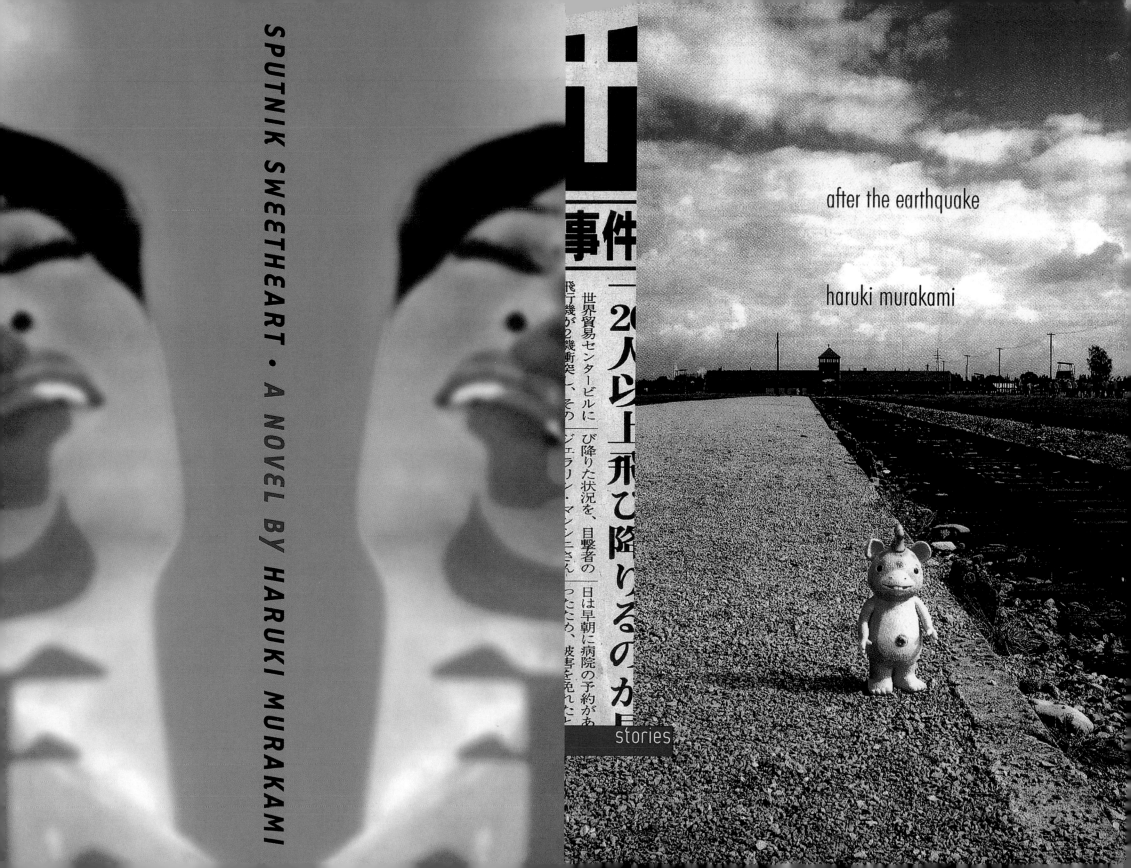

SPUTNIK SWEETHEART · A NOVEL BY HARUKI MURAKAMI

after the earthquake

haruki murakami

stories

AFTER MORE THAN TWELVE YEARS AT KNOPF HARUKI Murakami continues to astonish. And I've attempted to design jackets that do the work justice. I try to make them all completely different, but imbued with a common sensibility I've always gotten from the writing: that the unknown is worth investigating, and the weird can be truly beautiful. *Kafka on the Shore*, I believe, is his finest book to date. It also marks his first appearance on *The New York Times* Best-Seller List. **THIS PAGE**: Knopf, 2004. Photograph by Knopf interior designer Iris Weinstein. **OPPOSITE**: Knopf, 2005. Photomontage by Geoff Spear. Head sculpted by Eishi Takaoka. Geoff outdid himself with this one—the "sea" and "shore" are actually a square-yard sheet of rippled blue shower-door glass and a fistful of garden sand. The cat is a two-inch-high ceramic figurine and not even black. Before I knew of the book's existence I discovered the little wooden head sculpture on the website Giant Robot and just had to have it. Then, with it staring blankly from my shelf as I read the manuscript, I realized that it perfectly captured the spirit of Nakata, the mysteriously powered aging simpleton of the story.

after
the
quake

haruki
murakami

✄

Knopf

after the quake

stories

haruki murakami

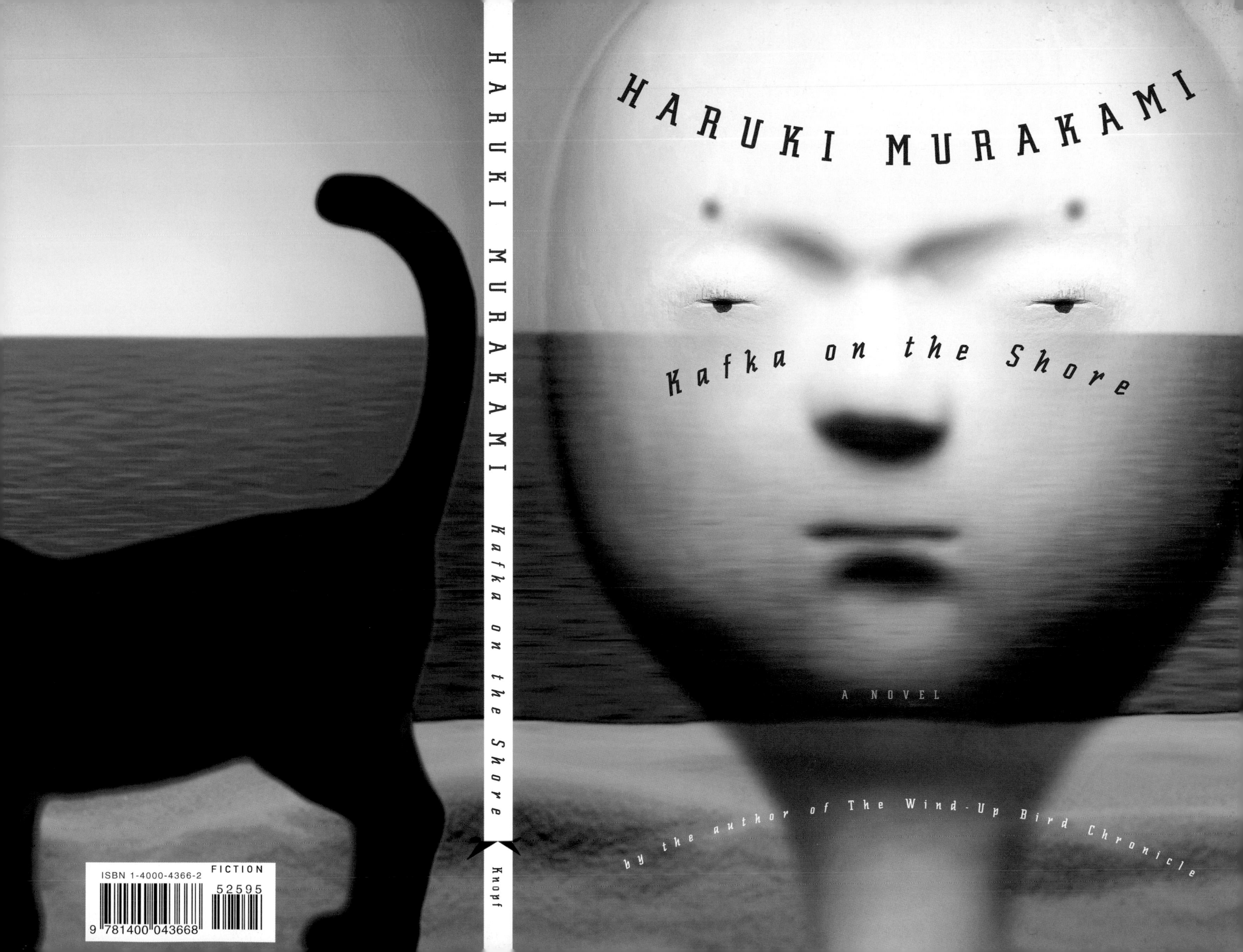

HARUKI MURAKAMI

Kafka on the Shore

A NOVEL

by the author of The Wind-Up Bird Chronicle

HARUKI MURAKAMI

Kafka on the Shore

Knopf

Say "cheese."

I HAD WANTED TO WRITE 'THE CHEESE MONKEYS' EVER SINCE I SAW PROFESSOR STANLEY Milgram's 1962 documentary, *Obedience*, at Penn State in freshman Psychology. I just didn't realize it until ten years later. A short visual chronicle of the famous scientific experiment at Yale, the film depicts unsuspecting volunteers who were coaxed to essentially torture and murder their innocent peers simply because they were being told to do so by someone in authority. It instantly haunted me, not only because it brilliantly exposed the potential for evil in good people, but also because the procedure itself was one of the most ingeniously constructed pieces of design I'd ever seen. I eventually came to understand that even though several stage plays and a song or two referenced the procedure, no one had ever written a novel about it. So I started taking notes, and constructing a story—let's say I participated in the experiment myself, which instantly put the setting in 1961. I didn't want to alter the facts or make it allegorical—it had to be *the* Milgram experiment, which he also exhaustively documented in a book, *Obedience to Authority*, published in 1974. As I fleshed out the narrator (me, essentially) I started working backward—where did I go to school, and what did I learn there, and from who? Why, Penn State, of course, studying graphic design, with Lanny Sommese and Bill Kinser and . . . a whole other story eventually emerged. To my knowledge no one had ever written a novel about learning graphic design, either, and there was definitely a book in it. A potentially very funny one (art school, *please*) but also one that could turn the design process into a narrative—and if anyone was going to write it, it was going to be me. Now, this took a l-o-n-g time to figure out, and for a good six years as I struggled with the structure and the characters and the text the only two people who knew about it were my agent, Amanda "Binky" Urban at ICM, and poor Sandy McClatchy. This was for practical reasons. There's nothing more cliché than idly mentioning at a party in Manhattan you're working on a novel or, worse, being asked how the work on your novel is going. I wanted it to arrive out of nowhere, fully formed, like Venus from the foam. Also, Binky wasn't going to shop it around to any publishers until I wrote the whole thing. "No one will believe you can pull it off without the evidence, sorry." She was right, of course, but it was not my style to toil on a project— for over half a decade—which may never see the light of day. It's one thing to learn a book jacket's been rejected; it's another to accept that the closest thing you could ever have to a child (without any of the diapers or vomit) will never be born. **SO, LONG STORY SHORT:** The first draft was finally finished in late 1999, and Binky offered it to our top five choices (including Knopf as a courtesy, but I didn't really want it anywhere in the Random House empire as long as I was working there—no nepotism accusations for me, thanks). Three rejected it, two made offers, and we went with Scribner and the editor Sarah McGrath. This was an ideal situation—Sarah had been Sonny Mehta's assistant a few years earlier, and we got along great. Plus she was also brilliant and loved the book. Since publication I've often been asked how the writing process compares to the design process. My stock answer is that they're quite similar—writing is just designing with words. That sounds too simple, I know, but I believe it's true. A theory: one of most misleading things about writing is that it's called writing. The actual writing is the last part that gets done after all the thinking—as when doing graphic design the final step is to make it look good, after you've figured out the conceptual strategy.

AND WHAT OF THE BOOK ON PROFESSOR MILGRAM? Well, it's still coming along, it's called *The Learners*, and it picks up three years after the events of *The Cheese Monkeys* take place. An extremely truncated version appeared in the summer of 2004 on *USA Today*'s website as part of its Open Book program. I'm about a third of the way through with it, and it's what I really should be working on instead of writing *this* . . .

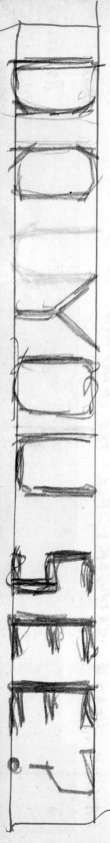

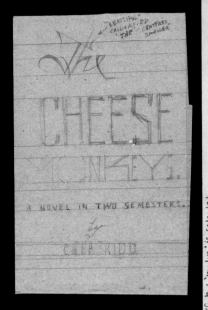

THE IDEA IS TO DO THE LETTERING "PROFESSIONALLY" BY HAND, AS IT WOULD HAVE BEEN BACK THEN. IN FACT, IT SHOULD LOOK LIKE IT *WAS* DONE THEN AND ONLY RECENTLY DISCOVERED — AGED, WATER-STAINED, ETC. — GEOFF WILL PHOTOGRAPH IT.

I SIMPLY DID THE TYPE AND DRAWINGS for Chip's book to his specifications; I had no idea what he was going to do with them. I did suggest a couple of things, though, both of which he ignored—the drawings were supposed to be extremely small, though he ran them extremely large, which is deeply embarrassing to me, since they're such horrible drawings.

—Chris Ware

FAR LEFT AND ABOVE: Early prepatory sketches of mine which were "rough guides" for Chris Ware to work his typographic magic. **RIGHT:** Chris's instructions, which I didn't choose to follow, much to his chagrin.

The ACME Novelty Library.
1112 North Hoyne Avenue, Chicago, Illinois. 60622.
Telephone: 773 227 2723.
Electronic Mail: weese@wwa.com

1/29/01.

DEAR CHAS. —

As always, apologies— firstly, for being such a whiner about this— I genuinely was not certain what it is you were/are looking for, and, being (having been?) your friend, didn't want to "screw it up." Also, this being your creative effort from start to finish, I felt a little odd stepping in and having to make any decision which in any way might smack of me, since I'd think you'd want the whole shnever to be unmistakably *you*, cover to cover. (Hopefully, I haven't done anything too "off" of your original idea here— if so, even more apologies—

Everything here (including shitty monkey/cheese drawings) should be sized at 50%. And as for "aging" or weathering." well... uh... maybe 'multiplying' a layer of old paper in photoshop is the ticket— or leaving it in one of the houseplants on your balcony for a couple of days. Note that top/bottom margins are consistent throughout— tho you may want to change this. Also: little drawings, as I was doing this, it occurred to me that perhaps if all the type was on the casewrap itself, it might work better thus leaving the little 'pictures' for the slipband, i.e:

This way, the blank field with the little pictures is what people would see/remember first... and it's definitely got a high "WTF" factor. Also, all the type on the case itself is consistent, and maybe more 'tactile,' esp. if it's photographed with stains, neatened, etc.

Also, if the band was matte laminate and the book was rough uncoated (à la Murakami) I think it would be an attractive 'combo.' But this is just a suggestion— I hope this is okay. Did I mention this was really hard to do? I hope this is what you wanted. My best wishes, thanks, and apologies, as always.

CHRIS.

The ACME Novelty Library.
1112 North Hoyne Avenue, Chicago, Illinois. 60622.
Telephone: 773 227 2723.
Electronic Mail: weese@wwa.com

FUCK! I just realized, after doing the whole thing, that I scaled it wrong. I thought it was looking sort of tall when I was working on it, and I just checked it — FUCK! It's one inch too tall when reduced. That means it should scale down at 44%, not 50%, and that there'll be an extra ¼" on either side now... maybe it'll work, though, since ok the type is centered, plus you could 'sqush' it slightly — FUCK!

Sorry about this... I musta added an inch when I was scaling and since it was lying on an angle on my table I didn't notice on an angle, huh? Well, let me know — Sorry, I'm so incompetent...

P.S. I gashed open my finger while doing this, by the way — just like in your story! What are you trying to do to me?!

The CHEESE MONKEYS.

A NOVEL *in* TWO SEMESTERS

BY

CHIP KIDD.

FAR LEFT: Scribner, 2001. All of the jacket "sleeves" had to be slipped onto the books by hand. **LEFT:** HarperPerennial, 2002. I followed through with my rebus idea for the title on the front of the paperback, using the quote from *The Onion* to tell readers what the title is if they couldn't figure it out. **ABOVE:** One of two fore-edge "messages." The other is "DO YOU SEE?"

356

Big in Japan.

VERTICAL INC. PRESENTED ONE OF THE MOST EXCITING new book publishing ventures I'd heard of in years: a small group of Japanese expats was going to buy bestselling books from their native country, translate them into English, and give them a new life here. They approached me to be their art director in 2002. At first I thought it was too much to take on, but their list turned out to be not just intriguing but manageable. And here was the opportunity to invent the look of a terrific publisher from the ground up. Vertically.

V ERTICAL.

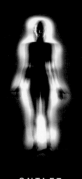

OUTLET

RANDY TAGUCHI

NAOKO

Naoko

a novel

Keigo Higashino

translated by Kerim Yasa

vertical.

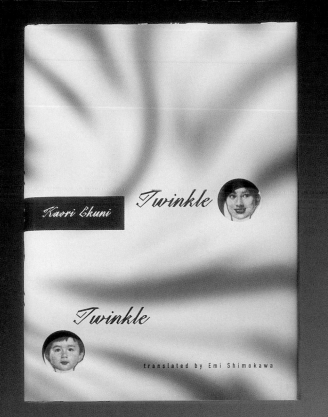

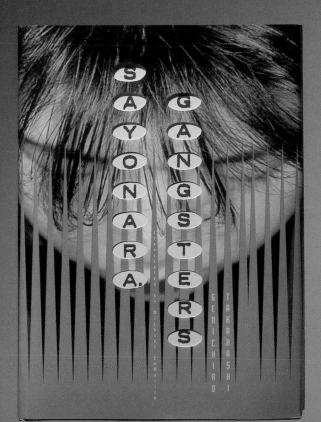

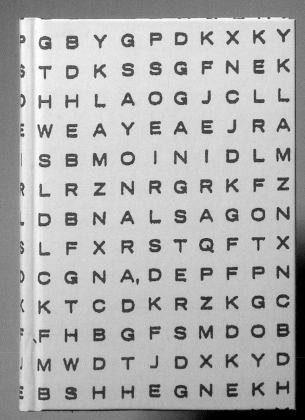

TOP LEFT: Vertical, 2003. *Twinkle Twinkle* features 2 die-cut holes. **ABOVE:** Detail from *Twinkle* case. **BOTTOM LEFT:** Vertical, 2004. *Sayonara Gangsters* is an experimental novel about a poet teaching a group of gangsters in Tokyo. The jacket works as a secret decoder—you can only read the title when it's wrapped around the book.

'ASHES' PRESENTED AN OPPORTUNITY TO WALLOW in my love of Japanese ephemera and sensibility, both new and old. The book tells a related group of stories about an aging don of the Yakuza (the Japanese Mafia). He spends a lot of time pondering life in bars (before shooting them up in a drunken rage), so I exploited this chance to use my collection of Japanese matchbooks from the '50s and '60s. The design is literally as layered as the stories, and the book has not one but two jackets (called "obis" in Japan) at different levels, which is common in modern Japanese commercial publishing. The uncoated, textured outer layer is meant to mimic a napkin, which may or may not have been cried on, but was definitely written and spilt on. That peels back to reveal the matchbooks, which are as glossy, varied, and colorful as the napkin is not, and that gives way to a detail of the main character, trying to rise above it all. Whether he does or doesn't depends on the reader. **OPPOSITE:** Vertical, 2003. **LEFT:** Pages from a scrapbook I found in Jimbocho, the antiquarian book dealer district in Tokyo. Finding such examples of period ephemera for sale is rare, especially in a city that was flattened not once but twice in the 20th century. **BELOW:** A supernaturally tinged title due for release in late 2005. **RIGHT:** Vertical, 2004. *Zero Over Berlin* is a novel set during World War II in which the Japanese attempt to smuggle an experimental fighter plane into Germany through restricted airspace.

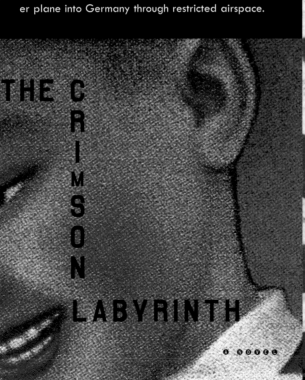

THE CRIMSON LABYRINTH

A NOVEL

zero over berlin

a novel

ioh sasaki

translated by matthew alt and hiroko yoda

DARK WATER

STORIES BY

DARK WATER

KOJI SUZUKI

KOJI
SUZIKI

V E R T I C A L

ONE NIGHT IN TOKYO, FOUR HEALTHY TEENAGERS DIE, ONE AFTER ANOTHER, OF HEART FAILURE. At first, an autopsy reveals Fugu. Intrigued by the coincidence, a journalist investigates and learns of a videotape that the four watched together a week before dying. Amid a series of bizarre and frightening images on the tape is a warning that the viewer will die in exactly one week unless a certain act is performed. The description of the act, of course, has been erased, and the journalist's work to solve the mystery assumes a deadly urgency. The *Ring* trilogy is not only a chillingly told horror story, but also a shrewdly intelligent and subversive commentary on the power of imagery and contagious consumerism. I wanted to use acetate in a way I hadn't before, with contrasting geometric patterns that formed moire patterns when laid atop one another. Rather than literally illustrating "horror," they create a sense of mesmeric disorientation. **PREVIOUS SPREAD AND THIS PAGE (LEFT TO RIGHT):** (Vertical is publisher for all) 2003, 2004, 2005, 2004.

ENTER A WORLD OF NIHILISM AND SELF-DESTRUCTION. ENTER A WORLD OF RAPE, INCEST, AND TRAUMA. ENTER A WORLD OF VIOLENCE, DRUGS, AND PROSTITUTION. ENTER AN INNOCENT WORLD.

AMI BELIEVES IN NOTHING, HOPES FOR NOTHING, AND TURNS TRICKS BECAUSE IT'S SOMETHING TO DO. HER JOURNEY FROM THE PIT OF DESPAIR TO THE PRECARIOUS EDGE OF SOMETHING ELSE CAPTURES THE PART OF BEING SEVENTEEN THAT NEVER MAKES IT INTO WORDS.

"A GIRL IS FINALLY FREED FROM THE CLUTCHES OF HER OWN DNA. THE SMALL STEP AMI TAKES IS, I THINK, A GIANT STEP FOR HUMANKIND." –KIYOSHI KUROSAWA, DIRECTOR OF *CURE*

JAPAN'S PRINCESS OF THE DISENCHANTED, AMI SAKURAI BURST ONTO THE SCENE WITH THIS RAZOR-SHARP NOVELLA WHOSE SHEER INTENSITY ELEVATES MISANTHROPY TO THE LEVEL OF ART. *INNOCENT WORLD* IS HER FIRST WORK TO APPEAR IN ENGLISH.

COVER DESIGN BY CHIP KIDD

VERTICAL BOOKS ARE DISTRIBUTED TO THE TRADE BY NATIONAL BOOK NETWORK, INC.

VERTICAL, INC., PUBLISHER, NEW YORK
www.vertical-inc.com

PRINTED IN THE USA
USA $11.95 CAN $16.95

ISBN 1-932234-14-4
51195>
9 781932 234145

INNOCENT WORLD

a novella by AMI SAKURAI
translated by Steven Clark

THE GUIN SAGA

Book One: The Leopard Mask

KAORU KURIMOTO

translated by Alexander O. Smith
with Elye J Alexander

FICTION

Set in the great human maelstrom of Tokyo, *Strangers* is a thinking man's ghost story. When Harada, a jaded TV scriptwriter, runs into his long-dead parents one night, he enters the womb of a city whose living inhabitants have perhaps lost their souls. Can Harada save his?

Taichi Yamada, one of Japan's most successful scriptwriters, transformed the TV drama in his country and has authored several acclaimed novels. *Strangers*, a contemporary classic, is his English-language debut.

Cover design by Chip Kidd.

vertical

$ 14.95
ISBN 1-932234-03-9
90000>
9 781932 234039

Strangers
Taichi Yamada

Strangers

a novel by **Taichi Yamada**. Translated by Wayne P. Lammers.

A RABBIT'S EYES.
A NOVEL BY
Kenjiro Haitani.
translated by
Paul Sminkey.

WHAT MADE VERTICAL particularly appealing was the prospect of designing Osamu Tezuka's extraordinary multivolume comic book interpretation of the life of the Buddha. I'd heard of it but had never read it because it hadn't been translated into English. But when its time arrived I was privileged to work on it. I gave each volume an obi (bellyband) as a nod to modern Japanese books. The art had to be chosen from existing material because, alas, Tezuka died long ago. Though often called "the Walt Disney of Japan," Tezuka actually wrote and drew everything. Determined to encourage readers to collect the whole series, I designed the spines so that shelved together they depict a progression of the title character from youth to manhood to old age.

ADVERTISEMENT

THE ART DIRECTOR'S CLUB, INC.

IN ASSOCIATION WITH

THE ACME NOVELTY COMPANY

—AND—

BIG GUYS IN PRESSED SUITS WITH PAINFUL HANDSHAKES AND LOUD BOOMING VOICES

PROUDLY PRESENT

MR. CHIP KIDD

SUCCESSFUL BOOK JACKET DESIGNER & EXPERIENCED TOASTMASTER

IN A LUNCHEON ORATION AT THE ART DIRECTOR'S CLUB, INCORPORATED

WEDNESDAY, NOVEMBER 2ND 1994. from 12~2 p.m. ADMISSION BEING ONLY $12.95 plus applicable taxes.

MR. KIDD HAS ENTITLED HIS PROGRAMME

"RUN WITH THE DWARVES AND WIN: MY LIFE IN BOOK JACKET DESIGN."

~AND IT IS CERTAIN TO BE A REAL DANDY.

FOR OVER 8 YEARS

MR. KIDD HAS DESIGNED BOOK COVERS FOR EVERYONE from POPES & KINGS TO THE SCUM of the EARTH.

HE REQUESTS YOUR ACCOMPANIMENT ON A "SPIRITED LITERARY JOURNEY WHICH WILL TRANSPORT YOU TO FABULOUS PALACES, MANSIONS, & SPACIOUS BARONIAL ESTATES, PRIVATE SOUNDPROOF PLEASURE CHAMBERS, SQUALLID TIN SHACKS CAKED with FILTH, DIVERTING THIRD WORLD PRISONS, AND LOCAL PUBLIC RESTROOMS, &c., &c."

MR. KIDD ASSURES US THAT THE ENTIRE SCHEDULE WILL BE ILLUSTRATED BY A LIVELY VARIETY of COLORED PICTURE SLIDES AND PUNCTUATED BY AMUSING QUIPS, NOVEL ANECDOTAGE, AND A BRIEF SONG of ADVENTURE, with SOUND EFFECTS.

PLEASE ARRIVE PROMPTLY with PROTECTIVE CLOTHING AND AN INSATIABLE WILL TO SATISFY, at any cost.

Amputees welcome.

250 PARK AVENUE, SOUTH, NEW YORK, NEW YORK. ~

The Greatest Friend on Earth.

IT'S HARD FOR ME TO TALK OR WRITE about Chris Ware without lending the impression that he's either the co-star in my latest movie and I'm a guest on *The Tonight Show*, or he's Elvis and I'm a lovestruck bobbysoxer. He would be rightly horrified by either analogy and could no doubt come up with better. I was an ardent fan before I ever knew who he was, giving copies of his unsigned 1991 debut story in *Raw* ("I Guess") to my senior students at S.V.A. as a brilliant example of how the interaction of form and content can be completely reinvented. Three years later I came upon *Acme Novelty Library #2* at St. Mark's Comics and decided that I just had to find out who this guy was and contact him. And I did (after searching the issue for his name with *Where's Waldo*-like effort), and my life hasn't been the same since— and how grateful I am for that.

The first project we worked on together was an invitation for an upcoming lecture I was to give at the Art Director's Club in New York (see left). Since then a LOT has happened, most notably the 2000 Pantheon publication of *Jimmy Corrigan: The Smartest Kid on Earth* and its tremendous critical and popular success. We've worked on plenty of other projects too, scattered throughout this book. Chris is a source of the kind of inspiration I never knew existed before I met him. His astonishing talent is matched only by his humility and generosity.

OPPOSITE, LOWER RIGHT: Chris Ware, fall 2001. Milwaukee, Wisc. Photo by yours truly. BELOW: Acme thank-you note. I can't remember what for. FAR RIGHT AND OVERLEAF: Jacket for *American Illustration Annual #14*, 1997. I was a judge that year and in charge of the cover and binding design. There was no doubt in my mind who I wanted to do it. The handling of the quotes on the flaps takes the form of separate ads, but they flow into each other as a single entity. OVERLEAF, TOP LEFT: My first letter from Chris, introducing his characteristic self-effacement. He means every word of it, though I don't recall that any of what he says was the case.

CHIP IS ONE OF MY BEST FRIENDS IN THE WORLD and has done more outrageously generous things for me than anyone I can think of, save perhaps my mother and my wife. I've got a house full of gifts from him, and I doubt very much whether I could still be drawing comics if it wasn't for his efforts on my behalf, starting in 1995 up until now. In fact, many cartoonists could say the same thing—I don't know if Pantheon would be publishing so many comics if Chip hadn't suggested it and brought his acumen and taste to the division. On top of that, he's one of the greatest living designers—a genius—all one has to do is walk into a bookstore and look around until something catches your eye, or your intellect, or both, walk over to it, pick it up, and nine times out of ten, it's Chip's. Or it's a ripoff by someone else of an idea he did a year before. (I'm amazed at the shameless plagiarism of the design world; a few years ago Chip was searching for a typefont that was "styleless," veritably transparent to the eye, and so he used the telephone book font for a book title. Now that look all but defines the nineties. Also, how many covers have been printed of a photograph of the title page of a book?) Other than Paul Rand, I don't know of any book designers who have shown such respect for the intelligence of the reader as Chip does—he almost always manages to pare down his ideas to the absolute essentials, finding a style for each project that is defined by and suited exactly to the content of the book or whatever it is he's designing, crystallizing his concept into something that effervesces both visually and intellectually. The last thing in the world Chip is going for is a look that he can apply like paint to everything he does. And he always takes his ideas farther than anyone—if he's designing a cover for a book that's completely tasteless, he won't do a tasteful nod to tastelessness, he'll genuinely try to make something that is genuinely tasteless, and, sometimes, eyeburningly painful to look at. But still good.

I'm almost sure that Chip trusts his instincts, like any artist does, visually and mentally feeling his designs as he works until it all suddenly falls into place—he's not working from one rule, other than make something that's good, and new, and he always starts from zero. Books look 100% different now than they did ten years ago, and I think it's because of his example as an artist.

—Chris Ware

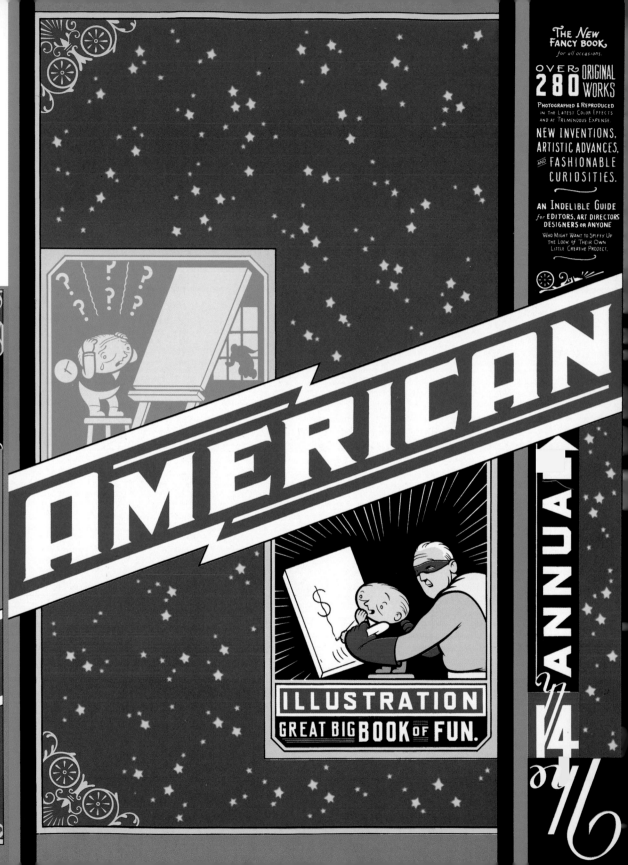

RIGHT: Prototype for the cover of *Jimmy Corrigan: The Smartest Kid on Earth*, 1999. I put this together to get the idea across to the Pantheon sales force of how the jacket would work. This kind of thing needs to be done many months before publication (for the catalog, planning meetings, etc.) and as an editor I don't like to waste the artist's time with it when he could be working on the actual art. Needless to say this is nowhere *near* as sophisticated as what Chris came up with, which is frankly a book's worth of material in and of itself.

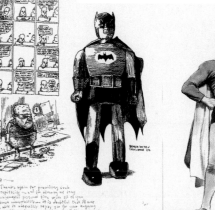

FedEx instructions:

SENDER'S FEDERAL EXPRESS ACCOUNT NUMBER

From (Your Name) Please Print
MR CHRIS WARE
Company
ACME SYSTEMS ANALYSIS
Street Address
~~CHICAGO~~ 1112 NORTH
↳ CHICAGO ILL

YOUR INTERNAL BILLING REFERENCE INFORMATION (optional)
PLEASE DON'T HATE ME

CHAS. —

Herewith all 380 pages of 'Jimmy Corrigan.' Hope it doesn't suck!

WHEN I SHOWED THE ARTIST DOROTHEA TANNING a copy of *Jimmy Corrigan* she refused to believe that anyone could single-handedly produce such a work in less than, as she put it, "a lifetime." It took him a mere six years, with frequent interruptions for bill-paying freelance work, myriad other personal projects, and the rigors of a weekly comic strip. When I pitched the book in a Pantheon launch meeting as "the *Ulysses* of comics" I meant it, and was confirmed as not out of my mind when it won the 2000 Guardian Prize for first fiction. I have no doubt that *Rusty Brown*, Ware's next epic-length work, will take the comics form to an even even higher level of achievement, which is saying something. **LEFT:** Instructions for FedEx. **RIGHT:** Detail of Chris's note upon delivering the final files for Jimmy Corrigan, 2000. Never fear, it didn't. Which is the understatement of the decade. **RIGHT:** Sketches from Chris after a stay in my apartment. The Batman Robot is from my collection. The Superman is based on a photo from the 1939 World's Fair.

'BATMAN COLLECTED' IS A LIFELINE TO MY TEN-YEAR-OLD SELF, a reassurance to that skinny little kid who endlessly pored over the shelves at Walden's in the Berkshire Mall that the book on Batman he was so desperately seeking would someday turn up. I owe its existence to several key people: first of all editor Steve Korté at DC Comics Licensed Publishing, Joe Desris (the foremost Batman collector at the time), and finally of course to Geoff Spear, who made it all come alive on the page. When I look back, it's truly astounding that DC gave me the freedom they did. What I originally proposed as a picture book about toys ended up equal parts memoir, pop-cultural history, art photography album, decadent design-o-rama, and opinionated exposition on one of their hottest and most venerated properties. By someone who'd never written a book before. Not one image was vetoed, as we presented extreme shots of bootlegs, wonky foreign knock-offs, and careworn toys that looked like they just lost a fight with the Joker. But Steve understood that our hearts were in the right place and he was heroic in his support of what we were doing, which was essentially making it up as we went along. Location shooting took us to ultra-glamorous locales like Cleveland, Tom's River (New Jersey), and Kenosha (Wisconsin). The entire book was shot, laid out, written, and edited in the space of a year, while we all also saw to our "day jobs." When I look at it now I have no idea how we pulled it off (which is how I feel about most of what I've worked on, this book included, no doubt). The ten-year-old me is just deeply grateful that we did. **ABOVE:** This chaotic spread was created for the sales blad and never actually appeared in the book. **RIGHT:** Geoff wonders what happened to his career as he prepares to shoot a Batman pogo stick.

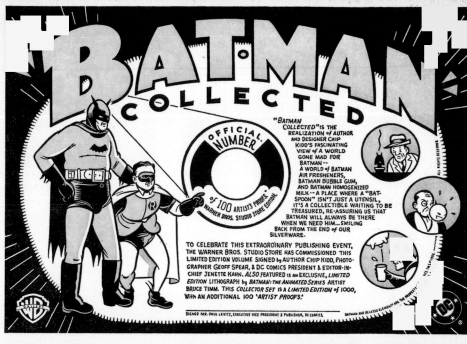

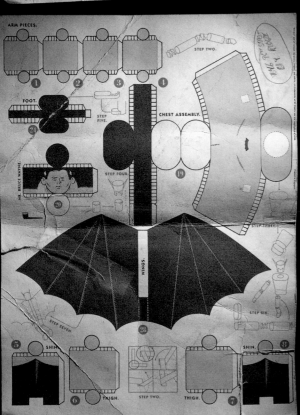

I DESPERATELY WANTED TO IMPLICATE CHRIS WARE IN 'BATMAN COLLECTED,' and the best way I could think of was to ask him to design one of his trademark build-it-yourself paper toys, to be included as an extra added bonus with the book. There is a dearth of Batman ephemera (other than comics) from the 1940s so I wanted something that looked like it was from that era, or earlier. Chris very kindly agreed and suggested a stereo-optic arcade movie viewer featuring a three dimensional Bat-Man flip-book movie. Sounded good to me! Little did I know what a gargantuan undertaking he had in mind. Chris went all out and when the drawings were finally finished they looked like plans for a nuclear reactor. I gave copies to my Dad (retired engineer) to build a prototype and it took him more than two weeks working the better part of each day. When the device was painstakingly completed I proudly unveiled it in a meeting at DC Comics for Jenette Kahn (then president). She picked it up, eyed it suspiciously, cranked it once, and set it down, declaring in her singsong voice: "It's not fun. Batman should be fun." End of meeting. On top of all that, Bulfinch's production department found it prohibitively expensive to pro-duce, adding tens of thousands of dollars we didn't have to our budget. Steve Korté somehow remained calm throughout the whole fiasco, but this clearly wasn't going to fly. So I made the dreaded call to Chris: he had to start over—a simpler idea, one piece of paper, three colors, folded, and we needed it yesterday. Bless him, he totally came through. And the movie viewer eventually landed on the pages of *Acme Novelty Library* #15. **LEFT:** For the paperback of *Batman Collected* I wanted to reprint the figure on the endpapers, but no one could locate the printer's original film. So we took one of the toys and "aged" it. Then Geoff shot it to play up the patina, and it went in the book that way.

ABOVE: Official Bat-Man Fetish Totem, assembled and pho-tographed by Geoff Spear. **OPPOSITE:** Shown for the first time—a selection of art by Chris Ware for the abandoned Bat-Man flip-book movie. If you cross your eyes and line up the pairs of drawings, you'll see that they actually are in 3-D.

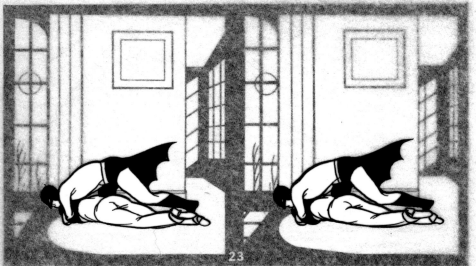
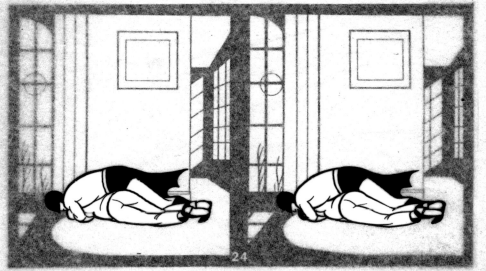

OPPOSITE: Chronicle Books, 1998, 1999, and 2000, respectively. For these sixty-year retrospectives of Superman, Batman, and Wonder Woman, I have to hand it to Chronicle and DC for allowing me to design the front covers without type (à la the Marlene Dietrich jacket). The images are details from the original comic covers from each character's first cover appearance, and when placed side by side in order of publication, they line up to make a continuous triptych: Superman's left shoulder blends into the right arm of Batman, whose cape connects to Wonder Woman's right shoulder. To emphasize the historic trajectories of the characters, we commissioned Alex Ross to paint fully fleshed-out renditions of them for the bindings underneath, so that you peel away the old to reveal the new. **THIS PAGE:** To accompany Les Daniels's text for the books, Geoff and I sought out rare ephemera from various collectors. These examples were used for the title page spreads and include an obscure Superman newspaper ad from the 1930s, a Batman splash panel from his second adventure in 1939, and an extremely rare promotional brochure used to solicit newspapers to run the *Wonder Woman* comic strip.

I HAD BEEN TRYING TO ATTRACT FRANK MILLER'S EYE FOR YEARS, first in the pages of *Batman Collected*, then in *Batman: The Complete History*, both of which feature sections on his work. But it was the Plasticman book (p. 382) that finally got his attention. He was quite taken with that project's reworking of existing comic book art and to my delighted surprise asked me to do the same for not only his collected edition of *Batman: The Dark Knight Strikes Again* but also for a corresponding reissue of his seminal *Batman: The Dark Knight Returns*. If any projects called for extremes of scale it was these, with Batman looming large over the rest of the assembled cast of characters. Miller's Carrie Kelly Robin/Catgirl is on the spine of both, as she is pivotal to each of the stories. DC was very nervous about the *Strikes Again* cover because they didn't think anyone would recognize it as Batman. Frank assured them it would work, and liked the result so much he asked me to redesign the covers for all of his *Sin City* titles (overleaf).

BATMAN®: THE DARK KNIGHT® RETURNS

FRANK MILLER

with KLAUS JANSON and LYNN VARLEY

FOR CHIP— FM '03

BATMAN: THE DARK KNIGHT STRIKES AGAIN

LEFT: DC Comics, 2003. The DC guys were nervous that no one would recognize this as Batman. Frank assured them that the title made it clear. **ABOVE:** Frank drew this image for me of the now classic Dark Knight and Carrie Kelly version of Robin as a "thank you" for working on his books (as if the pleasure wasn't all mine!). I colored it in Quark, just for fun.

FRANK MILLER'S
THE HARD GOODBYE.
SIN CITY
1.
THE HARD GOODBYE.
FRANK MILLER
SIN CITY
THE HARD GOODBYE
FRANK MILLER
1
SIN CITY
A DAME TO KILL FOR
FRANK MILLER
2
SIN CITY
THE BIG FAT KILL
FRANK MILLER
3
SIN CITY
THAT YELLOW BASTARD
FRANK MILLER
4
SIN CITY
FAMILY VALUES
FRANK MILLER
5
SIN CITY
BOOZE, BROADS, & BULLETS
FRANK MILLER
6
SIN CITY
HELL AND BACK
FRANK MILLER
7
SIN CITY

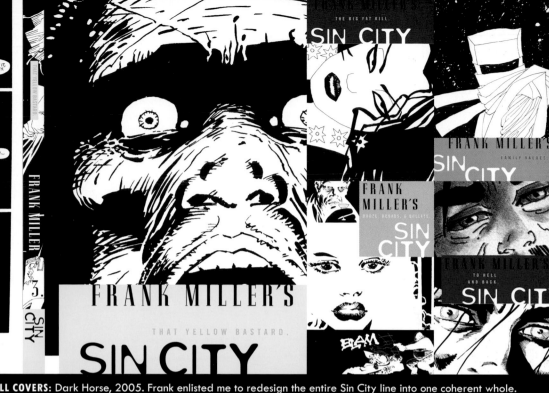

ALL COVERS: Dark Horse, 2005. Frank enlisted me to redesign the entire Sin City line into one coherent whole. **OPPOSITE RIGHT:** Shelved, the spines of all seven line up to form an image of Nancy, the cowgirl of every worthless Sin City sot's dreams. **BELOW:** Title page spread for *A Dame to Kill For.* She really is, apparently.

PANTHEON BOOKS PRESENTS

PEANUTS

THE ART OF
CHARLES M. SCHULZ

With an introduction by Jean Schulz

That round-headed kid.

THE EVOLUTION OF THE 'PEANUTS' BOOK IS RATHER COMPLICATED and even I don't know all the facts leading up to it, but in the early spring of 2000 I found myself in the boardroom of United Media in New York with Pantheon editor Shelley Wanger and a host of executives, discussing book ideas. Schulz had just died that February, and we talked first about doing some kind of tribute collection by other cartoonists. But that didn't seem to be enought about Peanuts itself to me. Whatever we were going to do, we were told it would have to be vetted by Jeannie Schultz, his widow, and Paige Braddock, his assistant at the time of his death. I was dubious—there seemed already to be a lot of cooks. But at the next meeting I was introduced to Paige and instantly we were like twins who had finally found one another. She was a fan of the "Complete History" superhero books so she knew exactly where I was coming from. Could I do that with Peanuts? Boy, could I. That June Geoff and I spent two weeks at Schulz's cordoned-off studio in Santa Rosa with assistant John Kuramoto, shooting everything in sight. Jeannie has since said that our timing was perfect: had we come any sooner it would have been too close to his passing, but had we waited any longer the studio would have been already dismantled for the forthcoming museum. As with *Batman Collected*, the amount of freedom I had on this project was extraordinary. Except for fact-checking not one page was touched. **LEFT:** Store display, 2001. **BELOW:** Pantheon, 2001. I wanted to show the characters literally up to their necks in playground anxiety. **OPPOSITE:** Shots from the book, all by Geoff Spear.

CHARLES M. SCHULZ CREATIVE ASSOCIATES
ONE SNOOPY PLACE • SANTA ROSA • CA • 95403 • (707) 546-7121

Chip,

Your appearance on the scene at #1 Snoopy Place began a whole new chapter in _my_ life. In a way I feel like a conduit between the past and the future. The focus on Sparky's life and work keeps my spirits high, and the privilege of collaborating with young, creative people charges my batteries

I feel honored to be able to say Happy Birthday to a friend!

Jeannie
Jeannie

PEANUTS

by SCHULZ

THE ART OF CHARLES M. SCHULZ

Schulz wrote the words before he did the drawings, and inked the lettering, using this C-5 pen tip.

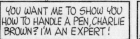

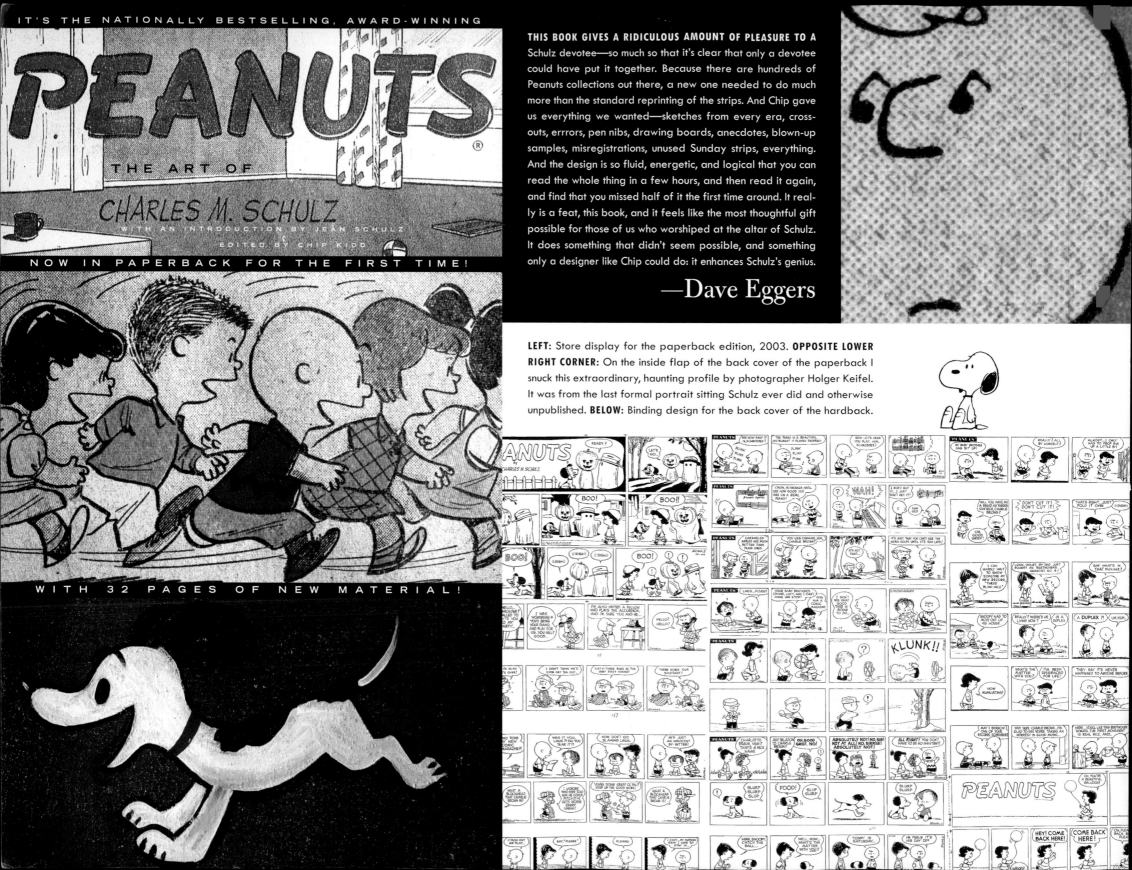

IT'S THE NATIONALLY BESTSELLING, AWARD-WINNING

PEANUTS

THE ART OF

CHARLES M. SCHULZ

WITH AN INTRODUCTION BY JEAN SCHULZ
EDITED BY CHIP KIDD

NOW IN PAPERBACK FOR THE FIRST TIME!

WITH 32 PAGES OF NEW MATERIAL!

THIS BOOK GIVES A RIDICULOUS AMOUNT OF PLEASURE TO A Schulz devotee—so much so that it's clear that only a devotee could have put it together. Because there are hundreds of Peanuts collections out there, a new one needed to do much more than the standard reprinting of the strips. And Chip gave us everything we wanted—sketches from every era, cross-outs, errrors, pen nibs, drawing boards, anecdotes, blown-up samples, misregistrations, unused Sunday strips, everything. And the design is so fluid, energetic, and logical that you can read the whole thing in a few hours, and then read it again, and find that you missed half of it the first time around. It really is a feat, this book, and it feels like the most thoughtful gift possible for those of us who worshiped at the altar of Schulz. It does something that didn't seem possible, and something only a designer like Chip could do: it enhances Schulz's genius.

—Dave Eggers

LEFT: Store display for the paperback edition, 2003. **OPPOSITE LOWER RIGHT CORNER:** On the inside flap of the back cover of the paperback I snuck this extraordinary, haunting profile by photographer Holger Keifel. It was from the last formal portrait sitting Schulz ever did and otherwise unpublished. **BELOW:** Binding design for the back cover of the hardback.

BOOK DESIGN STRETCHED TO ITS LIMITS

Jack Cole's Plastic Man could stretch and compress into any shape he chose (though always in his telltale red, black, and yellow costume), and thanks to Chip he literally morphed into a delirious book. Expanded from an essay I'd written in 1999 for *The New Yorker*, the book sported a cover made of plastic, printed on pages that bounced back and forth from coated paper to newsprint and followed no discernable grid. Column widths shifted throughout the text with type that was sometimes yellow on black, sometimes red on yellow, sometimes black on red.

I confess I was taken aback by the first layouts. When I signed on, I'd vowed to keep my control-freak tendencies in check, but the images gathered to accompany the text now stretched and careened with so little chronology or apparent logic that, while perfectly capturing Cole's mania, it made the left side of my brain ache. I tried to bite my tongue but blurted out to Chip that trying to follow the book was like listening to Charlie Mingus play "My Funny Valentine" without ever hearing the original version. Chip seemed so delighted with the analogy he forgot to be annoyed by my interference and, with the grace and flexibility of Plastic Man himself, allowed me to help rejigger the flow of pictures so that the madness of the layouts built to a crescendo in the last signature, a visual collage that suggested what was passing through Jack Cole's mind (the cartoonist shot himself in 1958) as the bullet did the same.

—Art Spiegelman

When I first read Art's Plastic Man piece I loved it but lamented that it wasn't illustrated properly due to space limitations. DC Comics editor Steve Korté was way ahead of me and proposed adapting it into a book—the first ever to emerge from the pages of both DC and *The New Yorker*. The design approach to me was obvious: what if Plastic Man turned himself into a book? **LEFT, TOP:** Chronicle Books, 2001. **LEFT:** One of the wackier page designs. **RIGHT:** Finale sequence.

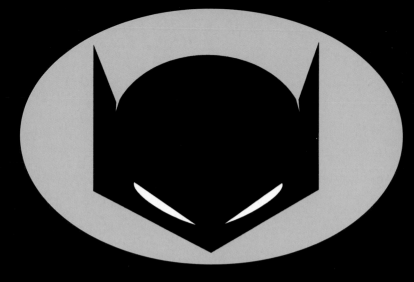

LOGOS ARE CERTAINLY NOT MY SPECIALTY, but how could I say no to creating a new symbol for you-know-who? DC wanted fresh, unified cover treatments for its monthly Batman titles (beginning in January 2000) and that included a trademark. I gave them a template and as they plugged in art and colors it was fun to see what they came up with month to month. I think these three covers are the most successful. The typeface is Champion (what else?) by Jonathan Hoefler. **ABOVE:** Sign of the Bat, 2000. **LEFT:** Art by Dave Johnson. The most elegant of the covers and the closest to my vision of how the redesign was to be implemented. **BELOW LEFT:** Art by Dave Johnson. **BELOW RIGHT:** Art by Brian Bolland, with the masthead incorporated into the drawing.

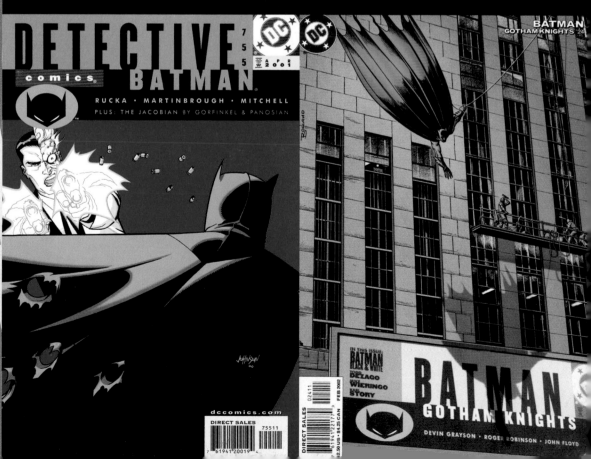

BATMAN:
ANIMATED

AS FAR AS I'M CONCERNED, YOU CAN GRAFT 'BATMAN ANIMATED' right onto the back of *Batman Collected*. One is the extension of the other. This project originated in 1997 with DC editor Charlie Kochman and Paul Dini, the head writer of *Batman: The Animated Series*. As a rabid fan of the show, I'd devoted the last twenty pages of *Batman Collected* to it—it's so beautiful and smart, and so much better than the movies have ever been. Coming up with an entire book's worth of material without duplication was no problem—producer/artist Bruce Timm and his staff gave Geoff Spear and me total access to not only everything in the Warner Brothers Animation archive but to their private sketches as well, a true embarrassment of riches. We could have done a good book on the storyboards alone. The most important thing I discovered while putting the project together was that a book about an animated show or movie is not about the animation or movement at all. It's all about finding the best production art prepared for the actual animating or filming to be done (in this case overseas in Asia) and presenting it in the most effective way. *Batman Animated* went on to win not one but two of the comics industry's Eisner awards, for design and best comics-related book. **LEFT:** HarperCollins, 1998. Art by Bruce Timm. **ABOVE AND OPPO-SITE:** Pages from *Batman Animated*. Line drawings by Bruce Timm, photography by Geoff Spear.

MYTHOLOGY.

THE DC COMICS ART OF ALEX ROSS.

CHIP KIDD
GEOFF SPEAR

introduction by
M. Night Shyamalan

FEATURING AN ORIGINAL
SUPERMAN-BATMAN STORY
BY ROSS AND KIDD.

www.pantheonbooks.com

ALEX ROSS MAY CLAIM THAT I'M A ROCK STAR (NEWS TO ME), but if that's the analagy then let's put it in perspective: I'm the Pete Best to his Paul McCartney. The first time I saw his work, it was like Superman and Batman just woke up from a long nap. I was an instant fan, but in 2002 I was reluctant to take on putting together a coffee-table book of his DC Comics work because I'd scarcely caught my breath from finishing *Peanuts*. But DC editor Charlie Kochman persisted, and of course I'm glad he did. Geoff Spear was up for it, and I think the resulting *Mythology* is as much about the committment to a brilliantly intense emotional vision as it is about superheroes. I cribbed the title from a long-since defunct toy store on the Upper West Side. **ABOVE LEFT:** Pantheon, 2003. **ABOVE RIGHT:** Humble beginnings any comic book fan can relate to. **RIGHT:** Store display.

CHIP KIDD IS A ROCK STAR. Not in the sense of a spoiled talent or artistic prima donna, but as a creative and visionary force that you should know to step aside and make room for. As one of the few people whose body of work was given a retrospective focus by Mr. Kidd (*Mythology: The DC Comics Art of Alex Ross*), I had the uncommon pleasure to see his vision applied to my world. Determining what to show and how much to show of it is his unparalleled skill. To put aside my own ego and watch how Chip interpreted and edited down ten years of my career was an awesome experience. When I didn't always understand the instinct behind including certain images, other's reactions proved him right. For example, a two-page spread was given to some decrepit old paper dolls I made of the Justice League when I was about 11. Not being necessarily representative of the greater worth of my creative output, I felt these childlike, cylindrical, colored paper construc-

tions made the younger me look the fool. Chip even included a phony exchange we never had on the pages to illustrate my reticence at having them in the book. Seeing the yellowed Scotch tape holding these crude figures together, shown in excruciating detail as photographed by Mr. Geoff Spear, made the 11-year-old in me want to shout, "I have better examples of my work!" Well, of course, the reactions of so many I would meet in touring to promote *Mythology* showed me how this was their favorite thing in the book. Chip tapped into the cultural zeitgeist of my audience and spoke to them about the common childlike enthusiasm we shared for our beloved superhero genre. Chip being a genuine fan like me helped a great deal, but his skill to put crap on a page and convince you it's art is his most impressive deception of all.

—Alex Ross

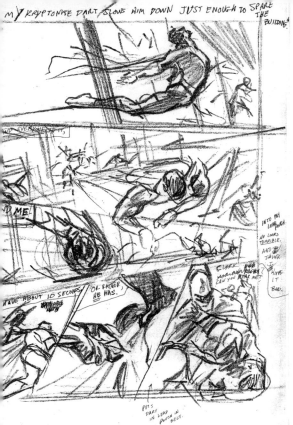

At top of img_4, handwritten: MY KRYPTONITE DART SLOWS HIM DOWN JUST ENOUGH TO SPARE THE BUILDING.

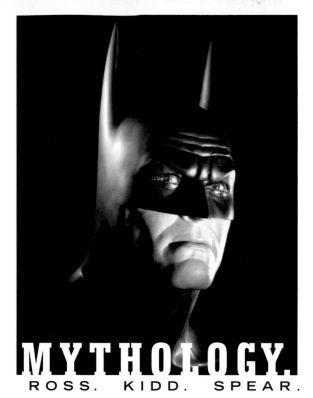

FAR LEFT: Sketch and finished painting, 2003. The highlight for me of working on this book with Alex was writing an original six-page Batman/Superman story for him to illustrate. On this penultimate page, Superman crashes into a crowded office building, with Batman close behind and desperately trying to save him. I asked Alex to put in "cameos" of me and Geoff as office workers, and there we are in panels 2 and 6. If you compare the dialogue scratched onto the sketch with the final book, you'll see it was changed. DC was very nervous about the idea of Batman using a potentially lethal gun on the Man of Steel, and demanded we alter the dialogue to indicate he's just trying to stop him, not kill him. Otherwise, the story was left alone. **LEFT:** Promotional bookplates I made to give out at the San Diego comics convention in the summer of 2003. Both shots are outtakes—ultra-realistic wax sculptures of Alex's versions of Batman and Superman—by British artist Mike Hill. We used four others from different angles in the book, but I didn't want these two going to waste. **ABOVE:** Prototype for the "ultra-deluxe" limited-edition hardcover, Pantheon, 2005. **NEAR LEFT:** Alex is making his Joker face—the one he uses as reference to paint Batman's arch enemy, and I'm making my what-did-I-just-sit-on face. 2004. **BELOW:** Sketch and finished art for the expanded paperback edition of *Mythology*, Pantheon, 2005.

387

MYTHOLOGY.
ROSS. KIDD. SPEAR.
OCTOBER 2003 • FROM PANTHEON BOOKS

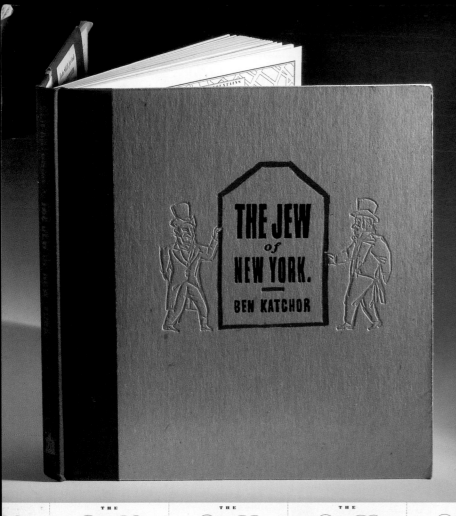

The you-know-what of you-know-where.

BEN KATCHOR'S 'THE JEW OF NEW YORK' UNWITTINGLY SPARKED Pantheon's return to comics publishing on a scale that would take it far beyond its initial foray in the 1980s with the enormous success of Art Spiegelman's *Maus*. In 1997 editor Dan Frank contacted me about a manuscript that had caught his eye by someone named Ben Katchor—did I know anything about him? What I knew from his weekly strip *Julius Knipl, Real Estate Photographer* was that Ben was a genius and I was a fan. Yes, please, let's do publish him, I said. The result was *The Jew of New York*, which I designed with Pantheon in-house staff member Misha Beletsky. Then I asked Dan, "Is Pantheon going to start doing this again, publishing comics?", to which he replied, "Should we? Who else is there?" And I told him: Chris Ware, Dan Clowes, Kim Deitch, Mark Beyer, Charles Burns—all of whom had works in the pipeline. So one by one we published them, and the "Graphic Novel Phenomenon" has steadily emerged as one of the few publishing success stories post-9/11. Soon enough, other editors brought in talents like Marjane Satrapi and David B. The arrangement for me is the best imaginable: Dan handles the business end of it and I act as editor and in some cases designer, depending on the artist's needs. What has been especially rewarding is the opportunity to expand my role at the Knopf Group beyond just designing jackets and into acquiring, editing, and publishing books that I truly love. **LEFT:** Pantheon, 1998. **LOWER LEFT:** Promotional bookmarks, designed with Misha Beletsky. **BELOW:** Pantheon, 2000. Designed by Dan Clowes. **RIGHT:** 2005. Logo for the Pantheon Graphic Novel program; one of the first drawings I published in years. **LOWER RIGHT:** Pantheon, 2005. Designed with Charles Burns.

...NOVELS.

ICE HAVEN

A COMIC-STRIP NOVEL BY
DANIEL CLOWES

LEFT: Pantheon, 2005. Designed by Daniel Clowes. Dan does all his own design work, and for this series of separate but interconnected strips that form a single narrative, he took the original format of the story as it appeared in his comic book *Eightball* and cleaved it horizontally in two. It completely transformed the pacing of the story. **BOTTOM LEFT:** Pantheon, 2002. Kim Deitch's *Boulevard of Broken Dreams* features Waldo, a reimagining of Felix the Cat with a real mean streak. Photostrip is of Kim Deitch and his wife, Pam, fall 2004. **BELOW:** Pantheon, 2004. The binding of this book of over 300 strips featuring Mark Beyer's hapless, helpless, and hopeless Amy and Jordan is designed to feel like it's falling apart, opening to expose the title characters, hiding in a corner.

The BOULEVARD OF BROKEN DREAMS

by *Kim Deitch*
WITH *Simon Deitch*

The BOULEVARD OF BROKEN DREAMS

DEITCH

PANTHEON

AMY + JORDAN

AND

MARK BEYER

MARK BEYER
Pantheon

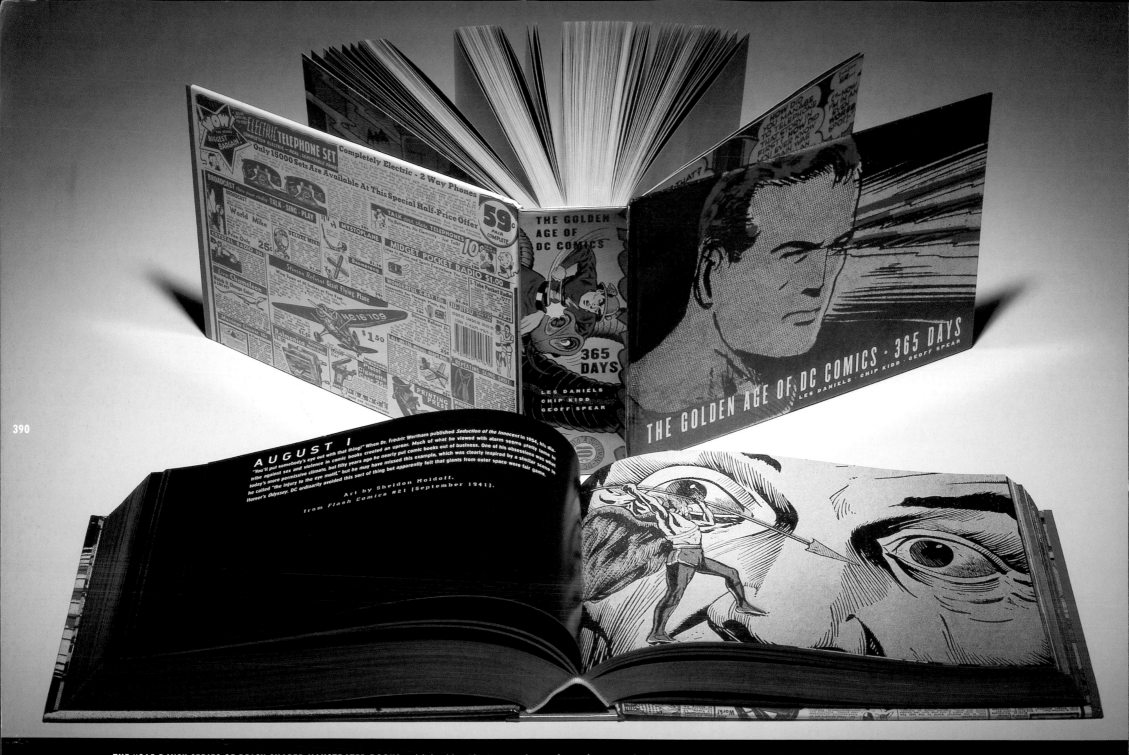

390

THE "365 DAYS" SERIES OF BRICK-SHAPED ILLUSTRATED BOOKS published by Abrams was born of a rather curious concept: an image assigned to each day of the year, but not as part of a calendar or diary. Nor do the pictures necessarily correspond to whatever day it is. Still, *365 Days: The Golden Age of DC Comics* was an extraordinary opportunity to comb through the archives at DC Comics and pick and choose among the thousands of vintage comics panels in order to showcase the best. Yet another project stoked by editor Charles Kochman, I didn't feel I had the proper time to lend it at first, but am thankful he urged me to give it a go. While not intended as any definitive history of DC's Golden Age, it nonetheless provides a good overview, thanks to Les Daniels's masterful text. Geoff Spear yet again rose to the occasion, camping out in DC's vaults to do more than 400 shots. **ABOVE:** Harry N. Abrams, 2004. All photos by Geoff Spear.

BIZARRO IS A COMICS GEEK CONCEPT stemming from the early 1960s. He is Superman's goofy opposite from a parallel backwards-planet, and was brought to renewed national attention in the early 1990s when Jerry Seinfeld built an entire episode of his TV series around the idea of a Bizarro Jerry. In 2000 some editors at DC decided to put together an anthology of "Bizarro stories" by alternative artists and writers who normally don't work in mainstream comics. Aware of my connection to Dan Clowes, they asked me if I'd approach him about doing the cover—I seriously doubted he'd say yes, but to my amazement he did. Then, in a move worthy of Bizarro himself, the editors rejected Dan's art on the grounds it made the book look like a retro-collection of previously published (as opposed to original) material. In return, Dan and I gave them a great big Bizarro "Thank you very much!"

FAR LEFT: Unused cover art for *Bizarro Comics* by Dan Clowes, 2000. **LEFT:** From *Bizarro Comics* (DC Comics, 2001). Splash page for the six-page story I wrote for the artist Tony Millionaire (see overleaf). **LOWER LEFT:** My script/instruction page for the second story I worked on with Tony, from the follow-up anthology, *Bizarro World* (DC Comics, 2005). **BELOW:** The finished page, with coloring by Jim Campbell.

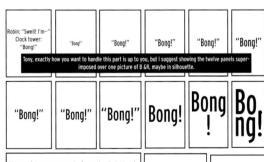

FANTAGRAPHICS WAS ON THE PHONE, "CHIP KIDD WANTS TO DESIGN YOUR BOOK, he loves your work." Chip Kidd! He's a genius! Why, this will be the most beautiful book ever made! The rough drafts came in the mail, and I eagerly opened them. These are going to be great! Alas, my eyes boiled in horror as I looked over the pages. Drinky Crow was upside down, a bottle was flying through the air. Logos and typefaces were strewn about the cover willy-nilly. On the back Uncle Gabby seemed to be twirling in space, wacky letters screamed MAAKIES, swirling all around. The endpages were scrambled with crazy kaleidoscopic designs, I grew dizzy. I got Chip on the phone, "These are terrible, what's wrong with you? Maakies is not about twirly-whirly pop craziness, it's old fashioned! This book should look like it came out of a lost sea captain's trunk, not from the knapsack of some crazed dervish!" Weeks later, the new designs arrived, and they were lovely. Antique paper and decorations culled from a hundred-year-old German bookmaker. It was breathtaking! The next year he produced the second Maakies book, it was spectacular! I flipped through the American Institute of Graphic Arts Year in Design, looking for boobs. There on page 132 was the layout of the Maakies book, it had been selected as one of the top 50 book designs of the year! Success! This year however, he got his revenge. The little bastard used the same wacky design I had rejected years earlier, but I could not deny it, the final result was beautiful!

—Tony Millionaire

TONY MILLIONAIRE USES A PART OF THE BRAIN I hope I never have to resort to, but if that time ever comes, at least I'll know the results can be tear-inducingly gorgeous, if utterly perverse. He has the hand of Ernest H. Shepard, the heart of A. A. Milne, the eye of Winslow Homer, and the whims of the Marquis de Sade. Luckily for us he keeps it all, gloriously, on the page. **THIS PAGE AND FOLLOWING SPREAD:** Fantagraphics Books, 2001, 2002, 2003, 2004. *Maakies* (Tony vows to take the meaning of the word to the grave, so don't ask me) features the rip-roaring adventures of a seafaring suicidal alcoholic crow named Drinkie and his friend Uncle Gabby, a gap-toothed ape in a bow-bedecked hat who waves his penis at the police, had his ass spackled smooth, openly discusses the intricate strategies of warring anal mites, and likes to rouse his crab lice into stirring sing-alongs. Fun for the whole family.

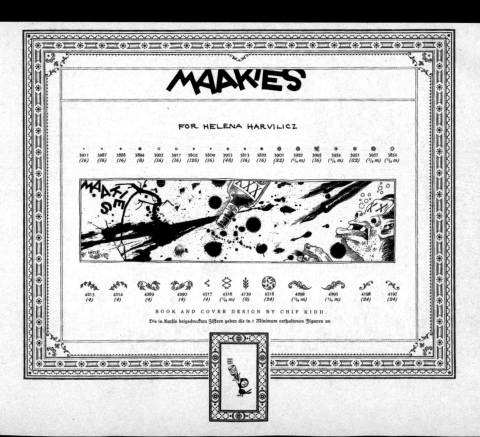

BATMAN: YEAR ONE

MILLER • MAZZUCCHELLI • LEWIS

DC COMICS

BATMAN YEAR ONE

FRANK MILLER

DAVID MAZZUCCHELLI

WITH

RICHMOND LEWIS

394

Starting over.

SO IT'S YEAR TWENTY AND COUNTING. WHO COULD HAVE GUESSED such a thing possible? And will there eventually be a Book Two? I can't imagine, but never say never. One thing I can say: there definitely won't be one if I don't get off my lazy ass and get back to work. **THIS PAGE:** DC Comics, 2005. Art by David Mazzucchelli. Features a diagonally die-cut jacket that slopes to the right and lops off the type, mimicking the plot's depiction of Bruce Wayne cutting through the corruption and decadence pervading Gotham City. This book's retelling of the origin of Batman is, to me, the single best story about the character ever committed to paper. The confluence of expertise in the writing, drawing, and coloring is superb and has yet to be bettered. **OPPOSITE:** Prototype designs for the covers of DC's re-launch of the Superman and Batman titles, called the "All-Star" line, set to appear in late 2005 and extend into 2006 and beyond. Up up, and away . . .

I DON'T WANT TO SAY GOODBYE TO ANY OF THIS, EVER. But that's the nice thing about books: when you get to the end, you can always go back to page one. And that's what I'm going to do. Right now.

—C. K.

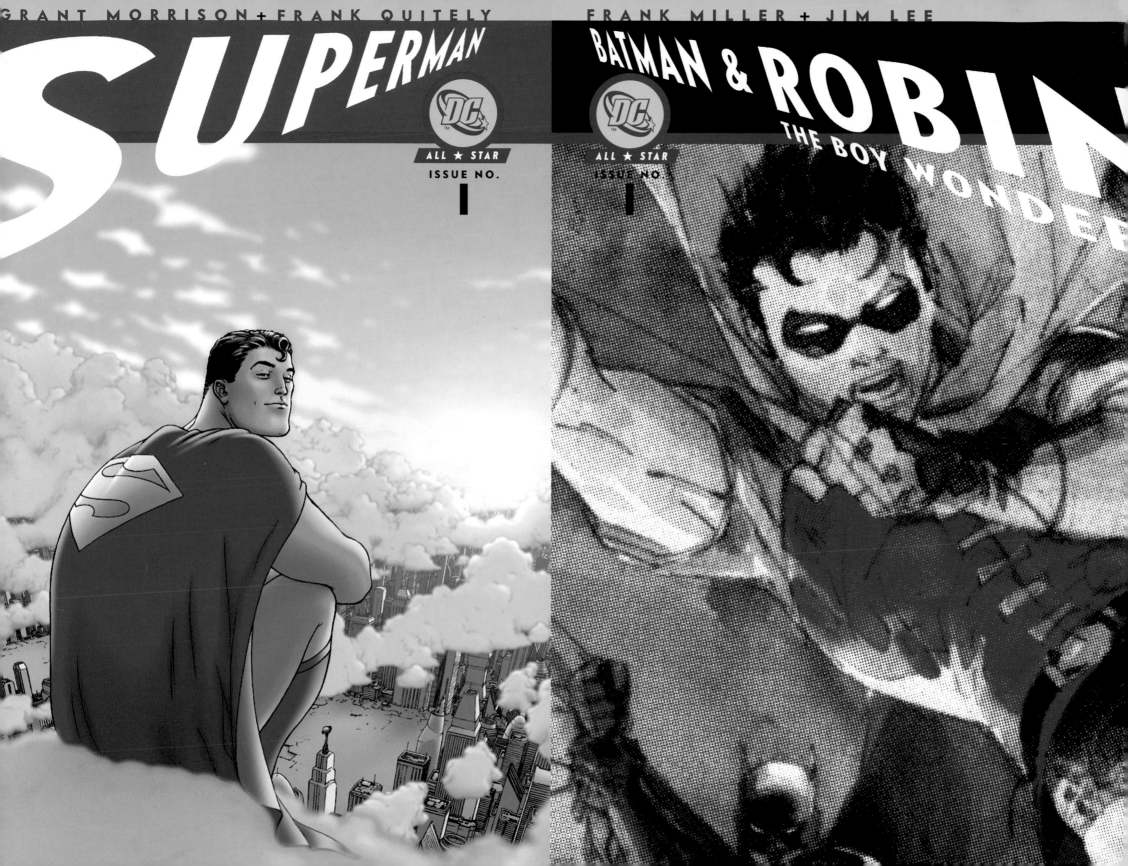

INDEX

396

™

www.pagesix.com

By JARED PAUL STERN
with PAULA FROELICH
and CHRIS WILSON

Richard Johnson is on vacation

Cash cow

WE are shocked — shocked—that **Regis Philbin**'s self-proclaimed flame **Maria Majerek** might be in it for the money. The former cheerleading coach, who revealed her alleged affair with Regis in the Enquirer last week, was forced into Ch. 7 bankruptcy in 1998 after running through her hefty divorce settlement, reports Foxnews.com's **Roger Friedman**. "She's a user," Majerek's most recent boyfriend, **Dennis Miller**, an Indiana contractor, told Friedman. The couple broke up in June, around the time her diary was sold to the Enquirer. Miller says she never mentioned an affair with Philbin.

Kidd stuff

GRAPHIC design genius **Chip Kidd** has turned out to be as adept at writing books as he is at designing them. Kidd, an art director at Alfred Knopf who did the jacket for **Joe Esterhas'** "American Rhapsody," just sold a novel to Scribner's for six figures. "The Cheese Monkeys" is a "thinly-veiled account of studying design" that he's been working on in secret for the past six years, he says. Meanwhile, Kidd, who put together two books on Batman memorabilia, recently edited two books of comics for Pantheon and is also art directing and designing a book on Charles Schulz and "Peanuts."

A NOTE ON THE TYPE

TWENTIETH CENTURY was designed and drawn by Sol Hess (1896–1953), in the Lanston Monotype drawing office between 1936 and 1947. The first weights were added to the Monotype typeface library in 1959. Twentieth Century is based on geometric shapes which originated in Germany in the early 1920s and became an integral part of the Bauhaus movement of that time. Form and function became the key words, unnecessary decoration was scorned. This clean cut, sans serif with geometric shapes was most appropriate. The lighter weights of the font family can be used for text setting; the bold and condensed fonts are suitable for display headlines.

BULMER was designed and drawn in 1928 by Morris Fuller Benton (1872–1948). After training as a mechanic and engineer, Benton joined the American Type Founders, originally as an assistant to his father, Linn Boyd Benton, famous in the printing trade for his invention of the Benton punch cutting machine. In 1900, Morris Fuller Benton became American Type Founders' chief type designer, where he spent his entire working life, retiring in 1937. Morris designed over 200 typefaces, including Century Schoolbook, Alternate Gothic, Franklin Gothic, and Cheltenham.

105 PHOTOGRAPHIC SHOTS WERE TAKEN, comprising over six hundred exposures. Thirty images were shot on 4 x 5 film, using a Linhof camera and Nikon 120mm Apo Macro lens. Seventy-five shots were digital, using a Canon 20D camera and 50Macro and 105Macro lenses.

FAR LEFT: I can't remember who in the office made this. It certainly covers a multitude of sins. **LEFT:** From the *New York Post*, August 8, 2000. Jared Paul Stern is a good friend, and responsible for occasional mentions on the ultimate gossip page. **BELOW LEFT:** Polaroid test photo by Tina Barney, at the late and lamented Rizzoli bookstore in Soho, early 1990s. This was for a piece slated to appear in *Vanity Fair*, but nixed at the last minute—they just ran images of jackets. I don't have the slightest clue who the other guy is, **BELOW RIGHT:** Now that this book exists, I'll be able to answer requests like this a lot easier.

Tina Barney 3/10/93

Dear Chip,
I'm a high school student interested in graphic design. I've seen your work in some design books + it's top notch! Could you please send me a brochure or something that tells me how I could see your book jacket designs? That'd be great. Thanks, + keep up the great work.

JOE IMMEN

COLUMBUS OH 43221

RANDOM HOUSE, INC.

CARD IDENTIFICATION NUMBER
1523

SOCIAL SECURITY NUMBER

EMPLOYEE NAME
KIDD, C

EMPLOYEE SIGNATURE

---

att: *Chuck Kidd*

Mr Charles Kibb
Knopf Publishing
201 East 50th Street   7th Floor
New York   NY   10022

Charles Klidd
Knopf Publishing
201 E. 50th 7th Floor
New York
NY.   10022

PHILIP MORRIS HOSSENFEFFER
PRESIDENT AND CHIEF OPERATING OFFICER
OF THE END OF THE 2 MILLENIUM A.D.

TO EVERYONE AT RANDOM HOUSE

One of the most important things we strive to do at Random House is maintain a sense of team spirit, and a feeling of membership in our community of colleagues. As a symbol of pride in Random House, we have created tattoos depicting the Random House logo. During the coming week, each of you will recieve a tattoo size book and body map. Price may vary according to size and location on body (when choosing placement, keep in mind that your tattoo will be used to gain admittance into the building). Nose or naval rings with the Random House logo charm in gold are also available, for an additional $1.75. Both tattoos and body ornaments can be ordered at the reception desk on the 15th floor. Be assured that all tattoos and body piercing will be administered on the premises by the nurse under the most sanitary conditions as required by the state of New York.

Following this initial distribution, new employees will receive their tattoos on their first anniversary with the company.

Please wear your Random House tattoo with pride.

CHRISTINE NAMES
DIVISION VICE PRESIDENT
PERSONNEL

TO EVERYONE AT RANDOM HOUSE

A memo on Random House stationery dated August 5th, allegedly sent in behalf of our Health Unit Nurse, Sharon Baird, was sent to many of you. It was apparently intended as a joke, but is most certainly erroneous and should be disregarded.

TOP LEFT: Random House ID, circa 1988. **TOP RIGHT:** More fun with name-mangling. This pretty much stopped after computerized mailing lists came along, which is kind of sad. **BOTTOM LEFT:** An office prank by me and Barbara, mid 1990s. This was before we had company-wide e-mail, when it seemed like every other day we were getting some hair-brained office memo. We made a zillion copies of this and stayed after hours one night, sticking one in every mail slot on every floor we could find. **BOTTOM RIGHT:** Personnel was not amused (big surprise). Unbelievably, their office was besieged by outraged calls from dozens of nitwits who fell for it. Oh, office life!

ACKNOWLEDGEMENTS

In addition to **SONNY MEHTA** and **CAROL DEVINE CARSON**, the real hero of this book is **MARK MELNICK**. He lived with it for a year and a half, organizing all the work with the kind of fresh wit that I thought I used to have. He is as brilliant as he is unflappable, excellent qualities to have when dealing with books. I cannot thank him enough, except by giving him his life back now that he's designed mine.

To all the great **TEACHERS** I've had, from Mrs. Wegter who read us *Charlotte's Web* in the third grade, to Michele Cambardela who nominated me for a senior high school class writing prize (based on nothing but intuition), to Lanny and Bill at Penn State.

To **BOB SCUDELLARI** and **SARA EISENMAN**, for hiring me when I had no experience, no New York schooling, no book jackets in my portfolio, and no clue.

To the **KNOPF ART DEPARTMENT**, the best in the business; you're a pleasure to see and work with every day.

To everyone else at **KNOPF**, past and present, who I've had the honor to associate with and didn't get a chance to mention in the text: Jane Friedman, the late Bill Koshland, Barbara Jones-Diggs, Kathy Grasso, Paul Bogaards, Tony Chirico, LuAnn Walther, Janice Goldklang, Ann Diaz, Jenny McPhee, Nicholas Latimer, Randall Keenan, Tracy Cabanis, Claire Bradley, Kathy Hourigan, Altie Karper, and Kathy Zuckerman.

To the **EDITORS** whose books have given me a reason to get up in the morning: Ash Green, Gary Fisketjon, Gordon Lish, Judith Jones, Carol Janeway, Shelley Wanger, Dan Frank, Marty Asher, Jonathan Segal, Ann Close, and Jordan Pavlin; outside Knopf—the late George Plimpton, Joni Evans, Ann Godoff, Sarah McGrath, David Remnick, Steve Korte, Charlie Kochman and Michael Peitsch.

To **ANDY HUGHES**, who for over two decades has been responsible for making all the Knopf books—and therefore their designers—look great. He is a magician and a saint.

To all the **ART DIRECTORS** who gave me work, chiefly Joseph Montebello at HarperCollins, plus Peter Kruzan, Doris Janowitz, John Fontana, Andy Carpenter, Phil Rose, Lisa Amaroso, Alex Gottfreid, Phil Rose, Rick Pracher and Richard Aquan.

To all of the **ARTISTS** whose work I've used—the photographers, illustrators, painters, cartoonists, sculptors and mark-makers—I have made every effort to credit you all within the text of the book. If there is anyone I omitted (which is inevitable), do please contact me for inclusion in future printings (how's that for optimism?).

To my fellow **GRAPHIC DESIGNERS** who have inspired and supported me throughout the past twenty years: Stephen Doyle, Michael Beirut, David Carson, the late Tibor Kalman, Paula Scher, Stefan Sagmeister, Milton Glaser, Steff Geissbuhler, Paul Sahre, Bill Drenttel, Seymour Chwast, Nicholas Blechman, Emily Oberman, Christoph Niemann, Michael Vanderbyl, and the uber-glam Peter Saville, who still doesn't know who I am and never will (sigh).

To agent extraordinaire **BINKY URBAN**, and to my naughty friend Paul Amador, who knows a thing or two about photography.

At **RIZZOLI**: editor Ian Luna (who had the idea to do this book in the first place), Charles Miers, Anet Sirna-Bruder, Ellen Nidy, Douglas Curran, Nikki Columbus, Chris Monroe, Julie Di Filippo, Julie Schumacher, Eugene Lee, Gloria Ahn, and Noriko Sakai. And here's to the memory of Steve Case.

Thanks to **SUSAN BIANCONI** at the Yale Review for her grace and invaluable assistance regarding my archives.

To my **FAMILY**—Mom, Dad, Aunt Sylvia, Walt, Mary, and the kids (Lauren, Sam, Tommy and Matthew). Your love means everything.

My apologies to anyone I left out by mistake. You know who you are, even if I don't.

Penultimately, thanks to all the **WRITERS**. I consider this entire book as my acknowledgement to you.

And finally to **J. D. McCLATCHY**: my bookmark, my index, my page count, my cover, my binding.

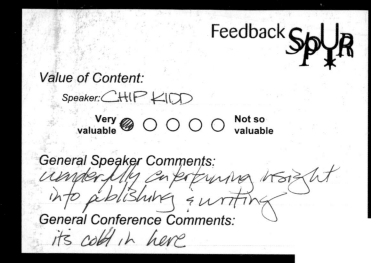

Feedback Spur

Value of Content:

Speaker: CHIP KIDD

Very valuable ◉ ○ ○ ○ ○ Not so valuable

General Speaker Comments:
wonderfully entertaining insight into publishing & writing

General Conference Comments:
its cold in here

TOP: Feedback from the Spur design conference in Colorado, 2001. **BOTTOM:** The highlight of my presentation at Typo Berlin, May 2005. Photo by Susanna Dulkanis. **OPPOSITE:** On the phone, as ever, in my office overlooking the heavenly Hudson, at 55th Street and Broadway. March, 2005. Photo by Chris Ware.

Feedback Spur

Value of Content:

Speaker: Chip Kidd

Very valuable ⊗ ○ ○ ○ ○ Not so valuable

General Speaker Comments:
Best speaker yet. Totally nuts.

General Conference Comments: